Jack Kerouac

SELECTED
LETTERS

1940–1956

Jack Kerouac

SELECTED
LETTERS

1940–1956

EDITED WITH
AN INTRODUCTION
AND COMMENTARY BY

Ann Charters

VIKING

VIKING
Published by the Penguin Group
Penguin Books USA Inc., 375 Hudson Street, New York, New York 10014, U.S.A.
Penguin Books Ltd, 27 Wrights Lane, London W8 5TZ, England
Penguin Books Australia Ltd, Ringwood, Victoria, Australia
Penguin Books Canada Ltd, 10 Alcorn Avenue, Toronto, Ontario, Canada M4V 3B2
Penguin Books (N.Z.) Ltd, 182–190 Wairau Road, Auckland 10, New Zealand

Penguin Books Ltd, Registered Offices: Harmondsworth, Middlesex, England

First published in 1995 by Viking Penguin, a division of Penguin Books USA Inc.

1   3   5   7   9   10   8   6   4   2

LIBRARY OF CONGRESS CATALOGING-IN-PUBLICATION DATA
Kerouac, Jack, 1922–1969.   [Correspondence. Selections]
Jack Kerouac : selected letters, 1940–1956 / edited with an
introduction and commentary by Ann Charters.
p.   cm.   Includes bibliographical references (p.   ).
ISBN 0-670-84952-9
1. Kerouac, Jack, 1922–1969—Correspondence.   2. Authors, American—
20th Century—Correspondence.   3. Beat generation.   I. Charters, Ann.   II. Title.
PS3521.E7357.48   1995   813'.54—dc20   94-12911

This book is printed on acid-free paper.
∞

Printed in the United States of America
Set in Sabon and Trajan

THIS BOOK IS DEDICATED
TO THE MEMORY OF
SEBASTIAN SAMPAS

"Comrade—
Curst be the wind-swept
                     stars
And the night be one
                     as thunder
You've had your share of
                     scars
Comrade! We shan't go
                     under—"

—Sebastian Sampas to Jack Kerouac
March 15, 1943

ACKNOWLEDGMENTS

The first person whose help I gratefully acknowledge in the preparation of this volume is Jack Kerouac himself. When he invited me to Hyannis to work together on his bibliography in the summer of 1966, he assured me, "I've kept the neatest records you ever saw." He was right. In his study was a meticulously preserved literary archive, as carefully organized as the archives I used a few years later while researching his biography in the Rare Book and Manuscript Room of the Butler Library at Columbia University, the Bancroft Library at the University of California, Berkeley, and the Humanities Research Center at the University of Texas at Austin. During our two days together in Hyannis Kerouac showed me everything I asked to see. I listed his publications, and he answered my questions about the circumstances under which he had written his books.

In Hyannis we never had any reason to look at the folders of letters that Kerouac had filed carefully away in his room, but if he had showed me his correspondence, I would have seen his letters and those from his friends systematically gathered and put away in manila folders. At some later point, Kerouac went through the carbons he had kept of his own typed letters to his friends, as well as the original letters he had written and never sent, and annotated a good number of them, supplying dates or comments. There is no evidence that he did this with a view to publishing his correspondence, but his work organizing his letters made mine much easier when I was asked to edit this volume. Whenever Kerouac's annotation is available, I have included it at the beginning or end of a letter, highlighting it with italics.

Also of key importance in the preparation of this volume is John Sampas, Kerouac's youngest brother-in-law and executor of the Kerouac literary estate. Sampas initiated the project and was extremely helpful. He allowed me access to Kerouac's letters in the archive. He also supplied information about the family background of his sister Stella Sampas, Kerouac's widow, and of his brother Sebastian Sampas, Kerouac's boyhood friend in Lowell, Massachusetts.

Sterling Lord, Kerouac's literary agent, was kind enough to let me include Kerouac's letters to him in this volume. They add an important new dimension to our knowledge of the development of Kerouac's literary career. Another significant source of new information was Kerouac's file at Viking Penguin, which my editor David Stanford made accessible to me. Adam Gussow, who has researched and written about the relationship between Kerouac and his editors Malcolm Cowley and Keith Jennison at the Viking Press, also filled in more of the story with xeroxes of Cowley's correspondence with Kerouac and Allen Ginsberg.

I offer special thanks to the writers who were close friends of Kerouac who gave me permission to include letters in this volume: Carolyn Cassady, who let me use an early letter from Neal Cassady to Kerouac; and Allen Ginsberg and William S. Burroughs, who let me include two of their letters to Kerouac documenting their close friendship. John Clellon Holmes also sent me a complete set of xeroxes of his extensive correspondence with Kerouac.

I thank the professional staff at several research libraries who helped me gather Kerouac letters: Kenneth A. Lohf at Columbia University (Kerouac's letters to Allen Ginsberg, W. S. Burroughs, Neal Cassady, James Laughlin, Carl Solomon, Lucien Carr, and Peter Orlovsky), John Skarstad at UC Davis (Kerouac's letters to Gary Snyder), Marilyn Kierstead at Reed College (Kerouac's letters to Philip Whalen), Cathy Henderson at the Humanities Center of the University of Texas (Kerouac's letters to Carolyn and Neal Cassady), and Francis O. Mattson, Curator of the Berg Collection at the New York Public Library (Kerouac's letters to his sister Caroline Kerouac Blake, Robert Giroux, and Alfred Kazin). Martha Mayo at the University of Lowell library kindly took the time to answer my queries about material placed on deposit there.

Many other people have also been helpful, especially the Kerouac scholar Dave Moore, who corrected errors in my commentaries and footnotes and checked many of my transcriptions of the letters. Michael Schumacher generously shared his xeroxes of the entire Kerouac/Ginsberg correspondence after he finished using the letters in his biography of Ginsberg. Allen Ginsberg let me read the unpublished manuscript of his annotated correspondence with Kerouac, which he compiled with the help of his student Jason Shinder at the Naropa Institute in Boulder, Colorado. I am particularly grateful to Professors Ellie DalMolin and Marie Naudin at the University of Connecticut, who looked over my transcriptions of Kerouac's Québécois.

Kerouac's first wife, Edith Parker, her friend Jim Perrizo, and many of the people with whom Kerouac later corresponded have also been extremely generous, including Robert Giroux, Elbert Lenrow, Gary Snyder, Philip Whalen, and Stanford Whitmore, who made available to me their letters from Kerouac. Donald Allen, Rod Anstee, Andreas Brown, Neelie Cherkovski, Maureen Croteau, Faith Evans, Lawrence Ferlinghetti, Russell Freedman, Mark Gisbourne, James Grauerholz, James Laughlin, Charlotte Mann, Barry Miles, Malcolm Reid, Kevin Ring, Mel Smith, and Jeff Steblea also shared material and helped with the project in various ways.

Finally, I wish to acknowledge the advice of my husband, Samuel Charters, who read my early transcriptions of these Kerouac letters and told me that from a reader's point of view, they would be more accessible if they were linked by brief commentary. Later in London my editor Tony Lacey of Penguin Books Ltd. also encouraged me to add commentary. Throughout the duration of the project my editor David Stanford at Viking Penguin has extended a steady and helpful hand. His assistant Kristine Puopolo has been responsive and supportive. Kerouac was such a voluminous correspondent that the total number of his letters is unknown. I have included about half of the letters from 1940 through 1956 that were made available to me. Kerouac's spelling in the letters has occasionally been corrected, as indicated in the Notes at the end of this volume.

Storrs, Connecticut

CONTENTS

1948

1949

1952

1956

INTRODUCTION

As anyone interested in literature knows, letters are important. They are what the literary critic Janet Malcolm has called "the great fixative of experience. Time erodes feeling. Time creates indifference. Letters . . . are the fossils of feeling. This is why biographers prize them so: they are biography's only conduit to unmediated experience. Everything else the biographer touches is stale, hashed over, told and retold, dubious, unauthentic, suspect."

The hundreds of letters Jack Kerouac wrote are the best repository of his "unmediated experience," a treasure trove for readers intent on appreciating his literary art. Since Kerouac wrote what he called "true-story novels" based on his direct experience, his letters bring us closer to the life he actually lived before he turned it into literature in the series of books comprising what he called the "Duluoz legend," the story of his lifetime.

Both his own letters and the letters from his friends were important to Kerouac, an indefatigible correspondent. He kept hundreds of letters, both those he received and, in the form of carbons and drafts, those he wrote to his family, friends, and literary associates. Many proved to be extremely useful to him. In June 1949, for example, when John Clellon Holmes asked him for information about Allen Ginsberg, whom Holmes wanted to make the central character in his novel-in-progress *Go*, Kerouac replied that he would "prepare a special brief on A.G. . . . One thing I have is several score letters from him full of information at various points in his life."

Nearly twenty years later, when Kerouac wrote *Vanity of Duluoz,* he went back to a letter he had written to his sister Caroline in 1941 and other letters from the 1940s to refresh his memory of how he had felt when he left his hometown of Lowell, Massachusetts, to attend school in New York City. Kerouac's mother and sister saved his letters to them as carefully as he saved letters from his friends, and this volume of his correspondence is further enhanced by the fact that Kerouac's widow, Stella Sampas, whom he married in 1966, was the sister of his boyhood friend Sebastian, who was killed during military action in World War II. The Sampas family kept the letters from Kerouac that Sebastian had sent home for safekeeping during the 1940s. They are a remarkable testament to Kerouac's early commitment to becoming a writer, with his friend Sebastian's passionate encouragement.

Even in these early letters, Kerouac's gift for mimicry is extraordinary, as evidenced in the different voices he assumed while writing to his various friends. He had a prodigious memory, and was able to quote conversations verbatim hours after he had overheard them. When he wrote letters to friends like Sebastian Sampas, Allen Ginsberg, or William S. Burroughs, he wrote with their voices in his mind, adjusting his style to each one. His letters reveal the apparent ease with which he projected different self-images, depending on the mirror each friend held up to him. In Kerouac's letters, as in his autobiographical books, the person writing and the person being written about were rarely a single entity.

Like many of his contemporaries, when Kerouac began to write his first published novel he consciously imitated the literary style of Thomas Wolfe. But in Kerouac's attempt to find his own voice, he was most impressed by the letters sent to him by his Denver friend Neal Cassady. In December 1950 Cassady wrote him a letter many thousands of words long, describing his sexual adventures in Denver. Kerouac felt that in the "muscular rush" of this letter Cassady had created a literary masterpiece, more important in the history of American literature than the novels of F. Scott Fitzgerald and Ernest Hemingway.

The day after receiving Cassady's letter, Kerouac was so inspired that he sat down "to write a full confession." The result, written in white heat between December 28, 1950, and January 10, 1951, was nearly a hundred typed pages—his own earliest memories of growing up in Lowell, in the form of a series of long letters to Cassady, some never mailed. A few months later, in April, when Kerouac returned to his work-in-progress *On the Road*, he made a completely fresh start by describing his adventures on the road with Cassady as if he were writing a letter to his second wife, Joan.

Kerouac's prose in his book was so similar to Cassady's style in his letters that Kerouac even incorporated a few passages from Cassady's letters to him in 1949 into *On the Road*. Later, when revising *On the Road* into what he called his "experimental" book *Visions of Cody*, Kerouac included a long letter he had written Cassady in the fall of 1951.

Kerouac wrote letters to his friends for the same reason that he wrote his books, for companionship. His first extant letter, written in 1940 to his friend Sebastian Sampas when Jack was eighteen, is a description of his life as a freshman at Columbia College. Besides writing to his friends, Kerouac also stayed in close touch through letters with his older sister Caroline and his mother, Gabrielle, with whom he lived most of the time, except for his brief stretches on the road or living with his friends. As the letters show, Gabrielle encouraged her son's dream of becoming a great American writer. Usually they were too poor to install a telephone in the series of modest homes they lived in, as when Kerouac wrote an excited letter to Ginsberg on December 15, 1948, to tell him about the rare event of a telephone call from Neal Cassady in San Francisco: Jack had to answer on the phone in the drugstore beneath his mother's apartment in Ozone Park in Queens, New York. It was years before Kerouac was affluent enough to afford his own telephone, and he continued to write letters several times a week. The habit continued until the end of his life, as he never stopped reaching out for the comforts of personal contact and companionship.

The letters in this collection begin in 1940 and continue to the end of 1956, the last year of Kerouac's anonymity before the publication of *On the Road*, the book that catapulted him to literary fame. I was guided in my commentary and choice of letters by my desire to let Kerouac tell the story of his life in them as eloquently as he did in his "true-story novels." His letters confirm what the critic John Tytell understood, that Kerouac "lived primarily for words and the rhythms of his work."

More completely than his novels, Kerouac's letters record every important turning point in his development as a writer. When he wrote his letters he had no thought of a biographer using them this way. Occasionally as an aspiring writer he half-jokingly told his friends that some day, after he was famous, strangers would read his letters. He was right. Kerouac left them to us as "the great fixative of experience" of a remarkable lifetime both on and off the road.

CHRONOLOGY

<table>
<tr><td>1922</td><td>March 12, Jean Louis Lebris de Kerouac born in Lowell, Massachusetts, third child of Gabrielle and Leo Kerouac, French-Canadian immigrants to New England</td></tr>
<tr><td>1939</td><td>Graduates from Lowell High School</td></tr>
<tr><td>1939–40</td><td>Attends Horace Mann Preparatory School, New York City</td></tr>
<tr><td>1940–41</td><td>Attends Columbia College</td></tr>
<tr><td>1942–43</td><td>Serves in U.S. Navy and Merchant Marine</td></tr>
<tr><td>1944</td><td>Meets Lucien Carr, William Burroughs, and Allen Ginsberg; marries first wife, Edith Parker</td></tr>
<tr><td>1946–48</td><td>Writes The Town and the City; meets Neal Cassady in New York City</td></tr>
<tr><td>1948</td><td>Meets John Clellon Holmes and invents the term "beat generation"</td></tr>
<tr><td>1948–50</td><td>Makes early attempts to write On the Road; first cross-country trips with Cassady</td></tr>
<tr><td>1950</td><td>Publishes The Town and the City; marries second wife, Joan Haverty</td></tr>
<tr><td>1951</td><td>February/March—reads manuscripts of Burroughs's Junkie and Holmes's Go; April—writes roll manuscript of On the Road in three weeks in New York City; October—discovers his compositional method of "sketching" or "spontaneous prose" and begins to rewrite On the Road as the experimental book Visions of Cody</td></tr>
</table>

1951–52	Writes *Visions of Cody* in New York City and San Francisco
1952	Writes *Doctor Sax* in Mexico City; works as a student brakeman and writes "The Railroad Earth" in San Francisco; daughter Jan Kerouac born in Albany, New York
1953	Writes *Maggie Cassidy* and *The Subterraneans* in New York City
1954	Begins study of Buddhism in New York and California; writes "San Francisco Blues" in San Francisco, "Some of the Dharma" in New York and North Carolina
1955	Writes *Mexico City Blues,* begins *Tristessa* in Mexico City; attends "Six Poets at the Six Gallery" reading in San Francisco
1956	Finishes *Tristessa* in Mexico City and writes *Visions of Gerard* in North Carolina; writes first part of *Desolation Angels* in Washington State and Mexico City; Ginsberg's *Howl and Other Poems* published by City Lights in San Francisco
1957	*On the Road* published by the Viking Press in New York; writes *The Dharma Bums* in Florida
1958–60	Writes sketches in *Lonesome Traveler*
1959	Narrates film *Pull My Daisy* in New York City
1961	Writes second half of *Desolation Angels* in Mexico City; writes *Big Sur* in Florida
1965	Writes *Satori in Paris* in Florida
1966	Marries Stella Sampas and moves from Hyannis to Lowell, Massachusetts
1967	Writes *Vanity of Duluoz* in Lowell
1968	February 4, Neal Cassady dies in Mexico
1969	October 21, Jack Kerouac dies in Saint Petersburg, Florida

1940

Apparently the earliest surviving correspondence by Jack Kerouac is a message printed on the back of a picture postcard of the Roger Smith Hotel in New Brunswick, New Jersey, that he sent to his hometown friend Sebastian Sampas. In Book Four of Vanity of Duluoz, *where Kerouac described his first year at Columbia College, he wrote that on Saturday, October 12, 1940—the day he wrote the postcard—he traveled with the Columbia freshman football team to New Brunswick to play in the opening game of the season. It was the first of the two freshman games Jack played for Columbia, but he remembered neither game with much pleasure. "We went down there and I sat on the bench and we lost 18–7. The little daily paper of the college said: FRESHMEN DROP GRID OPENER TO RUTGERS YEARLINGS BY 18–7 COUNT. It doesnt mention that I only got in the game in the second half, just like at Lowell High, and the article concludes with: 'The Morningsiders showed a fairly good running attack at times with Jack Duluoz [the name Kerouac called himself in* Vanity of Duluoz] *showing up well . . .' "*

TO SEBASTIAN SAMPAS

[October 12, 1940
New Brunswick, N.J.]

Hello Emerson,[1]

I'm sorry I haven't answered sooner and that you weren't able to come to New York. I'm sure you'll make it at some future date however.

Meanwhile, expect a document from me soon.

Jean Louis de Kerouac[2]

P.S: I spent the time on the way up here reading Saroyan![3]

---

1. Sebastian was a student at Emerson College in Boston.

2. Kerouac had been named Jean Louis by his parents, Leo and Gabrielle Kerouac, who were both French-Canadian immigrants; the French dialect *joual* (Québécois) was spoken in their home and was Kerouac's first language.

3. William Saroyan (1908–1981), Armenian-American author of the best-selling book of linked short stories *My Name Is Aram* (1940).

1941

Two weeks before his nineteenth birthday in March 1941, after he had recuperated from a broken leg the previous fall when he was tackled during his second freshman football game at Columbia, Kerouac began to write a series of postcards to Sebastian Sampas at Emerson College in Boston. Of all his Lowell friends, Jack felt a special affinity with Sebastian, remembering in Vanity of Duluoz *that Sebastian "was a great kid, knightlike, i.e., noble, a poet, goodlooking, crazy, sweet, sad, everything a man should want as a friend."*

TO SEBASTIAN SAMPAS

[February 26, 1941
New York City]

Sebastean—[1]

I'd like to have you drop me a card like this daily, and I'll do the same—of course, still continuing our regular documents. Good idea? Fouch[2] and I are going to do it also. This is to inform you of my suggestion. The second card is my first official Daily Chat.

Jean, BARON DE BRETAGNE[3]

P.S: I'm going to mail these cards to your college because your sister[4] may read these at home. I'm being boyish . . .

---

1. Kerouac spelled his friend's name both Sebastian and Sebastean.

2. Fouch and G.J. were both nicknames for Kerouac's Lowell friend George J. Apostolos.

3. When Kerouac boasted of his Breton French ancestry to Sebastian, his friend replied, jokingly, that he was really Sampas Sampatacacus, the Prince of Crete. In 1941 Kerouac addressed several postcards to Sebastian Sampas, Prince of Crete, Emerson College, Beacon Street, Boston, Mass. In *The Town and the City*, the character Alexander Panos, whom Kerouac modeled on Sebastian Sampas, is also called "the Prince of Crete." See Kerouac's letter to Charles Sampas, Dec. 27, 1949 (pp. 219–222).

4. Sebastian's older sister was Stella Sampas, who lived in the family home at 2 Stevens Street in Lowell, Massachusetts.

[February 26, 1941
New York City]
LETTER COMING

Sebastean—

J'ai vu "Mayerling" l'autre soir. C'est tout ce que vous avez dit—très triste, magnifique, et noble. Charles Boyer est une homme qui est extrêmement irresistible. (The suicide is PERFECT!)

I read Wolfe[1] at 4 A.M. this morning—"Four Lost Men"—he uses too much language, but hits the nail on the head, which counts. Am reading Jan Valtin's "Out of the Night."[2] Arise Masses!

J B de B[3]

---

1. Thomas Wolfe (1900–1938), American novelist, author of *Look Homeward, Angel* (1929), *The Web and the Rock* (1939), and *You Can't Go Home Again* (1940). Kerouac admired Wolfe above all others and took his autobiographical fiction as a literary prototype.

2. *Out of the Night* (New York: Alliance Book Corp., 1941) was a gripping autobiography by the German author Jan Valtin describing his torture by the Gestapo after he worked as a merchant seaman and undercover Communist agent during the years between the two world wars in Hamburg, Rotterdam, San Francisco, Seattle, London, Paris, Narvik and other cities. The jacket blurb of his book began, "Out of the depths of that political undertow, which for the last two decades has rolled beneath the surface stream of civilization, comes this shattering autobiography of Jan Valtin, the child of the generation nobody knows."

3. Jean, Baron de Bretagne.

[March 5, 1941
New York City]
DON'T TELL FOUCH

Sebastean—

Very sorry about the delay—unavoidable—typewriter broke down—helpless without it. Anyhow, I have something better than a letter for you—I hope you'll be pleased to know that I'm hitch-hiking home Thursday (6th), casually and poetically. I will stay till Sunday or Monday. So that we can get together and discuss over a banana split at Marion's, I am bringing a one-act play I wrote this morning at 3 A.M.

ZAGG[1]

[March 18, 1941
New York City]

Sebastean—   I

I'm sorry I didn't start sending cards sooner . . . but I had to buy a batch—and here we are.

I'm glad you read Valtin. However, read parts of the original to get wanderlust in your blood! Remember our dates—Nov. 18, 1950 'Frisco house of ill repute—March 12, 1946 Gray Sunday in Moscow with vodka and a room overlooking the roofs (Sam, please go to the library in Boston & look up "War & Peace" Chapter 3 or 4 dealing with a Moscow nite—please—the long "War & Peace"—I propose a date for the Casbah also. . . .

P.S.:[2]   II

Howie Marton is in NY for two weeks. The other night we sat in his Capitalist father's lavish study and chatted till 5 A.M.—I smoking Bourgeois 50c cigars. He would like very much to meet you. Why

---

1. A nickname given to Kerouac by his boyhood friend G. J. Apostolos.

2. Kerouac used a second postcard for this postscript.

don't you come down this weekend? Soon I'll have to start going to bed early on account of football. Howie & I took a stroll in Central Park that morning to watch the sunrise & the rosy skyline—and the famed Park birds . . .

J.

[March 25, 1941
New York City]

Sebastean—

My daily remittance hath arrived at last. Did you get my document? It is singular that we both thought of Spring at the same time. Last night, as I was coming out of "Philadelphia Story" I heard "I'll See You Again" from a cheap penny arcade—and I felt tears come to my eyes. It is the most beautiful of all songs, plus "The Man I Love" and "You Go to My Head" and others. Remember the night I left? I hardly studied this semester, yet am getting good marks. I roam the vast and rich web of the city almost nightly.[1]

[April 15, 1941
New York City]

Sebastian—

I shall write you a letter soon. I saw Walt Disney's "Fantasia" the other night. Wasn't it magnificent, especially Bach's Staccato [sic] & Fugue, the first one, and Bald Mountain and Ave Maria at the end? (I hope that's what the Bach number is called.) George came over the weekend, and we possessed the bodies of a few women; had a

---

1. In Book Four of *Vanity of Duluoz*, Kerouac described the spring of his freshman year at Columbia College, when he pledged a fraternity and sat "in an easy chair in the frat lounge playing Glenn Miller· records fullblast. Almost crying . . ." and read "Jan Valtin's *Out of the Night*, still a good book today to read. I wander around the Low Library wondering about libraries, or something."

little discussion on Union Square with a few Reds; roamed Greenwich Village; and sat by the Hudson on Sunday, ending the afternoon by gazing rapturously at some original Greek sculpture from the Parthenon frieze and some oils in the Museum of Art and watching the famed Fifth Avenue Easter parade! George also burped loudly in the face of a genuine burper.

Write soon.

Jean

TO SEBASTIAN SAMPAS

[May 5, 1941
New York City]

Prince—

Sorry if I let you down this last trip. With those guys around, I despise intellectual talk. It's not polite, nor considerate. I mean Scott and Salvey. And sometimes George isn't in the mood. I'm hoping to recrudesce my lost prestige as an intellectual this weekend:—Howie's coming in Saturday, and if you come down, we'll go through with our Manhattan interlude.

Zaggo

During the summer of 1941, Kerouac stayed home in Lowell, Massachusetts, often in the company of Sebastian Sampas, with whom he frequently hitchhiked to Boston. In Vanity of Duluoz *Kerouac described how they made trips there "several times to go see movies, lounge in Boston Common watching the people go by, occasionally Sammy leaping up to make big Leninist speeches at the soapbox area where pigeons hung around watching the argufyings." At the end of the summer, shortly before Jack began his sophomore year at Columbia College, he helped his mother, Gabrielle, pack up the family's household belongings in their rented apartment in Lowell and move to West Haven, Connecticut, where his father had found a job as a linotypist. It was the first time Kerouac's family had left Lowell, and the move was so stressful that Jack wrote a letter to his married sister*

Caroline from their new cottage in West Haven, asking her to keep Gabrielle company after he returned to New York City. Twenty-five years later, writing in Vanity of Duluoz *about this period of his life, Kerouac used the letter to his sister to refresh his memory of the experience. In the book he wrote that upon their arrival in New Haven, he and his mother had found that his father had rented "a place not even the cheapest landlord in Lowell or Tashkent would rent to the milkiest Kurd or horsiest Khan in Outer Twangolia, let alone French Canadians used to polished-floor tenements and Christmas cheer based on elbow grease and Hope."*

TO CAROLINE KEROUAC

> Tuesday afternoon
> [late summer] '41
> Seabluff
> [West Haven, Conn.]

Dear Nin . . .

We had a very tough time, but are finally settled down after much trouble. When we arrived in New Haven on that Friday morning, we found that the place Pop had picked was a hole [. . . .] Apparently he hadn't even seen it, but just picked it out from a Real Estate man's list. It was worse than anything on Moody street or Little Canada.[1] The sight of it made Ma sick. We started to look around for a place, on foot, in New Haven where there are practically *no* rents. Naturally, we didn't find one, and Ma, Burt,[2] and I walked around all day Friday (I guess it was Thursday, so from now on it's Thursday.) We finally had to store our furniture and stuff in a storage house. That night we stayed in a hotel with Pa.

Anyway, we found the New Haven rents really heavy . . . nothing under $40 a month worth living in. Pop mentioned a little place out near the sea, but said it was too far away. But we tried it, and found that it was near the trolley track (about 3½ miles from New Ha-

---

1. Franco-American neighborhoods in Lowell, Massachusetts.

2. Burt Stollmack, a friend Kerouac made as a student at Horace Mann Prep School two years before.

ven center) and that there was year 'round service from grocers, oil men, etc.

Well, Nin, we took it, and let me tell you about it. It's on the end of a street filled with cottages and houses, called Bradley Point. All the area around here is called Seabluff. The city is West Haven. We look smack at the sea, and on a clear day you can see Long Island 35 miles away. At the other end of the street is a little old shack called Barnacle Bill, a restaurant and a swanky one. Our street is filled with summer resort people—it is a summer resort, but a few people on the street live here the year 'round. To our right is a beach. Rowboats, skiffs, sailboats, and the like dot the shimmering tide. Around the point to the left, about a mile down, is the Savin Rock amusement center, something like Salisbury beach. In back of our street (and our house) there is a meadow which stretches 150 feet until it is cut by Ocean Avenue, a highway. Then the meadow continues until it reaches a cluster of palatial residences.

Oh, I tell you, it's *beautiful*. Every time you look out the parlor window you can see the ocean, and sometimes the high tide splash sprays over the sea wall across the street from our little cottage.

The cottage has five rooms, and modernistic ones too. Ma's bed faces the sea. We have a cute bathroom with sink and all. We have a shower bath in the shed adjoining the kitchen. We have a little attic where we can store our stuff. (By the way, the three bedrooms are upstairs.) We put the oil stove in the living room, and the parlor set in the front room which faces the sea. And so forth. You'll see for yourself.

It's not dangerous to live here in the winter because there is a breakwater a mile out. The waves are like those in one of the Great Lakes . . . . not tremendous breakers, but smaller waves about two feet high. And it will be a cozy little place when heated.

We are here only 75 miles from New York, and get all the stations there. There is grocer service, but the nearest grocery store is just around the little cove on the right (where the beach is.) We have gas, water, and electricity. This would have been a swell place for Tippy, but the movers said she jumped out of the truck when they stopped for lunch at Stafford Springs. Anyway, she's all right. We'll get another cat, and a dog too! The rent is $40 a month.

I have so much to say that I'm all mixed up. Anyway, you get the general idea. Now when you come down next weekend, if you're in a car find Ocean Avenue and stay on it till you get to Seabluff. Then, inquire about Bradley Point. We're at number 5, the last house on the street.

I tell you, Nin, this place is a resort. We look like millionaires, and what fun. Next summer, I'm going to get myself a job in New Haven and I will live at Seabluff, get myself a sailboat and a fishing set, and go fishing out beyond the breakwater. As a matter of fact, in a few days I'm going to borrow a rowboat and go rowing out. The day we moved, I went in for a quick swim in the cove and there was a high wind. The waves were rolling in on me in great grey mountains and I was being billowed high and then low, I grabbed a little rowboat which was anchored, and sat in the stern. Boy, did I get a thrill when it dipped its bow way up at a 45 degree angle, and then came down to slap the water hard, its bow now deep in a valley of waves . . . . and repeating with each wave.[3]

The beach couldn't be better. You can walk about fifty yards in high tide, and almost a half-mile low tide. If you come with Leslie, or in any car, find Ocean Avenue like I told you and ride till you pass the amusement park (Savin Rock) and reach Seabluff and a little beach. You'll have to come up the street with the car, come to think of it, so you'd better take a left on a dead end street off Ocean Avenue, which announces Barnacle Bill . . . . just a bit before Seabluff. If you come alone, by bus, make an appointment and I'll meet you.

Mom is working hard . . . . we all are. Pop isn't getting much work at the shop. Mom is a bit better, but she's very lonesome for you. As a matter of fact, I hate to leave her when I go to school because she'll be so alone here. It hurts me every time I think of it. Hurry over, Nin, and see the place. I'm praying that you'll decide to come home, because I can't bear the thought of leaving Mom all alone.

---

3. Kerouac described his days at Seabluff in *Vanity of Duluoz,* Book Five, Chapters 2 and 3. "As my poor mother huddled in the parlor of her new cottage she watched me walk right out into the sea and begin to swim."

That job at Sullivan's isn't so damn important . . . . there are millions of jobs around here for women. And above all, you'll live the life of Riley here. However, I'll let you decide for yourself when you come this weekend. Personally, I'm wishing with all my heart that you will decide to come to stay; then we will all be together. At any rate in the very near future.

Love,
Jack xxx Mom xxx Pop xxx

P.S.: Wait till you see the place!!

In mid-September 1941, soon after his return to Columbia, Kerouac dropped out of college after quarreling with varsity coach Lou Little, who refused to start him in the football season's opening game. With hindsight, Jack felt that his decision to leave college had been affected by the unsettled mood of the country at the end of that year: on December 7, 1941, Japanese fighter planes bombed Pearl Harbor and the United States entered World War II. Kerouac wrote in Vanity of Duluoz *that he "walked down the hot September streets of Brooklyn hearing Franklin Delano Roosevelt's speech about 'I hate war' coming out of every barbershop in Brooklyn. . . . This was the most important decision of my life so far. What I was doing was telling everybody to go jump in the big fat ocean of their own folly. I was also telling myself to go jump in the big fat ocean of my own folly. What a bath!"*

Before returning to his parents' seaside cottage in West Haven, Connecticut, Kerouac rode a bus to Washington, D.C., where he booked into a cheap hotel and wrote to Sebastian Sampas. He later told Sebastian that this letter was "probably the best thing I ever wrote, because I was young man-alone in South, tired, driven, mad, lonely, hopeless." Apparently the letter began, "I speak to you from the hearts of all the lonely young writers that have ever lived on the earth. I speak to you from their hearts because now I am one of them . . . suddenly, quickly, without a warning: I am one of them." Only a middle page of this handwritten letter to Sebastian has survived.

[mid-September 1941
Washington, D.C.]

II

. . . There, Sam, I must. And then? What then? . . . . I don't know, Sam. I don't know! I sit in this cheap hotel room on a very hot night—the sound of the trolley, the surging pulse of the city of Washington, the night breeze and no trees, no trees, yes no trees to sing for me. . . .

Oh Sam! I'm driven and weary. I'm mad, desperate. Yes—"My arms are heavy, I've got the blues: There's a locomotive in my chest, and that's a fact. . . ." I don't know what I've done—afraid to go home, too proud and too sick to go back to the football team, driven and weary with no place to go, I know not a soul, I saw the Nation's Capitol, the F.B.I. building, the National Gallery of Art, the Dept. of Justice building, "Dive Bomber" and a stage show, and I was lonely, sick, and cried. . . . [*incomplete*]

Back with his parents in the West Haven beach cottage on Long Island Sound, Jack wrote Sebastian Sampas that he lived "by the sea now, and an oyster steamer has been anchored for four days just outside my window. I can picture the men on board, working all day, and playing cards in the musty hold at night, and perhaps one of them, young, is writing. . . ." Kerouac had ambitious plans, he told Sebastian, to "write a novel, a play, a book of short stories, a radio script, and at least one deathless line," but after quarreling with his father about his decision to drop out of school to become a writer, Kerouac abruptly left home and went to Hartford to take a job that one of his friends had found for him. He sent a flurry of cards and letters to Sebastian, beginning the first one shortly after his train pulled out of the New Haven railroad station.

1 Warner St.
Hartford, Ct.
(New Address)
On a train in
New England,
just a few days
and it will be
Oktober [1941]. . . .

Sam—

I'm on my way to Hartford where I have landed a job as filling station man . . . $27.50 weekly. The train here is gliding out of New Haven. Men sit, and look out the many windows. They look at Oktober, the faint suggestion of mysterious and melancholy Oktober.

Since I returned from Virginia, I've bummed to Hartford and back, went down to New York for an amazing 24-hour sojourn, came back, and am now moving up to Hartford again where I'll share a room with old Mike, and will know man and his travails thru communion with him.[1]

I'll tell you later about my experiences in New York—"the sterile wink of lights" in front of a whorehouse, my vigil, and the pimp who fed my starving gullet which refused to break a deuce on anything but Venus; how I fell asleep in a mighty church; how I stood on a street corner and seduced New York City; how my intercourse with New York City ended in cold fever, weariness, emptiness, as all intercourses with a mistress do.

Now that I've a job, I shall be in the money, and will make arrangements to go to Lowell & Emerson. Your letter magnificent! Enclosed will find "FSSFMT."[2] You must read "Of Time & the River". . . . that's what I [incomplete]

---

1. See Kerouac's letter to Neal Cassady on January 10, 1951, about his life in Hartford and Manchester, Connecticut (pp. 295–300).
2. "FSSFMT" was apparently one of Kerouac's manuscripts.

[October 8, 1941
Hartford, Conn.]

Sam—   (Deeply grateful for your letter. . . .)

Got following writers from Hartford Library—Wolfe, Saroyan, Halper, Dos Passos, William James (Psychology). What men! And Wolfe the Giant—you must read "Of Time and the River"—all about Boston—Public Lib., Esplanade, Docks, etc. May go to Indiana soon to settle with Notre Dame.[3] If so, will take a room in Chicago hotel and write "Young Writer Remembering New York." Am going to perfect "Oktober" and send it to Orson Welles.[4] "FSSFMT" still at Harper's. . . .

Jean   YOUR LETTER SWELL

---

3. Kerouac considered transferring from Columbia to play football at Notre Dame.

4. Kerouac had written Sebastian Sampas from West Haven that he had seen Welles's film *Citizen Kane* and thought it was "really terrific."

1942

After Thanksgiving, 1941, when Leo and Gabrielle Kerouac left West Haven, Connecticut, Jack joined them back in Lowell. He wanted to enlist in the Navy, but before he was called up he took a brief job as a sportswriter with the Lowell Sun *newspaper and hitchhiked to Washington, D.C., with one of his friends. Then, in the summer of 1942, impatient to join the war, he impulsively signed up in Boston as a merchant seaman, taking out ordinary seaman's papers.*

Before receiving his assignment to a ship, Kerouac described the chaotic past months to a girlfriend named Norma Blickfelt, a Barnard College student he had dated in New York City. Apparently the letter was never sent, and when he sorted through his correspondence more than twenty years later, he wrote "Love Letter to Norma Blickfelt" across the top of the first page.

TO NORMA BLICKFELT

Wednesday Eve
July 15, 1942
Lowell, Mass.

Dear Norma—

Perhaps this letter may come as a surprise to you, since I've never written before. But please understand that, for one thing, I never really knew what to say—and further, I know full well that my handwriting is an unlovely sight. But now I must write to you, and I have so much to say that I sincerely hope I won't seem garrulous.

I've sent this Special Delivery, leaving it up to Uncle Sam to locate you for me.

After our 12-hour date last April (I thought it was wonderful), I went down to Washington, D.C., to visit a friend. Not long after, I went to work as a laborer on the New War Department project in Arlington, Va., simply to remain in the South and make a casual study of it. I stayed for a month and a half, and a fine time of it all I had. A Negro laborer went by one day with his shovel, singing the loveliest blues I ever heard—and I followed him all over the field, listening and smoking. One morning I hitch-hiked away from the project and spent the afternoon wandering through Virginia fields and villages. I returned in time to punch out at the time-clock—how was that for a day's work? But finally, I was fired because the field-boss could never find me. I took my last paycheck and headed further South, with visions of whole afternoons spent drowsing on a New Orleans river wharf, yawning, slapping off the flies, humming the blues. I had $60 (was earning $60-per week) and I think the cry of a train whistle made me decide to go on down. Halfway down Virginia's old land, I bethought me seriously about my responsibilities —going to work in order to return to Columbia. So I turned back.

Back home, I corresponded with Lou Little and made arrangements to come back to school in the Fall. Due to a temporary loss of my scholarship—I failed Chemistry my Freshman year, long before I really loved serious study—I had to save about $400 in order to pay my way until I should regain my scholarship status.

But one day, I met a very amazing young man from the Merchant Marine named George Murray. We stayed up all night, talking, until ten A.M. the next morning. When he left, on his way back to the sea (and Russia), I gave him my precious little leather-bound copy of the "Ancient Mariner."

A few days later, after long nights of thought, I went to Boston, took out my Seaman's papers, applied for a passport, and joined the National Maritime Union. I expect to be on the way to Russia within a short time. Every day, I hitch-hike down to Boston and spend part of the day waiting around the Union Hall for ships' calls. At sunset, I prowl around the docks, "drinking in the strong cod scent of the wharves," eyeing the anchored freighters and muttering: "There are ships, and there are cities." I repeat those words constantly. At night, in bed, I burn.

Murmansk, Russia—"a place more far than Fez, more strange than Cipango—." The distant Northern land, the homeless winds of the Arctic, the mist, the snow, the beautiful Barents Sea. What a strange call I hear from the sea! Perhaps my ancients, Breton fishermen, stir in my blood. Perhaps I am tired of dull, prosaic living. Perhaps I am a fool . . . but I must go. There is no need in my telling you of my impatience to get going, but perhaps you would like to know what [why] I choose to do this.

For one thing, I wish to take part in the war, not because I want to kill anyone, but for a reason directly opposed to killing—the

Brotherhood.[1] To be with my American brothers, for that matter, my Russian brothers; for their danger to be my danger; to speak to them quietly, perhaps at dawn, in Arctic mists; to know them, and for them to know myself . . . . an elusive thing, I speak of now, but I know it is there. I want to return to college with a feeling that I am a brother of the earth, to know that I am not snug and smug in my little universe. And I want to write and write and write about the Merchant Marine—the young men in its unsung service, youths with death in their eyes; irresponsible rogues who fear nothing, spend lavishly, and feed on Fate—As you know, these stories I could write may be in demand. I am on very good terms with *Esquire*—I believe they would be interested in such subject matter.

Further, there is the matter of money for school and some economic security for my family. (We are paid between $1500 and $2000 on returning from a trip to Russia—it takes about five months to complete.)

Oh, I know all about the danger and the extreme hardship. But I also know about Emerson's Great Necessity, and what he said about Fate: "A man's fortunes are the fruit of his character . . ."

What tension! Smoking a pipe below, heavily bearded, studying, awaiting the cry:—"Here comes Jo-Jo!" (Torpedo.) Some fellows develop what we call "torpedo fever." And what enormous meals we eat—and the Arctic tempests, machine-gunning the mines, docking at Iceland, Liverpool, Northern Scotland, and finally Murmansk or Archangel—drinking vodka with comrades of the Comintern, daily air raids, tramping through the outlying farmlands wearing a heavy sheepskin, red scarf, and boots, unloading the rich cargoes from America. . . .

If I don't come back, apparently I wasn't destined to become a great writer. That is why I think I shall come back.

When I return, I'll buy my mother a fur coat; I'll stock up with all the books I ever wanted, a huge collection including the *Encyclopedia Britannica* [11th edition]; classical records and Le Jazz Hot, from

---

1. The Brotherhood—a reference to Kerouac's idealistic political discussions about "the Brotherhood of Man" with his friend Sebastian Sampas and others in Lowell. See *Vanity of Duluoz*, Book Five, 1, and Book Six, 2.

"Tristan und Isolde" to Art Tatum; a wardrobe for school (I intend to re-enter for the second semester in January—one can leave the Merchant Marine at will); a trip to the *Esquire* people in Chicago, laden with manuscripts; two luxurious weeks in New York, seeing all the shows, etc.; a white Russian tunic for Sebastian, who, incidentally, will be very pleased when I bring him a small box of Russian soil from the U.S.S.R.—"the soil of Russia is the soul of Russia—"

And a million other things, the most important one being economic fortification of my home. As I see it now, this step is the only one for me.

Perhaps, when I return in the late Fall, you'll join me in seeing the shows, operas, concerts, and dining at the best places. How about Russian Art on Second Avenue, "where ex-Volga boatmen and deep-thinking pessimists weep into their vodka while guitars tinkle songs of home?" Sound O.K.?

Ah, but this is a rambling mess of a letter. Please allow me to apologize. So many ideas rush to my pen—such chaos! But after all, I *am* going to Russia . . .

But now, let's talk about you. I'll be anxious to hear whether or not you're at that children's camp near Poughkeepsie for the summer, and if you've succeeded in being assigned to care for blind children. If so, please let me know about your progress, experiments, and further plans. I would like you very much to answer this letter post-haste and airmail, so that I may hear from you before I ship off. Will you have time? I hope I'm not too forward in asking for an answer, because I remember you had given your class ring to a Columbia man last Spring. Disregarding that disconcerting factor, please try to send me a small snapshot of yourself and send it along—if you have one.

Those long nights below, I should like very much to brood over your letter and picture. You have the mind of a man, and the heart & body of a woman. *You* are dark and burning Helen. . . . I was still of a mind to go to your camp this summer and see you—and I was going to tell you these things—but now I must go down to the sea in ships. . . . And, somehow, I'm very sorry I can't see you till I return. We always had so much to talk about—remember that den in Chinatown, and the way you sang in German for me on the Ferry? I can still envision your blown straw-colored hair; your Norwegian eyes, your blue, engaging eyes—all silhouetted against the New York skyline. And the strong wind. . . .

This is a mad letter, I know. But I've always been this way.

Have you been reading Thomas Wolfe and William Saroyan? . . . and if so, what do you think of them? I took your advice and read Thomas Mann—he certainly is a great and true Humanist. Speaking of Humanists, I am a member of a young Humanist movement in Boston. We are obscure, and may never dent progress—but we have heated discussions and plenty of intellectual stimulation.

Now I must close this unwieldy document, for I have journeyed to the last page.

What is there to say? Howso? . . . Why? What a strange and beautiful life this is . . . as weird and lovely as the very sea. It is hard to say goodbye. There are many things I could say now, but I shall not say them, for, if ever I could never return, I should not be grieved for. That is why I go, quietly, with my plans, and commit nothing and expect nothing, but love everything.

Auf Wiedersehen,
Jack

Keeping his first letter to Norma Blickfelt as a "monument to my emotional 'teens," Kerouac wrote her again when he went off to sea. He sailed out of Boston harbor on July 18, 1942, hired as a scullion on board the Merchant Marine ship S.S. Dorchester *transporting a construction crew to Greenland. German submarines launched two unsuccessful torpedo attacks on the ship in the North Atlantic, as Kerouac later described in* Vanity of Duluoz: *"So I'm frying the bacon for one thousand men, that is, two thousand strips of bacon, on a vast black range, while Glory and the other assistant cooks are doing the scrambled eggs. I'm wearing a life jacket, O Baldwin apples. I hear 'Boom boom' outside. . . ."*

August 25, 1942

Love letter written at sea

Dear Norma—

You must excuse the stationery (and the pencil), but aboard these ships one is not always able to procure monogrammed and perfumed writing paper—I borrowed this sheet from the Puerto Rican night cook, who presented me it for so graciously composing a love letter for him.

How are you, Norma? Will you forgive me for not writing sooner. . . . I can't tell you very much, nor where I am, but I *can* say that I'm in the Merchant Marine, and in a very beautiful and enchanted land. I would have written to you sooner, but since at times things around here take on the aspects of war, I was not able.

Let me confess that I wrote you a long and dramatic letter before I shipped out, but I never mailed it. Of course, I was not able to visit you this summer as I had planned (at the Poughkeepsie camp), since I sailed out quite some time ago. But as to that letter, I shall preserve it as a monument to my emotional 'teens. (As I write now, the little Morro cook sits beside me eating oatmeal and Spanish chicken rice . . . it is morning, a grey drizzling dawn prevails, etc. etc.) . . . and I am in a most poetic mood. I'm studying like mad on this ship— *Outline of History*,[1] the Roman writers, some classics, Thomas Mann (what a Humanist!), and *The Shadow* Magazine.[2] Anxious to get back to dear old Columbia, if I can, in January. I took this trip in order to make money for school, but I misjudged the length of the voyage, and will not be back in time for the Fall semester. But what romance! . . . to stand on a deck bare-chested at dawn, and to listen to the pulse-beats of the ship's great, idle engine—Wolfe's "morning and new lands . . ." In the interim between this trip and January, I

---

1. H. G. Wells (1866–1946), *Outline of History* (1920). Kerouac wrote in *Vanity of Duluoz* that he went to sea "with a little black bag containing rags and a collection of classical literature weighing several ounces in small print."

2. *The Shadow* magazine was an American biweekly pulp magazine featuring the aristocratic hero crime fighter Lamont Cranston. Kerouac had read it avidly as a boy, and it was later an influence on his writing of *Doctor Sax*.

shall go down to New Orleans for a South American ship. As soon as I return from this run, I'm taking a room in the Village for a few weeks to write like mad (with Sebastian, of course), and take in the theatrical season. I'll call you up as soon as I arrive, and if Saroyan's on Broadway and the Russian restaurants go on tinkling songs of home while Russians weep into their vodka, we'll take that in together.

(Perceive—I have another sheet!)

How's Barnard? (You see, I don't know when you'll receive this note.) If not so, how's the camp? Did you succeed in being assigned to the care of blind children? Can there be such a thing as a female Humanist? (As Budd Schulberg[3] said, when a man finds a woman who can think, he blithely allows that she has the "body and heart of a woman, and the mind of a man.") Naive or not, that is you all over.

We did have a wonderful time last April, didn't we! Third Avenue (our penthouse, our little song), the Bowery, Chinatown, Union Square, the Harbor and your engaging little German singing, and the G.A. with its orgiastic Joe Colleges . . . (Shades of Elliott Nugent[4] . . .) Twelve hours together, twelve hours after almost two years, and now, months since April. I must make up for this when I return . . . after I left N.Y. last Spring, I went on South and wandered about in my own lonely way, from city to city, village to village, listening to the Negroes sing the blues, eating and working in lunch-carts, hopping freights and listening to the great American music of a train whistle. But I never did hit Asheville, N.C., Wolfe's home-town. I will next time. Suffice it to say I enjoyed myself, but the next time I wander America, I'll have money to do it more freely. And stories—I've millions of them, all ready to pop out. Now, more than ever, do I want to write. I've left aimlessness and paradoxical chaos behind me. . . . I'm developing an understanding of relations, which I believe is true knowledge, and I find the particular Genius of poetry

---

3. Budd Schulberg was the author of the best-selling Hollywood novel *What Makes Sammy Run?* (1941).

4. Elliott Nugent was a popular stage and film actor, playwright, and director.

(as Thoreau would have put it) quite redundant in myself . . . (entrez l'ego). I am either frank, or egotistical & vain, or all three. I don't remember Whitman having been self-depreciating, nor Wolfe with his long hours at the mirror, nor Saroyan indeed, nor Joyce,[5] etc. If anybody tells me I'm disillusioning myself, or harboring "pretenses to a higher mentality," or even "trying to rise from the 'people'," as my father claims,[6] I'll tell them they're damned fools and will go on writing, studying, travelling, singing, loving, seeing, smelling, hearing, and feeling. . . . Write to me, Norma; I miss you. Address: JACK KEROUAC A.P.O. 858 c/o Postmaster, N.Y. City. Forwarded Air Mail to us. Yours ever, Jack.

After the S.S. Dorchester *arrived in Nova Scotia, Kerouac wrote a quick letter to Sebastian Sampas on the stationery of the Allied Merchant Seamen's Club in Sydney.*

TO SEBASTIAN SAMPAS

[September 26, 1942
Sydney, Nova Scotia]

Sebastian—

Hello my comrade and cher ami! I shall be home soon—was not able to write before—and from Nova Scotia, here in the excellent Seamen's Club, I write. I'll be home for a week immediately after signing off the ship. Then I shall go down to Washington for memories of last Spring, Jeanie, G.J., Paul Myerson, Ed Dutton. Following this, with a possible dash down to Asheville, I am returning to N.Y.

---

5. Along with Wolfe and Saroyan, James Joyce was another literary influence on Kerouac at this time. See *Vanity of Duluoz*, Book Six, 2.

6. In *Vanity of Duluoz*, Kerouac dramatized the arguments between his parents about him after he dropped out of Columbia and came back to live at home. Gabrielle always took Jack's side in his quarrels with his father, telling her son, "Listen to me, dont listen to him, if you do, you'll be the same thing he is, he never did anything himself . . . he's jealous that you'll go out and make something of yourself. . . ."

for an apartment in the Village—at which time I expect you will join me (10 days of life) and enter the Merchant Marine also. At the expiration of my shore freedom, we can grab a tanker for Texas (be home for Xmas), or a coal boat to Newport News, Va. (several trips), or So. America, West Indies, Far East, Russia, etc. What say?

Are you still in the Navy Yard? I have further suggestions—we can discuss them my first week home, including everything under the sun from Picasso, Corot, Interpretive Dancing, and Prometheanism[1] to the subtlety of Johnny Koumantzelis and the Doris Miller affair, etc.

See you then. Fist up!

Your brother,
Jean

P.S.—Warmest regards to Connie, Eddie, etc.
P.P.S.S.—Was I drunk last night! Went up to the Collieries near Sydney and conversed biologically with a woman thrice, to the sound of sad mine-whistles. How Green Was My Wallet then—

When Kerouac returned to New York harbor on the S.S. Dorchester *in late October 1942, Sebastian Sampas was waiting for him on the dock and they returned to Lowell together. At home Jack learned that Lou Little, the football coach at Columbia, had invited him back to college. Jack accepted the offer and went back to school. On its next voyage the* Dorchester *was sunk by torpedoes, with the loss of several hundred lives. Impulsively, after a month at Columbia, where Kerouac again felt himself slighted by the coach ("If they wont let me play I aint gonna hang around"), he wrote Sebastian of his decision to go back to the Merchant Marine and described his vision of the freedom they would have traveling the world together.*

---

1. The Young Prometheans was a group of Sebastian Sampas's friends in Lowell who met informally to discuss politics, philosophy, and literature. See *Vanity of Duluoz*, Book Five, 6, for Kerouac's description of Sebastian's idealism.

Friday Eve

November, 1942

[New York City]

A relic of battered pasts and buried projects

Sebastian . . .

This is going to be a short letter, and to the point. I'm asking your advice, and not only that, I'm assuming that you will make an important decision yourself.

I personally have seen enough of the Navy regimentation here at Columbia. . . . I don't believe I shall join the Naval Reserve. My money is running low, and my family is once more in financial straits. And being truly myself, I am not too conceited about the prospects of a Naval officer's uniform. In brief, I believe I shall go back to the Merchant Marine for the duration of the war as ordinary seaman. I am wasting my money and my health here at Columbia . . . it's been one huge debauchery. I hear of American and Russian victories, and I insist on celebrating. In other words, I am more interested in the pith of our great times than in dissecting "Romeo and Juliet". . . . at the present, understand. These are stirring, magnificent times. I feel like a fool each time I think of Pat Reel.[1] And I am not sorry for having returned to Columbia, for I have experienced one terrific month here. I had a gay, a mad, a magnificent time of it. But I believe I want to go back to sea . . . for the money, for the leisure and study, for the heart-rending romance, and for the pith of the moment.

Sebastian, come with me, come with me! Your Maritime Cadet business will last 22 months . . . why, Man, the war will be over by then. Do you want to waste 22 months of your poet's life in strict, militarist regimentation at $65 per month? I certainly don't, for I also considered that branch. Don't you want to travel to the Mediterranean ports, perhaps Algiers, to Morocco, Fez, the Persian Gulf, Calcutta, Alexandria, perhaps the old ports of Spain; and Belfast, Glasgow, Manchester, Sidney, New Zealand; and Rio and Trinidad

---

1. Pat Reel was a friend Kerouac met a few months earlier aboard the *Dorchester,* who had fought for the Loyalists in Spain.

and Barbados and the Cape; and Panama and Honolulu and the far-flung Polynesias . . . I don't want to go alone this time. I want my friend with me . . . my mad poet brother.[2]

If you don't want to relinquish your present training position, which is perhaps forthcoming, then of course I shall go alone, but alone, Sam, and palely loitering.[3]

Think it over. This is not an offer . . . it is a suggestion to meditate upon, and to convey advice therewith.

Write immediately! . . . and tell me what you think. I shall be home for Thanksgiving. As soon as you take your papers out, we shall go down to New York or Baltimore and grab a nice clean tanker or freighter, not a rotten swarming tub like the *Dorchester*. We may come across George Murray, Joe Souzin, Hank Cru[4] (recently left for the Mediterranean, because he told me about the second front in Africa before he left, which was a week before it happened), and others. You may write the novel "A Seaman's Semen."

We can stock up with enormous quantities of books and plan huge study schedules, discussions, and debates. And I shall teach you chess. If we get killed, it is only in homage to Bill Chandler.[5]

Your Comrade,
Jean

---

2. In Book Seven of *Vanity of Duluoz,* Kerouac wrote, "Now that I look back on it, if Sabby could have got his Coast Guard papers on time & sailed on that ship with me he might have lived through the war."

3. A reference to the first stanza of John Keats's poem "La Belle Dame Sans Merci" (1820):

> O, what can ail thee, knight-at-arms,
>   Alone and palely loitering?
> The sedge has wither'd from the lake,
>   And no birds sing.

4. Henri Cru was a friend from Horace Mann Prep School.

5. Bill Chandler was a Lowell friend and talented cartoonist who shared Kerouac's desire to become a merchant seaman.

1943

Home in Lowell at the beginning of 1943, Kerouac recuperated from a bout of German measles and waited to be called up into the Naval Air Force V-12 program. Almost obsessively he worked on a novel titled "The Sea Is My Brother." He shared his view of himself as an aspiring novelist with another Lowell friend, Bill Ryan, who was studying engineering at Boston College.

TO BILL RYAN

Jan. 10, 1943
[Lowell, Mass.]

Dear Bill,

Received your letter. I was amazed at its size and bulk, but at the contents therein, I found what I had expected to find—a stripped prose flashing, at intervals, with deep insight. "I felt like someone who had been fighting a dummy in the dark and screaming; and then the lights go on, and there you stand, sheepish." (I quote from memory.) That's a very good bit of writing, and it serves to explain exactly how you must feel about the disillusionment of Mars; Sebastian kept saying one thing about it, "I've been cheated!" I think your attitude comes nearer to the truth. (He expected to find "the brotherhood.")

You remind me, Bill, of a certain type, or genre, of writer I have always deeply envied. The "lean, hardhitting writer" so well typified by a Sinclair Lewis or an Arthur Koestler or a John Dos Passos.[1] These writers seem to me to hit at the heart of things with a terrific force. Wolfe came close to the heart of things, but he is not the incisive, precise dissector; Lewis was. (Wolfe greatly admired Lewis for that.)

Before I go on, please don't assume that I am discussing Wolfe-Kerouac and Ryan-Lewis. I know it will sound like that; by saying this, I do not slip into an unconscious error.

Here's what I mean. We are two types of writers; one belongs to one school, to one aspect/attitude, one to the other. You went to

---

1. Sinclair Lewis (1885–1951), author of *Babbitt* (1922) and other satiric novels; Arthur Koestler (1905–1983), British author of *Darkness at Noon* (1941); John Dos Passos (1896–1970), author of the experimental *U.S.A.* trilogy (1936).

B.C. [Boston College] and I to Columbia. One of the truths you gleaned out of your college experience was a truth typical of your artistic makeup: you saw these engineering students and dissected them unmercifully. Lewis dissected Babbittry. Out of Columbia I only gleaned one truth: that formal education is not near enough an approach to Minerva. Wolfe, with his "subjective gushings," found life on the whole in America not near enough to Apollo.

Where the Lewis-school attacks problems one by one, with blistering satire, and leaves them smouldering in ashes, the Wolfe-school attacks no problems at all but writes over their heads, so to speak. I am not old enough as a thinker to presume an analysis of the distinction. But if you can faintly grasp the distinction as I have posed it, you might at least reach a level of understanding with me and agree in a fundamental sense. I have always wanted to write epics and sagas of great beauty and mystic meaning (and I believe I may grow out of that in time, as I seem to be doing now since pursuing psychology); you, I am certain, have always wanted to write satiric novels, on the majestic scale of a Tolstoi or a Dickens . . . despite what you said in your last letter about wanting to write a "slick" Army novel. You know yourself that you are lying; you will never turn "slick"; and not because you're a dreamy-eyed one, but because you love truth as fiercely as Wolfe loved beauty.

Your last letter served to strengthen these opinions I had of you as an artist: for I truly think you are an artist.

Incidentally, I've been trying to work out the third version of "The Sea Is My Brother" these past few weeks. You may not know this, but the little novel you read in Lowell that night has grown into a gigantic saga.[2] Wesley Martin has two brothers now, Peter and Big Slim. A hell of a lot happens: love, the tribulations of the generation, war, the sea, foreign countries, etc., etc. But after Wesley and Slim have perished at sea, their younger brother Peter stands on 5th Avenue in New York City watching a funeral of grandeur and high

---

2. In *Vanity of Duluoz,* Book Eight, 14, Kerouac wrote, "I'm home again with Ma and I start neatly handprinting a beautiful little novel called 'The Sea Is My Brother,' which is a crock as literature but as handprinting beautiful."

solemnity purr down the street. It is the funeral of J.B. Astorbilt, or someone like that: it is a hero's funeral, for J.B. Astorbilt had, a week before his death, contracted pneumonia on a flight to England for the government. High dignitaries pass by in black limousines, and the flowers are worth a small fortune. The Hearst Tabloid has a black band across its front page. The city is in solemn mourning. Peter enters a bar and writes an epitaph for his brothers on the back of a matchbook and then throws it away in the harbor waters. "Why?" asks the Great Asker.

I mention this passage, which I intend to close the book with, to illustrate what I meant a while back by "outgrowing" the adolescent side of Wolfeanism: the stone, leaf-door pattern, which has its place in any attitude toward history. A sort of melioration of dynamics with statics.

No one in America, notwithstanding, has ever said as much as Wolfe said. I am not going to discredit Wolfe, as so many fools are doing now in the light of contemporary history: it gives these fools a new sense of superiority to discredit the master, and it will last until they rediscover his essential greatness, which may be too late and may cause a great deal of mortification. Wolfe wrote about the essential and everlasting America, not the V-for-Victory America. Today's writers have to combine both Americas, if they chose of course to be in some sense timely. It is their choice; it is my choice for the time being—and I don't deny the reason: I would like, for a change, to have my stuff published.

It has always seemed to me a great injustice that the artists of the world are expected to produce, along with their "great" works, the commodities for consumption which all non-artists are expected to produce. [*At the bottom of this letter, Kerouac wrote, "1943 Unmailed letter to Bill Ryan of Lowell, who died in the South Pacific. JK."*]

Kerouac continued to correspond with Sebastian Sampas, who was in boot camp training to become a medic at Camp Lee, Virginia.

Monday Morning
2 A.M.
February 1943
[Lowell, Mass.]

Dear Sebastian,

I have just returned from work and this is the first time I've used my typewriter in more than a week—an ecstatic moment! (It seems to me now that my life is writing, be it only words without meaning: in the beginning, Logos.)

My job is at the Hotel Garage on Middlesex Street; it affords me plenty of time to read, despite the fact that I am at the beck and call of every customer that comes in in the middle of an intricate theory to have me park his car. But parking cars sustains a certain aesthetic satisfaction, the subtlety of giving an inch's grace to a sleek fender, and the exhilaration of jamming on the foot brake within certain disaster. (Today, G.J.[1] the Drunken Sailor was with me, and, as usual, I tried to outdo him in virility—I only succeeded in smashing a fender against a garage post while backing up at 30 miles per in the small space that I had to operate in; however, he enjoyed the madness immensely, and we must admit that there is a certain element of virility in ruining cars.) I must confess now that I have had little time to write you a letter from home, if none at all, but plenty of time to write to you from the garage office. The trouble is I want to write you good letters, neatly typed out and long, and I waited till I could find leisure time at home to undertake a "document." Yes, I shall outline our experience and our stage of development, but first I must chat about other things; however, I firmly believe we have found ourselves more successfully than any of the Prometheans,[2] which includes Yann, Connie, Eddie, and the whole shooting much

---

1. George J. Apostolos, a friend in Lowell since grammar school, had gone on to business college and was not part of the discussion group in Lowell called the Young Prometheans.

2. In addition to Sebastian and Jack, the Young Prometheans also included Cornelius ("Connie") Murphy, George Constantinides, Ed Tully, and Jim O'Dea.

[sic]: Mais c'est seulement mon opinion. (But my opinion is mine, and it is yours to reflect upon.)

Chat:—(Stream of Consciousness for the Sake of Informality):— As to GJ, I think he is the smuggest sonofabitch that ever lived, but I am humble and tolerant like you and let him rave on [. . . .] but he is not my friend, only a "pal." . . . Been reading your letter over and over: hemophilia was it? Blood all over the bed streaming from your jaw? What the hell is it? Serious? Honestly, Sam, you scare me with your stories about the hospital: I'm not afraid of physical pain (not Yet), but I don't want you to die because if you die how shall I do it alone? . . . Take care of yourself, and remember this one thing: You are big and strong and husky and a tough Greek and a Cretan warrior and a tawny lusty youth and nothing can kill you. (That's how I think you are and myself too . . . I think we're both rugged enough to withstand anything . . . clench your fist at the heavens like Beethoven.) (Because there is a hell of a lot to do, and not much time to do it, time flows by like a river and a wind is rising.) . . . Am reading "Theory of the Leisure Class" by Thorstein Veblen, the greatest Liberal of his time (died 1929); here's how Dos Passos tells about him in *U.S.A.* the book: "Veblen, a greyfaced shambling man lolling resentful at his desk with his cheek on his hand, in a low sarcastic mumble of intricate phrases subtly paying out the logical inescapable robe of matteroffact for a society to hang itself by, dissecting out the century with a scalpel so keen, so comical, so exact . . ." Veblen writes of the leisure class as the shrewd, exploiting group in society that holds the strings and glares to be called superior, that takes no part in production, only in the role of entrepreneur smoking cigars and being superior and smug and forgetful, in short, the enemy. But his scalpel, how can I possibly tell you about his lodestone mind without quoting him? but I shan't. You must try to read him if you feel the need to understand the sociological implications of the collective movement—the weary unstopping march of the common man, a world for brothers. You know the spiritual, Veblen will give you the sociological and psychological. . . . Jim O'Dea was home for two weeks, and I hung around with him and Billy Ryan, a B.C. engineering student who has dropped the course to take up writing (he happened on Tom Wolfe,[3] and bingo! presto! a new writer—he's good too, but a little too unimpassioned and so far uninitiated in the hard ways of the writer's world.) [. . . .] I see a lot of Yann[4] and Connie [. . . .] Yann, lost when he steps out of a barroom at Midnight for there is no more to drink, lost when he turns off a record of Beethoven's slow quartets, lost when he is unable to write, lost in a maze of house-keeping and boiler-tending and dish-washing, pauvre pauvre Ian [. . . .] By virtue of my youth and enthusiasm and fire, Yann tells me at night, blondly brooding, sad like Byron, he has been reborn: perhaps! But by virtue of his weary knowledge, his calm wisdom and pent, passive strength, I too have been reborn: I see within the realms of his truly great mind the wry diamond of Shakespeare's visage, the bejowled heaviness of Beethoven's face, the pale purple vistas of long-ago poetry, long-ago love, trees against the horizon, all the classic meaning of life, pent up in his pale brow like a submissive nightingale: Brahms, Schubert, Milton, the Bard, Donne, Beethoven (the heavy frown, the sneering sag of jowls, the eyes of thunder), Housman, Dante, Wagner, Wolfe, Elgar, Debussy. . . . I see them all, the High Priests of Beauty; and Ian, full of Beauty, drunk and weary with it, weighted with it, broods anciently in his Chamber of Beauty (the books, the music, the feasts, the discussions) and is lost. Is lost! Why? It is because he lives in an Industrial Age, an Age verging on Collectivism, on Use-Value and Proletariat and other Marxian terms, on the quiet dissection of Veblen, the fury of Wolfe, the deadly organization of Dos Passos, the wrath of six million Russians in the snow, the iconoclastic laugh of a Pat Reel—in short, Sebastian, I have learned from Ian, unconsciously, that my mission is to present Beauty to the Collectivists, and in turn, introduce the men of Beauty to Collectivism. . . . I am ambassador, mediator, soother, host.

And Ian is lost and does not believe that I can accomplish this, but you know I can. . . . shall I save Yann? Shall *we* save Yann? I think

---

3. Tom Wolfe: the novelist Thomas Wolfe.

4. Yann was the nickname of John MacDonald, a friend from Bartlett Junior High School in Lowell and a member of the Young Prometheans.

we shall. . . . Billy Ryan is a good kid and would like to meet you now that he has learned about you from me. He is mad about Wolfe, absolutely stunned him out of engineering. Speaking of that, I know of another kid at Columbia who has decided to become a writer from reading Wolfe! What more proof of his greatness? He is starting another Renaissance. . . . I am corresponding with Norma, and one morning I got a letter from her that almost made me rush to the window, open it, and shout out to the world: "I love Norma!" . . . for she is Helen; I shall enclose her next letter in one of the future letters I write to you; I have already sent her the leaf and the note you sent me ("the leaf unturned") in my last letter. (It was beautiful of you to do that . . . a leaf from Virginia of the old earth.) Yes, Norma is fair and some day I shall marry her and breed a brood of brats, all of whom shall be distinguished writers, humanists, humorists, satirists, essayists, critics, playwrights, poets, and all communists. (I shall marry Norma when I am 35, perhaps 40, perhaps 45, who knows? If she agrees to marry a wandering revolutionist, then perhaps I'll marry her sooner; but certainly not before 32 at least; there is a limit to the demands of society's laws.)

When I am thirty-three I shall put a bullet,

straight through me.
I wrote a letter to George Dastou tonight [. . . .] I am memorizing *P.M.*,[5] day by day. . . . I haven't heard from the Navy, and if I don't in another month, I shall go to see you in Virginia before I ship out to sea again. . . . the other night I saw little trees on Princeton Boulevard 'mid the tall, hardy, just pines: the little trees were leaning in the winter wasteland; they were wintering in bent and bitter misery. . . . I wrote a poem: "Tall pines standing like justice, the cold stare of stars between; I walk down the road, holding my ears, shelters from dry sweeps of brittle cold. 'Who has known Fury?' Wolfe had shouted, and the critic's winter eye (like these stars between the pines) had stared, amusedly. Come, it is warm in my house; we shall go there; soon the flashing sun will rise to overwhelm the petulant

---

5. *PM* was a tabloid published daily in New York City from 1940 to 1948. The newspaper was so progressive that it didn't accept advertising in its pages.

stars." (The critic in question: Alfred Kazin, "On Native Grounds,"[6] insulter of Wolfe—"naive, a grown-up boy looking at the world through his own eye." Kazin doesn't look at the world thru *his* own eye apparently because there was mud thrown there at a time when he possibly attempted creative writing and failed miserable.) I loathe critics. I saw Michael Largay the other night, we drank beer with Ian, talked, and made an appointment to go see him at his Boston apartment this Thursday with Billy Ryan—we shall feast in a good restaurant, take in a concert, get drunk and discuss all night . . . it should be a memorable evening. You see, they haven't cheated me just quite yet, and I am holding out as long as I can!

Sam! I have run out of cigarettes, you bastard! How can I continue?

Now I must end the letter in answer to your request which I now graciously fulfill. Our experience? It's been wonderful . . . you saw a lot of things that I didn't see and vice versa. But, in the end, like two normal youths, we saw the wrong, the root of the ill, and the cure. We cannot live in a world of vested wealth, property, privilege and selfish greed . . . in answer to the stale, flat reply of Catholicism, I say, like Shaw,[7] you can't save an empty stomach. You can find your soul in solitude, but why starve when the world is groaning at the bins? There are many brothers about us. Remember the NMU speech at Manhattan Center by Joe Curran? Henri [Cru] was with us, and we watched the colored girl with the two Jewesses, we clapped with the seamen, we saw the Union secretary in his leather jacket. We know too the art-killers among them, like Louise Levitas of *P.M.* who makes jokes about Orson Welles because she is envious of his genius, a repressed, lascivious Bitch. I remember Reel calling Wolfe a careerist because he wanted fame. I look all about my brothers and reflect what shall be done. And so do you. Our experience has been that we have discovered the Joy of Life, like Beethoven, who winds us his Ninth Symphony with a 200-person chorus singing together the words of Schiller's "Ode to Man" [sic] . . . a mightly

---

6. Alfred Kazin's *On Native Grounds* (1942) was subtitled "An Interpretation of Modern American Prose Literature."

7. George Bernard Shaw (1856–1950), eminent British playwright and socialist.

oath in song of communal brotherhood and immortal joy. Wolfe never knew this, he was a lonely man, he did not know that man was made to know man and to love him as his brother. It is the final thing, and we may not see it achieved, but we shall bring it about . . . ignorance, stupidity, bigotry, brutality: all must be tolerated, treated as in therapy, borne in quiet, repressed with slow, sullen, invincible truth! Your comrade, Jean

Write! Write! Write!

TO SEBASTIAN SAMPAS

Drunken letter
[undated—early March 1943
Lowell, Mass.]

Sebastian!

You magnificent bastard! I was just thinking about you, and all of a sudden, I feel

    very Sebastianish,

    very Bohemian!

    very Baroque!

    very GAY!   (TURN!)

I was thinking, in a flash of glory, about all the things we've done!!!—and all the others we're going to do!

AFTER THE WAR, WE MUST GO TO FRANCE AND SEE THAT THE REVOLUTION GOES WELL! AND GERMANY TOO! AND ITALY TOO! AND *RUSSIA!*

For 1. Vodka

     2. Love

     3. Glory.

We must find Pat Reel and get drunk with him; we must get tanked up with Phillipe: like Paxton Hibben, we must lay a wreath on Jack Reed's grave in Moscow—[1]

---

1. John Reed (1887–1920), a radical American writer who went to Russia and described the 1917 revolution in his brilliant book *Ten Days That Shook the World* (1920). He was buried in Moscow's Red Square.

Harvard boy—died in MOSCOW!

Sebastian you son of a beetch!

HOW ARE YOU?

I AM DRUNK!

Do you hear me? Do not die, *live!* We must go to Paris and see that the revolution goes well! And the counter-revolutions in GERMANY, SPAIN, ITALY, YUGOSLAVIA, POLAND ETC.ETC.ETC.

We must go to Bataan and pick a flower. . . .

SEBASTIAN!

SYMPATHY!

To hell with
  La Bourgeoisie!

No, *La Bourgueosie!* [sic]

To hell with
  Hearst[2]

To hell with
  Everything

That does not
  add up
    TO

Brothers living together and laughing their labours to fruition!

DECK THYSELF *NOW* WITH MAJESTY AND EXCELLENCY: CAST DOWN THE WICKED IN THEIR PLACE. . . .

Au diable
  AVEC

les cochons capitalistes,

y los cabrones
  cientificos!

STRUMBOUTSOMOUGAVALA
  with the Salops Riches! [sic]

SYMPATHIE!

C'est le bon mot . . .

C'est le seul mot . . .

---

2. William Randolph Hearst (1863–1951), dynastic American newspaper publisher.

La Sympathie et l'humeur—
J'AIME MES FRÈRES:
ILS SONT TRAGIQUES,
BEAUX, BONS, Beaucoup de noblesse—
A l'avant!
Sebastian:—

Red Wine, I have just written to Norma, my Gretchen, my Humanist—Socialist—Psychologist—Amorous love!

This isn't folly, this is me! I am mad with ardor for all things AND Sebastian!

THE LEAF UNTURNED

In a month or so, if I don't hear from the Navy, I shall ship out, I shall go to Camp Lee, and see you, I shall infuse you with new hope. You're not cheated! You're magnificent!

JEAN Louis le Brise de Kerouac, Baron de Bretagne, retired. AU REVOIR.

Sebastian Sampas's letters to Kerouac document their shared idealism in matters of politics, philosophy, and literature. They also give a sense of the debates with friends in the Young Promethean circle in Lowell, as in this letter from Sebastian to Jack shortly after Kerouac's twenty-first birthday.

TO JACK KEROUAC
FROM SEBASTIAN SAMPAS

March 15, 1943
[Camp Lee, Va.]

Jack,

You may or may not pardon this letter, but as I am writing it in the black heat of exasperation you may evaluate it as such. Your letter has caused me no end of annoyance, either to the defense of your ego or mine. I have asked you to look at things logically and instead you have done just the reverse.

Of course Promethianism hasn't arrived, but at least by working toward the right direction no harm can come of it. You claim that individuals such as ourselves have forged groups such as ours and have helped mankind, and you dismiss the whole issue. The great John Kerouac dissents and the whole issue is forgotten—

If you were dissatisfied with the procedure of Promethianism why didn't you cry out before—why wait until now? when all of us will be broken up before long—

If our viewpoints on society do not co-relate, God, man, you know how hard I have tried by weighing everything carefully to make them coincide.

I am sore, Jack, good and sore. You imagine me a comic—wallowing in a pseudo-tragic drama of seeing the disintegration of my friendships—I know not whether it is done through your purposely misunderstanding me or whether some more evil purpose is motivating your actions—

No one has tried to fuse many into One—We stressed time & again our own individualities, but simply that we would have greater strength in evaluating issues—

You know and have known from the beginning—if you wish to withdraw that is your privilege. I will always value your friendship but I will not lead a blind life—I want mine to have a purpose in uplifting mankind & you know as well as I that five heads are better than one. In doing so, I do not relinquish my prerogative for great artistry—

I have tried to help you and you turn against me, fearing that my helping you, automatically places me in a superior position.

For Christ's Sake, Jack, just when we are all arriving at some cohesion, you write a letter showing that you have misunderstood the thing entirely.

I myself do not know whether I shall be active in the Promethean Home. For all I know after the war I may be a seaman on some world-cruising ship.

I may be in Hollywood or the Village.

You haven't seen men who live their lives in vain—

Maybe the picture of being misunderstood and lonely, defying all mankind, appeals to you—it doesn't to me—

Wolfe was at odds with the world—so John Kerouac will be at odds with the world—

Do not choose, whatever way is easier.

Your letters have been unusually good—but I don't see anymore poetry.

[. . . .] I have not been just in this letter, Jack. I have only attempted to ward off certain tendencies you have—I had to speak candidly and it has hurt you but not as much as it hurt me—

Sincerely,
Sebastian

[. . . .] Comrade—

> Curst be the wind-swept
>   stars
> And the night be one
>   as thunder
> You've had your share of
>   scars
> Comrade! We shan't go
>   under—

Sebastian

TO SEBASTIAN SAMPAS

March 15, 1943
[Lowell, Mass.]

Dear Sam,

Just a short note to acknowledge receipt of your stirring recording. My mother played it when I was still in bed sleeping, and I woke up hearing your voice. My mother was weeping, Sam. When you quoted Wolfe, she thought you were sounding your own death-knell; she said "The poor little kid. Oh! this is an awful war." And she wept for you. I hope this will convince you that my mother is essentially a great woman, and that whatever rancor she may have held against you was not rancor, but something reflected from my father's profound theories on Sebastian Sampas.

Your performance was superb. One thing, though, you misunderstand what I said about Ed Tully. I told you I didn't consider it "important" I see him all the time. By that I meant I didn't have to depend on anyone, including Eddy, for my own spiritual survival; I can manage by myself, as I'm sure Ed can manage by himself. You thought I had rejected Eddy; all I did was delineate his weaknesses —we all have them—and as such point out why one must not depend on others, but should attempt to work out his own weaknesses. You see, Sam, you have too strong a dependence on the group—yes, we must stick together; but no, we mustn't depend on one another! When you say in the recording that perhaps "we were too immature to realize the importance of our discoveries" you are not saying anything; our "discoveries" were no more than the awakening of the social conscience; youths are going through the same process everywhere, and have been doing so since Homer's time. There have been "youth movements" by the millions, and none were "important" or "great discoveries" essentially because they were all alike—the awakening in the minds of sincere and intelligent young men of a social conscience, as I have said, and the need for purpose in a society ostensibly without. Ours was the Promethean Society, based on the Brotherhood of Man, and on the mass energies of several participants . . . as Connie once said, or Eddy, five twenty-year olds massed together equal a one-hundred-year-old sage. True. But it doesn't amount to a one-hundred-year-old artist, or a one-hundred-year-old scientist; the arts and sciences require labor, individual integrity, and as in the case of art, a singular love and understanding of mankind and the forces of society. Your understanding and mine of society differ; bring us together, and instead of two original artists, you have one vague jumble of an artist. This, I believe, is as silly as the whole thing was. I still can't understand what we thought we were doing; I do understand the fact that we were uniting in a Progressive movement of our own, and as to that, I'm not adversed to such an idea. That's allright; it's been done before and wrought good results. But not this immutable fusion of many into a One.

As to Connie, once more I was delineating his weaknesses and not rejecting him in the least. I saw him just last night. When I say he is a hopeless tyrant, I mean it; but I don't reject him; I learn his weaknesses; and I tolerate them. Please don't weep over the pseudo-tragic delusion you are developing about myself and the others [. . . .]

Oh, yes, you also bewail the fact I'm not writing any more. Well, that is not quite true; I am writing 14 hours a day, 7 days a week, before I go into the Navy. You may well read my book next summer, if you're in America, in published form . . . "The Sea is My Brother," about the Merchant Marine. Connie and Ian are enthusiastic about it: Connie: "Superb," Ian: "Rare work for your age; powerful, vigorous, with vivid portraits of American life; Wesley Martin is a lonely and a tragic figure." They are my only critics so far. I know you'll like it, Sam; it has compassion, it has a certain something that will appeal to you (brotherhood, perhaps). At any rate, I've written 35,000 words of it, working night and day and ruining my health, but I must finish it before the Navy gets me.

I failed to pass the Air Corps test, as you know. I'm glad now I'm going to be a gob after reading about the officers in your camp. Allright, said Dos Passos in *U.S.A.*, we are two nations.

Jack

After Kerouac failed the test to become a pilot in the Naval Air Force V-12 program, he was sent to boot camp at the naval base in Newport, Rhode Island. His sister Caroline ("Nin") had left her first husband Charlie Morisette and enlisted in the Women's Army Corps. With both their son and daughter in the armed services, Gabrielle and Leo Kerouac decided to move from Lowell to New York. In the process of packing up the household, Gabrielle wrote Jack an encouraging letter about what was going on at home.

TO JACK KEROUAC
FROM GABRIELLE KEROUAC

Wed. March 24 '43
[Lowell, Mass.]

Darling,

Just received your letter. Glad to know where you are and know that you are O.K. I'm also so glad you like it. I was worried. Now I feel better about it. I hope you will go through your training period with flying colors. If you get in the spirit of the thing and you are liked by your superiors you'll be tops there and I know you will. The Navy sent me a nice letter telling all about you and what you have to do there and how they train you so the parents will know what our son has to study. It sounds pretty good and they also tell me you will be by yourself and not see anyone for three weeks and so I should write to you to cheer you up. Well, I thought that was darn decent of Uncle Sam and now I hope everything will turn out O.K. out there for you. Right now Honey I'm very busy sorting out and packing things. Whew what a tough job. And its going to be very hard to sell my stuff. Had a break today. Aunt Leontine came to my rescue; she's going to be my *Salesman,* and believe me, in ½ a day she sold 2 articles. Well that helps. Glad to have her. I couldn't do it alone. She's not so *dumb.* Had a letter from Nin again today; she likes it out there and making good progress. Well Honey Mom has to go pack again so I'll end here. If you can write here again I'm going to be here till the end of next week. Sending you some letters that came today and a clipping you will recognize the boy. And that's about all. Au revoire [sic] darling XXXXX

Mom.

At the conclusion of a letter to Sebastian pontificating about his ideas on art and politics, Kerouac wrote a candid description of his behavior in the Navy barracks during his first weeks of boot camp.

TO SEBASTIAN SAMPAS

March 25, 1943
[Newport, R.I.]

Dear Sebastian—

I see now by your letter (which I have just received) that an argument of delightfully large proportions is on the fire. Very well, then, I am going to give you the works for a change; I shall moralize also.

(Morally, of course, we are of the same mind . . . we hate cruelty,

· 50 ·

ugliness, bigotry . . .) There isn't anything left for me to moralize upon. There is, however, much to chastise you for. I too want to correct my comrade.

You still haven't defined the poet as an *artist,* but we'll forget that for now—enough to mention that the poet is not a *fool,* unless it be in the minds of unresponsive "Philistines" . . . who misunderstand him, as you say. He is a lover . . . he loves beauty, and for this reason, his ideals point to beauty as he sees it . . . and any artist entertains a notion of beauty that you and I would both accept fervidly. And so, Sebastian, I want you to get more serious about your poet's station, more diligent, searching, and scholarly—forget the romantic "outcast" notions and continue observing the phenomena of living, with the patience and scrutiny of a scientist in his laboratory and not with a jumble of introverted, subjective half-perceptions. (I am not going "objective" on you—I am not a prim W. Somerset Maugham[1] devotee.) But if I retain vision in myself by removing my own single identity in experience—that is to say, distil myself off until only the artist stands—and observe everything with an unbiased, studious, and discriminate eye, I do more good, as far as creation goes, than the Byronic youth, like Joseph Kusaila, who identifies himself with the meaning of the world or if not that places himself in the center of its orbit and professes to know all about humanity when he has only taken pains to study himself. That's sheer adolescence! "War and Peace" was great because Tolstoi looked around instead of sitting there picking his nose in a garret. Dostoevsky understood humanity because it was more interesting and "poetic" to him than his own fucking "soul." And so forth. Who, then, is the fool? Kusaila or Tolstoi? Kusaila is not an artist, that's all. (Kusaila is a Soph at Columbia who announced in the Spec[2] that he was the "spokesman of mankind"—and two blocks away is a Harlem of 2 million Negroes he never will know about, let alone see.)

So much for our lives as artists. As men, you and I have been

---

1. W. Somerset Maugham (1874–1965), English novelist, author of *Of Human Bondage* (1915) and *The Razor's Edge* (1944).

2. The *Columbia Spectator,* undergraduate newspaper at the college.

generous enough spiritually to embrace Socialism or Progress. I am as rabid about it all as you are, don't kid yourself . . . and Seymour is quite the boy, too. But I'm looking at the workingclass movement askance, not because it's just that, but because it may not be in good hands. Pat Reel proved to be a very intolerant person. The American Communists, moreover, don't seem to rely so much upon their own initiative and native ideas than on simple Muscovite policy. Dos Passos has outlined the arid life of Party members, people who are iconoclasts from way down deep, who judge most literature as "Bourgeois inanity," and who have little if no belief in the essential "dignity and integrity" (your words) of men—only a mad desire to improve the material side of life, and perhaps, as Eugene Lyons[3] once put it, "with nostrils sniffing for power." (Even yours have sniffed, Sam, when you refer to your position at the Promenthean table— you said "you'd just as soon take a back seat," which indicates you had already conceived the element of "leadership" in our group.)

No! . . . that is not for me. If it meant the complete fruition of my present fears, I would prefer branching out as a one-man Commie party, or as a solitary radical working on no platform but the simple one . . . cessation of exploitation! (Even in the Army & Navy, Sam, they exploit the masses . . . don't you see that all those K.P. details are nothing but free labor? Prisoners of war don't go through as much crap and slave labor as do the poor kids training to die an orderly and disciplined death. Why don't the services hire their own labor instead of disguising their fairly Nazi labor policies under a heading of military discipline?) (P.S.—It's O.K. in wartime, labor is scarce; but not in peace time. However, I am no judge of militarism—I hate it too much to see it whole so far.)

To get back to my thread of thought (interruptions in the barracks), though I am skeptical about the *administration* of the Progressive movement, I shall withhold all judgements until I come in direct contact with these people—other Communists, Russians, politicians, etc., leftist artists, leaders, workers, and so forth.

---

3. Eugene Lyons was the author of *The Red Decade* (1941), a classic work on communism in America during the 1930s.

At this point, I must bring your statement to bear . . . it was: "Your letter is helping in clarifying our respective roles in the great coming upheaval." Does this mean you suspect I'm going reactionary? If you were to say that after having read this letter, it would mean you were destined to become another blind American Communist, instead of a *discriminating* one, in the vein of the great Liberal, Debs.[4] Commies like to use that term "Great Liberal" to refer to labor-fakers and that sort, or a Woodrow Wilson with briefcase and no organization, or a false liberal like Max Hirsch in "You Can't Go Home Again." Your role in the future depends as much upon your zeal as upon your understanding and vision. You have already hinted at my possible turnover . . . this is as typical of Muscophiles as anything. I am a Leftist . . . I couldn't be otherwise, I may not be a Party-liner. . . . they haven't done any good and most of them are a trifle too intolerant . . . and unless the Party improves here, I'll never join it. It too must suffer "change."

― ―

When I said—"read in the light of friendly argument"—I wasn't threatening, I was only expressing the wish you would not be angry with me. I hate friction; I do love heated, sincere controversy. You & your conclusions . . .

― ―

When I asked you about your pre-Army activities, I was asking you what you'd been doing *as a Promethean,* which should represent achievement of a sort in your field. (Your work at the Navy Yard has nothing to do with it, although it's more than I would have done.) All you did achieve was very little poetry . . . and all that time, Eddy, Con, Ian, George C. were all toiling at their fields. I wasn't . . . I was whoring around N.Y. . . . but I don't say, as well, that I'm a Promethean. At any rate, don't take me too seriously; I'm picking holes in you quite cheerfully, but at the same time it may help you to see. You would embrace a strict Promethean program, farm and all—with Murphy discharging the duties—and with regulations providing for orderly maintenance, upkeep, etc. etc. while

---

4. Eugene Debs (1855–1926), prominent American socialist.

way down deep the only way you want to write is to go prowling about Brooklyn's waterfront with me and write about it at five A.M. (as we did.)

However, a Promethean Farm would be good for vacations . . . but one can't really work there, live there, study there. If we had money, it might work, but even then, the ennui would be awful—an artist needs *life*. More on that later.

Sam, [can't I] read your poems? If you want to read the unfinished "Sea is My Brother," I'll mail it to you.

Well, I'll go to my watch now. I saunter through the barracks wearing blue peacoat, trousers, leggings, and bowcap, carrying a club and wearing a white belt, etc. I have to see that everyone is buttoned up, etc. Do you know what I actually do, Sam? I mind my own fucking business—they can have their peckers hanging out for all I care.

Au Revoir—
Buddie Jack

In Vanity of Duluoz, *Kerouac described how he grew "disgusted" with Navy discipline in the midst of "the dust and the yelling drill instructors" and "lay my gun down into the dust and just walked away from everybody forever more." He tried to appear in control of the situation when he wrote letters from the base hospital to his mother and his friends.*

TO GABRIELLE KEROUAC

John L. Kerouac
0-7 Sick Bay
U.S. Naval Training Station
Newport, R.I.
March 30, 1943

Dear Mom—

Although I tried to hide it, they found out about my headaches when I went to get aspirins a few times. I guess I wrote too much of my novel before I joined the Navy. Anyway, they've placed me under observation in the hospital, and all I do all day is sit around in the smoking room and smoke. My eyes hurt me—it may be the measles aftermath—or it may be an old football injury. I don't know.

Well, if I can't make the Navy, I'll try the Merchant Marine school—they're not strict there, and my eyesight is still *perfect.*

At any rate, I have an idea they're going to call you up about it. They're going to give me a nerve test tomorrow. Remember the night you noticed my hands shaking while I drank coffee? Well, I'm going to tell them about it—maybe if I give them all the facts, they can cure me, so when they call you up, tell them all you know about my symptoms—you know more about things like that than I do—and that way, they may know what to do. For my part, I feel fine—a few headaches don't really bother me—so don't worry about me.

I guess you'll be in Brooklyn when you get this. Boy, I'll bet you're feeling good . . . I can hardly wait till I see you in our new home, and I hope Pop comes home & finds a job in N.Y. soon, so that you'll have the old weasel around to argue with.

As I write now, we are waiting for "chow" and then I'll go to bed for a good night's sleep. The radio is right next to me.

Well, I'll write again in a few days. Address my letters to 0-7 Sick Bay instead of Co. 733.

Love,
Jack X X X

I told them about my accident in Vermont,[1] my football injuries, & everything, so that if I have anything, they'll discover it. Anyway, try to remember my symptoms and tell them about it. And don't worry. You know nothing bothers me.

'Bye

---

1. Kerouac was in an automobile accident in Vermont during the summer of 1940. He later told his friend Ed White that he never liked to drive a car because he was afraid of another accident.

Tuesday Night
[early April 1943
Newport, R.I.]

Dear Ian—

Excuse my tactless disregard of the laws of correspondence . . .
but I'm in an enthusiastic mood and I feel like pouring out this zest
and transmitting it to a worthy listener.

List! (Surely, I am dementia praecox—just this afternoon, I was in
such a melancholic stupor the doctor showed concern.) And now!
And *Now!* I feel fine and by God I'll tell the world & Ian
MacDonald.

My rake of an ami, I have been thinking in this hospital . . . and
I have devised new plans for my life. (This vanity is strictly between
us—I know the world cares very little what I have devised—but you
are mon ami, and I must tell you.)

The pathos in this hospital has convinced me, as it did Hemingway
in Italy, that "the defeated are strongest." Every one here is defeated,
even this "broth of a Breton." I have been defeated by the world,
with considerable help from my greatest enemy, myself, and now I
am ready to work. I realize the limitations of my knowledge, and the
irregularity of my intellect. Knowledge and intellection serve a
Tolstoi—but a Tolstoi must be older, must see more as well—and I
am not going to be a Tolstoi. Surely, I will be a Kerouac, whatever
that suggests. Knowledge comes with time . . .

As far as creative powers go, I have them and I know it. All I need
now is faith in myself . . . only from there can a faith truly dilate
and expand to "mankind." I must change my life, *now,* I have
reached 21 and I am in dead earnest about all things. This does not
mean I shall cease my debauching; you see, Ian, debauchery is the
release of man from whatever stringencies he's applied to himself. In
a sense, each debauchery is a private though short-lived insurgence
from the static conditions of his society. Sex, of course, is the universal symbol of life—I've discovered that all men, from aged veterans to sere academicians, turn back to sex in their last years as
though suddenly conscious of its deep and noble meaning, of its inseparable marriage to the secret of life. I shall change my life, yes; I

shall make new friends and I feel as well the time has come for my love to come along. Ian, I have been awaiting my Helen for a long time; when I find her, I shall adore her. (Perhaps I won't write beautiful poems about her, but I certainly will love her "with a love greater than love.")

Norma is on my mind . . . but I believe she dislikes me. I admit I am saddened by her attitude, but fortunately, we didn't go far enough to warrant any broken hearts . . . a little further, and I should be grieved.

I wonder if you've ever been perspicacious enough to peer beneath my blasé front as regards women . . . did I ever tell you that at sixteen, I was madly in love with a lovely Irish lass named, simply, Mary?[1] . . . Did you know about my reverence for the sight of her, my melancholy desire to steal to her house at night and regard her as she sat on the hammock? Oh lord, what a lovelorn Marius I was then!

She was a wench, hear, and she toyed with my heart—and broke it. I have not since played with fire.

Silence is the greatest wisdom . . .

Whimsically,
Jack

Sorry!—I have grown to hate rhetoric—or attempts at it—why don't men devise new ways of communication?

Written during the days of observation in the naval hospital, Kerouac's letter to his friend G. J. ("Fouch") Apostolos contained an analysis of what Jack called the "complex condition" of his mind, which he felt was divided into two contradictory parts, symbolized by his friendships with G.J. and Sebastian. "All my youth, I stood holding two ends of rope, trying to bring both ends together in order to tie them." Kerouac was also aware that for him part of the appeal

1. Kerouac fell in love with teenage Mary Carney during his senior year at Lowell High School in 1938–1939. His book *Maggie Cassidy* describes this period of his life.

of writing was that the act of creating a fictional world promised him the opportunity to weld "the divergent worlds" of his dual mind "irrevocably together."

TO GEORGE J. APOSTOLOS

April 7, 1943
[Newport, R.I.]

Dear Fouch—

Both of us are by now aware of having crossed mail in three unfortunate instances . . . your telegram arrived here *after* I'd mailed my embittered letter; and you sent it *before* you received the letter. In the same way, my latest letter, acknowledging your telegram, reached you *after* you wrote me your embittered letter. I suppose we may cross mail this time again, but at least we are not wallowing in misunderstanding now that we realize the vagaries our mail has suffered.

That's clear. What is also clear is that I was sore because you weren't writing. But what I *do* want to straighten out is the formality of my embittered letter . . . you see, this is a combination bug and nuthouse, and our mail is censored, our *outgoing* mail. I wanted to say my piece to you, but I had to do it in a scholarly fashion less the doctors disbelieve my arguments in favor of the better factors of my dementia praecox diagnosis, viz., logical mind, education, etc. But I don't care anymore . . . I'll write as I please, censorship or no.

At any rate, the cold formality of my letter need not be taken as unfriendliness; you were not obliged to write back in the same vein. I speak now *not* of the context of our notes—that comes later in the letter. I speak of the arch prose utilized.

Goddamn it, Fouch, I think you're still as crazy as the time you walked into the Zombie factory with me, arms outstretched, else how can I explain your ridiculous act of having a stooge write the letter for you. (Zaggo sees all, knows all.) If you had written it yourself, I'm sure it would have been more colorful, more creative, not to mention that I should at least have had the satisfaction of hearing from you rather than from that spineless cuckold whose cultural substance probably amounts to a packet of *Reader's Digest*s.

(This ghost-writer seems particularly eager to vilify the "intelligentsia"—and in calling them "soft-bellied," does he imply anything cogent? I'm sure he's one of these prim, sparsely-hued "moderns," who considers his ilk the backbone of the nation. Well, what about the brain of this nation?)

Anyway, Fouch, you dictated the letter, and I'll try to defend myself on some points. (But I still think that stooge is a piss-complected, broad-assed fartsack who never knew and never will know any objective enthusiasm for the world in which he was dropped with a hollow bang.)

[. . . .] What hurts me most was the unfairness of your stooge's remarks regarding Ian's admittedly totalitarian phrase: "It is safe to say, Sebastian, that Jack has come to regard George with lost reverence." I didn't write the damned thing. I only quoted it.

Anyway, consider the *tremendous* pressure these "intellectuals" foisted upon me against sticking with you. I'm sure you never were beleaguered with the voices of Mr. Coffee-Nerves, Inc., saying: "He's no good! Forget him! A vulgar influence! A smug rat!" and allied niceties. I still thought you were a good guy, and still do . . . and "lost reverence" at a time when you yourself confess you'd given me up as a reality and taken up as the "star of your memories."* (*Cop. 1943 Stooge Services, Inc.) Mull over that last sentence.

That stooge is indeed naive about the "wearing-a-mask" question; if he chose to lay down his copy of *Reader's Digest* and take up a good book on psychology ("Human Behavior & Human Mind"— Wells, Wells, & Huxley),[2] he would discover the light, a piercing shaft through his boor's armor, of this fact:—all persons wear a mask. I must confess I made stupid remarks about what your unmasking revealed—for now, to suffice, I may say I was shocked that you wore a mask; like everyone else of course (only recently have I learned this.)

I thought you didn't give a damn. But anyway, we wrecked our share of Hotel Garage cars, so that makes up for your downright

---

2. The actual title of this book was *The Science of Life* (1931), by H. G. Wells, Julian S. Huxley, and G. P. Wells.

covetousness of Lorraine. I never coveted a woman because she isn't worthy of a man's full concern—this does not deny *good* women of such treatment and affection, but Lorraine didn't belong in that category. I didn't understand why it hurt you to find that she and I were intriguing; but you explain it was your ego. Anyway, the whole Lorraine question can be truthfully summed up as a silent battle for sexual superiority. Admit that I confessed our relationship in the nick of time! Do you think, that night you trapped me at her house, I was there for a discussion on music?

One of the reasons for my being in a hospital, besides dementia praecox, is a complex condition of my mind, split up, as it were, in two parts, one normal, the other schizoid.

My schizoid side is the Raskolnikov-Dedalus-George Webber-Duluoz[3] side, the bent and brooding figure sneering at a world of mediocrities, complacent ignorance, and bigotry exercised by ersatz Ben Franklins; the introverted, scholarly side; the alien side.

My normal counterpart, the one you're familiar with, is the half-back-whoremaster-alemate-scullion-jitterbug-jazz critic side, the side in me which recommends a broad, rugged America; which requires the nourishment of gutsy, redblooded associates; and which lofts whatever guileless laughter I've left in me rather than that schizoid's cackle I have of late.

And, all my youth, I stood holding two ends of rope, trying to bring both ends together in order to tie them. Sebastian was at one end, you on the other, and beyond both of you lay the divergent worlds of my dual mind, and both of you the clearest symbols I could see. I pulled—had a hell of a time trying to bring these two worlds together—never succeeded actually; but I did in my novel "The Sea Is My Brother," where I created two new symbols of these two worlds, and welded them irrevocably together.

---

3. Duluoz, Kerouac's fictional surname for himself, was apparently modeled both on the name of James Joyce's autobiographical hero Stephen Dedalus and on the Greek family name Daoulas in Lowell. Raskolnikov was the central character in Fyodor Dostoyevsky's *Crime and Punishment* (1866). George Webber was the protagonist in Thomas Wolfe's autobiographical novels *The Web and the Rock* (1939) and *You Can't Go Home Again* (1940).

Maybe this will serve to explain a lot of things; I don't know. It is the price I pay for having a malleable personality. It assumes the necessary shape when in contact with any other personality.

Well, I've hastily scribbled a few words, and now it's time to turn in. I'll finish this letter later, after I've heard from you. Be sure to write!

I may not see you again—when I get out of here, I'm shipping right out, late this month.[4] Between trips I'll drop up to see you if I have at least a week in port at my disposal. I hope I can see you.

Incidentally, Big Slim[5] and I are going to Washington two days after we get out of here—for one night—to hit good old "G" Street. That, brother, is not my schizoid side.

Tell Stoogey do take care of himself and be a good boy.

Sincerely,
Zaggo

In an undated draft of a letter to his Lowell friend Cornelius ("Connie") Murphy, which Kerouac apparently never sent, Jack attempted what he called "a searing self-analysis" of his behavior in the Navy. On the last pages of the letter, his analysis ended in a series of aphorisms and a list of eleven books, from Joyce's Portrait of the Artist as a Young Man *to his own novel-in-progress "The Sea Is My Brother," with a thematic summary of their contents for his friend.*

TO CORNELIUS MURPHY

Wednesday Morning
[undated]

Dear Connie—

I think by now I can offer you a fairly authoritative explanation of my "case" here, and this only after considerable musing on the ramifications of the whole farce.

---

4. Kerouac went back to the Merchant Marines after the Navy granted him an honorable discharge with an "indifferent character" in May 1943. See Book Ten of *Vanity of Duluoz.*

5. Big Slim was William Holmes Hubbard, a former Louisiana State University football player whom Jack met in the Navy psychiatric ward.

In the first place, Connie, it was clearly and simply a matter of maladjustment with military life. On this, the psychiatrist and I seemed to be agreed upon in silence. I believe that if his queries had ended at that point, my diagnosis would have been psychoneurosis —a convenient conclusion which could have explained any number of idiosyncrasies in a protean personality. [. . . .]

This was the ground upon which I stood at the beginning of the end of my interview with the young psychiatrist, and is the ground upon which I should be standing right now. And, in view of my eagerness to get back to the merchant marine, I see no reason for being ashamed of my maladjustment. But the whole story doesn't end there.

The psychiatrist questioned me further, obviously in search of a blue-ribbon diagnosis. First he began to probe my emotional attachment, and found much food for thought there when I told him I wasn't in love with any girl, and didn't plan to get married at all. (This, of course, is pouring it on thick, but I wanted to see his reaction. He maintained a poker face & jotted down some notes—a superb performance!)

He wanted to know of my emotional experiences and I told him of my affairs with mistresses and various promiscuous wenches, adding to that the crowning glory of being more closely attached to my male friends, spiritually and emotionally, than to these women. This not only smacked of dementia praecox, it smacked of ambisexuality.

"Extreme preoccupation" is another symptom of dementia praecox, a characteristic, I am proud to say, with which I am stricken. I cheerfully revealed this, and he cheerfully jotted it down.

Next, he tried to detect "unreal ideas" in my makeup. What was the strangest thing I'd ever seen? In a voice like Sebastian's at his saddest, I gave vent to an image compounded of all the mysticism I knew, from Poe & Ambrose Bierce to Coleridge and DeQuincey. A gleam in his eye!

Next came an investigation of the "bizarre" in me. First, "bizarre delusions." Was I the center of attention in a group?

Of course!

"Bizarre hallucinations." Did I hear voices? Yes, as a matter of fact, I could hear voices accusing me all night, calling me pro-Fascist, reactionary, and Old Tory.

"Bizarre behavior." What were some of the experiences I'd had?

Well, being drunk for three months in Washington, for one. Quitting Officers' Training at Columbia University, for another. Spending my time writing.

And oh yes, dedicating my actions to experience in order to write about them, sacrificing myself on the altar of Art.

"Bizarre behavior" . . . and the full diagnosis of dementia praecox.

All this folly doesn't faze me, except for one item. Since I have "bizarre delusions," no one takes me seriously. Thus, when I asked for a typewriter in order to finish my novel, they only humoured me.

("The poor boy, now he's under the 'bizarre delusion' that he's a writer!")

I've taken the pains to place myself under a searing self-analysis. . . .

Gabrielle Kerouac was dismayed that Jack had gotten into difficulties in the Navy, unlike Leo Kerouac, who, as Kerouac wrote in Vanity of Duluoz, *believed that his son was right trying to avoid the military service ["Good boy, tell that goddamn Roosevelt and his ugly wife where to get off! All a bunch of Communists. The Germans should not be our enemies but our Allies. This is a war for the Marxist Communist Jews and you are a victim of the whole plot."] With hindsight in* Vanity of Duluoz, *Kerouac's conclusion was that he had been seriously handicapped by his "wise guy" attitude at the age of twenty-one, and that he "could have gained a lot out of loyal membership to that outfit. . . ."*

TO JACK KEROUAC
FROM GABRIELLE KEROUAC

Monday May 3 [1943]
[Ozone Park, N.Y.]

Hello Jackie,

How's my darling to-day, still in the "Hoose Gow" Hey. Well, I'm writing you again. This time is a little message from Nin. I quote from what she writes and wants me to convey to you this message. Here goes. This is how she puts it. I *quote:*

"Mom:

Can't you make Jack change his mind. He'd be a lot safer in the Navy. Tell him I think he should stick it out. He hasn't written to me yet, and I sent him a letter ages ago. Nin."

So see what big sister has to say to you. I thought you and her were corresponding regularly. Tell me Honey what seems to be all the fuss out there. At first I thought you were sick, but now pop tells me you refuse to go through the training, or in other words refuse to serve your country. Oh Honey *lamb*. That's not like you, don't you know that it will be an awful mark against you. You have good education seems to me you could have done something real good. The Navy is grand too, oh I dont know. Im all "mixed" up. You know how I dread the merchant marine, its so dangerous now, and this war is getting so tough. You could have streched [sic] time there, I dont know just what to advice [sic] outside of asking you to give it a "fair try," it cant be worse than the merchant marine. I know you are eager to help your *mom* and thats one way of doing it fast and profitable, and I admire your courage in doing so but if its going to make things hard for you, at the Navy, why dont you try and see if you will like it, it cant be that "*bad,*" as for me and *pa,* well sooner or later we'll manage somehow. *Pa,* as Ive already told you is coming here for a week and he will look around for work. There's plenty of printing jobs to be had. The only trouble is will they hire him. That we will soon find out. As soon as pa gets a job around here, [and we learn] its going to be steady, then Ill take a place of my own and try for a job myself. As I've said before there's lots of em *open.* I certainly wont remain here a minute longer than I have too [sic]. I suppose Ill be seeing you soon and when you come Ill have lots of things to tell you, not fit to write here so until then lots of courage Honey, and think carefully. As for me, whatever you do, I wont criticize your judgements after all your life's your own. But be brave and write to me and tell me all about everything and try and send a line to Nin soon—so good luck Honey and all my Love. Your *Mom* XXXXX

Sebastian Sampas visited Kerouac in the Navy hospital before Se-
bastian was shipped overseas as a medical corpsman. One of Sebas-
tian's last letters to Kerouac expressed ideas about the need for a
"new vision" of life and literature that prefigured the idealistic views
Kerouac would encounter again when he met Allen Ginsberg and
Lucien Carr in New York City less than a year later.

TO JACK KEROUAC
FROM SEBASTIAN SAMPAS

Wednesday
May 26, 1943

Jack—

Some of your criticism of my letter was sound, but I must take
issue on the majority of my points. Perhaps, writing hurriedly in the
few minutes I could spare, I did not express myself very clearly. You
quote a Russian,

"Dostoevsky was one of ourselves."

That is why you completely misjudged the man and his goal. You
are not a Slav. It is beyond the capacity of your Breton soul to understand him. I have known for a long time that the Russians are
children of another earth, not of this old earth, but seeds in a new
soil, earth-children of an unborn culture, great young souls—un-
found and formless—their music, their literature, the profound mel-
ancholia of an unfulfilled Destiny and not Western man's infinite
longing through individual endeavour for fame, intellect and riches
for a soul that has already died; their unbelievable dynamism, the
birth-pangs of a whole new world, not the death-throes of your over-
lived meaning.

Spengler[1] had an inkling of this. He recognized the Russian prime-

_____

1. Oswald Spengler (1880–1936), German philosopher and author of *The De-*
cline of the West (1922). In Lowell, Sebastian had shown Kerouac a copy of
this book belonging to his older brother Charles, a graduate of Boston University. William Burroughs introduced Allen Ginsberg to the book in New York
City in 1944. Spengler's analysis of European history as occurring in cycles of
cultural entropy contributed to the early Beat writers' apocalyptic vision of their
times.

symbol as the "plane without limit." I expressed the same idea in the paragraph above which I call "The Directive Determinant of Potential Actualization" which I fully understand but since I am writing in an alien (English) language I cannot make it more clear.

Your prime symbol, of course as well as all of Western mankind, is infinite space. You have had dreams of space as all Western mankind has had. Whether it be in great Gothic cathedrals, railroad stations, tunnels, the dome of heaven—whether it be received from a mountain-top or abyss, or whether it be pure infinite space. By this all else is conditioned. All individuality, difference, originality is really very much alike. And between the Western world and the Russian soul there is an unabridgable [sic] chasm.

You have misunderstood completely "Crime and Punishment." It is not of the suffering of mankind, not merely an investigation of the sources of mankind's misery. Read the last few pages. At the beginning of the book, Raskolnikov is the over-refined, polished, finished product of our Western World. It is only through great suffering that he forgets himself—his own, Razumikin's (who was a product of the Russian earth, a friend, a brother, and who never knew the Western World) and Sonya's.[2] In this great suffering he forgets himself. The "I" is young again and has lost itself in the "we," the "all," and he is one with all his brothers in the prime symbol or Russian plane. That is the epic. To quote Dostoevsky [in the final paragraph of the novel]:

> "the story of the gradual renewal of a man,
> the story of his gradual regeneration, of his
> passing from *one world to another,* of his
> initiation into an unknown life."

That is not a Western Man. For him there are only the futureless days. Tomorrow is stone and steel and bright lights. The Western

2. Sonya and Razumikin were characters in Dostoyevsky's *Crime and Punishment.* Through poverty, saintlike Sonya is forced into prostitution; she joins her destiny to that of the central character Raskolnikov at the end of the novel. Razumikin was a student friend of Raskolnikov's. Dostoyevsky formed Razumikin's name from the word *razum* (reason, intellect) and Raskolnikov's from *raskol* (split, schism, dissent).

Man appreciates Dostoevsky but he cannot see, he cannot livingly experience his world. All the depth of feeling which he arouses in the Western man is within the Western man—a part of him. Suffering and compassion he (the Western Man) can project, but it is not D's [Dostoyevsky's]. It is the Western man's. The Western Man understands Tolstoi, Lenin—but not D. He is an alien soul.

That is why I minimize D. To the Western Man he can convey nothing that is not already within him. The Russians he has not influenced; all true Russians are Dostoevsky. In him speaks their soul.

Spengler: "To call *the Faustian Culture* a Will-Culture is only another way of expressing the eminently historical disposition of its soul. Our first person idiom, our *Ego habeo factum,*" our dynamic syntax, that is—finally renders the way of doing things that results from this disposition and, with its positive directional energy, dominates not only our picture of the World-as-History but our own history to boot. This first person towers up in the Gothic architecture; the spine is an "I," ethical work upon an "I," justification of an "I" by faith and works; respect of the neighbor "Thou" for the sake of one's "I" and its happiness; and, lastly and supremely, immortality of the "I."

Now this, precisely this, the genuine Russian regards as contemptible vain-glory. The Russian soul, will-less, having the limitless plane as its prime-symbol, seeks to grow up—serving, *anonymous, self-oblivious* in the brother-world of the plane. To take "I" as the starting-point of relations with the neighbors, to elevate "I's" love of near and dear, to repent for "I's" sake, are to him traits of Western vanity as presumptuous as is the upthrusting challenge to heaven of our cathedrals that he compares with his plane—church-roof and its sprinkling of cupolas. Tolstoi's hero Neckludov looks after his moral "I" as he does after his finger-nails; this is just what betrays Tolstoi [. . . .]

Why is it that individual endeavor is pathetic to me? It is because I recognize no such thing as "individual endeavor." The ego, the "I," not only exists, it dominates. We justify, express the "I." It is the point of reference of the Western Man as exemplified in this dream of space. When comes this "I"? it comes from the All.

Children and primitive people are part of the landscape. They are one with wind and weather, sun and stars, soil, seed and season. But to them comes an experience of cosmic birth and dying and passing away.

The Western [man] senses an "other." He becomes an "I" and the sensing is an "I" that is not "I." The "all" resolves into an opposition of "I" and "other." The other he conceives symbolically in his dream of space. The "I" is lost and lonely in infinity. All the mighty strivings of our cultures resolve themselves into an attempt to express the foreign "other" in terms of an "I."

In all of us, Jack, there is a great spirituality, that flowers in our youth and should bear fruit in our maturity. That it does not is [because] there is a dissonance between ideals and life, between Civilization and the "landscape" whence it was rooted. Take out beauty in any form if it is only a medium. The Western Man seeks only completion in art. The "I" facing the "other" feels itself partial, incomplete. It seeks to include the "other," to conquer it, failing that, to lose itself.

All Western Men seek; if they are not concerned in the same meaning it is not because they do not feel as you feel, but that the form could not reach them.

Individual endeavour exists only as a cross-section of all the restless strivings of whole peoples. It is supreme only when it can express the soul-current common to all mankind (Western). That the All-Soul is manifest through this or that individual is a matter of chance, not intellect. In fact it would have been better had all the great works of our culture remained anonymous. We could have understood them better and more justly credited them. I am afraid there would be less "appreciation." Some of the people (and I certainly do not mean you) who cultivate a taste for Beethoven, Bach, Wagner, Goethe, Shakespeare, Dostoevsky, Tolstoi, Steinbeck, Dos Passos, Wolfe, etc. would not care for them anonymous.

There are no more worlds to conquer in the Western Civilization. It remains for the intellectuals of the Western World to re-arrange, to comment, to imitate but not to create, to actualize the fullest possibilities of the All-Soul. The form is set too thickly—its earth-roots are withered, the soul is dead. It's lifeless expression to one, a "craft" to another, a "taste." Prometheanism should help along this goal.

(Do not misunderstand. I do not say that you are not a great creative artist, but more about that in just a moment.)

Art is no longer livingly created or experienced. People cease to be concerned with its great symbolism. They are out of harmony with the pulse-beat of our becoming. To them it "is the hard reality of life, of living that is essential, not the concept of life, that the ostrich-philosophy of idealism propounds." Spengler. Soon the Western Civilization shall be as the Egyptian and Chinese have been for millenniums. In Eastern Europe there is little hope but in America "a wind is rising." Wolfe felt it. In the "hills beyond," the great open spaces (remember his Northwest Pacific trip), the uncrowded places, a new soul is in conception. The land is pregnant. A primitive man, crude, raw, unfinished—superb—is shaping in the heart of our land. He does not seek for "other." The meaning he knows is life. He and all his fellow-mankind are brothers in spirit. In him coarse, rough-hewn, lie all our hopes—his will be the civilization greater than all —all art will be an integral part of him.[3]

If you choose the Western World, it is well to remember that individual endeavor can achieve distinction only in harmony with its people—and its people have no soul, that they have a truth of their own which is not yours, but nevertheless true to them and unchangeable.

"The world's a stage and *all* men players." Choose the last act of one play, or the first of another. It remains for you to act your part, for the show will go on, with you or against you—

Remember this final quotation:

"The fates lead him who goes willingly and drag him who goes unwillingly."

I have finished re-reading this letter and realize its inarticulate spots but my time, Jack, is so god-damn limited. I was a perfect fool to let Joe May's misunderstanding of my letter affect me.

---

3. Sebastian's prophetic description of "a new soul" being shaped in the "great open spaces" of America anticipated Kerouac's description of Dean Moriarty [Neal Cassady] in the opening pages of *On the Road,* a man whose "wild yea-saying overburst of American joy" was "an ode from the Plains, something new, long prophesied, long a-coming. . . ."

I'm sincerely sorry if we disagree—am to be shipped to a P.O.E. [Port Of Embarcation] in a very brief time—I have to abandon all intellectual pursuits for the present—Write soon. I hope that this argument is not settling to a clash of "egos" so let's abandon it until we know our fate within the next month.

Goodnite.
Fraternally,
Sebastian

Spengler influenced me somewhat but the majority of the ideas are my own—not that it matters a god-damn. Probably I belong where you do and vice versa.

In June 1943, after Kerouac was discharged from the Navy, he joined his parents in their apartment above a drugstore in Ozone Park, New York. He also saw a girlfriend in Manhattan named Frankie Edith Parker ("Edie"), whom he first met in the fall of 1942, before he dropped out of Columbia. In September 1943 Kerouac sailed on his second ship as a merchant seaman, shipping out on the S.S. George Weems *on a bomb-carrying voyage to Liverpool. Aboard ship he wrote affectionately to Edie. She was then living in an apartment on West 118th Street near the Columbia campus with her friend Joan Vollmer, a Barnard College graduate. In* Vanity of Duluoz, *Kerouac called Edie "Johnnie" and described her as "radiant and happy to see me and young and she was the wife of my youth."*

TO EDITH PARKER

John Kerouac
Moore-McCormack Lines
Pier 32, North River
New York, N.Y.
[S.S. *George Weems*]
Sept. 18 '43

Hello You—

Daddy is now very far away from Mommy, and he is being a very good boy, as witness the amount of his draw: twelve dollars (equivalent). However, Daddy will make the best of it with his few sous and take long, lonely walks through the (1) desert, or (2) mountains, or (3) moors, or (4) jungle, or (5) steppes, or (6) plains. (I just realized that the censor might take all this for a code. Well, anyway, I'm safe.)

I hope Henri [Cru] is still hanging around so that we can ship out together next out. And how is Joan? And Alex? And Jimmy and Inez? And Ronnie? If you receive this Air V-Mail letter around the 25th of September, you'll have time to send me a line or two, by Air V-Mail, if you hop to it right away and reply posthaste. I'd like to hear from you while I'm here. Return address is on top of page.

I miss you very much, strangely enough. And I miss my jazz. A few nights before pulling out, I caught Ben Webster[1] at the Three Deuces on 52nd: he was wonderful. I suggest that you catch him there before he moves off—no one can beat his tone; he breathes out his notes.

It's been a long, dreary, grim, depressing voyage, as usual, but I had plenty of time to read several good books: I specialized, this time, on the English: Galsworthy,[2] Hugh Walpole,[3] Radclyffe Hall's "Well of Loneliness"[4] (which I recommend you to read), and Sir Philip Gibbs' stupid "Heirs Apparent."[5] I think Americans are much better novelists, today, than the English. Even Thomas Hardy, one of the

---

1. Ben Webster was a brilliant tenor saxophone soloist who joined the Duke Ellington Orchestra in 1940.

2. John Galsworthy (1867–1933), English novelist and author of *The Forsyte Saga* (1922), a long novel about three generations of the Forsyte family, combining in one volume the three Galsworthy novels *The Man of Property, In Chancery,* and *To Let,* with two additional stories about the Forsytes. In *Vanity of Duluoz,* Kerouac remembered that *The Forsyte Saga* gave him "an idea about sagas, or legends, novels connecting into one grand tale." He later developed this idea in a series of autobiographical novels comprising what he called the Duluoz legend.

3. Sir Hugh Walpole (1884–1941) was a prolific English novelist and literary critic.

4. Marguerite Radclyffe Hall, the English author of the best-selling novel *The Well of Loneliness* (1928), a thinly disguised story of her own life as a lesbian. Radclyffe Hall said that she wrote the book to promote "an understanding of the true nature of the homosexual, who is born and not made."

5. Sir Philip Gibbs (1877–1962), popular English writer.

very greatest English novelists, was no better and no worse, and certainly not as supremely powerful, as our Melville and his "Moby Dick." And I would much rather sit to a Hemingway, or a Thomas Wolfe [. . .] than to these Walpoles and Galsworthys and inane Gibbses. So much for my contribution to Allied unity.

I'm going to drop Seymour[6] a line from this port and have him get leave for late October, or early November, which is probably when I'll be back, so that you and he and Henri and maybe Fitzgerald and I can all get together. I'm very anxious to know what you're doing right now, so please write, as, you see, I love you. Also, I am very anxious that you don't get all fouled up in some ridiculous trouble or other, like the Dostoevskian creature that you are. So take it slow. Take good care of Woofit, of Sweeny, and of Joanie, and of Herbie. And did you pick up my radio at home? . . . if so, how did you like the folks. Write and tell me all about this action.

You and I are going to take a trip to "Galloway" (Lowell) when I come back; and what do you say to a trip to Grosse Pointe, or California, or something? I really want to do things like that. We'll have a lot of fun, so wait for me. Cheerio and goodbye.

Yours

Jack XXXX

6. Seymour Wyse, a friend from Horace Mann Prep School who was interested in jazz. He was called "Lionel Smart" in *Vanity of Duluoz*.

1944

After returning from England to New York, Kerouac worked odd jobs, dividing his time between his parents' apartment and Edie Parker's place at 421 West 118th Street. In his journal on January 4, 1944, he wrote that he "must have a split personality—when I get home in Ozone Park, can't remember a thing about 118th Street life." Two months later, just after his twenty-second birthday, he learned that Sebastian Sampas had died in a hospital in North Africa after being wounded on the Anzio beachhead. Writing half in English and half in Québécois, the language he still spoke at home with his parents, Jack composed a letter of farewell to his best friend. "A long time, a very long, long time ago, we were together, right? Together! This great name for love. . . ."

TO SEBASTIAN SAMPAS

[after March 12, 1944
New York City]

Sebastian—

It's raining—and the song has come—I'll See You Again. Where? Where, Sammy?

Mon pauvre, pauvre ami—ayez des pensées de moi, hein? Tu m'as tant fait mal au coeur—

I'm writing about Michael and Jeanne, Sam . . . help me. . . . Oh, vain is my illusion of your presence, vain, vain, as when you sang the words at Lakeview . . .

Jadis! Jadis! Jadis, on etait ensemble, non? *Ensemble!* Ce grand môt d'amour . . .

C'est tout parti. I bequeath thee this wraith of unsprung tears.

Sebastian, really, your death has never ceased making of me a damned sentimentalist like yourself . . . You bastard, you, I shan't ever forgive you!

Fraternally,
Jean

In the spring of 1944, Edie Parker introduced Kerouac to the people he called in Vanity of Duluoz *"the new characters of my future 'life' ": first Lucien Carr, a Columbia student Edie and Joan usually met at the West End Cafe on Broadway, a few blocks from their apartment, and then Lucien's friend David Kammerer. It was through Lucien Carr that Kerouac also met William Burroughs and Allen Ginsberg in 1944; both were Lucien's friends. On August 14, 1944, Carr fatally stabbed Kammerer with a Boy Scout knife for making homosexual advances to him, and Kerouac was arrested as a material witness. Leo Kerouac refused to lend Jack the $100 for his bail, but Edie lent him the money after he promised he would marry her. On August 22, 1944, Jack married Edie; soon afterwards he wrote her mother about their plan to start their life together at Mrs. Parker's home in Grosse Point, Michigan, while he worked to earn enough money to repay the loan. Edie added a note to Jack's letter, telling her mother that she hoped to find a job in Detroit and that when she came into her inheritance she planned to return to New York City to begin a career designing hats.*

TO MRS. PARKER

September 1, 1944
Ozone Park, L.I.

Dear Mrs. Parker—

Today Edith and I scoured around for the fare to Detroit. She wants to get going as soon as possible, and so do I. I particularly want to get to Detroit and to work as soon as I can, because being in debt like this weighs on me like a scourge.

My mother is of the opinion that nothing much can be done until the holiday weekend is over, Monday that is. Until then, we have ample time to pack and dispatch the varied business that goes with a change of this sort. We'll stay here at my people's house over the weekend. By Monday night, we should be ready to leave.

I could stay here in Long Island and work, but it is Edith's wish that I go to Detroit with her. After all, she opines, we are married now, and marriage does not call for immediate separation. I too think it is best that we be together and work, as it were, like a team. And as long as I am welcome at your home, under circumstances, by the way, highly embarrassing to me, we might as well go through with the plan.

I have firm intentions. I want to pay you back as soon as possible, and in the process, save for our own home here in New York. By the time the trial[1] is up, we should have saved enough to come back and get a headstart. In the meantime, I must reluctantly admit, I will find myself in a state of impatience and, again, embarrassment.

I was always of the opinion that we should have married once I was underway in a career, but Edith, impulsive and yet charmingly so as she is, did not wish to wait. The tragic events of the past few weeks, I believe, catapulted us into a badly timed union—but a bad beginning might augur a successful ending.

In the past year, I succeeded in securing employment (with Columbia Pictures) of a highly specialized type.[2] This, I feel, indicates that I can go far in time. But for the purpose of discharging these debts, I shall be willing to work at anything in Detroit. I'll try several things I have in mind first—the first day—and if without success, I shall settle with other employment. But there is no doubt in my mind that I can get along—and Edith as well.

I was aboard a merchant ship, in drydock, when the tragedy occurred. The ship was not paying, since it was in drydock, and consequently I found myself, when all this happened, broke as usual. I had counted upon my pay as a material witness, but that doesn't come until the case is disposed of—probably September 15.

That is about all I can say. Except for an additional thing—my father was very impressed with some letters of yours that Edie showed him. He was looking forward to meeting you when it was thought that you might come down to New York; it was with some disappointment that he learned you had changed your plans. He hopes to meet you in the future, and I was certain the meeting will produce amiable results. He is a man who professes notions about

---

1. Lucien Carr's trial was held on October 6, 1944.

2. Kerouac worked briefly as a freelance script synopsizer for Columbia Pictures on Seventh Avenue in New York City.

life and morals remarkably paralleling your own. Of conservative, Republican New England vintage, and from severely moral stock, he elicited great pleasure from your letters. My mother is sweet and charming, and I am sure you will like her, as she will you. I am sure that this marriage will succeed—at first, there is always the collision, social and moralistic, of the families. Later there is always the fusion of interests. At any rate, in a world where death is rampant, as today, marriage is the least evil—that much is certain.

Jack

While Jack was living with Edie in Grosse Pointe, Michigan, his mother wrote him from Ozone Park about the big "blowout" on September 14, 1944. This was a great Atlantic hurricane that swept up from Florida to Long Island and Boston with winds averaging eighty miles an hour. The hurricane was featured on the front page of the September 15, 1944, New York Times, *along with war news of Allied tanks crossing from Belgium to confront the German Army's Siegfried Line. Gabrielle found it hard to accept that Jack didn't "belong" to her anymore after he married Edie, but she continued to encourage his ambition to become what she called a "great 'writer.' "*

TO JACK KEROUAC
FROM GABRIELLE KEROUAC

Friday 9:30 P.M.
[September 15, 1944
Ozone Park, N.Y.]

Hello My Honey,

Just to let you know that we are O.K. after the big "Blowout" we had here. I thought you might worry a bit because Long Island was the worst "hit" despite all the damage it was not half as bad as the one we experienced in Lowell in 1938. Remember? Honest, I really enjoyed that fury. I stayed in my window throughout. The trees on the Boulevard[1] are all there none blew away only our mail box took a tumble. However, here's a few clippings of spots you know very well. At the same time I'm enclosing a clipping of Lucien Carr as we understand it.[2] There won't be no trial now. I don't know weather [sic] you know about it yet that's why I'm sending it to you right away. It should make you feel [better. You] have good stuff in you. As for me, Honey, I'm still not able to realize you have left me for good. I keep "searching" the Boulevard looking out the window for hours thinking I'll see you come walking up and waving to me. I dare say I miss you a lot now and more so now that I know you don't belong to me anymore but that's life and sooner or later I'll get used to the idea. I hope you will be very happy, Honey, and that nothing will ever stop you from being a great "*Man*". With the help of your new Mother and a good Wife you should become a great "writer." All the luck in the world to you Honey.

Well I must tell you what I did yesterday. Pa took me out. We first went to Jamaica for his glasses. Then went on to Chinatown, had a swell dinner at the "Port Arthur" restaurant. I bought *tea* also, and a few little souvenirs. Then to the Apollo. There we saw Jean Gabin and Simone Simon in the "Human Beast" in French. It was wonderful. It's a picture based on Emile Zola's books, I guess. The other was an English picture also very *good*. I enjoyed my outing very much, but I was missing having you there too. It seems so strange not to have you around New York. Oh well, and after moving way out here too. Just to enjoy all this with you. Now I'm beginning to realize what Bea always told me. It doesn't pay to *plan* anything. It never works that way. At any rate I'm staying here as long as I can work. We can manage o.k. I'll say good night now I have to write to Nin. I'm looking forward to her visit next month and yours too

---

1. Cross Bay Boulevard in Ozone Park.

2. The headline of the clipping about the Lucien Carr trial read: "Student Pleads Guilty to Killing Ex-Teacher." Carr's attorney was quoted as saying, "We believe we would have a fair chance of winning a plea of self-defense, but rather than risk a jury trial we have decided to plead guilty to manslaughter in the first degree." Carr, nineteen years old at the time of his trial, served two years in the Elmira State Reformatory.

if you can make it. So all my love and if you get a job soon let me know how you are doing. My best to Edie.

Love Mom. XXXXXXXX

Regarding himself as a "Prodigal Son" after he separated from Edie and returned to his parents in Ozone Park, Kerouac began what he called in Vanity of Duluoz *"a year of low, evil decadence," splitting his time between his parents and his friends around Columbia. With Lucien Carr gone, he saw more of Allen Ginsberg, whom Kerouac described as a "spindly Jewish kid with horn-rimmed glasses and tremendous ears sticking out, seventeen years old, burning black eyes, a strangely deep mature voice." Ginsberg borrowed books for him from the Columbia library, and Jack began to read literature and philosophy obsessively in an attempt to formulate a "New Vision" of art. Their literary hero at that time was Lucien's favorite French poet, Arthur Rimbaud (1854–1891). Kerouac pinned a quotation from Rimbaud on his wall that captured the spirit of their efforts: "When shall we go, over there by the shores and mountains, to salute the birth of new work, the new wisdom, the flight of tyrants, and of demons, the end of superstition, to adore . . . the first ones!?"*

TO ALLEN GINSBERG

Thursday
[October 1944
Ozone Park, N.Y.]

Dear Allen,

Let you not to the marriage of true minds admit impediments— love is not love which alters when it altercation finds[1]—O no! 'tis an ever fix'd lark . . .

———

1. Shakespeare's Sonnet 116 begins:

> Let me not to the marriage of true minds
> Admit impediments: love is not love
> Which alters when it alteration finds,
> Or bends with the remover to remove.
> O no, it is an ever-fixed mark . . .

Our wedding anniversary fell on the day of the liberation of Paris.[2] I suppose this news Lucien now views morosely—he who wanted to be in Paris among the first. That event will have to wait now . . . but surely it will come about. I'd like to go to Paris after the war with Edie, Lucien and Céline[3]—and a little money for a decent flat somewhere in Montparnasse. Perhaps if I work hard now, and establish my fortune swiftly, I can realize that transcendent ambition. You yourself might lay down your legal labours[4] for awhile and join us there. The New Vision would blossom. . . .

But this is all speculation, meditation, nay, emasculation . . . Thanks for the letter. It moved me at times. I find in you a kindred absorption with identity, dramatic meaning, classic unity, and immortality: you pace a stage, yet sit in the boxes and watch. You seek identity in the midst of indistinguishable chaos, in sprawling nameless reality. [. . . .]

Lucien is different, or at least, his egocentricity is different; he hates himself intensely, whereas we do not. Hating himself, as he does, hating his "humankindness," he seeks new vision, a post-human post-intelligence. He wishes more than Nietzsche[5] prescribed. He

---

2. The liberation of Paris occurred on August 25, 1944.

3. Céline Young had been Lucien Carr's girlfriend.

4. Ginsberg had entered Columbia with the idea of becoming a lawyer so he could do legal work for labor unions.

5. Friedrich Wilhelm Nietzsche (1844–1900), German philosopher. In November 1944 Kerouac, using a piece of string as a tourniquet, wrote out a quotation by Nietzsche in his own blood: "Art is the highest task and the proper metaphysical activity of this life." In a diary entry for November 16, 1944, Kerouac confided:

> I wrote close to half a million words since 1939, when I first began to write. Poems, stories, essays, aphorisms, journals and nine unfinished novels. . . .
> Art so far has rationalized my errantry, my essential Prodigal Son behavior. It has also been the victim of an ego craving fame and superiority. I have been using art as a societal step-ladder—which proves that my renunciation of society is yet incomplete.
> Self-Ultimacy I saw as the new vision—but I cravenly turned it to a use in a novel designed to gain me, the man of the world, respect, idolatry, sexual success, and every other thing that goes with it.
> Au revoir à l'art, then.

wants more than the next mutation—he wants a post-soul. [. . . .]

I prefer the new vision in terms of art—I believe, I smugly cling to the belief, that art is the potential ultimate. Out of the humankind materials of art, I tell myself, the new vision springs. Look at "Finnegan's Wake" and "Ulysses" and "The Magic Mountain."[6] [. . . .]

Well, goodbye . . . and write: tell me more about the shadow and the circle.

Ton ami, Jean

---

6. James Joyce's experimental novels *Ulysses* (1922) and *Finnegans Wake* (1939) and Thomas Mann's *The Magic Mountain* (1924) were European novels discussed by Kerouac and Ginsberg in their conversations about the New Vision. In his notebook Kerouac listed the authors they were reading to deepen their understanding of the "conflict between modern bourgeois culture and artistic culture." See *Vanity of Duluoz,* Book Thirteen, Chapter 5.

1945

At the end of 1944, as Kerouac wrote in Vanity of Duluoz, *William Burroughs returned to New York and advised him to "stop this nonsense" with Ginsberg, trying to discover a New Vision in literature. Edie also came back to New York from Michigan, and Jack joined her in the Upper West Side apartment she shared with Joan Vollmer. After Burroughs moved into the apartment, Kerouac collaborated with him writing alternate chapters of a novel about the Lucien Carr–David Kammerer slaying. Jack described the book in a letter to his sister Caroline after she sent him money as a gift for his twenty-third birthday. Nin had married her second husband, Paul Blake, and they planned to live in North Carolina when he returned from military service. Writing his sister, Kerouac glossed over his dissipation from the drugs he was taking with his friends, later described so graphically in* Vanity of Duluoz. *In his letter Kerouac's account of how he felt living with his parents, "a sort of mopey dullness," gave a clear picture of his life with Leo and Gabrielle. The situation would change after the discovery of his father's fatal illness.*

TO CAROLINE KEROUAC BLAKE

March 14, 1945
[New York City]

Dear Nin—

This is not only by way of being a letter of thanks for the birthday gift but a heart-to-heart letter I've long been planning to write and never got around to simply because I didn't have much sheer *news* to give you about myself. Since nothing constructive ever seems to happen to me—for reasons which I shall subsequently explain, harrumph—I never can find anything to write about, especially to you, who am [sic] a vigorous and busy person. Well, anyway, something did happen to me—I got a birthday present from my sister. I don't deserve it and you know it, but on with the letter.

I hear you don't take Henderson Nor'Calina to heart, but you were saying to Gin that you wanted to raise your children in a rural atmosphere and Henderson is rural if anything. I liked the place in one way, but for romantic reasons and not practical ones: the South enchants me anyway, but I don't know if I'd want to live there. Passed through Henderson at night in a car, stopped for a beer, and could smell the honeysuckle. Well, I suppose you and Paul can decide where you want to live after the war, but if he wants Henderson, you might reconsider your original opinion about the jernt. If you want country life, there it is. Weekend excursions to Washington in a car are within the pale of possibility, or to Raleigh south. At least the country around there is beautiful. So here I am making conversation where I have a little news to give you.

The news is about the book Burroughs and I wrote. It is now in the hands of the publishing firm Simon & Schuster and they're reading it. What will happen I don't know. For the kind of book it is—a portrait of the "lost" segment of our generation, hard-boiled, honest, and sensationally real—it is good, but we don't know if those kinds of books are much in demand now, although after the war there will no doubt be a veritable rash of "lost generation" books and ours in that field can't be beat. An agent has taken pains to make our contact at Simon and Schuster and we should know whether or not they will publish it within two weeks. If *they* don't want it, we simply take the book to another publisher, and so on ad infinitum. Columbia Pictures wants movie rights on it, even though I told them it wasn't movie material, but they said if it were published and by any chance became popular, they wanted the title and a few scenes just for good measure. This is all too optimistic. What will really happen, I can see it, is an endless trudge from publisher to publisher until some two-bit firm takes it.[1] So that's the news I have, and it's only problematical.

If the book is published, Bill and I will immediately begin on a second novel. We make a good team. On top of that, I will begin to finish that novel I've been writing ever since I was nineteen (when you used to giggle in the kitchen with Dixon, remember?) If that happens, I know exactly what to do. But if the book is not published, and nothing happens to anything I write, I frankly will be up against a stone wall again.

---

1. Burroughs and Kerouac ultimately dropped the idea of publishing the book, although Kerouac continued to try to sell it until 1952. See his letter to Carl Solomon on April 7, 1952, pp. 341–342.

I'll explain now what I mean by stone wall *again*. Have you noticed how my life operates in cycles? How I flit from, say, Edie to the merchant marine (usually abortive attempts) to home and writing and then back again to Edie in a continuous blind circle? A psychoanalyst I recently met is much interested in all this and claims that what I need is an operation—a psychoanalytical operation on my will—before I can get out of this ever-revolving prison circle. He says I don't want to be successful, that something destructive in me, in my subconscious mind, works against all that, which explains why I never finish important projects or why I don't stick to jobs or to anything for that matter. And what is most fantastic, that the reason I have this subconscious will to failure, a sort of death-wish, stems from something I did before I was five years old and which stamped upon me a neurotic and horrible feeling of *guilt*. Now all I remember about Gerard, for instance, is his slapping me on the face, despite all the stories Mom and Pop tell me of his kindness to me. The psychoanalyst figured that I hated Gerard and he hated me—as little brothers are very likely to do, since children that age are primitive and aggressive—and that I wished he were dead, *and he died*. So I felt that I had killed him, and ever since, mortified beyond repair, warped in my personality and will, I have been subconsciously punishing myself and failing at everything. And it wasn't until I took off on my own that the failure really began, for up to the age of eighteen and my freshman year at Columbia I was being directed by my elders and by a pre-decided career of football and journalism. When I went off on my own, exercising my own malicious and destructive will against myself, I really hit the rocks. But psychoanalysis can make me remember the kind things Gerard did to me, and the kind feelings I had for him—which would thus balance against the terrible guilt complex and restore normalcy to my personality.[2] Nothing else can

2. Kerouac's older brother Francis Gerard Kerouac (1916–1926), who died of rheumatic fever, was a profound influence on Jack's life and writing. In *Visions of Gerard* he wrote, "For the first four years of my life, while he lived, I was not Ti Jean Duluoz, I was Gerard, the world was his face, the flower of his face, the pale stooped disposition, the heart-breakingness and the holiness and his teachings of tenderness to me, and my mother constantly reminding me to pay attention to his goodness and advice."

make me remember the kindness I felt for Gerard, since I've been trying like hell, and all I can remember is that slap in the face. Psychoanalysis is a sort of ingenious method which helps you to remember by piecing clues from dreams, by semi-hypnosis, and so forth. So one of my definite plans, if the book is published, is to get that much-needed operation. My case if anything very closely resembles the case of Peter Slavek in a great contemporary novel by Arthur Koestler, "Arrival and Departure," and my personality is almost like that of another writer, Carlton Brown, who describes himself in "Brainstorm." And of course, throughout Freud, Adler, Karen Horney, and Krafft-Ebbing, and all the other psychologists, I can find more data. I'll bet now that you think I'm nuts because I'm looking into these things. The truth is I've studied these people long ago, but now for the first time, I find that their knowledge can help me. So now they're not just books, but salvation.

So you see, Nin, my aimlessness and laziness are not just ingrained in my personality—they were put there by the hard nature of life when I was just four or five, and can be extracted again, like a bad appendix. The only thing I don't like about all this is that I lose self-respect, I feel as though I don't have a mind or will of my own. But then I realize that, well, anyway, get operated on for the hell of it—because if I start to exercise my so-called will on my own again, it will blindly lead me back along the rounded rut of that circle I'm in. Gadzooks, I'm sick of that circle.

I've asked Edie for a divorce, but nicely. No news until I get her answer, but possibly she's keeping the letter [. . . .] If we do get divorced, I'll go on seeing her occasionally, for we are both wacky in a way, and we should never have gotten married but just gone on knowing each other in a casual sort of way. I don't know what she's thinking [. . . .] The happiest days of my life, I can tell you, were spent living with her at Columbia when all the kids were around, including Lucien. You'd wake up in the morning and find the house full of people talking or reading books, and you'd go to bed at night with most of them still there and getting ready to curl up on couches and pillows on the floor. What the hell, I don't know, but to me a home in the suburbs is a sort of isolated hell where nothing happens. I like to open my doors to the "foaming winter" and to lots of people and let them troop through my house. You may never see them again, I think, and I like people anyway. If I had a million bucks, I'd have a mansion, with thirty rooms and the house would be full of my friends all day long, with concerts going on in the record room and bats going on in the wine cellars. I am not inclined to what one might term the Bourgeois way of life. Well, in case you don't like this happy picture of domestic life in my mansion, let me say that I might not want that after being psychoanalyzed.

So that's the news about the book, about Edie, and about my tentative plans.

Mom and Pop are fine. Pop turns on the radio full blast so that he can start talking to you at the top of his voice. Mom has her quart of wine hidden in the closet, though God knows why she should hide it. And I sit around in a sort of mopey dullness. First thing I'm going to do if I ever sell books and things is give them money to start their store. Mom's thinking of California already, and if I do well in Hollywood, why I think, why can't they start a store in some leafy pleasant California town? We'll see what happens. Meanwhile, as you saw for yourself, they're doing very well and they love you very much indeed.

Well, I guess that's all. One more thing I guess. You and Gin didn't like Burroughs, hey? Nobody can actually *like* Burroughs. I think he studied occult Yoga magic with which he could throw a cold curse on everybody around him. He's a cold fish all right. If the book isn't published, he's going to go in the American Field Service. "What?" you say to him, "are you getting patriotic at last?" And he answers, "Oh, nothing of the sort, I just want to knock the gold teeth off the corpses on the front and collect them in a bottle." That's the way he says he is. Bashful, he will never admit any emotion short of that gold-teeth business. Actually, he'd wince if a fly died. When he first came to Harvard he had an ugly picture of an old ugly house on his wall and someone asked him why he had the damned thing hanging up on his wall and he said, "Why, I like it because it's ugly." That's him, all right. No one can actually *like* him, as I say, but he's nice enough.

Well, sis, see what you can make of all this, and thanks a million for the gift, it will come in very handy indeed. (Quart of Imperial?

Lobster at King of the Sea? Who knows?) Now good night and please write soon. I'll let you know the good news if any, and bad news if is . . .

Send my regards to Paul. I don't know what to write to him about, because after all he's in the South Pacific expecting me to sail into view or something and what can I say. I'll write to him if you think I should.

All my love,
Jack xxxx

By the late summer and fall of 1945, Kerouac was spending more time at home in Ozone Park, where he nursed his father, who was dying of cancer of the spleen. Jack began to receive letters from Ginsberg analyzing their relationship. After Allen was suspended from Columbia in March 1945, he had decided to get his papers as a merchant seaman. Early in August 1945 Ginsberg wrote Kerouac from Paterson, New Jersey, asking about Burroughs and explaining his view of himself as "a Jew (with powers of introspection and eclasticism attendent [sic], perhaps)."

TO ALLEN GINSBERG

August 23, '45
[Ozone Park, N.Y.]

Cher jeune singe:[1]

I shall answer all your stupid questions, as there is nothing else to do. Bill's now at Sheepshead,[2] has been there since Monday the 20th. Of course he won't look you up right away—that's his system, he wants us not to think that he is too eager. He'll look you up in good time, unless you happen to run into him. Don't be too surprised!—

---

1. "Dear young ape."

2. Burroughs had also been trying to get his merchant seaman's papers at the U.S. Maritime Service Training Station in Sheepshead Bay, Brooklyn, where Ginsberg had enrolled at the Telephone Center.

Now, he was in New York five days before he called me up, or that is dropped me a line, telling me he was around. I immediately went to see him, not being wary of my own eagerness. He was not living in a flophouse this time—he lived in a Park Avenue hotel at $4.50 per day. It did not adjoin a Turkish bath (I'm still answering your questions) but the place itself was a well known Turkish bath, as the saying goes.

I've scoured your letter for further questions, and there are no more. Strange!—I had had the notion that it was full of whys and whats. All well and good . . . there is no Why. There is Mystery, of course, but no Why. The mystery is this: that there should ever have entered our heads the notion of Why! That's the mystery, among others. Death is a mystery almost as enigmatic as life. But enough of that.

You were right about my "peckerhead romanticism." Of course. I perfectly agree with you. Now it is all settled. We can begin worrying our little heads about something else now.

The other night, the last night I saw Bill, that strange thing happened to me . . . I got very drunk and lost my psychic balance. It doesn't always happen, remember, but sometimes it does, like that night. Gilmore had some fellow come to our table . . . we drank . . . all went to his apartment, where we drank much more. Even Bill was a little silly. We were all silly. I hated the guy. You know of him, he was with that large party at the Cafe Brittany that night we were there with Gilmore and Uncle Edouard, that large noisy American party, shot through with ensigns and society girls. I shall have to tell you about that night I lost my psychic balance. Only one thing did I carry away with me from the welter of silliness . . . a book! I stole a book. "Voyage au bout de la nuit" by Céline.[3] In a remarkable English translation. And also, I carried away with me much drunkenness. It was the second time I saw Bill, and still we did not talk. For awhile we were alone, in a restaurant, and it occurred to me we had nothing more to talk about. That's the way it has developed;

---

3. Louis-Ferdinand Céline (1894–1961), French novelist; Kerouac had taken a copy of his *Journey to the End of Night* (1932).

that's what it's come to. We have nothing further to talk about. We've exhausted the possibilities of each other. We are tired. Another few years, an accumulation of new possibilities, and we will have something to talk about. As for you, my little friend, there is always something to talk about because you are so unutterably vain and stupid, and that always leaves a splendid electrically charged gap for argument. Merde à toi!—that's what I say.

In view of all that, I suppose we can meet at the Admiral, providing you are serious about meeting me there. As to eating there, I don't know. The place has deteriorated, service and food and all. It's a disgusting biological change, like cancer. Bring along the Trilling letter.[4] I may as well begin to find out what kind of a fool he really is . . . whether he is a bigger one or lesser one than you or I or anybody else.

It may surprise you to know that I have been writing in prodigious amounts. I am writing three novels at this very minute, and keeping a large diary to boot. And reading! . . . I have been reading like a madman. There's nothing else to do. It's one of those things you can do at the moment when all else isn't any more interesting, I mean, when everything else can't exactly prove to be much more worthwhile. I intend to do this sort of thing all my life. As for artistry, that is now a personal problem, something that concerns only me, so that probably I won't bother you about that ever again. All well and good. A line from my diary: "We are all sealed in our own little melancholy atmospheres, like planets, and revolving around the sun, our common but distant desire." Not so good, perhaps, but if you steal that line of mine, I'll actually kill you, for a change.

Bye bye petit,
Jean

5:30 à l'Admiral, Samedi . . .

---

4. Letter to Ginsberg from Lionel Trilling (1905–1975), literary critic and professor at Columbia to whom Ginsberg had shown his poetry. Ginsberg had written Kerouac that he still saw Trilling from time to time, and that he'd been invited to Trilling's apartment.

In his early letters to Burroughs, Kerouac kept up his guard almost as if in awe of what he described in Vanity of Duluoz *as his friend's intelligence as an "observer weighted with more irony than the lot of 'em." There Kerouac wrote he felt his "saving grace" in Burroughs's eyes was "the materialistic Canuck taciturn cold skepticism all the picked-up Idealism in the world of books couldn't hide . . ."*

TO WILLIAM S. BURROUGHS

Sept. 2, 1945
133-01 Crossbay Blvd.
Ozone Park, L.I., N.Y.

Dear Bill,

I have recently had the great pleasure of receiving Ginsberg as a visitor to my house, whereupon I learned that you would be returning to New York within the next month. Allow me to congratulate you on your speedy recovery and to express the heartfelt wish that in the future there will be fewer rocky bumps on the road of life for you. In temperance is wisdom; moderation is the key to all sound accomplishment. Let us hope that the whores of evil no longer loiter on the doorsteps of your path beckoning you into the brothel of despair, and that hereinafter you may present them with the most rigid manifestations of a firm and manly will. Ad astra per aspera.

Yours truly, J. Kerouac

In his last two letters to Ginsberg in 1945, Kerouac expanded on the subject of their friendship and his sense that, while dependent upon the others in their group for emotional support, he was different from them because of the intensity of his desire to be a writer: ". . . my art is more important to me than anything. . . . I've long ago dedicated myself to myself. . . ." On September 4, 1945, Ginsberg had written Kerouac a letter saying that he refused to quarrel over Jack's "unexplained attacks on my 'stupidity and vanity,' which distressed me rather than amused or wounded, whatever you were aiming at.

What is the matter? At any rate, don't shepherd your artistic prob-
lems back into the cave; I'd like to hear of them."

TO ALLEN GINSBERG

Thursday night Sept. 6 [1945]
[Ozone Park, N.Y.]

Dear Allen,

Your little letter moved me, I must say . . . particularly the line,
"I was so sick that I found myself worrying about the future of man's
soul, my own in particular." There you elicited the true picture of
things terrestrial . . . namely, disease and loss and death. I like the
way [Rainer Maria] Rilke faces these facts in his un-Bourgeois way,
and I must say I don't particularly approve of forgetting the facts of
life and death in an orgy of intellectual pseudo-synthesis . . . Shelley's
"dome of white radiance"[1] has become a sort of rose-coloured dome
now, shedding technicolor pinkness on us all. However, I don't think
there's much point in telling *you* all this because I know you don't
represent the average intellectual softy. Or punk.

Some of my most neurotically fierce bitterness is the result of re-
alizing how untrue people have become . . . and you must admit that
I am in closer touch with public vulgarity than any of us. Although
Bill [Burroughs] reads the *Daily News* also, I go him one better, alas,
and take the trouble to listen to the radio . . . *and* suffer myself onto
P.M. as well. Archetypal morality in its modern high-pressure Orson
Welles and Hearst regalia—you see, there are no right and left dis-

---

1. Percy Bysshe Shelley (1792–1822), author of "Adonais," an elegy on the
death of his friend the poet John Keats (1795–1821). Shelley's poem includes
the stanza:

> The One remains, the many change and pass;
> Heaven's light forever shines, Earth's shadows fly;
> Life, like a dome of many-coloured glass,
> Stains the white radiance of Eternity,
> Until Death tramples it to fragments. —Die,
> If thou wouldst be with that which thou dost seek!
> Follow where all is fled! —Rome's azure sky,
> Flowers, ruins, statues, music, words, are weak
> The glory they transfuse with fitting truth to speak.

tinctions, and never were, in spite of what I think the Lancasters[2] and Fritz Sterns would say—have become for me a kind of windmill to my Quixote . . . I think of what Joan Adams and Kingsland[3] would say about all this; this makes of me a most ludicrous figure. I'm wrestling with the passe . . . that's what you're probably thinking. Well, let's have no more of this for now . . .

News of Burroughs is what you want. . . . I haven't seen him and I don't know where he is. However, I've mailed a card to the University Club in the hopes that it will be forwarded to him, and he may let me know where he is. Gilmore's roommate, Francis Thompson (!), is under the impression that Bill is still in New York . . . Gilmore[4] himself is staying at a cottage on Cape Cod writing a novel. The reason why Bill disenrolled from Sheepshead is because he wanted to go in the MM as a purser, and very likely they wouldn't see it his way . . . Francis believes that Bill is going to try again. That about sums up all I know about Burroughs for the present, but the moment I'm in receipt of his new address, it shall be sent on to you. There remains but one additional item re Burroughs . . . Joyce Field says he is "leprous." That I must tell Bill . . .

I was moved by your letter, I repeat. Partly because you'd been and still are sick . . . Partly because of Trilling's letter, which represents something I'd like to happen to me someday, namely, to be liked and admired by someone like him. Although there's something a little wearying about his emphasis on "effect" in poetry, that letter he wrote you is certainly a marvellous example of how an entrenched man of letters can inspire confidence in a young poet. There's something French about it . . . I mean, it smacks of [Stéphane] Mallarmé encouraging the young author of Le cahier d'André Walter; or of

---

2. Bill Lancaster was Ginsberg's roommate at Columbia before Ginsberg's suspension from college in 1945 for writing "Fuck the Jews" on his dirty windowpane and for letting Kerouac spend the night in his dormitory room. Ginsberg was readmitted in September 1946.

3. John Kingsland was a friend of Ginsberg's who often visited Joan Vollmer's apartment. Joan had separated from her husband, Paul Adams, after the birth of their daughter Julie in the summer of 1944 and was studying at the School of Journalism at Columbia University.

4. Bill Gilmore was Burroughs's friend at Harvard.

[Paul] Verlaine praising the tempestuous provincial lad in a letter addressed to Charleville; or of [André] Gide bestowing his warm appreciation and admiration on the young and unknown Julian Green. I say all this gauchely in my haste, but honestly I envy you. I think we none of us realize the importance, nay the sweetness, of admiration; it is one of the dying virtues of character. Look for instance at the way Lucien is neurotically resented all around Columbia by a lot of bloodless fish who couldn't out-argue him or something, or who couldn't get away with wearing red shirts and stroking white masks on the streets, as he did. A recent visit at Columbia, where Carr is still very much in evidence, reveals, I suppose, and to coin a pat and disgusting phrase, the neurotic nature of our times . . . Here are all these jerks snarling out of the corners of their mouths at everything—and particularly at Lucien.[5] There is none of the loving perception of "Look! Look!" . . . no one grabs your arm eagerly to seduce you sweetly with a point . . . there is no Germanic enthusiasm, no thick guttural cries . . . just so much monotonous epigram-making, and as far as that goes, there are no Oscar Wildes at Columbia.[6] [. . . .]

I asked Edie to meet me at Columbia this weekend. There's going to be a sort of get-together, which will include Edie, Joan, John, Grover, Céline, Kahn, myself, and I hope, Burroughs—if I can locate him. We will drink a toast to you, I'll see to that. Though Kingsland may giggle and Burroughs smirk and Edie turn up the corner of her mouth and Joan make a crack and Céline smile sweetly and Grover make a pun, I'll suggest a toast to our bed-ridden little copain.[7]

---

5. Lucien Carr was still in the reformatory.

6. Oscar Wilde (1854–1900), Irish novelist and dramatist imprisoned for homosexuality, was a gifted epigrammist.

7. In Book Thirteen of *Vanity of Duluoz,* Kerouac described a scene at Joan's apartment "around September 1945" when Joan's husband, Paul Adams, unexpectedly arrived from his military service, "fresh from the German front," and was surprised to find her and her friends "all high on Benny sprawled and sitting and cat-legged on that vast double-doublebed of 'skepticism' and 'decadence,' discussing the nothingness of values, pale-faced, weak bodies, Gad the poor guy said: 'This is what I fought for?'. . . . Of course we know the same thing was going on in Paris and Berlin of the same month and year, now that we've read . . . Sartre and even, of course, Auden and his Age of Anxiety."

Your curiosity regarding la soirée d'idiocie is understandable. True, I did feel remorse. So much so as to cancel an appointment with Burroughs for the next day, which probably bored him altogether. He has no patience for my kind of neurosis, I know . . . But since then I've been facing my nature full in the face and the result is a purge. You understand, I'm sure. Remember that the earlier part of my life has always been spent in an atmosphere vigorously and directly opposed to this sort of atmosphere . . . It automatically repels me, thereby causing a great deal of remorse, and disgust. There is a kind of dreary monotony about these characters, an American sameness about them that never varies and is always dull . . . Like a professional group, almost. The way they foregather at bars and try to achieve some sort of vague synthesis between respectability and illicitness . . . That is annoying, but not half so much as their silly gossiping and snickering. If they were but Greeks, things would take on a different tone altogether. I am repelled, then, largely by these social aspects, an overdose of which I got that night. As to the physical aspects, which as you know, disgust me consciously, I cannot be too sure . . . whatever's in my subconscious is there. I am not going to play the fool about that. My whole waking nature tells me that this sort of thing is not in my line. It keeps on telling me. It drums in my nature, telling me, until I begin to suspect its motive . . . But I shan't worry my pretty little head about it anymore. I think that in the end it will just be a matter of "Drive on!"—you have heard that story about Phil the junkey, haven't you? I shall let my neurosis dissolve in the white fire of action, as it were. Strangely, the thing that annoys me the most is the illusion everyone has that I'm torn in two by all this . . . when actually, all I want is clear air in which to breathe, and there is none because everybody's full of hot air. [. . . .]

You shouldn't have been "distressed" by the tone of my last letter. It was only a mood . . . and a not malevolent one either, not at all. It was all done as an older brother. Sometimes you give me such a feeling of superiority, say, moral superiority, that I can't restrain myself . . . Other times, I feel inferior to you—as I doubtlessly do this moment. I'm afraid that you'll never understand me fully, and because of that, sometimes you'll be frightened, disgusted, annoyed, or pleased . . . The thing that makes me different from all of you is the vast inner life I have, an inner life concerned with, of all things, externals . . . But that would be discussing my art, and so intimate is it become that I don't want to babble about it. You may deplore the fact that I'm "shepherding artistic problems back to the cave," but it's certain that that's where they indeed belong. The bigger and deeper this inner life grows, the less anyone of you will understand me . . . Putting it that way may sound silly, it may particularly amuse Burroughs, but that's the way it is. Until I find a way to unleash the inner life in an art-method, nothing about me will be clear. And, of course, this places me in an enviable position . . . it reminds me of a remark Lucien once made to me: he said: "You never seem to give yourself away completely, but of course dark-haired people are so mysterious." That's what he said, by God . . . Then you yourself referred to a "strange madness long growing" in me, in a poem written last winter . . . remember? I just thrive in this, by God. From now on, I think I'll begin to deliberately mystify everyone; that will be a novelty.

After all my art is more important to me than anything . . . None of that emotional egocentricity that you all wallow in, with your perpetual analysis of your sex-lives and such. That's a pretty pastime, that is! I've long ago dedicated myself to myself. . . . Julian Green, among others, has one theme in all his work: the impossibility of dedicating oneself to a fellow being. So Julian practises what he preaches . . . There is just one flaw: one yearns so acutely to dedicate oneself to another, even though it's so hopeless . . . There's no choice in the matter.

I was telling Mimi West last summer how I was searching for a new method in order to release what I had in me, and Lucien said from across the room, "What about the new vision?" The fact was, I had the vision . . . I think everyone has . . . what we lack is the method. All Lucien himself needed was a method.

I understand Trilling's impatience with the High Priest of Art . . . There *is* something phoney about that. It's the gesture adopted when the method doesn't prove to be self-sufficient . . . after awhile the gesture, the Priestliness, begins to mean more than the art itself. What could be more absurd?

But let's not let the whole matter deteriorate, as I feel it will in mentalities such as Trilling's—that to adopt art with fervor and single-minded devotion is to make the High Priest gesture. No, there's a distinction to be made, without a doubt.

So goodnight for now . . . [. . . .] I'm keeping Trilling's letter for awhile in order to show it to a few people; this must make you realize that the quality of my friendship for you is far purer than yours could ever be for me, you with your clay-pigeon complex. There's nothing that I hate more than the condescension you begin to show whenever I allow my affectionate instincts full play with regard to you; that's why I always react angrily against you. It gives me the feeling that I'm wasting a perfectly good store of friendship on a little self-aggrandizing weasel. I honestly wish that you had more essential character, of the kind I respect. But then, perhaps you have that and are afraid to show it. At least, try to make me feel that my zeal is not being mismanaged . . . as to your zeal, to hell with that . . . you've got more of it to spare than I. And now, if you will excuse me for the outburst, allow me to bid you goodnight. I've spent two hours on this letter and now I must write to Cornelius M., one of the Galloway Prometheans, who is now in Germany with a radar unit. He never liked me, but he wants to know all about the Carr case, that's evident . . . Perhaps I can worm my way back into the confidence of Allan M. this way, because they were bosom friends. His great grudge against me is that I'm irresponsible and amoral. I'll spread it on thick. Write soon.

Jean

TO ALLEN GINSBERG

Nov. 13, 1945
[Ozone Park, N.Y.]

Dear Allen—

I feel an indescribable need to talk to you . . . Not because I'm high on Benny,[1] and alone in the cursed kitchen, but as a matter of

---

1. Kerouac broke open Benzedrine inhalers, took out the soaked papers, and rolled them into little balls, which he soaked in Coca-Cola or coffee.

mood. I want to confess that I've grown very fond of you again. I'm quite aware of the nature of my previous "dislike"—that it was an essential pose for me, as much as your superimposed masochism has been essential for you. It has suddenly been revealed to me the extent of our common madness, and I mean not only you or me, but all of us. Particularly since our madness sets itself no vital goal, but only a kind of sustained and unrelieved heaviness of personality. We don't want to move, we are caught inert in the contrived intertwining stupidity of the common preconceived notion of ourselves. Bill, whom I love dementedly—he has the grandest mirror in which I can stare at myself—continues to be Bill, and it is so ridiculous for me to persist in my own stubborn sameness of self, since he himself does not deviate, and the whole thing is one interminable duel fought dully in the same misty light of a dawn that idiotically hangs suspended in the east. There we are, with our unvarying pistols, firing the same shots at each other, wearing the same facial expressions, a puppet show run by a mad bore, and it's never going to end.

And, likewise, there's you and I, and then Bill and Hal [Chase],[2] and Hal and Céline, and Joan and Bill, and Edie and myself, and so on. *C'est une chose formidable.*

Benny has made me see a lot. The process of intensifying awareness naturally leads to an overflow of old notions, and voilà, new material wells up like water following its proper level, and makes itself evident at the brim of consciousness. Brand new water!

The art of my past is all farce, or at least mostly. It is neurotic and cunning concealment of what I really know, and don't or didn't want to know.

I was given to see—and forgive my naiveté—how Hal, in the "episode of the Wolfeans and the non-Wolfeans,"[3] operated his own self into an external sham calculated to hide his real fears. [. . . .] Thus I had an inkling of myself too, the moment I had the first real inkling of Hal. I saw that it was very easy to get all tangled up in these

---

2. Hal Chase was a student at Columbia studying anthropology; he had rented a room at Joan Vollmer's apartment.
3. The "episode of the Wolfeans . . ." refers to the literary discussions at Joan's apartment about Thomas Wolfe and other writers.

compulsive falsehoods, and in spite of the charming pathos of such techniques per se—for they are of the stuff of life—I rather preferred, once I was given the chance through these insights, to climb up on the next level and proceed from there. What a strange journey it will be. At last I shall be clever!

It must also be confessed—and this should be hard to say, since at one time you provided us all with an eminent sense of moral superiority—that you are the least shammish and confused. Bill, of course, is stark raving mad . . . I wonder if you realize it. Thus, I've seen you flare out into a sudden glory before my eyes, and I like to tell you about it. Anyway, things in general are not always—now, you see, I'm falling into a state of narcotic imbecility.[4] Too late! Au revoir,

Jean

---

4. A month later, while walking over the Brooklyn Bridge with Ginsberg and Hal Chase, Kerouac collapsed and had to enter the Veterans Hospital in Queens to treat the thrombophlebitis in his legs, a condition resulting from taking too much Benzedrine. Ginsberg's response to learning that Kerouac was ill was to send him a poem, "To Kerouac in the Hospital," which began: "Death can make us gentle, pain will kill/ The animal, subdue the aggressive/ Pride of the disastrous, healthy will. . . ."

At the end of *Vanity of Duluoz,* Kerouac wrote. "I began to bethink myself in that hospital. . . . I began to get a new vision of my own of a truer darkness. . . . [Then] partially well, I went home and, in the general vanity of Duluoz, I decided to become a writer, write a huge novel explaining everything to everybody, try to keep my father alive and happy, while Ma worked in the shoe factory, the year 1946 now, and make a 'go' at it."

1947

After his father's death in the spring of 1946, Kerouac began the book that was to become his first published novel, The Town and the City. *He worked on the manuscript for two years (as he later wrote in* Vanity of Duluoz*) "in solitude, in pain, writing hymns and prayers even at dawn, thinking 'When this book is finished, which is going to be the sum and substance and crap of everything I've been thru throughout this whole gaddam life, I shall be redeemed.' "*

There are no Kerouac letters from 1946, but on March 20, 1947, shortly after he turned twenty-five, Kerouac wrote his sister in high spirits to thank her for her birthday gift. He also casually referred to his plans for his "proposed Western trip" that summer, when he would be midway in his work on The Town and the City. *This was to be the journey to visit his new friend Neal Cassady in Denver described in Part One of his next book,* On the Road.

TO CAROLINE AND PAUL BLAKE

March 20, '47
[Ozone Park, N.Y.]

Dear Nin & Paul—

Thanks a million for remembering my birthday and for the buck, with which I intend to get me ten glasses of beer this Saturday night. Say!—about next summer I'm all set to go! If I understand right Paul will get us a shack on that lake for 2 weeks: just think of all the things we can do: broil a lot of delicious fresh fish over a *charcoal fire* in the yard, and big steaks and chops too. Do nothing but fish in the daytime, eat at sunset, drink hi-balls at night, go to the dances around. Just swim, read, eat, sleep, hunt frogs and anything else, hang around, spin the bull, eat, sleep, swim, eat—drink—how long is this going to go on?

I'm glad Paul's finishing his schoolwork for now, and I knew he'd get high marks—seeing as how he's married to a smart "kiddles." Will you work in Kinston now? I'll be glad when I finish my book (next Fall) and when Paul is all set with his work: then we can work out more vacations, bigger ones, and perhaps even work out some angles, like that Alaska pipedream—on a smaller scale. Incidentally don't worry about my book, the more time goes by the better it gets

(I keep working on it every day in the week)—and I'll hand in *500* pages in May, which *may* get me a contract and some monthly checks to begin with. "Life is short and Art is long . . ."

Incidentally I may not go by N.C. in June on my proposed Western trip—gotta get back East for our summer vacation a month later, don't I? And Nin, if you can come here this month, great!—Mom is always dying to have you around and I'm always dying. (That's known as an *execrable* pun, meaning ptoo!) Yipe! the end of the page. And what did it get you? Thanks for the gift again. So long.

BROTHER JACK

P.S. My typewriter's busted—longer letter next time.

The following month, Kerouac wrote Hal Chase about his prepara-tions for his first trip west. Chase was from Denver and had intro-duced Jack to his Denver friend Neal Cassady in December 1946 when Cassady came to New York. Excitedly planning his trip, as he wrote in On the Road, *Kerouac had "been poring over maps of the United States" for months, "even reading books about the pioneers and savoring names like Platte and Cimarron and so on. . . ." He told Chase he had "begun a huge study of the face of America itself," and he wrote later in* On the Road *that he noticed there "was one long red line called Route 6 that led from the tip of Cape Cod clear to Ely, Nevada, and there dipped down to Los Angeles. I'll just stay on 6 all the way to Ely, I said to myself . . ."*

TO HAL CHASE

Sat. afternoon April 19 '47
[Ozone Park, N.Y.]

Prince Hal—

Well I was hugely *pleased* to hear from you and to learn about your plans for next summer. And I certainly hope to be around for that trip to the western slope: because that is the sort of thing my attention has slowly been turning to in the past few months.

In connection with that I might as well outline something which I had planned to tell you about in leisurely conversation, namely, that lately my interests have been undergoing a startling change, and I was pleased (once more) to learn that you yourself have been reorganizing or possibly just naturally turning your mind to new interests. [. . . .]

My own development in the directions above hinted center around a new interest in things rather than in ideas. For instance, all my reading in the past few months has been of a very practical nature. Here's a list: Parkman's "Oregon Trail,"[1] another book concerned with that trail and also every other important trail in the country (don't ask me why: I'm crazy about this kind of reading now), a history of the United States, a biography of George Washington, a history of the Revolutionary War (campaigns and maps included)— and last but not least, I have begun a huge study of the face of America itself, acquiring maps (roadmaps) of every state in the USA, and before long not a river or mountain peak or bay or town or city will escape my attention. Now what does all this mean? I know some people who would regard it as a kind of recidivous childishness. And yet I know some people who would regard it as a step ahead. Because, after all, what is the ruling thought in the American temperament if it isn't a purposeful energetic search after useful knowledge. The "livelihood of man" in America instead of the vague and prosy "brotherhood of man" of Europe. My subject as a writer is of course America, and simply, I must know everything about it. What does a thorough investigation of the "history of thought" yield to a man of purpose? What does the study of thought amount to if you yourself don't think new thoughts?—and how are you going to think new thoughts if you don't at first fire yourself with a new purpose? Well, my purpose is Balzacian in scope—to conquer knowledge of the U.S.A. (the center of the world for me just as Paris was the center of the world for Balzac)—my purpose is to know it as I know the palm of my hand. And as to the business of resentment, might I not say,

---

1. Historian Francis Parkman (1823–1893); a new edition of his book *The Oregon Trail*, handsomely illustrated by Thomas Hart Benton, was published in 1946.

like Washington said—"Envious of none, I am determined to be pleased with all." This is so far from the Raskolnikovs and the Julien Sorels[2] of Europe that it isn't funny: I feel too lazy to expand on it, but you can see it in a flash. It's the difference between a culture of turmoil, resentment and inter-human struggle, and a culture of livelihood, purpose, land, and natural struggle. *[Unmailed letter to Hal Chase 1947]*

In a letter to Burroughs in mid-July 1947, Kerouac described his plans to hitchhike from New York to California. The previous year Burroughs had been arrested in New York City for forging prescriptions; he drew a suspended sentence on the condition that he return home to his parents in St. Louis for three months. Joan Vollmer remained with her young daughter in the West Side apartment, along with Herbert Huncke, a Times Square hipster junky. They later joined Burroughs in Texas, where he had bought what Joan described in a letter to Edie as "a nice broken-down 99-acre farm a little north of Houston in New Waverly, Texas" in order to plant a marijuana crop. Ginsberg had come to Denver to be with Cassady, with whom he had fallen in love, and they planned to visit Burroughs on his Texas farm.

TO WILLIAM S. BURROUGHS

July 14, 1947
[Ozone Park, N.Y.]

Dear Bill—

My old friend Henri Cru recently blew into N.Y. with a couple of steeazicks[1] from Panama as big as your thumb: however this is not the purpose of this letter. It seems that we are going to ship out together, he is now in San Francisco arranging for rather good jobs on a ship (Chief & Assistant Electricians), and I am going out there

---

2. Protagonist of Stendhal's novel *The Red and the Black* (1830).
1. Steeazicks: marijuana cigarettes.

in three days, hitchhiking from New York. What I would like you to do is this: if Neal Cassady or Allen are at present visiting you in Houston, would you kindly let them know that I will be passing through Denver around the 23rd and 24th of this month, and if they are not enjoying your hospitality just right now, perhaps you could do me the favor of dropping them a penny postcard wherever they are (I assume you have their addresses). That is all. Neal, particularly, whose address is always changing, would be glad to hear word from me, and meet me somewhere. I keep losing track of him, like his landladies.

Say hello to Huncke and Joan for me, both of whom I miss quite a bit, as well as you. On the way back from a Pacific run I should see my way clear to drop in on you. Also I would like to see this Fall's Texas-Rice game, which is always a killer (among us football characters.)

I just spent an interesting two weeks in the deep South and I wish you could have seen some of the things I saw. [. . . .] I saw a lot of snakes and alligators at the Okefenokee swamp in Georgia, one alligator was 900 years old and just lay there in the sun like it's been doing since Alexander Nevsky. I don't know why I mention all these things, but I get a kick out of it. Am enclosing a newspaper clipping about an ideal landlord, just the type we were always looking for in New York.

I wish you would write to me once in a while and tell me about your life on the ranch. When are you going to grow grapefruits or something? I'll drop you a note from my San Francisco address, and you make sure and write me a long letter there. And don't forget to drop a line to Neal or Allen.

As ever,
Jack K.

When Kerouac left home on his first cross-country trip, he kept in touch with his mother in Ozone Park by sending her postcards to mark his progress on the road, reassuring her that he was eating well and taking good care of himself. As he said in On the Road, *while hitchhiking to Denver his favorite food was apple pie and ice cream.*

In Davenport, Iowa, "I went to sit in the bus station and think this over. I ate another apple pie and ice cream; that's practically all I ate all the way across the country. I knew it was nutritious and it was delicious, of course."

[July 24, 1947
postmarked Shelton, Neb.][1]

Dear Ma—

I've been eating apple pie & ice cream all over Iowa & Nebraska, where the food is so good. Will be in Colorado tonight—and I'll write you a letter from Denver. Everything fine, money holding out.

Love, Jacky XXX

P.S. You ought to see the *Cowboys* out here.

[July 24, 1947
Cheyenne, Wy.]

Dear Ma—

Sending this card the same day as the Nebraska card, from Wyoming—Cheyenne, Wyoming, where they're now having "Wild West Week." Travelled 600 miles today . . . am now ⅔ of the way to California, money holding out. Having great trip.

Jacky XXX

---

1. In Part One, 3, of *On the Road,* Kerouac wrote that in Nebraska he and his hitchhiking friend Eddie were "stuck in Shelton. . . . I had a cold. I bought cough drops in a rickety Indian store of some kind. I went to the little two-by-four post office and wrote my aunt a penny postcard. We went back to the grey road." He called Gabrielle his "aunt" in the novel.

[July 28, 1947
Denver, Colo.]

Dear Ma—Just arrived in Denver. I'll rest here at my friends' houses for a few days and then go on to California. You should see the beautiful mountains out here. The climate is clear and cool and sunny. I'll write a letter tomorrow.

Love from Jacky XXX

TO GABRIELLE KEROUAC

Denver
July 29 '47

Dear Ma—

My friends were all wonderful to me here, feeding me and giving me places to sleep, but now I want to get on to San Francisco and make some money. I haven't a cent left and I'll need $25[1] to take a bus to California from here, because hitch-hiking is impossible across the desert and the mountains. And Henri Cru will be expecting me by Monday.

The easiest way for you to send me the $25.00 is to go to a Western Union office in Brooklyn when you come out of work, and *wire* me the money to 1475 Cherry Street, Denver 7, Colorado—care/of White. That way I'll get it fast, and also you won't have to walk all over Ozone Park to find a Western Union office.

Boy, it's been a lot of fun around here. When I get Alan Temko's[2] typewriter tomorrow (he's that boy from Richmond Hill) I'll write and tell you all about it. I had about ten girlfriends; went up to the mountains; saw an opera; ate swell food, venison steak, at Hal's house; the weather is nice—and I'm staying in a swanky apartment

---

1. In *On the Road*, Kerouac wrote that in Denver he "sent my aunt an airmail letter asking her for fifty dollars" so he could take a bus to San Francisco.
2. Alan Temko, a Columbia student interested in architecture and literature.

with showers and food and everything. But I want to get going[3] so I can make a lot of money sailing in the Pacific and come home in the Fall and finish my book. Gee, and you can't realize how much I miss you, and the house, and writing in my room. But I'll be back in a few months and we'll save money. I hope Nin or Bea[4] are visiting you—if so, give them my love. Write me a little letter right away.

Love, Jacky XXX

My address:—

> Jack Kerouac
> c/o White
> 1475 Cherry St.
> Denver 7, Colorado

When Kerouac joined his old prep school friend Henri Cru in California, he learned they wouldn't be able to ship out as merchant seamen. Instead Cru invited Kerouac to work nights in Marin City with him as a security officer in a barracks for overseas construction workers. There was a typewriter in the office, and Kerouac settled down to write his friends long letters about what he was doing in California. Neal Cassady got one of the first letters, dashed off, as Jack told him, his "first time at a typewriter for weeks." In the letter Kerouac reflected that he hadn't been able to spend more than a few minutes with Cassady during his short time in Denver, yet the visit confirmed his feeling that they shared an "animal-relationship."

When Kerouac wrote On the Road, *he based the character of Dean Moriarty on Neal Cassady and recalled that when he first met Cassady in New York, Neal "reminded me of some long-lost brother. . . . All my other current friends were 'intellectuals' . . . But Dean's*

---

3. Kerouac described his "mad" days with "the whole gang" in Denver, and his "itching to get on to San Francisco," in Chapters 7 through 10 in Part One of *On the Road.*

4. Kerouac's cousin Beatrice Rouleau, who had often visited the family in Lowell.

intelligence was every bit as formal and shining and complete, without the tedious intellectualness . . . a western kinsman of the sun."

TO NEAL CASSADY

Aug. 26, 1947
Marin City, Calif.

Dear Neal—

This would be "one of those big mad beer-drinking" letters except that I ain't drinking no beer—but it will be a *long* letter. Could you possibly imagine the circumstances under which I write this letter? —wearing a badge of the local police department, with a blue hat on my head, blue pants, gray shirt, a club on the desk, a .32 automatic on my belt? Yes, Neal, I am a cop[1]—it is one of the funniest things ever to happen to me. I can hardly wait to tell Burroughs about it. But anyway, I'm not drinking beer as I write this, but I have all night to myself and a wonderful silencer typewriter and a whole office and the stationery this is written on. It would be a huge, unbelievable letter, full of subconscious scribblings and mad thoughts, except for the fact that I also want to write to Burroughs, Allen, and Lucien as well as you tonight: four very important characters. And whatever you do, don't think ill of me for being a cop, if only temporarily. I do *not* do my duty. I am a cop looking like some fugitive from Charley Ventura's Sextet.[2] I stare at the women on the grounds, fingering my genitalia, and move on shuffling my feet like a Dostoevsky character. See me that way, not as a cop. (I don't believe I ever wrote such nonsense to a human being before.) But see this— the first time at a typewriter for weeks, and you being an old typist, and you know the feeling you get, just writing anything that comes to your head, "scribblings-away," etc. You just like to see the words come out on the page, small and neat and all in straight lines, and

---

1. In Part One, Chapter 11, of *On the Road*, Kerouac described his job in Marin City: "I was sworn in by the local police chief, given a badge, a club, and now I was a special policeman."

2. The Charlie Ventura sextet was a jazz group led by tenor saxophonist Charlie Ventura.

whatever you say almost doesn't matter, and the person you're talking to in the letter is like a person sitting right nearby to whom you make all kinds of silly little remarks and noises—like when you and I were standing in the lobby of the Denver U. Playhouse and we were wrangling and making noise about the joke, the one about tongue in cheek. Just farting around like two kids sitting by a railroad track on a hot afternoon, like two similar kids I saw in Nevada, just sitting there and being together. But think not for a moment that I'm reverting to that "animal-relationship" kick with which I bored you so much last winter.

Just now, as I was writing this to you, the red light in one of the buildings here went on, signifying some trouble in the dormitory. Henri Cru and I rushed out with our clubs, gun and flashlights, laughing like hell and goosing each other on the way, and when we got there, it was a woman who dropped her keys in the toilet bowl and couldn't get back in her room. Henri wrote up the report on the incident as follows:

"The female occupant of room J-110 switched on the
red light. She had accidentally dropped her keys in the
toilet bowl and flushed water. Readmitted her to her
room." (I copy verbatim from his report.)

I suggested that he add: "Officer Kerouac suggested that Officer Cru reach down in the toilet bowl with his hand to probe for the strayed articles." There you have an idea of my job. $45 a week, 5 days, sleep on the job, nice fresh air, etc.

But to get back to us. Pay no attention to all the rigamarole in the first paragraph and I will settle down and write a good letter.

First, practical matters—I may myself go to a purser's school in Frisco, for 3 months, and thus graduate as a purser, with $250 per month in prospect, and a stateroom to myself on any ship. This would enable me to write at sea and make money to send home to my mother, and travel, and so forth. It all depends on whether I can get into the school or not, in view of my past record. But if I can, I'll go. In which case, if you came to Frisco, I could still see you and Allen, but couldn't ship out. The shipping is slower out here than in New York. It seems as though you and Allen might do better sticking with Burroughs, altho I am dying to have you with me here. But I can't imagine what you could do out here short of just working and living here. Allen could ship out but you'd have trouble. However such problems are always surmountable—but they don't seem important enough to surmount, unless you *really* want to come out here for kicks and to be around my orbit. There's a part of Frisco that's very Greenwich Villagey, but that's not too much in itself, and the rest of the town is rather boring, nothing like L.A. or Denver. One thing though—everybody looks like a junkey, but I can't be sure. When I say everybody I mean the people on Turk street and Fillmore and Jones and Geary and Howard etc. Anyway, I don't want to foul you guys up. I'm particularly anxious that you and Allen and Bill get together so that you may form a permanent friendship and keep things boiling for me to enjoy when I get back—purely selfish. Now if I cannot get into purser's school, I'll work here a while longer, and return to New York and you and the others, and finish my novel[3] in Ozone Park. Either way it's okay. One thing, though. If you're in the chips and Burroughs feels good, all three of you could come out here for kicks sometime. But remember that I'd love to have you out here, but don't want to cast a pall on wonderful Burroughsian plans. If you and Allen want to sometime, you can hop a freight and come out here free (the experience would be good for Allen.)—and then go back free. Whichever you do, stick to Burroughs. This is all I can think of: when you write again, tell me what you really want to do, give me some of this [sic] great *decisions* of yours and Allen's that I may meditate upon them. Whatever happens, I'll be seeing you in December in N.Y., and that's great.

Now to get down to real matters, not merely practical, but real. In Denver, when you and Allen held that long rapport on Logan street, I wasn't hostile to you, but simply in the dark as to what you were both talking both [sic]. You were high, you were using private terms, you spoke swiftly, incessantly—and I was sober, confused,

---

3. *The Town and the City.*

sad, and meditative.[4] You understand that already anyway I think. But one thing that really disappointed me was that you and I didn't once have a chance to talk. The night we picked up the Colombian girl and the Scott Fitzgerald decadent flapper from Dallas (with the languid eyelids), I really would have preferred eating that pork chop alone with you, and conversing over several beers. But we will get around to it again. Because the private terms you use with Allen are not really understandable to me—I who have to conduct private terminologies with the Burfords and Chases and Whites[5] of the world —and moreover, you and Allen seem to enjoy my confusion, or are indifferent to my intellectual understanding of you, desiring mainly my emotional presence and what you called "dignity." Which is allright with me, except that it has led to Allen's misunderstanding of me, and yours too in a slighter way. Allen exclaims that sadness, as a key to me, would transform me and redeem me completely in his eyes, which is really silly considering that we've known each other for years, we sang in the Octoberal winds together. But you understood me more quickly. Not that I want to obtrude myself upon either of you, boasting of my sadness, although you'd enjoy and accept such a thing, but, in this coy and deviating little way, I say, wistfully, that I wish you would really understand me and yet not require that I consistently lay myself before you—my soul, that is, which, not in the least inert or sullen, is only quiet and sad. (I hope you won't show this letter to Burroughs, as he considers himself too grown up for these things, and I want to keep his respect through other means.)

Another thing. Or perhaps the same thing. My intellectual understanding of you and Allen, and similarly before of Joan and Bill, was always played down simply because of this quietude and sadness.

---

4. See *On the Road:* "A tremendous thing happened when Dean met Carlo Marx . . . Their energies met head-on, I was a lout compared, I couldn't keep up with them." In the novel the character of Carlo Marx is based on Allen Ginsberg.

5. Ed White was another of Hal Chase's friends from Denver, who attended Columbia after his discharge from the Navy. Hal Chase, Ed White, and Alan Temko were all in Denver the summer of 1947. Bob Burford and his sister Beverly were friends of Ed White living in Denver.

And as a consequence, in vicious circles, I actually almost become sullen and inert, as a reflex. Yet my real feeling for you and Allen, and for Joan and Bill, is one of pure affection. How long it took me to realize that!—and in so doing, realizing myself. Pure simple affection—yet tagging after you,[6] trying to play your games, thinking that I cannot really play them well (like Edie thought). But whether I can play them or not—and I can if I want to, emerging from meditation and rue, the rue being so general and world-wide, so much! —whether I can play these intellectual games or not, does not matter, since my affection is enough in itself, if only it will be *detected*. I have no such trouble, of course, with Hal and Ed and others like that, because of certain social, emotional intertwining harmonies, too subtle to mention at one crack in a letter. This is the long way of saying that I can get along with birds of my own feather. But I refuse to believe that anyone in the world is not of my own feather, really, in the long run, I refuse to believe it with vanity, unhappiness, and longing. Life must be rich and full of loving—it's no good otherwise, no good at all, for anyone. If I feel affection for someone, and am blocked by superficial things such as intellectuality or "social difference" (as a Temko would love to believe and have sanctioned by an act of Congress)—if I feel affection for someone and it's all warped by the things of this world, which is not my kingdom, then it's really time for me to arrange matters myself, following the impulse of my affection, and letting that impulse work both ways, since it's the main thing. All confused, perhaps a little insincere, but who knows?—since all this I would have said long ago.

Is this a lot of hot water? Not from this point of view: that we will all die some day and it would be one hell of a joke if we all died in darkest ignorance of one another, oh brother my brother, what a travesty it would be, turned on ourselves. Very monstrous. My experience in these matters of mutual ignorance ended at the death of my father. I really and actually believe now that, while my father was alive, I loved him more than any son has ever loved his father.

---

6. See the opening chapter of *On the Road:* "But then they danced down the streets like dingledodies, and I shambled after as I've been doing all my life after people who interest me. . . ."

How do I know? Well, I can't measure it, I don't know what others have felt. But those who reveal their feelings to me reveal things that are nowhere nearly as intense, perpetually agonized, loving and maddened, as my feelings were and are for my father. It's incredible. I cannot forget him one bit. I never never will. And my mother also, living and later dead. And all of us dead. Can't you see it? And all this has been transferred to other intimate human friends. (I have my little demon beings)—this strict, severe, stern love. It is the *only* thing. And while my father was alive, all this, lying unconscious in me, was covered over with stupid intellectual malices and stupider worldly malices. The hatred I had for his face!—and now, what a terror it is to learn that this hatred for his face was a mad love for it. How can such things be? Why do we have to learn these things at the expense of someone's happiness, and of your own? Don't you see how stupid it is. We are stupid, stupid—that's the main thing about us. We don't doubt enough, we form too many convictions, like idiots we live by them. It were far better that, instead of perfecting our attitudes, or perfecting our position in the world even, we would spend time perfecting doubt—develop a perfection of doubt, become saints, saints. Allen needs doubt (of this kind)—he needs that to see Hal clearly, who himself is the greatest doubter of all (along with Lucien in those lines). Allen does not doubt enough. You yourself Neal—perfection of doubt, but widen your range, widen your range. What vanity this is—but perhaps I have achieved a real true tone. Now you know a little of what I feel and think.

I can't think of anything else to say. You're not here to feed me, start new levels of thought, ask questions—but I wish you were.

I wish you could read the stupid 40,000-word screen story I wrote here when I arrived. What a huge job! . . . and in six days. Because I hate the story, it might be good at that . . . "in the swamp the fishing would be tragic." (an association).[7] I'm writing a letter to Allen also, analyzing his poem from my own vortexes and whirlpools of consciousness. Also I plan to write a huge letter to Burroughs, in the style to which we are accustomed, detailing the events of my life

---

7. A reference to Ernest Hemingway's story "Big Two-Hearted River."

out here in California . . . in the Céline tradition . . . but that is a monstrous job. It must be art or Bill is lost from me forever. For me, in this life, it's got to be a world of gold and rich darkness, *the* world of gold and rich darkness, or nothing. That I'll have to explain to you someday. It's a tremendous personal subject of mine.

I guess by now you've left Carolyn.[8] A nice girl. But hardly your type—she's too pale and furtive. You need some girl like Edie now —a girl giggling in the sheets at morning, not just smiling. Write!!

Yours truly,
Flatfoot

P.S. Flying down to Los Angeles next week, Hollywood, San Diego, Tijuana and Agua Caliente Mexico. How's that sound? Will send you a card from T-town.

Kerouac's pleasure in being back at the typewriter after six weeks on the road is suggested in the letter he wrote Allen Ginsberg right after finishing his letter to Cassady. Speaking to Allen "as father to son," Kerouac offered a reading of Ginsberg's poetry and encouraged him to get over his unhappiness at Cassady's neglect of him in Denver.

TO ALLEN GINSBERG

August 26, 1947
Marin City, Calif.

Dear Allen—

A short, pithy letter. Having just written a long letter to Neal, in which a lot of information is contained to which you may refer, with my permission, and Neal's. I'll send you my permission in the morning.

About your poem "Last Stanzas in Denver"—and about your wonderful, though, I suspect, high letter—(which begins, "Helen, see,

---

8. Cassady had a teenage wife, LuAnne Henderson, whom he had taken to New York City the previous winter, but back in Denver he had met Carolyn Robinson, a Bennington College graduate studying theater at the University of Denver, and they had fallen in love. Kerouac called her Camille in *On the Road.*

is on vacation—") I'm looking her up tomorrow. Donkeshurn.—anyway—My impressions of your poem:

> "Art is illusion, for I do not act—
> dwell or depart—with faithful merriment.
> My thoughts, though skeptic, are in sacrament,
> Holy prayer for knowledge of pure fact."

Qu'est-ce que ça veux dire?—To me it means, and to me alone (altho I'll be better on your other stanzas), to me it means that you are sad, but passing it off to art, which is not real life, faithful merriment, and so on—and you yet use it in search of pure fact, or the reality you wish, the reality you wish *embodied* in yourself. I too can be ambiguous. You admit at last to sacrament, which you denied on 92nd street, and which I counter-denied and confronted you with, and surprised you, surprised you in the act of being sacramental yourself, and what a look came over your face—of musing and wondering and frantic intellectual chasing after vague submerged truths. You were asking yourself—"What's this? I thought it was figured out." You saw the dualism, and you don't like dualisms, you're after fact, which does not exist, anyway, except for a moment, and then time changes it. But anyway you're sad, and you admit sacrament. So.

"So I enact the hope I can create/ a lively world around my deadly eyes."

A beautiful line which might have been written about you by Ed [White] or Hal [Chase], but which is not too true. You're vain about your reputation as an Uncle Edouard or even a Strouvilhou [sic]. Your eyes are not "deadly"—they're only the eyes of a poet and a Jew of the ancient kind, not the new city jew, but the old prophet jew: not the political jew but the jew of the wilderness . . . really "of the mountains."

"Sad paradise[1] it is I imitate, / and fallen angels whose lost wings are sighs."

---

1. Ginsberg's "sad paradise" in this poem may have suggested the name Sal Paradise to Kerouac as his pseudonym in *On the Road*.

Here you're piqued at Denver and all the children of the rainbow everywhere, they are a "sad lot," you muse, really a sad lot. (As I write this Henri Cru keeps rushing up from the stockroom downstairs with old Bowery and Mission street suitcoats that have been left here by vagrant workers-to-be in the company. So far nothing fit for Hollywood and similar sadder paradises. Henri is always [. . . .] looking for some way to redeem our humble wages. Thus the parade of suits, smelling of stale whiskey and the ends of the night, Skid Row, puke, sperm, and sadness.) Yes, you're piqued at Denver, and of course, always at the world, almost psychotically, but sincerely and rightly—according to your personality. Don't pull your head back into the shell, never. The fallen angels love you and what they do to you, what unhappiness they cause you, is no less than that which you cause them just by being, as all of us do. It's really piquant—to put it superficially. I feel whimsical and lightheaded now, at five in the morning.

"In this unworldly state wherein I move/ my father and hope are hellish currency."

So you find from the Hal experience, and Temko's condescension, White's aloofness. Your kingdom is not of this world, therefore you're found to be hellish—but mistakenly of course, of that I'm sore convinced. They don't understand you, that's true. You say it very well. It's only that they are not seeking love as you are—that you must understand. You must doubt your disappointment in them, that is, you must doubt whatever irks you about them, doubt their valuelessness: for they have value, and they have hope, on their levels, they will be reached by you. Form no ideas about them. Forgive everything!

"In counterfeit worlds, I coin small charity/ about myself, and trade my soul for love."

Please be fairer and juster with them, and with yourself! They are not so counterfeit, and if you trade your soul, why, that's your metier. Accept your metier of course.

In what you're trying to do is contained all that's best in the world: it's a wonderful life you're weaving for yourself, the way I look at it: but the way you look at it, not so wonderful, just impulsive, necessary, matter-of-fact. It's you. I can look at your strivings objectively and love them aesthetically and also emotionally. But I can see why you fail so miserably sometimes: because you're not clever enough, really, to play the games that lead to consummation. There are all kinds of things in your way with which you cannot cope, because you despise those things: social things, psychic differences, etc. Don't doubt for one moment that Hal doesn't understand and realize you, as he did once. But now he hasn't time anymore. He's moved on to another level, one which he considers more mature and businesslike, and meanwhile, his understanding of the human personality enigma is still keen, though not so active, yet still very keen and getting keener. His mind is on geological changes: he's playing at something else: let him play. He's making different mudpies than you are, on his own side of the yard. But we're all in the yard together. And something that happens in that yard can bring us all together again. Everyone has his own brooding vision, be sure of that. A little less Yiddish contempt and more Jewish understanding. Be fair, be just, forgive everything. Forget a word like skeptical and use the word melancholy. Forget the facts and think of the *things,* all the things. What is a fact in a whole world of things! It is only a vanity, a word, an intellectual term. There are all the things, all the appurtenances of the world, through which you move with love, as best as you can, doubting even your love as you doubt your hate, equally, doubting, staying fair, just, forgiving, rich and large. Not like Whitman so much as like Christ . . . (to conciliate your dislike of Whitman.) "So spake Chesterton"[2]—meaning, I speak as father to son. Your poem is bitter but the beautiful sadness emerges and saves it. I welcome thee, a new Sebastian! Because Sebastian is really a perfect being. "Absent thee from felicity awhile."[3] (an association.) But

---

2. Kerouac is probably referring to Lord Chesterfield (1694–1773), famous for his letters to his son, rather than the writer G. K. Chesterton (1874–1936).

3. From Hamlet's speech to Horatio in Act 5, Scene 2 of *Hamlet:*

> If thou didst ever hold me in thy heart,
> Absent thee from felicity awhile,
> And in this harsh world draw thy breath in pain,
> To tell my story.

really, be happy and don't waste your energy comparing yourself, your mistakes, with the stupidities of others. Why man we're all stupid. This is not a football game . . . this is people walking around in the sun, then in the night, and this is the forest of Arden.

Adieu, adieu, goodnight,
J.

All this advice of mine is ashes when you consider the last line written in your letter to me, the line that says, "Is there ever really need to close my heart?" Well, that alone will save you, has saved, will continue to save you, me, and everybody in the world. Enough on the subject of hearts. We must next speak of the soul, which is conscious of powerful Octoberal winds and the joy of the earth itself.

Kerouac's letter the next night to his sister and brother-in-law in North Carolina was more down-to-earth about what he was doing in California, but again he dreamed about traveling the world working as a ship's purser, a job he imagined would give him "a private stateroom in which to write."

TO CAROLINE AND PAUL BLAKE

Aug. 27, '47
Marin City, Calif.

Dear Nin and Paul—

Well here I am in California, after a long hitch-hiking, freight-hopping trip across the country—and I stopped in Chicago, Des Moines, Denver, Cheyenne, Salt Lake City, Reno, and am now in San Francisco, working as a police guard in a settlement for overseas construction workers, while waiting for a good 'round-the-world ship.

Paul, my partner Hank [Henri Cru] and I went out hunting with our police guns (.32 automatics) in the hills around here, but we missed more shots at the pheasant than you could shake a stick at. One time we were kneeling in the bushes and here come a parade of pheasant not six yards from us, and we shot out our clips, and missed. Some shooting. But we need a rifle.

There's not much trouble on the police job, except with happy drunks, and you just lead them to their rooms. You would laugh like hell if you could see me in my police uniform.

What I want to do is go to a purser's school and then, making a good record there, getting on one of two ships, the Pres. Monroe or the Pres. Polk, as purser, $280-a-month and a private stateroom in which to write. These two ships go around the world three times a year, to the following ports of call—from 'Frisco to Honolulu, to Yokahama, to Shanghai, Hong Kong, Penang, Cebu, Bombay, Suez, Marseilles, Boston, New York, Panama, & back to 'Frisco—going to all these places three times a year. Just think of it! Why I could go around talking about my friend Mimi from Marseilles, my friend Geisha from Yokahama, and my friend Cleopatra from Suez. Me and Somerset Maugham!

While I'm here this Fall, I'm going to see some California U. and Stanford games. Also I'm going to take a run down to Hollywood to try to sell a 40,000 word movie story I wrote last week. And, when there, a little run-down to Tijuana Mexico won't hurt. And on my way back home in December I'm going through Oregon, Washington, Montana, Dakota, Minnesota, Wisconsin—great states I have to see.

I'm sending money home to Gabe[1] for rent, but if I could sell that story, even for a few hundred dollars, it would be great. Incidentally, Nin, I'm going to look up Lon McAllister.[2] He has a cottage at Malibu. And I have my Columbia Pictures contacts—and several others, through a big Denver wheel connected with M.G.M. I hope something happens, but the main thing is to finish "Town & the City," because that's the inevitable good one.

Write and tell me what you're doing, etc., and Paul, if you're still

---

1. In *On the Road* Kerouac wrote, "Lately I'd been sending so much money to my aunt that I only bought four or five dollars' worth of groceries a week."
2. Hollywood movie actor.

planning to build that inboard boat. And when you plan to see Gabe again, in N.Y. or South, so I can plan to be there with you. So long keeds.

Love, Jack

WRITE!—J.K.—P.O.Box 819, Marin City, Calif.

As the weeks lengthened for Kerouac on the job in Marin City, he later recalled in On the Road *that he became increasingly lonely. He wrote long letters to Cassady and Ginsberg, who were visiting Burroughs in Texas. Jack was casual in his reference to his lack of success with girls in his letter to Neal, but in* On the Road *he wrote that "I tried everything in the books to make a girl. I even spent a whole night with a girl on a park bench, till dawn, without success."*

TO NEAL CASSADY

Sat. Sept. 13, 1947
3 A.M.
[Marin City, Calif.]

Dear Neal—

I am bugged because I can't use that wonderful typewriter here except on nights when I'm on duty alone or with Henry, 2 nights a week. However, it isn't too fair for me to dash off huge letters to you in sixty minutes, while you have to labor on top of a cardboard box for hours trying to keep up with me. Isn't that true, man? I am very happy at the volume of our present correspondence. I like your letters immensely, especially the last one, in which I was afforded all kinds of mad strange glimpses into your present circumstances. It was better than my letter because it dealt with real and interesting things—I will try to maintain your neat standards of reportage. Incidentally, I can hardly wait till this winter when we'll be in New York and we'll start a new phase in our lives, and the wonderful others too. One of the first things you and I should do is go in the coat-selling business—I have 14 tickets, and you must try to get the

· 125 ·

rest from Allen. We've got to work out a surefire coat-selling plan. Also, it will be interesting activity. I am getting very practical now, thanks to temporary necessity and Henry's influence, but it will undoubtedly wear off when I get back to finishing "Town & the City."

Anyway, Neal, you mentioned a few plans of your own but that you hadn't formed a "pure certainty" about any of them. Let me know about them, and I will venture suggestions and the possible dove-tailing of my own plans with them. We must make this another good year, like last winter. And in any case, whatever you do, you must keep reading, studying, and even writing. You must fashion your own education, and do so with that superhuman determination of which you are so capable. Intelligence doesn't go as far in the practical world so far as the *appurtenances of intelligence,* in other words, "education." Very phony but necessary and real, too. Burroughs will be good for you in these respects—he has *finish.* Yet understand that these things are not as valuable as your own tremendous insight. Let me just say this: Hal Chase and Ed White are well aware of these appurtenances of intelligence, and use them to good advantage, graciously and cleverly. I myself don't need these things because I'm a writer and I'm independent of that world because of talent, but yet every now and then I fall back on them, as in business letters, or in a recent letter to Justin asking for suggestions *re* Hollywood. Yet why am I rambling on like this. Well, hell, I just want you to read a million books, that's all. I want to see you remain the same Neal who rushed from work straight to the library, in Denver, educating yourself, and never stopping. You must start reading Balzac, incidentally, but don't let me rush you and bug you. I like a guy whose [sic] always rushing around doing a million things everywhere and knowing everybody, yet at the same time continuing his inner development, which is what is going to determine the lines in his face some day, his *soul.* I rush headlong like an old schoolmaster tonight. And you with a book under your arm everytime I see you!

Well, now, to get on: the five wasted days and the mad 90-mile drives to Houston in a jeep certainly gave me a boot. I hope, however, that Allen has not fallen out with Bill for any reason. Why was he shipping out?—for money? I am sore at Allen, however, for kicking your girl out of the hotel room—it's too much like Mother Kammerer,[1] and silly, especially if the girl is all messed up mentally. I will question him on the matter, and if he objects, reverting to Trilling intellectual dignity and indignation, I will kick him in the ass. Seriously, though, keep writing good letters full of such information and mood. You must also tell me how Burroughs is. Huncke is always the same, but let him start to tell you stories sometime—he is the greatest storyteller I know, an actual genius at it, in my mind.

You wanted to know about my job. Henry fixed it up. I am an actual sworn-in officer-of-the-law, on special detail guarding dormitories for an overseas construction company. I am a member of the Sausalito Police Department. On my days off, when I go into 'Frisco, I pack a gun and bring my badge along. I do this for the hell of it, and the last time, drunk, I came real close to shooting up a street-lamp. What's amazing is that I have a right to carry the gun. It's silly I know, but variety and amusement. Every time I meet a girl I whip out the old roscoe and pretend I'm a New York gangster and scare the hell out of them. Also, one night I pulled it out on a fag and told him I was "Nanny-Beater Kelly" from Chicago. Naturally I'm off my nut, especially as I do all these things by myself, wandering along the foggy Embarcadero, going into bars and so forth.

I've met a lot of girls out here, and at least two of them are anxious for me to fuck them, but I never get around to it. I'm sending 75% of my pay home, which leaves me very little to spend. Henry and I steal a lot of food, and the rent is cheap. But one of these women out here is extremely beautiful, Odessa by name, hard to get but worth it. She would take a trip to Hollywood with me if I could afford to take her down—I told her I knew all the producers. But saving money is my present obsession, and anyway I am going to bang Odessa's roommate tomorrow afternoon at four, before Odessa gets home.

There's another girl whom I'm investigating with a view to putting her on my marriageable list for the future. She's fine—just like Edie, yet better-looking by far (a real beauty), and young, about 21—an eager, warm-hearted little creature with violet eyes, a simple, child-

---

1. A reference to David Kammerer.

like, yet well-behaved manner, and the blushing, flushing look of modesty and fineness. She's just fine. I would be like a father to her. She was born in British Columbia on a farm, and comes from Seattle. She's working in San Francisco getting the sophisticated fling out of her system—that is, anti-farm life, all that. I wrote her a mad love letter the other night. But I've got to learn more about her. Her face is all moonlight and Keats, man, and she's like a baby—but not small: well-built, and about 5:5.

Now then, to give you an idea of what I do around here when I'm not working, today Henry and Dianne (his girl) and I spent a whole day in San Francisco Bay. We hired a rowboat and rowed out to an old ghost ship in the middle of the bay, an old freighter used as a buoy to warn navigators of the shallow water around there. We went aboard, Dianne took all her clothes off and sunned herself (she is one delectable little blonde, too, a natural blonde I am privileged to say), and Henry and I explored the ship with our flashlights, from captain's quarters to bilges. Henry made estimates on the copper we could strip and rushed around with crowbars. I had a gleeful time just exploring the ship—and I made up my mind to live on this abandoned ship for three days & three nights before I leave 'Frisco. Take tonight for instance, as I write this letter: there's heavy fog in the bay and all you can hear are the mournful foghorns everywhere.[2] I want to be alone aboard the ship on a night like this, with just foghorns and rigging-creakings and candle-light and my own thoughts, and memories of Jack London & everything. It is the most isolated thing in the world. I'm bringing bread & butter sandwiches, tomatoes, cucumbers, a thermos of milk, a pint of whiskey, candles, matches, blankets, and pencil and paper—and I'm going to have Henry row me out and not come back for me for three days. He dared me to do it, he thinks it is a frightening experience. This is what I'll do when I'm ready to leave.

---

2. See On the Road, Part One, Chapter 11: "There was an old rusty freighter out in the bay that was used as a buoy. . . . It was an old, old ship and had been beautifully appointed, with scrollwork in the wood, and built-in seachests. This was the ghost of the San Francisco of Jack London. . . . I said to Remi, 'I'd love to sleep in this old ship some night when the fog comes in and the thing creaks and you hear the big B-O of the buoys.' "

Think!—if you were out here, we could live on that ship rent-free. There's an old woodstove and we could cook. Water is the only problem, but easily solved. We'll just keep this ship in mind, this ghostly Admiral Freebee—that's the name of it. It'll be here for hundreds of ghostly years.

Now here are my plans for returning home, Plan "A," and Plan "B"—

Plan "A," the original plan, was to go down to Hollywood, place my movie story on the market (I received great connections through the mail recently), and see L.A. to my heart's content, see it just as you told me to see it, and my way too (walking at night). Then, a run down to Tijuana, Mexico; then back to L.A. to check on my business—all in three days, then back to 'Frisco and my job: to work a few more weeks at my job, save up about $75.00, leave, and ramble slowly northward, on freights and hitch-hiking, through Oregon, Washington, Idaho, Montana, North Dakota. ("The great unknown Montanas, the mysterious Dakotas, the undiscovered places of America"—): on through the powerful October-lands of Minnesota and Wisconsin, on to Chicago again, Detroit, and New York—all very slowly, eating huge meals in hungry diners and great breakfasts in the morning places of men, man, in some of those Northwest hotels in backwoods towns, sleeping 20 hours at a crack in a big creaking bed, moving on—

Plan "B" depends on whether Bill would like to have me go along with the party from Texas. I assume Bill, Huncke and you are to drive back in the jeep. If so, and since I did a lot of driving coming out to Denver, I could come along and help. So from Hollywood and Tijuana, I could move out across Arizona, New Mexico, Texas—then Arkansas with you people, Missouri, Kentucky, etc. Don't you see, man, I absolutely refuse to go back home the way I came! To do this, I need to know *exactly* when you're leaving, and if in the jeep. I already wrote to Bill about it. Let me know soon: and prod him to write.

I think it is amazing how Bill put you to work on his ranch. What the place probably needs is an old hand like yourself, "Horseskinner" Cassady from Arkansas. I wish I were there, I'd really go to work too—just for the hell of it. Tell me more about it. And tell me all about Joan & Julie. Suffer, man, suffer!—labour on that cardboard box.

About Hal, all I know is that he's sick again, this time with blood poisoning. Ed White wrote and told me, so I wrote to Hal to distract him. Ed's on his way back to Columbia. It will be great there this Fall, with Ed and Livornese,[3] and later Hal, and Ginger around, and Jack Fitzgerald[4] around and everybody. I feel like writing a huge novel about *all* of it. Just think—these people I mentioned, and us, and Bill, Joan, Huncke, Allen and Lucien & Céline, and Vicki and Normie,[5] and all the places & things of New York. Where could I begin? It's wonderful when you don't know where to begin—what a great city New York is, in the final vision of it. It's the Paris of the greatest civilization of the time. We are living at just the right time —Johnson and his London, Balzac and his Paris, Socrates and his Athens—the same thing again. And the amazing thing is that everybody is bored, which makes it all the more interesting. I haven't even begun to live and write. The only thing I'm worried about is the inevitable Siberia I'm bound to get, like Dostoevsky, which will make me grow up.

Your pal,

Jack   WRIT BY HAND

TO CAROLINE KEROUAC BLAKE

Thurs. Sept. 25 [1947]

[Marin City, Calif.]

Dear Nin—

I've got a few minutes to myself tonight so I thought I'd write you a letter on this typewriter. I'll be leaving for Hollywood Oct. 6, where I'll just place my story in the right hands, and then continue on home

---

3. Tom Livornese, a student at Columbia who played jazz piano.

4. Jack Fitzgerald, another Columbia student.

5. Vicki Russell was a friend of Herbert Huncke's; "Norman" was a dock-worker in New York City who sold Burroughs his first supply of morphine syrettes (see Burroughs's autobiographical novel *Junky*).

via Tijuana Mexico and Texas and then all the way up to Minnesota and Wisconsin, just to see the country. Before that I might take a run up to Seattle Washington, just to see the place. If I do all this, and I'll certainly do 90% of it, I'll have seen 41 states in all. Is that enough for an American novelist?

So, I'll be home the last week of October and I'll be glad, because I haven't had much time or privacy to write out here in San Francisco. That's all right though, it was interesting to be here and see what the people and things are like. My conclusion is that California stinks. Really. I think Iowa and Kansas and Michigan and places like that have it all beat, not to mention, of course, great states like Nawth Calina and New York and Colorado. But the thing about California is this: everybody is on their high horse trying to imitate Eastern high society, and that includes *everybody;* all the girls are debutantes and all the men are out for nothing but the "best." Of course, they're all Okies, and terribly conscious of it. Not that there's anything wrong with Okies. But it's really funny to watch these Californians trying to put on the dog. And they all do it. San Francisco considers itself the most refined, enlightened, cosmopolitan city in all the world. People go around with a sneer of refinement on their faces. The women are terrible. They're all somehow pale and secluded, they come out in 70 degree weather in fur coats. They all consider themselves tremendously intelligent. They're proud of their San Francisco opera, to which they all go in the newest long hemline gowns, the men in full dress, although it is certain they know nothing of the music itself—which is what opera is supposed to be, music. They go to the races all decked out like the Edwardian elite that used to go to Eton, the first thing you know they'll be going to the races in carriages horse-drawn. Of course, in New York and other places, the racetracks are packed with gamblers half-shaven and wearing loud ties. But in San Francisco, city of enlightenment and culture and good manners, people go to the races to be seen in the latest fashions and to lose all their money. It is a shallow place. It's all show. There is nothing substantial. It hasn't got the beautiful spirituality of the South, nor the brooding Eastern qualities, nor even the good health and vigour of a Kansas City—it's got nothing. But it was interesting being here and watching the show. Just to indicate how phoney the place is—the favorite pastime of the San Francisco crowd is to listen to radio mysteries at night. You tune on the radio at six o'clock, and it's all bang-bang mysteries and murders until midnight. People haven't got thoughts of their own out this way in California, they have to fill the room with a lot of noise and screaming and semi-sophisticated dialogue.

I think I'll like L.A. a little better . . . it'll be more like Times Square, if anything.

However, I'm not saying anything against the West, just California. Colorado is wonderful, and Texas too, I imagine. I'm going there on the way home.

Enough of this. I just thought I'd amuse you with these few things, and since you've been out here yourself, you might draw your own conclusions. I hope Paul writes to me soon. He sure is a busy little bee these days. Is he going to build that boat? I imagine he hasn't got time. I see, also, where you got that job you wanted last summer, when Paul argued that his wife wouldn't work. Well at least it means more money in the house. I guess Paul will be owning the company if he keeps this up. And I'm wondering if you got a new dog or a cat. I feed five cats where I live here . . . I have them living in a box under a hole in my floor, little baby kittens, and the mother and father. Some stuff. At any rate, I'm glad to hear everything's going full guns. There's plenty of time for Paul to make good, and I mean good. And there's plenty of time for the little Paul Blakes to start arriving. Eat a lot and sleep a lot. I want some nephews sho nuff. Did you hear about Ma buying a refrigerator?[1] Ice cubes!—drinks for Paul when you visit us! How was Jean Bergeron—is she marrying Charley? Anyway, this is a kind of letter. Or is it? Bye for now. Love—

Jack XXX

P.S. I found out that I'd have to ship out before being eligible for a purser's school, so I had to abandon that plan.

My screen story is fair to middling, and I won't be mad if they

---

1. In *On the Road*, Kerouac wrote, "My aunt and I decided to buy a new electric refrigerator with the money I had sent her from California; it was to be the first one in the family."

don't buy it. Writing for the screen is pure plot and dialogue, while my best writing is descriptive, such as in novels. But we'll see. About Lon McAllister, I don't know if it would do any good to see him, but I will certainly look him up when I write something really good for the screen. As it is, I'll concentrate on the Columbia Pictures connections. As you say, the novel is more important & promising now, and I'll get to see L.A. if nothing else.

Well so long, keed. All my love,

Jack XX

Kerouac's letters to his sister and his friends from Marin City suggest the confusion of his travel plans at the end of the summer. He stayed in California after he picked up a "Mexican girl" on the bus to Los Angeles, so he missed the rendevous back east with Cassady, who had driven a jeep from Texas with Burroughs and Huncke. After Jack returned to Ozone Park, Neal wrote him apologetically from San Francisco, where he was living with Carolyn Robinson, to say he couldn't wait in New York any longer. In On the Road, *Kerouac wrote that "he had left, two days before I arrived, crossing my path probably somewhere in Pennsylvania or Ohio, to go to San Francisco. He had his own life there. . . ."*

TO JACK KEROUAC
FROM NEAL CASSADY

c/o Robinson
561A 24th Avenue
San Francisco
Oct. 5, 1947

Dear Jack,

I waited for you until Monday night and when you didn't show, since I had to go, I left.

I want you to know, purely and simply, it just could not be helped—in reality, I sense I felt more disappointed than you may have; for you had the pleasure of a reunion with your mother to take the edge off my desertion, but I had no one.

My conviction that Carolyn was enough is, I find, correct—so, don't worry about your boy Neal, he's found what he wants and in her is attaining greater satisfaction than he's ever known.

Since arriving I have begun to note little thoughts, actions, etc. written them on scrach [sic] paper and along with my attempt to recall *all* my past life and record it in a semi-outline (similar to a diary) is, I'm sure, enough writing to occupy my time this winter.

No work life as yet, but whatever I get will be the same as I always do get, somehow, the job seems to have a tendency to be short on cash and long on ennui, boredom . . . or, as I used to say (ahem) in my New York period (ahem)—*Drag.*

Please, do be kind-hearted and find the necessary love within yourself to be forgiving; in a typically Kerouacian growl send me a short and gruff note demanding to know "what in the hell I meant by running out of town when *I* was acomin' with new records, ideas *and* addresses, besides, Neal—goddamit—you owed me a ride in that f—kin' jeep." Then, Jack, I'll be happy again and we'll *really* carry on. Come on now, give me a new lease on our friendship, and thereby, find one yourself. *You* listen to *me* for awhile; I've made you carry the brunt of the load in our letters and since you don't have the drive to talk to me (because I've let you down intellectually and your heart has no warmth anymore, although you like to think it does), to you *I* will talk, yes, even over your protests—I accept the load for [a] while.

When I left town Bill and Huncke had sort of fallen out, the main reason seemed to be that Bill had taken up with Garver[1] and, perhaps you didn't know, Huncke dislikes "Mother" Garver. Joan was still leading Bill about and hasn't dropped Bennie either. When I read the portion of the last letter you sent me to her—Vicki, that is—she said, "Are you sure that dream sequence was concerning me, not Stephanie?" and after I reassured her, she continued her Vicki-like bursts of enthusiasm over your impending arrival. This, little kiddies, is the end of our semi-annual, one-minute news and views on the latest N.Y. gossip.

---

1. William Maynard Garver was a junky in New York City who stole overcoats to support his heroin habit. Huncke was living on Burroughs's farm in New Waverly, Texas, when Cassady and Ginsberg visited there.

Christ! I'm getting corny.

[. . . .] Allen, as you know, was in Africa.[2] The day I left N.Y. I heard from Eugene[3] that he had sent his father a cablegram from aboard his ship saying he'd be [back] in the middle of November. Lets hope everything works out for him this season; he really has a rough go.

I am finding it easier to led [sic] a more productive life, having escaped the fixation on my *need-to-write* (have you?). I now find I'm relaxed enough to start plugging away at it; this seems to fit my temprement [sic] to a greater extent than the old, frantic, unreasoning drive—which, when not let out, started to rot in my gut; sterility followed. I, most certainly, don't wish to force a rehash of all this on you, but really now, Jack, are you healthy? Have you not found yourself at times, dissatisfied with your present—shall we say, Philosophy—toward your Art? I know after 5 years of overbalance—no matter how good the cause—one finds himself cluttered up with so many trite, and otherwise, things that it becomes increasingly difficult for one to function properly or attain to that which they have been striving—this seems, almost always, in direct inverted ratio to the degree of character one has to push with [when] is added the degree of fixation and narrowing—inevitably—of outlook. So, since your great sense of humor prompts you to assume mouth-twisting, cigar-clenching, gruff-voiced mannerisms; it naturally follows that since you've also taken on a semi-stock, reactionary mask—to escape all the mad discussions etc., which, being overdone in youth have produced in you a strong reaction—you, now, find yourself blocked [. . . .]

I stop this silly, overdone and presumptuous bullshit—sorry, Jack.

Nov. 8, Just got a great letter from Allen, he calls me down plenty & I'm sure he's right; no doubt,

---

2. Ginsberg signed aboard a freighter bound for Dakar, Africa, after a lover's quarrel with Cassady in Texas. By mid-November 1947, Ginsberg was back in New York City, where he assumed legal responsibility for his mother, Naomi, in Pilgrim State Hospital (she was divorced from Allen's father) and signed the forms authorizing her prefrontal lobotomy. Allen had turned twenty-one on June 3, 1947.

3. Eugene Brooks, Allen's brother—a lawyer in New York.

you agree with him; well—I agree with both of you—but, not enough to come back to New York until next year. So, *that's settled.*

Drop me a line & tell me what you & Allen did—in one paragraph he cryptically states, "Jack & I wandered"—I, of course, can imagine what happened (depending on how drunk you got)—up & down the avenues, sitting in bars, etc.

> Your Pal (I hope)
> Square John Cassady

Carolyn Cassady quotes part of this letter in Chapter 10 of her memoir Off the Road. *In Chapter 11, she also cites a December 1947 letter from Neal to Jack that Carolyn felt would "affect Jack profoundly" after he finished* The Town and the City *and tried to discover a way to write fiction free from the influence of Thomas Wolfe. Then Neal wrote Jack:*

> *There is something in me that wants to come out; something of my own that must be said. Yet, perhaps, words are not the way for me. . . . I have found myself looking to others for the answer to my soul, whereas I know this is slowly gained (if at all) by delving into my own self only. I am not too sure that the roots of the impulse to write go deep enough, are necessary enough for me to create on paper. If, however, I find writing a must (as you've seemed to) then I know I must build my life around this necessity; even my most indifferent and trivial hours must become an expression of this impulse and a testimony to it.*
>
> *I have always held that when one writes, one should forget all rules, literary styles, and other such pretentions as large words, lordly clauses and other phrases as such. . . . Rather, I think one should write, as nearly as possible, as if he were the first person on earth and was humbly and sincerely putting on paper that which he saw and experienced and loved and lost; what his passing thoughts were and his sorrows and desires. . . .*

1948

Back at work on his novel in Ozone Park, Kerouac kept up a stream of letters to his friends and family in the winter and spring of 1948. He had returned home, he wrote at the end of Part One of On the Road, *to find his "half-finished manuscript" on his desk. "The first cold winds rattled the windowpane, and I had made it just in time."*

Friday Jan. 2 '48
[Ozone Park, N.Y.]

Dear Allen—

In a recent letter from Neal there is this quote—"I understand that you and Allen had a couple of serious evenings together—and, he delicately hinted that perhaps the seriousness of the talks was the thing that was keeping you from seeing him more often—'sat so?"

I was really surprised when I read that, because actually, since those talks I've called you at your W. 27th place at least 20 times, or a dollar's worth of phone calls, and almost every time your landlady hung up on me in disgust, as though she were mad because you receive so many calls. Her husband too does that, hangs up without really calling you. I even went up there late one night with Lou [Lucien Carr] and we tried to get in through the back alley and the roof and everything. I thought of leaving a little note in the front hallway, saying—"The circle completes itself inadequately."

But even more important than that, Allen, is the fact that since those talks, which impressed more than anything ever before in our relationship, I've been telling everybody about you and about those talks and about your marvellous vision of life. You can ask Vicki, or Huncke, or Ed and Tom, or Jack Fitz, or anybody, although it would be silly for me to press you to that. Indeed, I've even been waiting for you to visit me at Ozone—and lastly, most greatly, I wrote a long letter to Hal in which among other things I told him that I was convinced you had a great soul (to try to impress Hal with the force of my own impetus—no smugness). I told him that he was missing out on something great in you if he continued to act in such a way as to keep you on your guard with him. Ed White read the letter. In fact I've been praising you to such a point that you yourself would look with disfavor on it. Do I care? I'm mad about one thing. I want to straighten you out on one thing***if you wrote a letter to Neal in which it was hinted that I was shying away from you due to "seriousness," when actually I was looking for you all the time, then for Christ's sakes why don't you stop reaching solepsistic conclusions about everybody, especially me [. . . .] I am not afraid of you, as you so desire me to be apparently, as a matter of fact I like you more than ever, as a man as well as a poet, and I intend to be your brother as long as I live. It's only your poor defenses that annoy me and the way you continually insist on being the knowing diabolic watcher of my soul. Go ahead and peer into it, that's what I want you to do [. . . .] There's only one thing that I won't have, of course, and even you agreed with me that this was the way to do things in the world of love, remember? That was the last barrier, for I always felt uneasy about your queerness, felt that I was being smug for not joining you in that, but you yourself told me that you agreed with me on that point at the conclusion of our big talk, in front of the 23rd street subway entrance [. . . .]

It seems to me that both you and Neal are making yourselves obnoxious with your condescending attitudes towards the rest of us. I think that I'm easy-going enough on the surface to take it all in, but this explains why the others are shying away from both of you. I continue to be amazed at the tremendous amount of critical energy being expended on you two guys. What are you doing that everyone should be so conscious of both of you, with such annoyance? [. . . .] Incidentally, Huncke is brooding again, and it seems that Huncke is never so great as when he's beat down and brooding and bitter. I really believe this cruel fact. I see him all the time. For awhile when he got out of jail, he was happy, glowing, something was "swinging in him," as Vicki expressed it, but now things have caught up with him again, and he seems to become great again, a real Huncke figure again in the world, angrily waiting in Bickford's[1] for the circles to complete themselves, and broke all the time [. . . .]

---

1. Bickford's Cafeteria was a popular meeting place on Times Square.

We had a big New Year's Eve party at Tom Livornese's house in Lynbrook. There were Jeanne and Jack Fitzgerald, Ed White and his beautiful Nicki from Detroit, Tom and his girl Mary Lou Brown (a very talented pianist, she played the Apassionata for us), and others, including Stasia. We had a recording machine and made mad jazz records all night, singing and riffing with the piano—"How High the Moon" and "Lover" and "Born to be Blue," etc. Some of it is actually great jazz. During the course of the night I discovered a new mode of singing that is greater than Sarah Vaughan,[2] although I haven't got the voice or the technique to carry it through—however I'm certain that this mode of singing is the singing of the future. I really am tremendously prophetic about jazz, Tom realizes this. This mode of singing combines Tristano[3] with Vaughan. Incidentally if you're still dubious about Tristano's greatness, ask Freddy Gruber and Vicki about him. And when I went to see Tristano I overheard some of the cats discussing him in the john—cats with beards and artistic-looking manners and real Bohemian hipness, etc.—and they were saying that they couldn't stand anybody else any more.

"Once in a while," said a bearded guy, wonderful looking cat, "I get nostalgic and listen to a little Bird,[4] but I can't even stand that any more." They agreed that Tristano was more profound than Stravinsky, which I think is a gross understatement. He is very close to Beethoven, as all the musicians agree. On opening night, Tristano's audience included us, and Leonard Feather the *Esquire* critic, and Pete Ruggolo, [Stan] Kenton's arranger, and Neil Hefti and dozens of other great musicians. The guy is standing the music world on its ear.

But about the party, soldier Fitzgerald and seaman Kerouac were the last ones still up-and-drinking at 8 in the morning, and it was really funny. Fitzgerald went upstairs to try to lay all the women he could find in the beds, the house was deathly still, suddenly I heard

---

2. Sarah Vaughan, jazz vocalist.

3. Lenny Tristano, blind jazz pianist.

4. Charles "Bird" Parker (1920–1955), legendary alto saxophone player who developed an innovative and influential jazz style.

a tremendous slap in the face, and heard Fitz clomping back down the stairs and suddenly a huge explosive commotion as he fell down the stairs.

So on and so on. I was fooling around with Stasia on the chair and Fitz comes up to us, grabs her, and says, "Listen Stasia for kris-sakes did you ever have an orgasm? do you like orgasms? does it make you feel good inside to have a nice orgasm?"

"I'm sorry," she replied, "but that's a personal matter."

"Well, Goddammit, that's what I mean!" yelled Fitz at his wit's end.

Incidentally I bought a ticket for "Crime and Punishment" on the stage, with John Gielgud and Lillian Gish, for Jan. 7th, matinee. Also I'm now only six weeks real good work away from the conclusion of "Town & City," which is run up to 280,000 words at present and will wind up at 333,000 wds. But what a job, what a two-yeared burden! Jesus. Another thing . . . well, I guess there isn't another thing, I'm all pooped out and I have to get on with other things. I'll be seeing you around, and inasmuch as I can't call you at your place, drop me a card or something or meet me at Vicki's sometime or in Bickford's and so on, or Bill's. Do you know that I labored out a copy of a fragment of my novel for Neal and he wrote back a month later, not even mentioning it?—and wrote back one measly stupid page. Well, I guess for some reason or other I get pissed off at some-body every now and then and today it's Neal. Anyway so long and write me a long letter before I see you.

Jack

P.S. By the way Donna Leonard tried to look me up at Xmas but I was in No. Carolina.

Unlike his relaxed, enthusiastic letters to his close friends, Kerouac consciously adopted a folksy, convivial tone in his letters to his sister and brother-in-law. In the spring of 1948, after being supported by his mother for two years while he wrote his novel, he also hastened to agree with his family's conservative political views, distancing himself from the idealism about the "brotherhood of man" he had shared earlier with Sebastian Sampas.

TO CAROLINE AND PAUL BLAKE

March 16 '48
[Ozone Park, N.Y.]

Dear Nin & Paul,

Thanks so much for the trousers. You wouldn't believe it but I was going to buy a pair just like that this spring, small-checked—and here I find them given to me as a [twenty-sixth birthday] present. Youse must have read my mind.

Now when are you going to send us pictures of your new house? And how do you like Rocky Mount? There's a college there of some kind, isn't there?—and I remember it being a big lively town, our train stopped there on that Saturday afternoon before we met you at Wilson and thousands of people were shopping on a long busy Main Street. The farmers were chewing the fat in feed and hardware stores, the women were chopping their gums in Five-and-Tens and department stores, the children were hopping around in search of Superman, Eskimo Pies and penny candy. I'll bet you like it better than Kinston, and it won't be so *warm* there in the summer off the coastal flat and near the hills. Not far from Henderson either.

Gabe and I are waiting for Little Moe just as anxiously and happily as you are, and I personally hope it's a boy to start off with, so that fifteen years from now when Paul tries to get me up to go fishing at dawn, he won't have to curse me in solitude at the crick, he'll have his son beside him, a-listenin'.

Paul, what kind of big executive have you become in Rocky Mount? You remember you were just about ready to quit the telephone company when they sneaked that promotion over on you. I guess they were reading your mind and they didn't want to lose you. Well, now you're all set, more than anybody would dare to imagine for a guy your age. No doubt they're still making you do the work of ten men, but that's why they promoted you I guess, they needed *ten* big executives.

How's my sad dog Bill? I'll never forget that foray in Henderson last Christmas with the dogs because I was so sick all I could do was trudge along in back of you and Frank.

Gabe is planning to go down and see you when the baby comes. We were going to go down to see you in Hal Chase's little car (a Rocky Mountain-goat) in about three weeks, but Hal's girl Ginger wanted to come and it would have been too many people, especially as she's in the habit of donning her ballet shorts and dancing all over a body's house. But at the same time, since Gabe is going in July, there's no need to go now and spend the money she can use in July. Depending on circumstances, I may come with her in July or I may be out West again, I don't know yet.

There'll come a time when a trip to No. Carolina won't be such a rare event—especially if some publisher gives me an advance on my story. It's pretty nearly finished now, three hundred twenty-five thousand words to date, twenty-five thousand more to go, a month's writing, and I'm showing 90% of the manuscript to Scribner's late this month. No publisher has seen my book yet, only one agent, that woman, last year, so here goes, it'll be its first important reading. I've added a lot to it, it's okay. But now I'm worried, as far as my book is concerned and 2½ years' work on it, by news of another war. As long as they don't blow up the publishers and the printing presses, okay. When it's printed I'm all set to enlist in the infantry, I've got no more to write for another 2 years. The war scare I think is just for the sake of squeeze-playing Congress into voting Universal Military Training and the Marshall Plan. It's a dirty administration with dirty tricks—creating "emergencies" for its own political ends, and all tied up with the brass. I think we should *arm* and just dare anybody to attack, but I don't think we should be the aggressors, that wouldn't pan out.

However, a war against Communism, if and when it comes, is a war against the *real* enemy of American life: the psychology of neurotic malcontent. The only trouble is, fighting Russia alone is not fighting the Communism in England and France and China and India and—America. Therefore it's a little mixed up—war wouldn't pan it out. But if there was war, and that would be tragic, I would be inclined to *believe* in it a little more than that last fiasco—which was just Communist-inspired on one hand, and uselessly directed against the German race on the other. That's what I didn't like about that last war, and I told them that, too. As far as I was concerned, and Pa too, Washington *needled* Japan into it. It makes no difference now, and made none then, if the Far East was to be dominated by Japanese Imperialism or by Russian Imperialism as now. All that is none of our business if we stand here laughing at them and armed. When they settle their issues, we could join them in the only *real* "ideology" the world will ever know—the Livelihood of Man instead of their so-called hypocritical "brotherhood of man."

Ta-ra! Speech is over. Take to the hills, men, and bring your shootin'-arms and a wagonload of black-eyed peas and a few hawgs—and nails (to make a *still* stand up).

We shall see. As the commentators say, 1948 is a fateful year. But I never did see any kind of "fateful year" that could make any real difference to people who are truly *living* and minding their own business (unless they get killed, that is)—but as to that, you just can't wipe out the human race try as you may, and everybody's tried it from Genghiz Khan on up to Henry Wallace[1] and the pugnacious little Forrestals[2] of this world.

Be seeing you soon, maybe this summer, and thanks for those swell trousers again. Now on the money *I* make *writing* I can't exactly observe all the birthdays like Diamond Jim, but I can send you a keg of nails soon with which to build that still in the hills, remember. And a couple of clay jugs. But enough—so long for now and don't forget those pictures of your new house.

Love,
Jack

---

1. Henry Wallace (1888–1965), United States vice president from 1941 to 1945.
2. James Forrestal (1892–1949), secretary of defense from 1947 to 1949.

Writing to Allen Ginsberg from Gabrielle's apartment, Kerouac confided his belief that they were both "creative geniuses." He also shared his concern that neither he nor Ginsberg had heard from Cassady in several weeks.

Saturday night
[April (?) 1948
Ozone Park, N.Y.]

Dear Allen—

Distractions, excitement, and evil influences prevented me from absorbing what you were saying about Van Doren and the proposed publication of your doldrums.[1] Thus, sit down and write me a letter about it. I'd love to see you about it only I'm so near to the end of my book that I tremble at the thought of leaving it for one moment. Exaggeration—but I can see you next weekend. Meanwhile I'd like to hear about it, more about it, circles of it briefly.

Meditating on the yiddishe kopfe[2] heads I wonder if you were right about my taking "Town & City" to Van Doren[3] instead of a publisher. Tell me what you think about that in your considered well-groomed Hungarian Brierly[4]-in-the-bathrobe opinion. It seems to me perhaps that if I took my novel to publishers they would glance at it with jaundiced eyes knowing that I am unpublished and unknown,

---

1. Ginsberg had shown a manuscript of his poems "The Book of Doldrums" to Mark Van Doren, a critic and professor at Columbia University whose literature classes Kerouac had also attended. In *On the Road*, Kerouac described Carlo Marx—the character based on Allen Ginsberg—living in "the room of a Russian saint; one bed, a candle burning, stone walls that oozed moisture, and a crazy makeshift ikon of some kind that he had made. He read me his poetry. It was called 'Denver Doldrums.' " In an early letter to Kerouac, Ginsberg complained that he suffered from what he called "ventriloquism," imitating other poets' voices.

2. "Jewish head."

3. In his letter, Ginsberg had offered to show Kerouac's manuscript of *The Town and the City* to Van Doren.

4. Justin Brierly, a Denver lawyer, teacher, and Columbia alumnus, who had befriended Hal Chase when Chase was in high school.

while if Van Doren approved of it, everything would be quite different. I imagine that's what you think, too. We creative geniuses must bite fingernails together, or at least, we should, or perhaps, something or other.

Have you heard from Neal? Reason I ask, if I go to Denver on June 1st to work on farms out there I'd like to see him. It's strange that he doesn't right (write)—and as I say, he must be doing ninety days for something, only I hope it's not ninety months, that's what I've been really worrying about.

Hal has been reading my novel and he said it was better than he thought it would be, which everybody says. As a matter of fact I don't know much about it myself since I never read it consecutively if at all. Hal is still amazingly Hal—you know, Hal at his best and most *mysteriously intense* self. What a strange guy. With a million unsuspected naivetes jumping over the monotone of his profundity. And it is a real profundity.

[. . . .] So when you see Van Doren—tell him I plan to take my novel (380,000 words) to him, tell him I *will* take it to him in the middle or end of May, completed novel: tell him it's the same one I told him about 2-½ years ago and go and tell him that I have laboured through poverty, disease, and bereavement and madness, and the novel hangs together no less. If that isn't the pertinacity or the tenacity or something of genius I don't know what is. Go tell him that I have been consumed by mysterious sorrowful time yet I have straddled time, that I have been saddest and most imperially time-haunted yet I have worked. [. . . .] Tell me of Huncke. Man of enigma-knowledge and despair of aggression.

J

P.S. The thing I like about Van Doren is this: he was the only professor I personally knew at Columbia who had the semblance of humility without pretensions—the semblance, but to me, deeply, the reality of humility too. A kind of sufferingly earnest humility like you imagine old Dickens or old Dostoevsky having later in their lives. Also he's a poet, a "dreamer" and a moral man. The moral man part of it is my favorite part. This is the kind of man whose approach to life has the element in it of a moral proposition. Either the proposition was made to him or he made it himself, to life. See? My kind of favorite man. I have never been able to show these things to anyone from a fear of seeming hypocritical rather than sympathetic, or sympatico. Thus, if he should happen to like my novel, I would get the same feeling that Wolfe must have gotten from old Perkins[5] at Scribner's—a FILIAL feeling. It's terrible never to find a father in a world chock-full of fathers of all sorts. Finally you find *yourself* as father, but then you never find a son to father. It must be awfully true, old man, that human beings make it hard for themselves, etc. [. . . .]

P.S. More, much more, but I'm tired. So long.

Finally, in early May 1948, Kerouac finished The Town and the City *and began to make plans for the future while he waited for a publisher to take the book. Excitedly he shared his thoughts with Cassady about living together on a ranch. As Kerouac wrote later in the opening pages of* On the Road, *he envisioned Cassady as "a young Gene Autry—trim, thin-hipped, blue-eyed, with a real Oklahoma accent—a sideburned hero of the snowy West."*

TO NEAL CASSADY

Friday May 7 [1948]
[Ozone Park, N.Y.]

Dear Neal—

Big rainy day, thoughts of Neal in Frisco, thoughts of Neal trying to get a job as a brakeman on the hobo's favorite RR, the Southern Pacific . . . How wonderful it is to recall that months and months ago, years ago, you were here in Ozone Park tempting me and taunting me and pushing me to continue writing Town and City, and I went on blasting away at it just to impress and more to please you.

—————
5. Maxwell Perkins, Thomas Wolfe's editor at Scribner's.

That was the turning point of that novel . . . that was when I got to doing it, towards getting it done, wham, wham, wham . . .

And guess what? IT IS NOW FINISHED . . . IT IS IN THE HANDS OF SCRIBNER'S.[1] What an amazing thing to realize that *you*, more than anyone else, can be said to be the biggest pitchfork that got me howling and screaming across the pea-patch towards my inevitable duties. It's that wonderful Nealish creativeness that did it. Others may criticize, others may hurt me, others may suggest darkly, others may not care, others may watch without emotion—but you yell and gab away and fill me with a thousand reasons for writing and getting a big story done. And to think that you haven't been back to glance at it? Why didn't you read some of it when you were waiting for me last October!

The truth is, you know, that I have only ONE chapter to finish, and you may be saying to yourself, Oh yes, that everlasting last chapter, and I agree with you, I even admit it's going to be, somehow, the hardest to write, the last two hundred feet to the peak of the unclimbable Everest. But in ten days I'll be able to say, FINIS.

And now, by Jesus Christ, I'm going to become a rancher, nothing else. I've made up my mind to become a rancher, I've learned all about it in books, and am going to learn the rest this summer working on ranches in Colo., Ariz., or Wyo. All I want is about 300 head, a spread that cuts enough alfalfa for them, a winter pasture, two houses for me and whoever joins me in partnership, etc. etc. Just a small outfit that me and a partner can run without hiring cowhands. Also grazing permit for a national forest . . . if not that, I'd need a fortune to buy my own grazing land wouldn't I. But who knows how much money I might make. Chances are I won't make much, not enough, in which case I'd look high and low to rent or lease such a spread. And proceed to live a good life in the canyon countries, lots of forage, trees, high sharp mountain air . . . and marry a Western girl and have six kids. That's for me now. I can start working on

---

1. Kerouac's first choice of a publisher for *The Town and The City* was Scribner's, which had published Thomas Wolfe's novels.

that plan as soon as I collect on royalties, which would be, with luck, sometime next year. And writing other books later I could eventually buy the spread I might lease. A real humble start, then working towards something conclusive, secure, richly satisfying. As for partners, I have my boyhood pal Mike in mind, who, right now, is grubbing away on a small farm in Massachusetts and is just about the poorest guy in the world. Mike has five kids already, he's 27. He's a wrangler, and can do anything with his hands, a natural born farmer or rancher, and a master mechanic to boot. The simplest best guy in the world, you'll meet him someday. Hal met him, and says, with reservations, that he could be a little more sensitive . . . but who gives a shit about that in the long run, when life runs its natural courses and all those fancy campus words fall back into the campus limbo where they belong. All I know is that when I was a kid palling around with Mike, it never occurred to me that he was insensitive, or that I was sensitive because I wrote 11-year-old novels in my room. Either Mike as a partner . . . certainly Mike as a partner . . . or Paul my brother-in-law, both of them . . . the more the merrier, and even you if you ever wanted to *settle* and do something consecutively for years, maybe your whole life. Why roam around . . . Why not roam from a base? Think of it. Well, right now all this is just a dream, but so was the novel when I started it and you were around to prod me. Write me a postcard or something and let me know *what* you're doing and if everything is okay and how Carolyn is.

Your pal
Jack

With The Town and the City *completed, Kerouac next turned his hand to writing a much shorter piece of fiction, a recommendation for Cassady to help him get a job as a brakeman on the Southern Pacific Railroad. Living in his mother's apartment, Jack began to brood about the problems of finding a girlfriend and earning a living, as suggested in his next letter to Ginsberg.*

Tuesday night May 18 '48
[Ozone Park, N.Y.]

Theme: All the young angels rolling to the
music of celestial honkytonks.
(in a rollerskating rink)

Dear Allen—

Thanks for writing. I'll be seeing you perhaps this Friday night, but now I don't want to discuss your letter in detail due to the fact that it's a lot of ancient material with me. [. . . .] As to the novel, I already handed it in to Scribner's two weeks ago, and they're reading it now; no word yet.

But here is news that will interest you a lot, I heard from Neal. Oh these are the sweet dark things that make writing what it is . . . Anyway I heard from Neal, and I had to fill out an application blank for his employer attesting to his character. Assured that I piled it on in the best Bill Burroughs letter-manner. I think I said that he would be of "great initial value to your organization and purposes," etc. The job is as a brakeman on the Southern Pacific railroad. From which I assume—and I guessed right—that Neal got in trouble, got three months, and they're getting him a job out of a jail agency of some sort. No peep out of Neal himself, however. The Southern Pacific is the most wonderful railroad in the world incidentally . . . on a Sunday morning, riding down through the sunny San Joaquin Valley of grapes and women-with-bodies-like-grapes, I reclined on a flatcar reading the Sunday funnies with the other [ho]bos, and the brakemen smiled at us and waved cheerfully. It is the hobo's favorite road. Anybody with any sense in California can ride between Frisco and LA endlessly on that road, once a week if they want to, and nobody will ever bother them. When the train stops at a siding, you can jump off and help yourself to fruit if you're near a field. So wonderful Neal is working for a wonderful railroad, in the Saroyan country—(if there's any beastly murderousness it's not my fault or Neal's or Saroyan's.) The Santa Fe brakemen will kill you if they catch you and if they have enough clubs. But not the SP.

I had a season, Allen, I had a season. It lasted exactly four days.

She was eighteen years old, I saw her on the street, was riven, and followed her into a rollerskating rink. I tried to rollerskate with her and fell all over the place. Young and beautiful of course [. . . .] you can't imagine how madly in love I was, just like with Céline, only worse, because she was greater. But finally she rejected me because "she didn't know me, she didn't know anything about me." I tried to get her over to my house to meet my mother for God's sake but she was afraid I was trying to trick her, apparently. Sweet love softly denied. She thought I was some sort of gangster . . . she kept hinting. She also thought I was "strange" because I didn't have a job. She herself has two jobs and works herself to a bone, and can't understand what "writing" is. Tony Monacchio[1] and I found Lucien dead drunk in Tony's room after a party—on the night that Lucien was supposed to fly to Providence for his 2 week vacation. We helped him to the Air Lines bus. He was bleary-eyed, blind, wearing brown-and-white saddle shoes like a Scott Fitzgerald character of the '20s. [. . . .] I mean he was really sick. Tony said to him, "Jack's girl is sweet and beautiful but dumb." And Lucien out of this dizzy sickness of his, said—"Everybody in the world is sweet and beautiful but dumb."[2] Allen, these are the things, these are the things, don't worry about the *theory* of writing, not at all. Then Lucien thanked us for escorting him to the "airplane" as he called the bus, and there was a farewell. That afternoon my little girl rejected me. So now, how are you? How's everybody in the sweet beautiful dumb world?

Jack

After Kerouac's sister Caroline gave birth to her son Paul in late May 1948, Jack and his mother went to visit her in North Carolina. A short time later Kerouac came back to Ozone Park to type another copy of The Town and the City. *He wrote Gabrielle about how well he was managing in the apartment by himself.*

---

1. Tony Monacchio was a friend of Lucien Carr's.

2. Kerouac liked Lucien's comment so much he inserted it into his revisions of *The Town and the City.*

Tuesday June 15 '48
[Ozone Park, N.Y.]

Dear Ma—

Well I got home Sunday night at midnight and went to bed, and Monday I went to the bank and took out the money, paid Mrs. Parisi (who sends her regards), paid the insurance till Aug. 1st, paid the electric bill ($6.40), mailed you a couple of letters from Aunt Marie and Leontine, bought groceries, and settled down to typing. I called up my connection, Ed Stringham[1] is his name, and he is arranging for me to meet the critic as well as the chief editor of Random House soon, the first one this week.

All the food was okay and I'm eating everything but the chicken, which is frozen solid and allright. The screens were put up by Parisi while we were gone.

I called up Evelyn and told her how everything was with Nin and little Paul.

So I guess I took care of all those details. Now I'm sending you your money—and write me a letter and tell me how things are going now. I'll be glad when Nin feels better, and glad for you when they let her come home so you can have her at your side. Although you're away from the house I feel very confident because you're with Paul, otherwise I might worry. And as for me I've got my typing, my baseball games, cool weather, my books, and my midnight snacks. And tell Paul I'm betting .340 as of today. Tell him to write a little note informing me how he's getting along with the radio shack. So that's all for now, Ma, and have a good vacation while you're down there.

Love to all,
Jack

---

1. Ed Stringham was a new friend in New York City.

While Gabrielle Kerouac was away in North Carolina, Jack began to feel what he called a "yearning lonesomeness" in the empty apartment. His mood was exacerbated after he received a letter from Cassady with the news that he and Carolyn were expecting their first child. (They had gotten married on April 1, 1948.) In his letter Neal had enthusiastically supported Kerouac's dream of buying a ranch. Neal also understood that Jack looked forward to making a home for Gabrielle on the ranch, since he had promised his father to take care of her for the rest of her life. Neal had written Jack that "I know your mother (you must bring her) and Carolyn would get on together famously—and for us to build a ranch, a great spread, together, would be better than renting rooms for $50 the rest of our lives. . . . Your mother (Bless her) and Carolyn (Bless her) are exactly alike. . . ." Jack's response was to take a "night off" from retyping The Town and the City, *cook himself a big meal of curry with rice "just so I can fill the house with the odors of food and consequence," and sit down at his typewriter to answer Neal's letter.*

TO NEAL CASSADY

Sunday midnight
June 27, 1948
[Ozone Park, N.Y.]

Dear Neal—

Finally hearing from you reassured me that nothing had really happened to you, because you see I thought you were in some kind of external trouble. Now allow me to congratulate you with all my heart and love on your marriage and the impending birth of a child. Carolyn is an amazing girl—I talked to her in Denver, you know—and now that she has become great, as you say it so wildly, that initial difference between the two of you must undoubtedly be ironed out, that is, her kind of serenity, and your restlessness and blood-brother craziness. I am truly so glad.

Your letter is so stupendous . . . however, I want to start from the back of it, the part about ranching, and then work backwards to the other parts. I've taken this night off (from typing my ms.) to write to you, and later to Burroughs in New Orleans[1] . . . (altho that will be a different kind of thing, of course.) You dig?

Because you see, now that you actually speak out on a definite plan, a real actual plan, my confidence in our friendship is finally solidified. (Real stuffy words . . . I just ate a huge meal and I'm smoking and writing, you see that situation.) To show you how, with such pitiful dumbfoundment, I need a life-situation like a ranch, I'll describe my feeling tonight . . . Alone in the house. My mother has been down South for three weeks taking care of my sister who just had a baby by Caesarian, a little three-pound thing. She won't be back for two weeks. In great sadness I stay alone in the house rounding the end of my 3-years work, the final typing of the manuscript, which will be shown to the critic Alfred Kazin sometime this summer. Alone in the house . . . cooking, sweeping floors, washing dishes, working, sweating, sleeping, terrified dreaming, and the most yearning lonesomeness. You know that I have hitch-hiked around and have been alone in weird cities and places, and waked up in the morning not knowing who I was (particularly one time in Des Moines.[2])

But to be alone in a *house of home* is the last unhappiness. I think of it. The house is empty, it broods, it's haunted . . . all those things. So I start cooking big meals, curry with rice, just so I can fill the house with the odors of food and consequence, and lone, I sniff the air and think. Neal, what I want is a big home with about twenty people in it, whole families at the same time, something going on all the time, someone leaving, someone coming, someone building a

---

1. After losing his driver's license and being arrested for public indecency, Burroughs had moved from Texas to New Orleans with Joan Vollmer, her young daughter Julie, and their baby son William Burroughs, Jr., who had been born in Texas. Kerouac gave Burroughs the pseudonym Old Bull Lee in *On the Road*, writing that his "final study was the drug habit. He was now in New Orleans, slipping along the streets with shady characters and haunting connection bars."

2. See *On the Road*, where in Des Moines Kerouac had felt himself "at the dividing line between the East of my youth and the West of my future," when he fell asleep in a hotel room and woke up to "the strangest moment of all, when I didn't know who I was. . . . I was just somebody else, some stranger, and my whole life was a haunted life, the life of a ghost."

shelf, someone mending a fence, someone sewing, someone cooking, someone reading, someone eating, so on, and on, on, on . . . I want all the Shakespearian gamut of things in one big tumultuous house. I don't want to be alone in a garret and I don't want to be an "artiste"—I truly know how to live, I think, and that's the way it must be. And in your saying you want a home . . . "to go and come to . . . to grow old in . . . to make into a great place . . ." etc., you express part of my own similar feeling. (It's so wonderful to know you, Neal, really.)

You say "start right away." I agree with you. So I will outline the prospects: First about my mother, she's willing to take off for California any time, just so she can go to California. Ditto with my brother-in-law, a big hunter and carpenter and mechanic and everything. But all of us are poorer now than we ever were. So the prospects of selling my novel enter into temporary consideration. How will I do it? When Alfred Kazin reads it, and if he likes it, as Allen thinks he will and everyone thinks he will (everyone being a whole bunch of composers and agents and whatnot who are amazed by my book now)—if so, he tells a publisher and I get a contract on the spot. But the real consideration is how much money I'm likely to earn, and that might not be much. At the least, $5,000 in the first two years . . . and then of course it might be more. Leaving that aside for a moment however, supposing, and it is likely, that in the Fall I got a $2,000 advance from a publisher. This is a practical supposition according to what they tell me. That would be enough at least to move out to California, to pay the movers (if, however, it is more practical to move our furniture.) To pay the movers and get settled a bit. And my book being finished, I shall be proudly ready to work at any job and to work like a fiend. You understand that. And by the way, in those circumstances, it would only be my mother and I. It wouldn't be to Paul's advantage to follow me out there unless I had some real dough to start something truly secure . . . because of course he has a sick wife and a baby now, and debts from the hospital. (He cried when he heard of the debt, by the way . . . and I was so moved and sorrowed by that, I wrote to him and told him there were worse things than debt, which is true of course.)

So just picture it. A few thousand dollars . . . we move out there.

I'm ready to work, my mother is ready to work. It's all so beautiful and problematical. Originally, by the way, I intended to move to Colorado someday, but *northern* California is the greatest country, especially for ranching or farming due to the climate. And San Francisco, I finally admit, is "my city, my Parisian city across the desert." When I was there last year I was very lonesome . . . but how I was hungry! how I prowled by Trantino's and the Fisherman's Wharf and smelled the food and the fog so Boston-like. And how amazing it was that you had to cross Wyoming, and Utah, and the Nevada wastelands, to get to this secret white city on hills, at night, and all the mysterious women in doorways, and foghorns blowing. Man, and the little jazz places on Broadway. It's really much more than Denver, of that there's no doubt. And there are just as many wranglers in Frisco as in Denver . . . and where you find wranglers, I say, you find real country and real people.

If worse should come to worse, we could ship out and leave the women to take care of the place. Henri Cru is shipping out of Frisco now on a big luxury liner, back and forth to China I think, via Hawaii. The point being: in time I'll make a lot of money writing, from "Town and City" I might conceivably get high-paying scenario jobs in Hollywood. In time I'll have something like a fortune, you'll see. But not now, that's plain (altho you never can tell how "Town & City" will sell, it's got everything.) So, working on railroads or ships, we'd make a go of it at least for awhile. To start a real great spread will be long work and a lot of patience . . . but someday we can *really* do it. Others have done it. I have great confidence. Down in North Carolina two weeks ago I helped Paul build a shack for his radio equipment . . . and who would have thought that *I* could put up a whole wall in one afternoon, as I did, sawing away and hammering and measuring and nailing and sweating. I mention all this in connection with real human confidence and calm, and that ever-present beauty everywhere that's killing me nowadays.

And finally, to get these things off, here's the time element: I may have that $2,000 any time from this summer to next winter. Now what I want you to do is write and communicate your thoughts on all this. This is all I know now, my willingness, even my willingness to start "right away"—(by that I mean, even before I get an advance.)

. . . my willingness and my hue of circumstances. And my hope that you really mean this and that you won't suddenly "buy a typewriter and leave." Do you recall that?

Your letter, by the way, was so good that I suddenly realized that you and I may be the two most important American writers someday. This is according to my judgment. But the tone of my letter is so sad . . . let's go "backwards."

Two weeks later Kerouac wrote another letter, this time to both Neal and his wife, about his plans to live on a ranch, since Carolyn had taken him seriously and been skeptical about the prospect of their living together as a group. In this letter Kerouac admitted his idea "was but a metaphor, and the whole thing a fanciful lyrical dream." Then he went on to elaborate on the theme of his vision of the ideal home, including facilities for their friends, who were to be what Kerouac called their "beat" visitors.

TO NEAL AND CAROLYN CASSADY

July 10 '48
Ozone [Park, N.Y.]

Dear Neal & Carolyn—

Believe me I appreciate your apprehensions about a "Shakespearian house" and all that; I was excited, the letter was a preamble to things; and actually such a house was but a metaphor, and the whole thing a fanciful lyrical dream, formal and poetic, full of speculation and vagueness.

Beyond a loving statement of purpose, then, here are some (I hope) actualities. Don't worry about the unavoidable, true, and Biblical matter of female incompatibility. It will boil down to various friendly encampments on the same land. A real stock-ranch always has two houses and other buildings; a farm sometimes has more than one house, if not, things can be managed till something is put up, really. To speculate some more, in an early stage of the project it would be (if everyone was there) my mom and sister and husband and son in one house, Neal and you and son (daughter?) and myself and Edie-type wife in another house . . . the "younger element" and all that. Perfect compatibility. My wife, if not Edie again, will be someone like her . . . "wild" . . . "crazy" . . . etc. . . . rushing off to mad bars, yet at the same time a sunny housekeeper.

And by a ranch (if it is possible at all) I mean a real stock-ranch from which we might conceivably make a fortune some day, which would enable you Neal, as well as me, and Paul, within a few years, to work exclusively for ourselves in partnership . . . no railroads, no telephone companies (Paul's a wire-man), and for me, no dependence on shifting literary fortunes.

If not a stock-ranch (and I know that ranching, though the oldest thing in California, has gone into a decline there since the droughts of 1870), there are a thousand other endeavors pleasant and healthful and profitable and beautiful—fruit-farming, wheat-farming (particularly steady—as Hal says, "Wheat is like time.")—and apple-growing and so on. *Partnership* in such endeavors means protracted vacations for all, rotation of responsibility and duties, opportunity to travel, a real workable routine. That's why I wouldn't want to go at it alone. And there's no fun alone, as I say. If I make money, here is the great investment. If not, still, it's something to sweat for, something really cooperative, and free.

A ranch, say. In Mendocino county, or around Clear Lake, or the Russian River valley around Ukiah, or even Eel River. I even saw some stock-ranches near Stimson beach, in Muir woods. All wonderful country not far from Frisco.

A good bull, some cows and yearlings . . . this after one conceivably gets property . . . maybe a thousand acres or less for grazing, or (if there are National Grazing Forests in Cal) (find out for me Neal), then all you need is 100 acres or so for alfalfa, for interim feed . . . and a grazing permit in the forests. You grow and grow. $400-per-head . . . with a small herd of only 50, you can cut out 20 in the fall and sell at the stockyards for $8,000 . . . and the next year, growing the herd to 350, say, you cut out 70 head and sell for $28,000 . . . you see how it grows. Money makes money, however. I'm talking big here. But see how it grows and works.

You can always truck-farm while waiting for the herd to grow and steers to fatten. And then, of course, the real work of castration of steers is the work of waddies, or vaqueros in Cal, and branding and all that, and roping and wrangling. But Paul (former Wake Forest fullback) and you and I are athletic enough to learn all these things ourselves in time.

All this I look forward to. But at first, the first two years, no such set-up is possible. All I know is about Colorado ranching. I don't know what gives in California. Find out, boy. (About National Grazing Forests, property, permits, water, etc.) I'm going to buy a Frisco paper tonight and dig the acres and ranches section.

Meanwhile, here's what the thing would be. I come out alone, at first, to establish things and look around. To work while I see how my book sells, maybe to study a little agriculture on a G.I. [Bill] setup in college. To begin another novel. Then when I'm earning from some job or other—(and I can get a job on a Frisco newspaper for one thing, thanx to Temko and others)—my mother can come out. Then, after we've saved a little, and get a tract of land . . . for farming perhaps at first, with quick returns (this is all problematical) (we don't know) . . . then the others can come out. Paul can get a job on the Frisco phone companies, a great linesman. We could live apart for awhile . . . you in Alpine Terrace,[1] and so on, and us elsewhere. When we had all saved enough money to really get some good land, then we'd start the cooperative project, either ranching or fruit-farming or wheat or whatnot.

Is that better?

As for our wandering friends, I'm sure their interest eventually will be as "beat" visitors . . . that's great too. We can fix up an outbuilding, a dormitory, get them drunk, put them to work, talk, have big jazz-record parties in our basement which will undoubtedly have a pool table surrounded by bookshelves. And perhaps someday we'll be lolling back on the porch looking at our valley of cattle and broiling steaks in the yard and entertaining our mad friends.

So we'd all work, save our money, and look around for a land project. When the next Depression hits, we'll have food and home-

---

1. The Cassadys were living at 160 Alpine Terrace in San Francisco.

steads. Also, in time, as I say, we'll be free to work for ourselves exclusively.

Paul is a "hound-dog man"—that's what they call them in Texas. He'd sell his wife my sister for a hound-dog. A great hunter . . . and if it's a ranch, and inasmuch as wildcats and coyotes and sometimes wolves prey on the stock, he'd be of great value in that respect among others. A great worker. We'd never see him . . . he'd be always down in the valley baying in moonlight with his dogs, returning wild-eyed with a wolf-scalp, a real hound-dog man. There's a guy who could almost make a living on bounties if they still had bounties. But I'm just rattling along joyously and irresponsibly.

The first stage is myself coming out alone. And how much the book sells, if at all. That's the real initial stage. Maybe by next winter, maybe this Fall, who knows. Working . . . on newspaper at $40 to start, unless I too could hit on the railroad or other jobs. There are many. I'll come out, as Mark Twain says, and drat that man's truth—"to begin to take advantage of the opportunity to begin."

Okay? You see it's all speculation, and we're both sick of it. We'll keep it in the realm of planning instead. These are my plans. God help us if I make a lot of money . . . we'll be reactionary cattle-barons—and if so, where else would I want to invest my money? In cocktail parties in New York? You dig? And if I don't make big money, we'll go at it like human beings.

Carolyn is certainly not blocked . . . she's wise. We must give women their age-old privilege to love each other perversely and run the world thereby. Their "cattiness" is love as old as Eden's snake. We'll understand and fixit. Now let's knock off from all this specu-lation awhile and relax and be cool and enjoy. Write me a pure letter full of things.

Partner Jack

As the summer wore on and Kerouac failed to interest anyone in his novel after Scribner's and other publishers turned it down, he wrote to Cassady with increasing desperation about what he was going to do, while giving Neal the latest news of the unsettled lives of their mutual friends Ginsberg and Burroughs.

Sept. 5 '48
[Ozone Park, N.Y.]

Dear Neal,

Well come on, man, do I have to urge you to write me another letter? I'm getting lonesome for word from you in your own words. Every time there is a long lapse in your replies, I get to wondering if I said anything that offended you or hurt you or even bored you, and I rack my brain and get real paranoiac. This time I'm thinking: Neal must think I have abandoned him in my future plans and he's saying "Oh fuck him." Not that it is a great privilege to be included in my "future plans," only that it means the extent of my feeling, as you undoubtedly know (whether the plans are sensible or not, you see.)

I want to see those stories you mentioned, too. And I would really truly want to hear about your "San Franco demon," as you termed it. This interests me—also, I see no reason why I should be excluded from such things, unless you reserve a certain area of your experience for certain levels, and you have plopped me into one of those levels, and therefore excluded me. May I suggest that this is a Wolfean technique of living—in the sense of "creating levels"?—thereby anticipating the organic confusion and variety of life with a strict iron-clad "concept." Relegating certain men to a certain level, but only from subjective evidence, and so on, and so on.

Since my book is finished I've been reading and thinking, and feel a certain clarity coming on. Also, since the book is out of the house, I have easily determined how to reduce a few hundred pages—by "easily" I mean, with clarity and relaxation. Right now it is being read by MacMillan . . . next on the agenda, Doubleday, Little Brown, Random House, and perhaps the critic Alfred Kazin will read a selection of chapters. I am running into crass commercialism now and what is even worse than that, the sour-grapes mentality of "literary people"—reviewers and editors and such-like. But that is old hat, I expected it, I don't give a shit—just as long as eventually I make a living from my writing-work. After that the coast is clear on the worklife level.

In connection with worklife, I almost got a job on United Press, but didn't anyway . . . and now I'll have to decide on something. I could go to sea in the Army Transport command (as a typist, you see)—or I could get a job, try to get a job in the lumber yard in back of my house in Ozone—or try longshoring, try to get a union card . . . and so on. Or go to Frisco. But I've got to stick around to see the book through all the various hands, so I can't leave town until at least after New Year's. Also there's going to be revising work. So that's the *work* at hand preceding others.

At that time, though, I'm almost certain I'm at least going to take a trip to Frisco. I'll be seeing you one way or the other within a few months. Things aren't clear yet on this subject . . . and so on.

I haven't seen Allen in a long time, he left town and went home to Paterson, but does not write and send me his address. I'm thinking of hitch-hiking out to Paterson and surprise him. Huncke stole all his stuff and that helped in depressing Allen . . . Durgin must have asked him to leave the 121st street place, too.

And so, write, and begin a new chain of "evidence"—I saw Burroughs one night before he went back to Algiers, La. He has lost most of his human qualities . . . that is, the ability to blush occasionally, or get excited about something. He sits and stares, or giggles idiotically with Allen, and looks sick. However I think that makes him even more fascinating after all, and I'm mad because he paid no attention to me.

As always, Jack

Kerouac had told Cassady that he couldn't leave New York "until at least after New Year's" in his effort to sell his novel, but a few weeks later he visited his sister and brother-in-law in Rocky Mount, North Carolina, to work at the parking lot they ran at the autumn county fair. First Jack wrote a quick note to his brother-in-law to

say that he was coming down, and later he took advantage of some
slow rainy days in Rocky Mount to write two letters to Cassady.

TO PAUL BLAKE

> Thursday night
> *Fall 1948*
> [Ozone Park, N.Y.]

Dear Paul—

Okay boy, I'm a-coming down to work on your parking lot and I'm glad it came up . . . It's just the sort of thing I was waiting for because I wanted to get out of New York awhile. Seems like I always want to "get out of New York awhile" now.

I'm sorry to hear about Bill. It's a good thing you didn't lose Bob, too. He's a beautiful dog. You can get him another partner in time. I bet he's lonely now.

Of course now I'll be able to see Paul Jr. and guess who envies me?—No one but "Grandma."[1] And I'll see Ann[2] too. I'm sure I'll have a great time & here's hoping we get enough customers to pay for your lot. What rates?—how many customers a day?

We'll have things to talk about; also oil up the football, hey? I'm glad you thought of the idea. I'll hitch-hike down around the 24th. Tell Nin I'll be seeing her.

> As always,
> Jack

---

1. Gabrielle was called "grandma"—"mémère" in Québécois—after the birth of her grandson.
2. Ann B. was a neighbor of the Blakes whom Kerouac dated when he visited his sister in North Carolina.

Rocky Mount, N.C.
Oct. 2 '48

(FIRST LETTER)
(Intentionally martyred)

Dear Neal—

Where are you, man?—why is it you don't write to me when you know there's so many things that have got to be said. Here I am sitting in a shack, writing on a board table, as it rains, and as the radio plays colored music in this land where the colored are pushed back & scorned & "kept in their place." And, Neal, there's a woman called Mahalia Jackson who sings real sad, while, in the background on another station, there's white audience laughter from some contest show in Nashville, Tenn. You see how it makes me feel, don't you? I didn't come down here to mourn the Negro's lot, but I do. I'm down here to run a parking lot which would have earned a couple hundred bucks if it hadn't rained. The lot is right in front of the county fair. Now it's all mud, & I'm still broke.

I hitched down here a few days ago.

I'm really bugged because you stop writing sometimes. There's no need for that, just write steady like I do. Take a little time out for a buddy whose feeling is constant and real. You didn't tell me about your baby daughter. Do you think I expect you to "hero-worship" me?—to expect anything? I only expect you to believe in everybody, including me, and to believe in everything, like a child, a bird; like I do. Love to all. Write soon.   Jack

(Write to Ozone)

Oct. 3 '48
[Rocky Mount, N.C.]

(SECOND LETTER—fat & satisfied)

Dear Neal—

Okay—we'll wait and see about your R.R. job in Nov. and if you lose it, I'll come out to go on Standard Oil with you. I don't think my bookwork will hold me back once I get an agent. (But don't be *positive* it might not hold me up?) We'll *both* see in November.

The ranch information I will file away for future use. My brother-in-law's all hip on idea. No doubt, 'tho, that none of us have enough money for such an idea yet. But later . . . yes! (Wait!) (My book! my book!—it's great!)

Neal, I feel real good. As Lucien said to me the other week, on Washington Square, "And you know, boy, it gets more & more joyous all the time." Yessir! Not without grounds, either. When you knew me I was so locked up in a rigid "picture" of life that I refused, I absolutely refused to participate or believe in anything that did not fit in that picture. That picture was of all life not rooted to earth (actual farms, mind you) as being corrupt. Naturally, of course, beyond the *blithest* doubts, my mind was mad then—tho not my heart, for I continued loving. But I was insane. What you did was respect my heart, my "dignity." Well, I really like you, Neal, and even when I had the insane ideas which served as an artificial incubator for the novel, I liked you—especially when I saw you sitting in my father's chair one night puffing on a big cigar, with your "Western" vest, reading the papers, smiling. I said to myself, "Not only is Neal a mad character (as categorized in my "picture of life") but he is also a man with a sense of enjoyment (joyousness) and satisfaction and he knows how to work and make his way, and all those Chases and Temkos don't like him only because they don't feel it necessary to consider him their social & cultural equal (AND I DO? PITY POOR NEAL), which is a vanity in them I cannot understand yet. (No, I cannot buy it, either.) I said to myself, "Neal is a real good kid at heart, he's had a tough time and he has to fight, and he fights a sly fight the others consider obvious because it is nowhere as sly as theirs."

Tell me I'm wrong, put up your dukes, Neal. I *know* this is true. It is also true that I must learn indefatigable ways of fighting from you, and you must learn sadness from me. I think I'm almost ready to say I no longer "care" what you think about me, now all that concerns me is what I think about you—it's *you* that counts. I want to be normal, dammit. Normal people are not self-conscious so much as I've been. [. . . .] Forgive me, I'm *green*. I try to please and therefore

I am all wrapped in my picture of myself as a clever pleaser—No? Pride prevents me from continuing enough to say, "Help me learn to be natural." (This suggests queerness . . . it is too "sissy . . . and it ends there on a note of social hysteria.) He-he! But listen . . . do you realize (this is apropos) that a new literary age is beginning in America? Sinclair Lewis et al sum up people by their social & cultural "positions." This is American Lit. in general . . . especially Lewis & magazines, and leftist writing, all. But, with the advent of Dostoevsky the Russian Christ, we young Americans are turning to a new evaluation of the individual: his *"position" itself,* personal and psychic. Great new age, truly, much further advanced than Sovietism. The Prophets were right! Nature Boy is only an American beginning of the last human preoccupation—the position of the soul among all the souls in the Forest Arden of the world, *the* crux of life.

Right?

Moreover [. . . .] I consider queerness a hostility, not a love. "Woman exists because there was man—the penis exists because first there was void—(cunt)—therefore, "I have one of my own" (a void, or a penis)—"You have one of your own—you do not *really* wish mine without envy, hostility, aggression, and inverted desire." These are my views. . . . (SILLY) (SELF-CONSCIOUS TOO) . . . and I'm not saying them for *your* benefit (don't have to) so much as for "posterity" which might someday read this letter, all my letters (as Kerouac). Posterity will laugh at me if it *thinks* I was queer . . . little students will be disillusioned. By that time science & feelings intuitive will have shown it is VICE, VICIOUS, not love, gentle . . . and Kerouac will be a goat, pitied. I fight that. I am *not* a fool! a queer! I am *not!* He-he! Understand? And forgive me for dramatizing the idiotic thoughts I have at moments. They're of no use to you. I am the Sly Idiot, I refuse to be accused of concealing anything. I am sad, and mad, and I wish I could be sensible like you & Paul & my sister & my mother & Ann etc.

Jack

P.S.—Neal, all your doubts about the semi-fertilized intelligence of my mind must be confirmed by this letter. Are they? And what would others say? Neal, pretty soon I'm going to start saying & doing what I please and cease trying to be a "model" truth-speaker for mankind. The prophet is always false to himself, therefore hates himself. Right? Tell me.

Might as well tell you about Ann B . . . then. She is just sweet, Goddamit:—sits there in the house rocking my sis's baby while I'm outside with an axe putting up parking-lot signs. Then, I come to her window (she's watching me) and I look at her thru the window, she looks at me (beautiful eyes), we say nothing, just look, deep look. Also I want to lay her real bad. How can I explain? I fear I'm too trampish for her, no money, wild, drinker, full of "he-he!" while she just sits & rocks the baby. Also, she's hard to win, almost in love with another boy. What'll I do? I want to marry her, I think. Who could be better? A nurse, beautiful, pliant, quiet, sensible, but ready for a good time; very shy, looks away, blushes, murmurs her words; a womanly flush on her cheeks, the popping-at-the-seams shape of a real gal in calico; and, finally, on couch, a shuddering cannonball. I'd marry her tomorrow if I had dough, and could. But I hate her because I have a rival to her (young doc). She loves the situation, of course.—Next door, a young couple:—young wife looks like Lu-Anne, husband like us . . . he's barefooted in new hardwood house, casual, khaki pants, drinks like fish, goes to work in morning. "Lu-Anne" listens to radio, writes letters. Great marriage. I want a girl who'll be all things. Ann may have to learn these things, see? These are my doubts. As to love, who have I ever loved? I am too insane to love anybody else but me, but I have decided to change. Therefore, I think I will chase Ann (I'm mad about her anyway) and marry her. Real sensible, practical girl. I feel like a fool beside her, she feels "why should I want her?" So on. What a life!

Ah well, thanx for writing, Neal.   WRITE AGAIN.   J

Back in New York City after Rocky Mount, Kerouac applied for funding from the GI Bill to attend courses in American literature at the New School for Social Research. As he bragged to his friend Hal Chase, he had also embarked on several new writing projects, in-

cluding his first attempt at a work of fiction about hitchhiking he called "an American-scene picaresque, 'On the Road' . . ."

Tuesday Oct. 19 [1948]

[Ozone Park, N.Y.]

Dear Hal,

Twice I went up to the campus[1] to look for you, without avail, and each time I called Ginger no one was in. Where are thou? Your address, your plans for weekends,—send them on a post-card.

To get $75 a month I now attend the New School a terrible school where the restraint of the lady-students goes hand in hand with weary utterances from the front of the class—except in the case of one Russian professor who says "willage" and claims his allegiance to the peasants, to [Nikolai] Gogol, to the Ukraine, and is pulling the wool over all their eyes like a professor in Dostoevsky. But goddamit I need $75 a month.

Ed White and Burford and Jeffries and I are planning to go to the Sorbonne in February and we've all made preliminary arrangements. Something is bound to happen, to obtrude in our plans, but surprisingly it might just as well not. Just think what it would be to go to Paris with those guys!—as Burford says, "to show the existentialist drek the *real* meaning of anarchy."

If it doesn't pan out I won't care too much inasmuch as I'm writing three new novels and a big essay on Wolfe (for my own satisfaction.) The Town & City novel, completed last summer, is being read by a critic, and then will be read by Random House, Knopf, H-Mifflin, Little Brown, etc. The three new novels are entitled "Doctor Sax" (dealing with the American Myth as we used to know it as kids—and incidentally I crave to go over the whole subject of myth with you)—and "The Imbecile's Christmas" . . . the imbecile who believes

---

1. The Columbia University campus at 116th Street and Broadway, New York City.

everybody, believes in everything, makes no judgment of good and evil, can't drive a car . . . and finally an American-scene picaresque, "On the Road,"[2] dealing simply with hitch-hiking and the sorrows, hardships, adventures, sweats and labours of that (two boys going to California, one for his girl, the other one for Golden Hollywood or some such illusion, and having to work in carnivals, lunchcarts, factories, farms, all the way over, arriving in California finally where there is nothing . . . and returning again.) These ideas and plans obsess me so much that I can't conceal them, like Goethe[3] did: they overflow out of me, even in bars with perfect strangers. I mention them here in the same obsessive way altho in this case it is justified.

Drop a card. I swear it's eerie the way I couldn't find you on the campus, altho I saw your car, I think, a Colorado plate, a coupe, at 2 in the morning in front of Warren Hall.

In July 1948, Kerouac met a new friend in New York, an aspiring novelist named John Clellon Holmes. Their conversations about literature and postwar social change helped Kerouac formulate the term "beat generation." As Kerouac was to recall in his 1959 article "The Origins of the Beat Generation," he and Holmes "were sitting around trying to think up the meaning of the Lost Generation and the subsequent Existentialism, and I said, 'You know, this is really a beat generation,' and he leapt up and said, 'That's it, that's right.'" In a letter to Ginsberg, Kerouac told him about plans to meet at Holmes's apartment before going off to another party.

---

2. In this early attempt to write *On the Road*, Kerouac was working on a chapter he titled "Tea Party." He started it on sheets of paper captioned "Employees Semi-Monthly Time Report" that he'd saved from his job the previous year with the Housing Authority of the County of Marin in California.

3. Johann Wolfgang von Goethe (1749–1832), German poet and dramatist, author of *Faust*. In "Beatific: the Origins of the Beat Generation" (1959), Kerouac wrote, "My hero was Goethe and I believed in art and hoped someday to write the third part of *Faust*, which I have done in *Doctor Sax*."

[postmarked November 17, 1948
Ozone Park, N.Y.]

Dear Allen,—Sorry I bothered your Pop the other night with mad midnight call. Let's change that appointment to Friday night if you can make it, at John Holmes apt. 681 Lexington (56th St.), apt. 4C. Everybody will be there. Big party[1] at Stringham's (Stringham taking off cast.) Livornese, Monacchio, literary agents, Holmes, and that Normie Schnall character told you about (who writes "lush" rococo novels and blasts) and many others, including an artist. This is for 9 P.M. but you can go earlier (to Holmes.) Then all to Stringham's. If you can't make this let me know pronto. I am devising new seasons for you, man. Arrive! arrive! Here is my new theory: live more, and write more. So work, write, live, work, write, live.

Bring the monster. And wait till I tell you what Levinsky[2] does in my new novel.

Jean-Louis

At the end of 1948, still unable to find a publisher for The Town and the City, *Kerouac sent a letter to Cassady after Neal had written that he'd lost his job with the railroad. Neal had asked Jack to look for work with him on an oil freighter. Jack immediately offered to "go out in my own miserable hitch-hiking way" to join his friend on the West Coast. As usual when Jack answered Neal, his imagination was stimulated into making elaborate plans to merge their future lives together. The publishers' rejections of his manuscript over the previous six months had made Kerouac "refuse to go on banking on the fantasy" that he could make a living with his writing, though he was determined not to give up his plans to be a writer.*

---

1. Kerouac described the parties with his "New York gang of friends" at the beginning of Part Two of *On the Road*. "We went to Tom Saybrook's [John Clellon Holmes's pseudonym] first. Tom is a sad, handsome fellow, sweet, generous, amenable. . . ."

2. "Levinsky" was Kerouac's name for Ginsberg in *The Town and the City.*

Dec. 8, 1948
[Ozone Park, N.Y.]

Dear Neal,

Let's hope this letter doesn't cross-mail with one of yours so that you can answer me directly. In my last letter I expressed my love and friendship for you and yours. Now in this letter I revert again to my old habit of making plans . . . only this time it is less a plan, more a direct suggestion.

You've lost your job with the S.P. railroad, Neal, and now I presume you are looking around for something else in 'Frisco. And have found something.

I haven't got your last letter with which to refer to your suggestion that I come out to join you because dear Allen stole it (it's okay.) But in one of your letters you mentioned an "in" with Standard Oil.

Neal, how about you and I sailing for Standard Oil for awhile? . . . a real slow boat to China, at $200-per-month each. If you agree to do this, I am ready to take off for the Coast any moment; and if you wish, I can come out first thing in January. Any time. I have the money to go out in my own miserable hitch-hiking way, of course.

This is why I want to do this. (1) Little, Brown has rejected my novel because "it is too long," etc., and I refuse to go on banking on the fantasy that I will make a living writing. Only charlatans, journalists, and phoneys do that. I'm through—although I'll go on writing. (2) My sister and Paul and the baby are coming to live with us in Ozone Park. Here at home they'll all be working and saving money for the farm-day. I want to pitch in and send part of my pay home. We will all live cheaply here, and save.

If you and I sailed for six months or a year, together we could amass savings amounting to no less than $1200 in six months, twice as much in a year. This, along with the grand my mother has in the bank, and the grand my brother-in-law is getting back from his house, and possibly another grand they might save in time, would give us 4 or 5 grand to start a farmstead with. (In Cal., of course.)

How does this sound to you? Fantastic? At least one thing . . . it is quite possible for us to start a farm on a thousand or two, both of us being able-bodies, and Paul to boot; and it is much better than working for employers all our lives. I've been through all this before, won't bore you. Want your immediate reply about you and I shipping out.

Do not hesitate to tell me if you're reluctant to sail, thus leaving your family behind for long stretches. You may not want this at all —and Carolyn most certainly will not enjoy the prospect of it. Tell me the score on that.

But if you're in tough straits as I am (we all are) perhaps you have to do something like this. Going to sea means saving large sums of money (with which to start a farm.) However, if you have ideas for working in 'Frisco, and ways and means of saving, that would be fine too. Also, ideas of your own about what to do with your savings, of course.

I am not entirely giving up on my writing-prospect, but no longer banking on it, not a moment more. Actually I am closer than ever to publication because the letter from Little, Brown was most flattering and referred not to the worth of the novel but the printing costs in this day and age. But I have no opportunity to moon about "the age." I have started 2 new novels, as you know, and wouldn't be surprised if I made plenty of dough in 5 years. But these next five years are not to be wasted "waiting" for these cocksucking bastards with their sheep's brains who will some day come bleating all over my premises. I am so mad that I keep entertaining the thought of going into a racket, i.e., safe-cracking in publishing houses. Justice demands it. I won't get the screwing Melville got. Nowadays critics bewail the cloud of "despair" that came over Melville after *Moby Dick* because he stopped writing. No reason to despair, nobody paid any attention to *Moby Dick* (a mediocre book after all.) It is only "history" that today critics cream all over *Moby Dick,* the dear perceptive things. Neal, if you want to go into safe-cracking with me, tell me. Or a year's stretch in the South Seas. Anything. Please respond to your desperate and loving (and determined) eternal friend.

Jack   (TURN)

P.S. And there is always a job with an overseas construction unit, at a one-year contract, which would net us each about $5000 for the year, or $10,000 together (certainly enough to start something, providing we don't die of malaria or elephantiasis.) What do you say, man? There's a number of big companies right in Frisco, especially the one I guarded for in Marin county, sending out guys on one-year-contracts to hell-and-gone all over. Write write.

P.S. Poor Allen is having the same troubles . . . he has "nothing to sell" and is wandering around N.Y. trying to get a job.

> However I still insist that sex is
> the basis of life (altho you wouldn't
> know it, would you?)

P.S. There's an ad in the paper just tonight in N.Y. about overseas jobs. The typist-clerks, lowest, get $4380 for a year—the mechanics get $5500. This is all clear, as you know. One of the requirements is to have a driver's license. This I could get. If you have had yours revoked by any chance, I guess that's the gimmick. But we can get around that. Just think how well we could make out if we spend one miserable year in Iceland or Okinawa working, and come back with enough money to start a real good paying little farm. Even Paul is desperate enough he would join us for that year . . . the three of us would come back with a mint.

> Neal, you may say I'm impractical, but I think this is a very practical idea. We're not saving anything now, or getting anywhere. Come on, admit it!—how much have you saved from your big S.P. checks? While you're gone for a year Carolyn could even live with my folks (but please don't misunderstand me, I don't wish to plant such a fantastic idea in her head unless she'd want to.) I'm sorry if I intrude on something . . . But the mere thought of you and I (and Paul) coming back with 12 or 13 grand is hounding my harassed brain. I tell you, if something like this isn't worked out, and if someone doesn't come in on it with me, I'm going out to crack safes. If they don't want to accept the good in me, by God I'll give them back the worst . . . with interest. I'm having the same dreams as Lucien now . . . machine-gunning people. Come on, Neal, tell me what you think! I'm depending on your great sense.

P.S. Fine tea lately from a cat named Herb. Also, will see Huncke soon and give you lowdown. Vicki living with second-story man in Queens. Got great letter from Burroughs[1] saying he is making money with his pea, lettuce, and cotton-crop, and plans to leave U.S.A. for S. America or Africa, after sojourn in N.Y. soon. Wants me to visit N.O. [New Orleans]—will do so on way to the Coast. Says he is having feud with "terrible nest of Dagoes" next door in Algiers [Louisiana]: will help him . . . Says he has bought "piece of swamp" and that "hunting, or rather, shooting is now his favorite pastime." Is getting that Chinaman off his back, too. Good. And don't forget that I have got my own Chinaman off my back, namely Mr. Faust. Don't forget! Also, Hal off my back. Fuck him seventy eight times. Fuck the literateurs too. Fuck the whole lot. Have met great gal—the greatest yet—Pauline[2] is name. The very greatest of all. From PA.— a model, married to a mechanic; poor, beautiful, gone, like me, has great kid, is lonesome (husband doesn't like to get his fingers wet; she calls him the Minute Man). Glorious body and face.

J.

Several days before Christmas 1948, Kerouac wrote Ginsberg to tell him the exciting news that he'd had a long-distance call from Cassady on the drugstore pay phone below his mother's apartment. Jack hadn't seen Neal for more than a year, and Cassady had called to say that on an impulse he had scraped together his savings, hit his friend Al Hinkle for a loan, and bought a brand-new maroon 1949 Hudson to drive to New York so he and Jack could celebrate New Year's Eve together.

---

1. Burroughs was living in Algiers, Louisiana, across the Mississippi River from New Orleans. He wrote his letter to Kerouac on November 30, 1948.

2. Kerouac based the character Lucille on Pauline in *On the Road*, saying, "I knew my affair with Lucille wouldn't last much longer. She wanted me to be her way. She was married to a longshoreman who treated her badly. . . . I had nothing to offer anybody except my own confusion."

[December 15, 1948
Ozone Park, N.Y.]

Allen,

I am aware that Reginald Marsh,[1] and his cool change from tense faults and naturalism, to God's-eye view of man in the Godreal world, is great. (SPOKEN IN A DEEP VOICE.)

[. . . .] Do you know what I think?—People in this century have been looking at people with a naturalistic eye, and this is the cause of all the trouble. I think women are beautiful goddesses and I always want to lay them—Joan,[2] Barbara, all—and I think men are beautiful Gods, including me, and I always want to put my arm around them as we walk somewhere [. . . .]

However, I hate you. Because years ago you and Burrows [sic] used to laugh at me because I saw people as godlike, and even, as a husky football man walked around godlikelike, and Hal did that too, and still does. We long ago realized our flesh happily, while you and Bill used to sit under white lamps talking and leering at each other. I think you are full of shit, Allen, and at last I am going to tell you. [. . . .]

Thinking of getting a job in a gas station, I shudder as before. I'm lost. If my book doesn't sell, what can I do? As I write this to you I am on the verge of falling dead from my chair. Just now I felt myself swooning. It is too much, too close to death, life. I must learn to accept the tightrope. [. . . .]

Now that I have more or less settled that, and expressed my appreciation of our new life and regard for each other, let me go on to the next "great" thing: (you see, I used "beautiful" and "great" only in quotes now to show you I am conscious of our former hypocrisy)—

It is this, "dear" Allen . . . (you see? but you don't have to see any more, we have dead eyes now, we'll be quiet)—

Neal is coming to New York.

---

1. Reginald Marsh (1898–1954), American artist.
2. Joan Vollmer, Burroughs's common-law wife.

Neal is coming to New York.

Neal is coming to New York for New Year's Eve.

Neal is coming to New York for New Year's Eve.

Neal is coming to New York for New Year's Eve in a '49 Hudson.[3]

I have almost real reason to perhaps almost believe that he stole the car, but I don't know.

The facts: last Wednesday, Dec. 15, he long-distanced me from San Fran, and I heard his mad Western excited voice over the phone, "Yes, yes, it's Neal, you see . . . I'm calling you, see. I've got a '49 Hudson."

Etc. . . I said: "And what are you going to do?"

He says: "That's what I was going to say now. To save you the hitch-hiking trip out to the Coast, see, I will break in my new car, drive to New York, test it, see, and we will run back to Frisco as soon as possible, see, and then run back to Arizona to work on the railroads. I have jobs for us, see. Do you hear me, man?"

"I hear you, I hear you, see."

"See. Al Hinkle is with me in the phone booth. Al is coming with me, he wants to go to New York. I will need him, see, to help me jack up the car in case I get a flat or in case I get stuck, see, a real helper and pal, see."

---

3. Several months later, in August 1949, after trying unsuccessfully to place his first novel with a publisher, John Clellon Holmes began to write *Go,* a novel based on what he called "the people & events" in his life during the preceding year. His first meeting with Neal Cassady in New York after Cassady's nonstop cross-country trip in the new Hudson epitomized what Holmes described in Chapter Five of *Go* as "this beat generation, this underground life." Cassady, Kerouac, Ginsberg, Holmes, and others appear in Holmes's autobiographical fiction, which Kerouac read in manuscript before rewriting *On the Road* in April 1951 (*Go* was published in 1952). Holmes wrote Ann Charters on June 23, 1987, that the "plot" of *Go* "presented itself to me ready-made. . . . So the form—properly a roman à clef, I suppose—came of itself, though I had to learn how to use it, and found that simply telling the truth wasn't half enough. It still had to be brought to fictional life. Here my primary influences were the Russians—Dostoyevsky above all. Tolstoy, not so much, I was dealing in extremes of spirit, excesses of behavior, violent emotions or lack of them. . . . I was actually in the process of going *backwards* from modern literature—being self-educated, I could go where I liked—and was deep in 'the great days of the novel' during the writing of *Go.*"

"Perfect," I said.

"You remember Al?"

"The cop's son? Sure."

"Who? What's that, Jack?"

"The cop's son. The officer's son."

"Oh yes, Oh yes . . . I see, I see—the copson. Oh Yes. That's Al, that's right, you're perfectly right, that's Al, the copson from Denver, that's right man, see."

Confusion.

Then—"I need money. I owe $200 but if I can hold off the people I owe it to, see, by telling them or perhaps by giving them $10 or so to hold them off. And then I need money for Carolyn to live on while I'm gone, see . . ."

"I can send you fifty bucks," I said.

"Fifteen?"

"No, fifty dollars."

"All right all right fine. See." And so on. "I can use it for Carolyn, and to hold off these people I'm in debt . . . and my landlord. Also I have another week's work left on the railroad so I'll make it. It's perfect, see. Reason why I call is because my typewriter broke down, and it's being traced (sic! I'm only exaggerating here)—and I can't write letters, so I called."

Anyway, how crazy it was. So I agreed to all our new plans, of course; I had been writing him asking him to go to sea, but this is better we both agreed, more pay, too. $350 a month. And Arizona, see. He says he traded in his Ford and all his savings for the '49 Hudson. That car is the greatest in the country in case you don't know. We talked about it more than anything else.

But come Saturday, and I'm in New York with Pauline my love, and Neal calls up again and beseeches my mother to warn me not to send the money to him in name but in another name he would mail me, and another address. I had, however, already sent the money to him airmail registered . . . but only $10, I couldn't make my mad happy miscalculation of the phone. My mother's report includes a certain remark he seemed to have made without connection, viz., "I ain't there." (?)

Secondly, when I sent him the $10 I asked him to pick me and my Maw up in North Carolina on the way East,[4] we could use the money saved to our advantage and to return to Frisco and Arizona. He agreed to this with my mother over the phone, altho he mentioned going to Chicago too, which is pretty far North off the Carolina course. But he apparently will do that . . . both.

I know nothing. If he stole the car, or what's with Carolyn, or his landlord, or something, or debtors (creditors?), and what's with the cops, or that phoney address he wanted to send me. All I know is that he is tremendously excited about the car, and that "He's off," of course.

So I expect to see him in North Carolina around the 29th of December, and we will be back in New York for New Year's Eve, and of course you're going to begin right now arranging a big BIG party in your York Ave. place for New Year's Eve inviting everybody[5] . . . especially Stringham and Holmes etc. We will rotate the party to the Holmeses and your place and Ed's and Lucien's and then Stringham, the Holmeses (I will have Pauline), and of course Lou and Barbara; and Herb Benjamin for tea and for kicks. I will try to get Adele for Neal.

However, if you wish, don't arrange anything, inasmuch as *it is no longer necessary* to arrange things anymore; we have changed. Use your judgment. Meet me at Kazin's Wednesday night and we'll

---

4. Kerouac wrote in *On the Road,* "One day when all our Southern relatives were sitting around the parlor . . . gaunt men and women with the old Southern soil in their eyes, talking in low, whining voices about the weather, the crops, and the general weary recapitulation of who had a baby, who got a new house, and so on, a mud-spattered '49 Hudson drew up in front of the house on the dirt road. . . . A weary young fellow, muscular and ragged in a T-shirt, unshaven, red-eyed, came to the porch and rang the bell. I opened the door and suddenly realized it was Dean."

5. In *On the Road,* Kerouac wrote, "The parties were enormous; there were at least a hundred people at a basement apartment in the West Nineties. People overflowed into the cellar compartments near the furnace. Something was going on in every corner, on every bed and couch—not an orgy but just a New Year's party with frantic screaming and wild radio music. . . ."

talk. On the other hand no, meet me at Tartak's at 4 Monday after-noon (today if you get the letter Mon.)

If . . . well, to hell with it. That's it.

Jack

p.s. You may not believe this but as I write, a little child is looking over my shoulder . . . a real little child who is visiting us with his aunt, and who is amazed because I type so fast. Now what that little child is thinking is it, see.

1949

In January 1949, Kerouac's first cross-country trip with Cassady in the brand-new Hudson became the story of Part Two of On the Road: *"And what a trip it turned out to be! I only went along for the ride, and to see what else Dean was going to do. . . ." Jack mentioned his obsession with "the myth of the rainy night" in the narrative before he described setting off from New York with Cassady and his friends to visit Burroughs in Algiers, across the river from New Orleans, but he didn't reach what he considered the geographical source of his vision until he parted from Cassady in San Francisco,[1] made himself ten bologna sandwiches "to cross the country with again," and rode a bus back to New York City. When Kerouac passed through Butte, Montana, he scribbled an enigmatic "rainy night" postcard to Ginsberg.*

TO ALLEN GINSBERG

[postmarked February 7, 1949]
Butte, Montana
Return address:
"The Bitterroot Mountains
   —Root of Rivers
      & Rainy Nights. . . ."

Dear Sweet Levinsky—

Here I am at the sources of the rainy night, where the Missouri River starts—and the Powder Snake Yellowstone and the Big Horn & others—to roll in the tidal midland night down to Algiers bearing Montana logs past the house where Old Bill sits. The rainy night is a river (NO LAKE)—The rain is the sea coming back—and waters so fluid flow in their appointed serene beds with satisfaction & eternity (like men really do) to the Gulf of the Night. There are the hooded mountains & the caped rivers, etc.

Jack

. . . MORE, MORE, MUCH MUCH MORE. . . . (I GOT IT.)

---

1. See Kerouac's letter to Cassady, Jan. 8, 1951, pp. 275–280.

In mid-February 1949 Kerouac returned to his mother's apartment in Ozone Park after the long cross-country bus ride. On his second trip to the West Coast he'd been away only a month, and he was home in time to resume his classes at the New School. He also plunged back into work on the early drafts of On the Road *and* Doctor Sax. *The manuscript of* The Town and the City *continued to collect publishers' rejection slips, until finally, at Ginsberg's urging, Kerouac showed a few chapters of the novel as well as two early chapters of* Doctor Sax *to his old Columbia University literature professor, Mark Van Doren. Van Doren was so impressed with Kerouac's work that he telephoned the editor Robert Giroux at Harcourt Brace to recommend that they publish* The Town and the City. *At the end of March, Giroux wrote a letter of acceptance to Kerouac and offered him a $1,000 advance on the novel.*

TO MARK VAN DOREN

Mar. 9, 1949
[Ozone Park, N.Y.]

Mr. Van Doren:

The completed novel (*The Town & the City*) is 1,100 ms. pages long and has that sort of structure that cannot be represented in piecemeal chapters: these few chapters, however, may show the substantial elements of the theme and its main preoccupations (*The Soul of a Family* is its other considered title.)[1]

—included afterwards are the first two chapters of *Doctor Sax: the Myth of the Rainy Night,* which is about children and glee; townspeople; a river flooding; and mysterious occurrences, in and about a "castle of life" (with many levels, from dungeon to attic) where "concentrations of evil" foregather (wizards, vampires, spiders, etc.) for a Second Coming in the form of a giant serpent coiled under the castle miles deep. Doctor Sax is the caped fighter against

---

1. In January 1950 Van Doren gave Giroux the following endorsement of Kerouac's novel: "John Kerouac is wiser than Thomas Wolfe, with whom he will be compared. In his first novel he is serious, warm, rich and mature. He is, in other words, a responsible writer, and much may be expected of him."

these evils (chiromancer, alchemist of the night, and friend of the children): the Old Wizard (modelled after the original 15th century Faust) his arch-enemy and leader of the gnomes, Zombies, and heretical priests of the castle. There are naturalistic elements interwoven, such as Doctor Sax being, by day, disguised as the football coach of the local high school and referred to in the sport pages as "Coach Doc Saxon, the Wizard of the Merrimack Valley." There are also fumbling, awkward, apprentice vampires who never quite step into the supernatural sphere; a masquerade play for the children in which real gnomes and monsters appear onstage without their realizing it; one great monster, Blook, who is actually terrified of the children; and giant Mayan spiders that appear with the flood a natural phenomena; and many goings on on various levels, including the scholarly absorptions of a certain Amadeus Baroque who eagerly seeks to understand all this. It turns out "t'was but a husk of doves," the serpent, from which, on golden Easter morning (after climactic midnight events, dins & earth tremors, featuring Doctor Sax's sudden tender change of mind in the rainy night of the river), beautiful doves fly forth—and everybody "good or evil" was mistaken.

J.K.

On March 29, 1949, Kerouac wrote his friend Ed White to tell him that The Town and the City *had been accepted by Harcourt Brace.*

TO ED WHITE[1]

Mar. 29, 1949
[Ozone Park, N.Y.]

Dear Ed,

Well, boy, guess what? I sold my novel to Harcourt Brace—(after one rejection from Little, Brown)—and got a $1,000 advance. Mad?—I tell you it's mad. Mad?—me mad? Heh heh heh. As Hal says, I'm just chuckling all over . . . chuck-ling, that is. Also, my

---

1. This letter was published in *Mano-Mano* magazine, 1971.

personal editor is the boss of H-B himself, Robert Giroux, a fine young man of 35 or so, prematurely gray-haired, who read my novel (it almost seems) with my eyes. Ah Ed, I feel good. My mother and family feel good. I am redeemed in so many ways that I realize now I've been living under a cloud of inferiority complex. But aside from that kind of bull, just think what it means to me and the family. Later, I'll have saved enough to buy a homestead, get married, etc., and I have nothing but books to write. Shit!

So there you are in France, and here I am in Ozone Park, and— presto!—why aren't I in France? First, how long will you be there? Knowing this, I can plan. I keep thinking I may get a fellowship within a year; maybe I ought to wait for that. I have a school year of G.I. [Bill] left, however. I have a long time to try and get a job on a ship. Many angles. [. . . .]

In your letter you said you watched the children in the parks & gardens. That's for me—to sit in a Baroque park, at red dusk, in Paris, watching the amazingly charming children play, with you: & commenting like we did that day on Central Park West. With Burford get the great girls that are there (let him do the open-field running, I'm the coach.) [. . . .] And all together, one, two, three, four, sweep down to the Cirque Medrano in Montmartre and see the circus as it was intended, the French-Italian circus of rueful, cosmic, Shakespearian clowns. And scraggle in the streets of Rancy, where Céline raged. And what about this here Cote d'Azur? Jumps? Women in diaper suits? Fine, I'll take one. Ed, who have you seen? [. . . .] No see Hal, who can come and see me any time he wants, of course. Yes, I sold my novel, & I'll come to Paris sometime; just let me know your plans. Right now Giroux and I are working on some revisions in his office, in the evening. (By the way, the chapter you & Hal didn't like is undergoing a cut.) My contract includes a Hollywood clause—what? Lana Turner and me? bosh! I command you, as King of the Thousand Dollars, to write me a long and informative epistle, Sirs.

BET-A-THOUSAND KEROUAC

With money from the sale of The Town and the City, *Kerouac persuaded his family to move with him to Denver. His decision to "go West" was the natural continuation of his earlier plans to buy a ranch, which he had discussed with Cassady. Also, in the spring of 1949, Kerouac's desire to leave New York and make a new life for himself in Colorado was strengthened after the arrest of two of his friends. Burroughs was arrested on a charge of possession of drugs and firearms in New Orleans, and Ginsberg was held as an accessory to a crime in New York City: he had let the heroin addict Herbert Huncke use his Manhattan apartment to store stolen goods. In April Kerouac wrote a letter to his friend Alan Harrington, a young novelist on the periphery of the group, about his reaction to the fact that all his "geniuses [were] in jail."*

TO ALAN HARRINGTON

Apr. 23, 1949
[Ozone Park, N.Y.]

Dear Alan—

Glad to hear you're well along on Hamtrack[1] . . . it sounds as though you're almost ready to throw a finishing push to the whole thing, like a man at the top of a hill with a big rock. Work saves all. Work is perhaps more important, the work we do as writers, than what we actually say . . . who knows? I'm reminded of this tonight due to the fact that so many of my friends & acquaintances are suddenly in jail, which is not much of a contribution to one's soul . . . (sometimes.) The total effect of my selling the novel, and many misfortunes befalling these friends, & all the misfortunes of the world, has been to make me go home and sulk over my gold, and make maxims about "work" and the "soul."

I am in a particularly stupid state of mind, now.

So I start to work in earnest on my 2nd novel this week. "On the Road." I think. All my geniuses are in jail, Alan—Burroughs, Huncke, Allen (innocent Ginsberg), the big redhead Vicki, maybe

---

1. An early manuscript. Harrington's 1966 novel *The Secret Swinger* would include a portrait of Ginsberg as the dissolute bohemian poet Muchnik.

Neal & LuAnne, for all I know. I am no longer "beat," I have money, a career. I am more *alone* than when I "lurked" on Times Square at 4 A.M., or hitch-hiked penniless down the highways of the night. It's strange. And yet I was never a "rebel," only a happy, sheepish imbecile, open-hearted & silly with joys. And so I *remain*. It is all ominously what you said about my "innocence"—even though that Lucien business years ago, when everybody went unscathed except me (that is, me, & the actual pale criminal.) But now (as I promised myself) I want to go on to *further considerations*—no more John Garfield[2] parts mixed with a dash of Myshkin. Now I'll be the Invisible Man, the Shroud, Doctor Sax, the Night-Bird Hiding in the Living Trees . . . and a poet, a true writer. I am very glad I know you. But don't tell me to "clarify my ideas." I'm only interested in the history (genesis & tendency) of ideas, & the relativity of ideas, & the *meaning* of ideas & ideation—that is, put forth in this statement: "What do we *mean* by all this?" (ideas and all other forms of absorption we may have.) [. . . .]

I'm going to Colorado in June. My family & I are ready to move out there if we can find an abode. I am extremely weary of New York—there is no mystery left in it for me. I have grown dull-hearted, too. It is all a matter of "further considerations" now. I will soon become a great bore, too. I've nothing to "say" anymore. All I've left is . . . lies.

Excuse me for not ever being serious with you. It's my own way of finding out more about you. You can't pin a wriggling fish like me. Also—no deviation here—I've been thinking of going back to my 1st wife, Edie. In any case, enough about me. It's very sad the way I feel I must "carry on" before you & Johnny & Edward. It's only because I don't want you to understand me. And I'm in a strange mood this night so many people I know are sitting in actual jails. If all this sounds like Dostoevsky, realize at least that I intend it so, in my upset-mindedness . . . for "clear reasons" that are not half as important as the fact that I'm actually *doing* it. See?

Maybe that's what life is, a wink of the eye, and winking stars . . .

---

2. John Garfield was a Hollywood movie actor starring in gangster films.

and maybe also the hi-ball I'm presently drinking: (He-he!) Also the glee of little children.

I've just read "An Unfortunate Predicament," a long story by Dusty-what's-his-name [Dostoyevsky]. I studied it carefully and found that he begins with "ideas" and then demolishes them in the fury of what *actually* happens in the story. This letter is a similar venture. However, nothing detracts from the fact that this is a mad letter. "So be it! So be it!" [. . . .]

Jack

After his arrival in Denver, Kerouac was welcomed as a promising "soon-to-be-published" novelist by people he knew who were associated with Columbia University. His letters to his friends were filled with the exhilaration of experiencing a dream come true.

TO HAL CHASE

Sunday May 15, 1949
Denver

Dear Hal

Just arrived in Denver this afternoon, spending a total of 90c on the trip, with the intention of making my home out here come hell or high water, and practicing the asceticism that is necessary to accomplish this, ahead of time.

However there were wonderful gratuitous developments. I was looking for Ed White's father's phone number and casually (failing to find it in the phone book) called Justin Brierly . . . who immediately came out to pick me up. So that I was no longer walking the streets beat, but riding in a chariot. Ed White had been at work for me in Paris. He had written to Justin about my book, etc. And as I write this letter to you tonight, on the Y typewriter, for a dime, I am drunk on some of Justin's Scotch. We went riding all over Denver with Dan, drinking and talking about everybody. It was interesting and mostly sad.

[. . . .] Coming towards Denver this afternoon on the plains I had the definite feeling of . . . finding my world at last. Somewhere near Deertrail Colo. the sun was blushing through storm clouds upon a territorial area of brown plains where only one single farmhouse stood . . . so that the farmhouse, as I conceived it, was receiving the blush of God Himself. Come what may, mush or whatever they call it, my idea of life is that it's at least not the way it's lived in the East.

And the East is really effete. When a cowhand got on the bus at Hugo, and smiled at all of us in there, a whole busload of people, I knew that he was more interested in mankind than 10,000,000 New School and Columbia professors and academicians. Say anything you want, I like my people joy-hearted.[1] It is the sickly-heartedness of the East that has finally driven me away from there.

I feel very happy. I'll make it allright. [. . . .] On June 15 I'm returning to N.Y. to attend a cocktail party by the Book of the Month Club, and may be selected by that worthy cause, and may make mints.

If not I don't care . . . so long as I'm where I want to be, which is the West.

Excuse this mad, drunk letter. You certainly deserve a better correspondence. I would be immensely *consoled* if I were to hear from you again, before you came home (your mother wanted to know when)—and I could write back a more coherent letter.

And one more comprehensive. And one explaining the sadness and truth of the Lamb. In any case keep on la-bour-ing . . . and when you do come home, I'll be waiting to see you.

Your buddy,

---

1. See Part One of *On the Road*, where Kerouac went into a "homemade diner" for cherry pie and ice cream on his first trip west and heard "a great laugh, the greatest laugh in the world, and here came this rawhide oldtimer Nebraska farmer with a bunch of other boys into the diner. . . . He didn't have a care in the world and had the hugest regard for everybody. I said to myself, Wham, listen to that man laugh. That's the West, here I am in the West."

June 10, 1949
[Denver, Colo.]

Oops—Tip my cup, roll my bones,[1]
    all my oops are doopsing.

Dear Gillette,

    Your big letter occupied my mind for a whole day here in what was then my hermitage. In answer to your questions about what I think about you, I'd say you were always trying to justify your ma's madness as against the logical, sober but hateful sanity. This is really harmless and even loyal. I can't say much about it, after all what do I know? I only want you to be happy and to do your best toward that end. As Bill says, the human race will become extinct if it doesn't stop doing what it don't want to do. As for me, I think you are a great young poet and already a great man (even tho you get sick of my evasive golden-ness.) (For which there are dross-ish reasons, you know; and you know.)

    I'm no better off than you are with respect to doing what I want. I have to work on a construction job now and can't stay up all night dreaming up the mouthings of the Lamb. (But there is something else in this business of Forest-of-Ardening around people, all day, at work.)

    [. . . .] Reading over your Holier Than Thou poem last night (or Lines Write in Rockefeller Center), I saw something weird, in comparison to my own lines. For instance, let's start with my recent "crazy" poem, then yours.

> "The God with the Golden Nose, Ling,
>   gull-like down the Mountainside did soar,
>   till, with Eager Flappings, above the Lamb
>   so Meek did Hang, a Giggling Ling.

---

1. See Ginsberg's poem "Fie My Fum," written as a collaboration with Kerouac and Cassady in 1949. Ginsberg's letters to Kerouac in May and June 1949 contain several drafts of the poem. Allen also sent him Neal and Carolyn Cassady's current address in San Francisco at 29 Russell Street.

And the Chinamen of the Night
from Old Green Jails did Creep,
bearing the Rose that's Really White
to the Lamb that's really Gold,
and offered Themselves thereby, and
the Lamb did them Receive, and Ling.

Then did Golden Nose the Giggling Ling go down
and He the Mystery did Procure—
all wrapp'd in Shrouds that greenly swirl'd,
which barely He, nor Chinamen, could hold,
so Green, so Strange, so Watery it was:
but the Lamb did then the Mystery Unveil.

Saith the Lamb: "In this Shroud the Face
is Water. Worry therefore not for Green,
and Dark, which Deceptive Signs are,
of Golden Milk.
Beelzebub is but the Lamb."

Thus did the Lamb his Mouthings end.

I find that your lines evoke yourself, and mine, myself . . .
which is proper. "Not a poppy is the rose" has a strange lech-
erous sound; not only that, but "up-in-the-attic-with-the-bats" and
the line about the superfine poppy. Not that I want to go into that
. . . but, poetically, the combination of sensual hint, wink-of-the-eye
lechery, dirty ditty goes with your work. This is comparable to
Herrick:
"A winning wave, deserving note, in the tempestuous petticoat:/
A careless shoe-string, in whose tie/ I see a wild civility." Picture
Herrick's picture of the petticoat, etc. Enuf of this.
I live west of Denver, on the road to Central City.
When I can, I now read French poetry: De Malherbe, and Ra-
cine the French Shakespeare. But I have little time. Brierly gave
me Capote to read. He winked at me today during a big lun-
cheon at High School among teachers and labor leaders and ty-
coons.

As I run miserably around Denver I wonder what Pomery[2] [Cassady] would do.

I'll write a longer letter next time. It's always "next time" now with us . . . why? Because there's too much to say.

The family is here, the furniture is here, and cats, dogs, horses, rabbits, cows, chickens, and bats abound in the neighborhood. Last night I saw bats flapping about the Golden Dome of the State Capitol. If I were a Bat I'd go and get Geld. Up-at-the-dome with the goldy bats. There are so many beautiful girls around, I ache. A little girl has fallen in love with me . . . a pity. A crush for an older man, me. I gave her classical records and books, and am become a dancingmaster. Dancingmaster Wink.

I rode in a rodeo; bareback, this afternoon, and almost fell off.

I decided someday to become a Thoreau of the Mountains. To live like Jesus and Thoreau, except for women. Like Nature Boy with his Nature Girl. I'll buy a saddlehorse for $30, an old saddle on Larimer St., a sleeping bag at Army surplus; frying pan, old tin can; bacon, coffee, beans, sourdough; matches, etc.; and a rifle. And go away in the mountains forever. To Montana in the summers and Texas-Mexico in the winters. Drink my java from an old tin can while the moon is riding high. Also, I forgot to mention my chromatic harmonica . . . so I can have music. Thus—without shaving—I'll wander the wild, wild mountains and wait for Judgment Day. I believe there will be a Judgment Day, but not for men . . . for *society*. Society is a mistake. Tell Van Doren I don't believe at all in this society. It is evil. It will fall. Men have to do what they want. It has all got out of hand—began when fools left the covered wagons in 1848 and rode madly to California for Gold, leaving their families behind. And of course, there ain't enough gold for all, even if gold were the thing. Jesus was right; Burroughs was right. Why did Pomery turn down Dancingmaster's help to go to High School? I saw their graduation exercises last night and the 18 year old valedicto-

---

2. Kerouac named Cassady "Cody Pomeray" in *The Dharma Bums, Desolation Angels, Big Sur,* and *Book of Dreams.*

rian, using a false deep voice, spoke of the fight for freedom. I am going to the mountains, up in the eagle rainbow country, and wait for judgment day.

Crime is not what men want either. I have often thought of robbing stores and didn't want to do it finally. I didn't want to hurt nobody.

I want to be left alone. I want to sit in the grass. I want to ride my horse. I want to lay a woman naked in the grass on the mountainside. I want to think. I want to pray. I want to sleep. I want to look at the stars. I want what I want. I want to get and prepare my own food, with my own hands, and live that way. I want to roll my own. I want to smoke some deermeat and pack it in my saddlebag, and go away over the bluff. I want to read books. I want to write books. I'll write books in the woods. Thoreau was right; Jesus was right. It's all wrong and I denounce it and it can all go to hell. I don't believe in this society; but I believe in man, like Mann. So roll your own bones, I say.

I don't even believe in education any more . . . even high school. "Culture" (anthropologically) is the rigamarole surrounding what poor men have to do to eat, anywhere. History is people doing what their leaders tell them; and not doing what their prophets tell them. Life is that which gives you desires, but no rights for the fulfillment of desires. It is all pretty mean—but you still can do what you want, and what you want is right, when you want honestly. Wanting money is wanting the dishonesty of wanting a servant. Money hates us, like a servant; because it is false. Henry Miller was right; Burroughs was right. Roll your own, I say.

It will take me a long time to remember that I can roll my own, like our ancestors did. We'll see. This is what I think.

So leave my bones alone. I think that is a wonderful poem. Write me another. Write me that coherent long letter. All is well. Go, go; go roll your own bones. Bone-bone. Roll-bone your own go-bone, etc.

> Quelle sorcière va se dresser sur le couchant blanc?
> Quelle bone va se boner sur le bone-bone blanc?

> Jack

P.S. May have to come to N.Y. soon . . . good.

> I heard a night-bird warbling in a living tree;
> and a queer house there was that yakked at me.

Do you know what about Blake? He talks affably and cheerfully about those things in the Bible that we never could understand. "They wandered long till they sat down upon the margined sea, conversing in the visions of Beulah . . . Nine years they viewed the living spheres, feeding the visions of Beulah." Who is Beulah? Beulah is the mystery of the Bible, huh?

A month after Kerouac's arrival in Denver, he found his dream "collapsing" about him. As he told John Clellon Holmes, his family was bored with their life in Colorado and wanted to return to the East Coast. The only prospect that gave him pleasure was the thought that he could show "the West" to his editor, Robert Giroux, who was coming out to visit him in July. When Kerouac later described his weeks in Denver at the beginning of Part Three of On the Road, *he emphasized his isolation in the city, where he "felt like a speck on the surface of the sad red earth."*

TO JOHN CLELLON HOLMES

> 6100 W. Center Ave.
> Denver 14, Colo.
> June 24, 1949

Dear John (and Marian[1] dear, and Ed, and George):—

Just got your vast letter and read it once over, and am starting in this reply right away out of SHEER EXUBERANCE. (Exuberance-bone, that is.) First off, I can't hide the following fact from you any longer: turns out that my big ideal Homestead idea, which wasn't a bad idea at all, is collapsing around me. It seems that I had underestimated the madness of everyone. My móther is bored and wants to go to Radio City, and wants her job back in the Brooklyn shoe

---

1. Marian Holmes was John's first wife.

factory; so she wrote, and they gave her the job back, and she's leaving for New York next week to go back to work. My brother-in-law doesn't know where the good fishin' is in Colorado, so by God he's going back to North Carolina. I have spent my entire one thousand dollars in this huge madness. I am so hog-tied by all this that I am not doing anything, just sitting in the sun while my sister and brother-in-law work. I am doing a lot of writing however, and my editor Giroux is flying to Denver July 15 and most likely will have me fly back with him (or something) because he's only coming for 3 days, to stay at my house. I will have to sub-lease this house to some sucker, and then take it on the lam to Frisco, where Neal is hiding on Russian Hill in a queer house with crooked roofs. There, I will get a job as a fry-cook and dig some bop (there's none in Denver.) After that I am going to Pharr, Texas, which is way down near Monterrey, Mexico, to see Burroughs who is there, at present, as he says, "immobilized in this valley of heat and boredom." I will set there awhile, and make runs to Monterrey. Also, I have to go to the Southern Colorado country, somewhere near Alamosa, to see Hal Chase, who got a $1000 grant from Columbia to dig. If I can, I'll go to Butte and get a job as a fry-cook or student miner, and gamble awhile (for material.) Then, in September, I'll come back to New York, where my mother will already have an apartment (through her shoe factory lady friends) and become a bloody New Yorker again. But I'm glad. It's my forest of Arden after all, right?

You remember my telling you, John, about the great classless mass of Americans who never read the papers? Here in the foothills of Colorado I have been running around with a bunch of them. [. . . .] One woman had flaming red hair, no teeth, and rode a snow white circus horse. She says to me, "I hate these goddamn women who don't say SHIT when they have a mouthful of it." Then a cowboy who joined us in Horse Heaven hills began doing tricks on his pinto, such as standing up in the saddle. She shouted in a loud voice, "By Christ if I tried that on my stallion I'd land my ass on a rock!" There were tourists, women and children, gaping at us. "The dumb sonof-abitch ain't got no more sense than a mule. He'd asoon SHIT in my face as look at me!" This went on all day. We made plans to go riding to Arizona this summer, although I haven't seen her but once since, and she didn't really recognize me. I saw her this second time at a Tex Ritter movie. It seems there's a huge class of Western mad-people out here to go to Class C Westerns just to hear Tex Ritter and Roy Rogers sing "Twilight on the Prairie" and to watch the horses and the gunplay. In their conversation they continually make allusions to "Roy" and "Dale Evans" (his leading lady) and "Trigger" (his horse) just as we make allusions to Dostoevsky and Whittaker Chambers.[2] They sit there and watch the Myth of the Gray West, on rainy days in Larimer Street movies. Drunken cowboys snore in the balcony; little kids titter and throw popcorn. Everybody believes in Roy Rogers and Gene Autry. It's very beautiful. Then I start thinking about the mad beret-characters who actually make these movies in crazy California (the tea-head Mitchums, the horn-rimmed directors, the bag-eyed leading ladies who lead dissolute lives in motels, the seedy beat-up companies with their mad Neal stand-ins who leap from horses to railroad cabooses)—it's crazy. I have come to believe now that life is not essentially but completely irrational. I should like anybody to challenge this CLEAR idea. I have seen proof of this. Ginsberg is right: everything is a big balloon.

[. . . .] I rode in a rodeo. We ran around like an Indian attack, in a wild circle. I went to the movies of this rodeo to see myself ride. There I sit, in a big sombrero, like a impostor Hipster smoking a weed. Honest. All hunched over the saddle, leering at the air. There's a close-up shot of me drinking from a beer bottle in the saddle. It's ridiculous. I have been hunched over my typewriter since I was eleven, that's what it is. I don't think I'll be a rancher. I'll live on a barge in the Hudson River, right by the Fulton Fish Market, and play my chromatic harmonica which I will soon buy in a Larimer Street pawn shop.

Sometimes I go out in the alfalfa field and sleep. I take walks with my dog and throw him in the irrigation ditch just for kicks. I buy eggs at a farm for 24c a dozen, and heavy cream. There are sunflow-

---

2. Whittaker Chambers was the author of *Witness* (1952). In 1948 Chambers told the House Un-American Activities Committee of the existence of a "Red" underground in federal offices and implicated State Department employee Alger Hiss as a spy.

ers and prairie-snowballs and long green fields, and snow mountains: as I said to somebody, "I am Rubens and this is my Netherlands." I've been drawing pictures of the scene. I hitch-hike to Denver and lurk on Curtis street, in the poolhalls and the 10c movies, and drink huge beers in Larimer Street saloons. I go riding around at night with Justin W.B. [. . . .] He is going to take Giroux and I to the opera, free. One night he drove me around Denver (the first night, in fact) and he had one of his bright boys with him, and spotted that damn spotlight of his into people's windows to explain the Denver interior decorating trend. "Provincial," his bright boy sneers. They show me castles in the night, bought by fabulous mining barons; explain everything to me. I prefer talking about Neal and the others [. . . .] I have to make my choice between them and the Rattling Trucks, and I chose the Rattling Trucks, where I don't have to explain anything, and where nothing is explained, only real. REAL REAL, see? Shee?

I haven't had a cent in my pocket. Maybe Giroux will soon give me an advance on "On the Road," which is become a novel by now. In any case, enough about all this, and on to other matters.

[. . . .] Perhaps the greatest thing I ever learned was from my Lowell boyhood buddy George Apostolos. George was the funniest guy in the world, and still is, I think. I mean, I really *learned* things from him—style, tone, the way to look at things. He himself is just a dumb Greek, you see. We had a pal called Iddyboy . . . a huge moronic French-Canadian built like a bull, who [had] the kill-instinct in him. George had practically hypnotized him, and sometimes would go into a wild witch-doctor dance to get Iddyboy excited, and then turn him on me. (When George had a bone to pick.) I would have to defend my life with this bull . . . he would froth at the mouth in direct ratio to George's white eyeball-poppings. (Never mind, never mind, the words.) So one time George and I promoted a six-fight boxing card in the yard of a parochial school. Iddyboy was in the main bout. Geo. and I went through many crazy preparations to be his "seconds" in the ring, that is, we got striped polo-shirts, cigars, derby hats, pails, sponges, blackjacks, everything to look the part as we had seen it in B-movie boxing pictures. We were going to really give him the works in his corner; splash water, puff on cigars, jam the mouthpiece in his teeth, swagger, lurk, dart in and out of the ropes, count money. George (to show you his utter and complete wonderful madness) was even going to imitate the sound of the warning buzzer ten minutes before the round. You've heard those on the radio. "B-a-a-a-a-a-a-!" Only George used to make this buzzer-sound last twenty seconds. "Ba-a-a-a-a-a-a-a-a-a-a-a-a-a-a-a-a-a-a-a-a-a-a-a-a-a-a-a-!" even until the round started.

Iddyboy knocked out his adversary in .21 seconds of the first round and there we were, no chance to perform before a screaming mass of children. I remember this with amazement. Why did we want to do this? What is meant by "Ba-a-a-a-a-a-a-a-a-a-a-a-a-a-a-a-a-a-a-a!?" Why does Ginsberg refer to Blake's "Visions of Beulah" [sic] as "Beulaaaaaaah"? What is Rabelais talking about in his Crazy-Book? And the *Decameron*? What got into Céline when he wrote the first chapter of "Installment" which ends with him lifting his mother's skirts and roaring with rage? What is Shakespeare talking about when he has those mad servants singing crazy little jingles? Or Lear's fool?

You shee, there's something to it.

All my serious passages in "On the Road" (and in Town & City), as I re-examine them, turn out to have this crazy "Ba-a-a-a-a-a-" sound [. . . .]

Et cetera. Your request for objective information on Allen is really a big order. You ought to just invent them out of your own larger naturalistic fund of information than he has. In any case I may see you soon—if I go back with Giroux, I'll definitely go to Provincetown, and I can answer your questions one by one. If in the Fall, and if that is too late, let me know in your next letter and I'll prepare a special brief on A.G. The only trouble is that if I ever prepared such a brief, I would immediately want to use it myself, as I always come up with such Golden Bones. One thing I have is several score letters from him full of information at various points in his life.

I've been thinking about you and have come to a pass where I feel qualified to suggest that, among other things, you should write immense novels about everybody, using the New York scene and the New York types (that is, us.) But on a more social plane. Do you think you can write accurately about a madman like Allen? I should

like to see you invent a potpourri out of [Alan] Ansen,[3] [Bill] Cannastra,[4] Allen G., the people who come to your parties, the San
Remo[5] the bars, the mad parties, big swirling vortexes like [Dosto-
yevsky's] *The Possessed,* not concentrating too much on one individual, but painting a large impassioned portrait like Dickens, only
about the crazy generation. Because this is the *Crazy Gen.* If you do
write the Allen novel[6] . . . revelation is revolution . . . be sure to
introduce everything else you can think of. This I believe to be your
special genius: to see everybody as a whole. That's why you listen to
everybody at parties. What Allen does at parties is wink at everybody. He's up to something else. But you're concerned with the Can-
vas of it. Now if you really think I ought to send you objective
information on Allen, tell me outright. What can I say? Born in Paterson in 1926; his mother was a Communist who went mad; spent
childhood at crazy Communist picnics upstate; his father a school-
teacher. Saw green faces in his window at night. His bucolic life
consisted of one little arbor near the Paterson Gas Works, where he
hid every afternoon, trembling. Burroughs is his Father. Neal is his
God-Bone. Lucien is his Angel. He goes around looking for confir-
mation of coy loneliness, as we all do. He is justifying his mother by
playing madman. His father represents hateful sanity. In one of his
visions he heard a great machine descending from the sky. And all
that. It can be invented. The thing you've got to worry about is, i.e.,
why do I, John Holmes, do this?—what do I mean by saying these
things? Do you understand what I intend to mean? you shee.

Oh balls. I'm a bigger bullshitter than any of them.

[. . . .] Anything else? Okay, I hang up. Write me another long
letter, John—See you this September. If I overlooked anything in this
letter I'll catch up to it next time. Have a drunk on me.

Jack

---

3. Alan Ansen was a writer portrayed as "Rollo Greb" in *On the Road.*
4. Bill Cannastra—see letter to Neal Cassady, November 21, 1950 (pp. 235–
236). Cannastra was called "Finistra" in *Visions of Cody.*
5. The San Remo was a Greenwich Village bar.
6. In *Go,* the main character "Stofsky" is Holmes's portrayal of Allen Ginsberg.

Alone in Denver at the end of June 1949, Kerouac wrote a letter to Elbert Lenrow, who had been his professor at the New School, telling him about the books he was reading and writing that summer. Jack found that he had drifted into "a kind of Melvillean thing" in his attempt to work on the novel he was calling "On the Road." In his letter to Lenrow, Kerouac suggested his dissatisfaction with his writing style when he commented that he felt Ginsberg leaning over his shoulder and saying, "You have never sounded more pompous."

TO ELBERT LENROW

June 28, 1949
6100 W. Center Ave.
Denver 14, Colo.

Dear Mr. Lenrow:—

I guess you must have wondered what got into me last May when I suddenly took off from New York. This was only a swift decision on an old idea I had, to establish some kind of "homestead" for myself and family—an idea I had been harboring for years. And inasmuch as there was a lot of prevarication all around, I suddenly packed one night and went, and prayed on the bus that I might have luck in Denver finding a house and all such matters. You know this already: the reason why I could not go to the Museum on your kind invitation, with Allen, that Friday night.[1]

Since then I have learned a few other things that don't seem to crowd a brain I thought was already surfeited with knowledge of such things. The whole idea has really collapsed. It is more interesting than anything else—that is, sad, or disillusioning—it is extremely interesting to learn that a man ought to get his own family instead of trying to surround himself with a second-hand synthetic one; to learn that a woman like my mother, for instance, who has been working in shoe factories since childhood (13), and who had been "yearning" to live in the country and become a grandmother, suddenly learns, on her own hook, that she prefers going back to the

---

1. Lenrow had invited Kerouac and Ginsberg to a screening of Carl Dreyer's film *The Passion of Joan of Arc* at the Museum of Modern Art.

shoe-factory and to the denser and richer excitements of a city, an industrial city whether it is New York or some New England mill city. Yes, my mother is going back to New York this Sunday; has managed to get her job back through friends; and is going to find an apartment. At the same time, my brother-in-law prefers North Carolina (his home) to Colorado, and refuses to go fishing out here out of some kind of pique. In the midst of this, I go right on writing "On the Road" and as a matter of fact feel a little freer than before, which is worth the advance I spent to do all this. It's very funny and the upshot of it is, we had a good vacation in Colorado, with all our furniture and appurtenances, and are all going back.

In September I'll be a New Yorker again, and hope to see you then.

Meanwhile I hope to get another advance on the second novel "Road." Robert Giroux, the Harcourt editor, is flying out here to Denver July 15 either to work on the novel a bit, or just rest prior to returning to N. Y. with me for further revision. I've made plans to give him a good time, through a "cultural tycoon" I know here who runs the famous Central City opera festival in the mountains. This year they're showing Strauss' "Die Fledermaus," which is a charming piece of froth, and beautiful music (I saw a German film of the thing once). At the same time the editor likes outdoor life and here, out in the foothills west of Denver, there are numerous horses to ride for free (friends, you know, crazy horsepeople who go to Roy Rogers movies and refer to that Myth of the Gray West just as people in the New School refer to Stendhal and Turgenev)—much fishing, and so forth. It will be very interesting to be with Giroux awhile and talk to him. He's been too busy so far to get to know me, and I him. Our revision-work, by the way, is going to be very light; it seems that Giroux is proud of my prose (as I frankly am, that is, considered in the light of development, as a first novel). (And everyone had predicted I would have to write the thing over completely.) In any case, that's the story of my life this year.

Incidentally, referring back to "praying on the bus," on second thought now, I assume that my prayers are yet to be answered, that, insofar as I was successful in securing a house in Denver in good order, *that* in turn led to the present denouement, and an opening of my eyes, and a freeing of familial burdens of a sort, which will therefore inscrutably lead me to the real import of the prayers. Right now I have in mind going back to see my first wife, and bringing her to Paris with me next Spring when my royalties come in. In Paris I'll write my Indulgence in Mysteries—"Doctor Sax."

At this moment I can just feel Allen Ginsberg leaning over my shoulder and saying, "You have never sounded more pompous." I don't know why. Actually, as I type this, I'm listening simultaneously to a baseball game and carrying on a desultory conversation with others in the house. So I hope you'll pardon me, Mr. Lenrow. I've yet to develop a "style" for *you*.

I'm eager to see you again and learn further things from you and from your marvelous collection of great works. In your one apartment all the Royal Guts themselves. And those pleasant evenings are matchless.

A word about my present reading, and other things: Alain-Fournier's "Le Grand Meaulnes" (The Wanderer). This is a volume I took furtively from a book-stall in Hollywood, of all places, in 1947, on a night when I sat in a parking lot behind Columbia Pictures studios and made myself a trans-continental lunch out of a loaf of Pumpernickel and slices of cold meat. I intended to read this book all the way to New York on the bus, but ended up "reading the land," as I always do when traveling. But just this week I returned to Mr. Fournier, and find a strange kind of affinity with his efforts, with his whole stock of symbolistic "ritual" (to be dry about it), with his self-pathos and reverie concerning a childhood that must have been greater than his adult existence. I can see who Meaulnes is—a hero, some kid he knew, with a dash he envied; combining that with the magical beauty of Defoe's Crusoe, also a dashing hero; combining the whole thing in fact with the pathos of childhood and the pathos of first reading "Crusoe"; mixing in the slushy schoolyards, the boredom of the classroom, the sudden magic of the blacksmith shop in the French village. "I Haunted a Basket-maker's Shop," the title of one chapter, openly referring to Crusoe; then the strange adventure to the shrouded manor, the pretty girl, the mystery and the sadness of the fete. Another chapter heading: "The Fall Into an Ambush"—this fin-de-siecle, Beardsleyan, sensitive Frenchman shooting his bolt for Stevenson and Defoe instead of Maldoror and Rimbaud, yet retaining the intentions of his generation, symbolism, because this is nearer home to him whether he likes it or not. Do you know what I think?—the significant writers so-called are merely men who can write extremely well, who come up in a generation, asking, a little wearied by silly furors, "What is it you want me to write now?" With Fournier, who really wanted to write a Robinson Crusoe, his question was answered, "Symbolism"—and he labored to make ends meet. Otherwise no one would read him today, or in his own day. And of course, besides, a person always wants to address his fellow men in their own language. It's only that these grand figures like Fournier are conscious of the fact that any language could just as well do for their more eternal purposes, while the mediocre asses go around thinking the manners and moods of their generation represent the very last thing.

For 50¢ I snatched a copy of the complete poems of Spenser, in Denver. "Oh that I might be there, to helpen the laydes their Maybushe beare!" "And in a Dongeon deep him threw without remorse." Remember the night you showed me Gerard Manley Hopkins' notebooks, and I brought your attention to his labours on the mere word "horn"? In the same way now, Spenser has sharpened my appetite for such pursuits (someway) and I conduct private philologies of my own in a notebook, concentrating mostly on tremendous words like "bone" and "door" and "gold" and "rose" and "rain" and "water." The fact that I don't feel "horn" yet indicates a poetic immaturity so far. "And in a Dongeon deep" is so much more tremendous to me, now, than the vague *horns* of secular poesy—but the time will no doubt come. Also, from Spenser, I have been kicked off into poetry-writing of my own; mainly, though, from reading mad Blake occasionally. Recently, also, I read Matthew Arnold's Study of Celtic Literature, and everything in my intention seems to begin to focus. I found a name in Celtic lore, Keinvarvawc. Pretty close hey? From things like Celtic Literature it is possible to pluck up perfect golden bones of images . . . such as the Doors of Bran, who told his lieutenants they would be happy only if they refrained from opening certain doors. This like telling oneself not to open the horror-doors, the dark-doors of futile melancholy . . . a kind of spiritual relativity (happiness is just as sensible, allowable, good, as true, as actual, as unhappiness) . . . why break your head? save it. In strange and Chinese connection with this, therefore, I find that the Gaelic "dorch" means *dark,* the Dutch "Door" means *fool,* and so on:—most of it facetious and full of fun, and fruitful of images. In connection with this, finally, by reading Rabelais, I come to the divine tricks of "facetiousness" and "fun" and therefore, anything goes, one point of reference (as in relativity science) is as true as another, and go to it. *Take liberties* with your art. Here is the latest full title of Doctor Sax to be written in Paris (my Pierre & the Ambiguities, my Ulysses):—

"The Book of the Myth of the Rainy Night; or, the Crazy-Book of Doctor Sax; with Variorum Notes and Hints, etc."

(That's not all. "With an Introduction by Mustapha Nightsoil (that being Carr and Ginsberg) (in Company) Containing Elegies, Riddles, and Roses. etc." And so on. Meanwhile I'm making On the Road a kind of Melvillean thing, in spite of myself. Here, for instance, are excerpts written today: "So by and by all the lights but one dim hall-light were out, and the men were shrouded in May-night sheets, preparing their minds to sleep. Some desultory conversation murmured vaguely among the steel." (This is in jail.) "It was, to be exact, the one moment of true and sad sincerity: for of course men in bed do grow tender and full of wonder, some child-comprehension steals their hammered iron wits, wistfulness and true sighings come by in the dark, and they stare round-eyed at the secrecies and shadows, preparatory to their polite and slumbrous entry in them.

"Red lay like this, idly shuffling his cards on his chest before turning over to sleep, listening to the strange, soft, and demented conversations that carried on here and there down the hall: this night like every night, and his last night turning it into something perhaps beautiful at last, but even so more fatal and hopeless. Poor jailmen! Wished the Chinamen of the night from old green jails to creep? The Chinese prisoners in the cells to his left were silent—Billy Ling and the Hoo-Kang boys; four Oriental mouths held closed and sealed, or perhaps just secretly quivering with the quivering motion of the earth they could feel spite of steel and shelved suspension.

"To his right Eddy Parry seemed to moan, alone; to roll his own bones on the hard, hot pad; unless he moaned to someone in the next cell further. Old Dad and Chazz Williams hooted crazily about something, then suddenly talked with equal incomprehensible verve about something, in low, earnest, at last excited tones. A monotonous drone arose from further, where (other conversations going on). From the other side of the tier, muffled, sad-like voices of men like Yogi and the Hook, and Big Czech and Rocco and all the gunmen of Blood Inc. came swimming on murmurous waves, as if the jail—a ship in full sail—were at sea, on an ocean May-dark, wound about with salty roses, glowing slowly on golden waters, off raven coasts somewhere, some World's East, and the voices in general complaint were the voices of old Sea Sisters in the hour of reverie. The voices diminished as the cradle softly-seeming rocked. And when the silence increased, then it was possible for Red and anyone else who was awake and listening, to hear the great sea-roar of New York outside: the rumorous Saturday night stretching its tides far over the wash of the vast eventful plain—with its towering Knight-island, and basins, and outreaching apian dark flats to Rockaway, and to Yonkers cliff, to blue-shawled Jersey, and the Jamaican night of ten million secret and furiously living souls to which Red, now considering it, half-drowsy, would soon return, himself a secret and furious and excited motion in that ocean antique. For what reason?"

This is uncorrected. "Apian," by the way, is a word culled from my "beat" collection of books (Allen's opinion) that I showed you last winter; from the Celtic book by Arnold. It means "watery" or "water-issued."—the "apian land" of the Greeks being therefore IS-LANDS. There is something of course distinctly watery about the Rockaway plain south-east of Brooklyn. Therefore, an example here of how I am working; and studying.

Also I'm reading the Letters of John Keats.

Can you tell me what profit there is in reading Cicero's Offices? I started that last night, and was mystified, and dropped it; returning in favor of Blake's Visions of Beulah. Incidentally, I now have Boethius; and was depressed by the story of his life before I read the Consolations, and stopped right there. How grim it seems—to be executed in the days of Roman Law; in jails, too, unlike my old green jails of Chinamen and hipsters.

Have you seen your millionaire madman with the airplane? Are you enjoying your summer (wherever you are)? I hope this reaches you soon and that you can find time to write to me. It's a lonely spot here (I've no car) . . . and I appreciate letters.

I look forward to seeing you in September.

From a recent letter from Lucien:

"Dear Buddy-bone, has-been queen of the May-bone, Have I met some fine girl yet! The insufferable impudence of the question! Why you tarnished-assed old spent-your-money-bone! Yes I have met a fine girl, the girl to end all girls—all woman and a yard wide. And it ain't one of these here brittle, horseshit New York mannequins, either-bone. No siree-bone! This here heart-of-my-heart hails from North Carolina—she's sweet as honey on the outside and a combination-to-end-all-combinations-bone of generosity and determination on the inside. You want a vignette of this woman-bone, you say. You old fart head, you. Why this woman would bust out of a vignette like an unbroken filly out of a loading chute, stomp on it and kick it over the moon just out of deviltry. Bone, bone, bone, bone, bone, bone. BONE."

In Chaucer, by the way, "bone" is PRAYER. "Lawdy dem bones, dem bones, dem dry bones." And Ginsberg's latest poem: a skeleton lamenting, take my flesh, take my eyes, take my love, take my life, "but leave my bones alone." To which I add: The God-Bone will prevail. Isn't this interesting?

And from a Ginsberg letter recently:

"I harken back to your letter to say, that the dirty ditty in my work comes from the feeling that I have that all I and other people secretly want . . . also it's happened to me several times that while walking up a rainbow, when I get to the other side I find not a pot of gold but a bedpan, full. But I am not disappointed, because shit is gold. What else would gold be, but that, and rain? and water? So that the key has been to remind them (people) that the shroudy stranger has a hard on; and that the key to eternal life is through the keyhole; and so I make great big sensual hints; and not dirty jokes, mind you, but serious hidden invocations . . . And not only that, I'll have this long serious conversation with them, just as if the two of us were in the same head."

There's much more, of course, but just look at those crazy-simple expressions . . . "walking up a rainbow," "conversation in the same head," etc. I had told Allen that the tone of his poetry was like a dirty ditty, a New Jersey joke, as against my false Biblical tone in this line:

"Worry therefore not for green,   (And that was his
And dark, which deceptive signs are,   answer). No
Of Golden Milk.   more paper. As ever,
   Beelzebub is but the Lamb."

               Jack

In July 1949 Kerouac wrote to Ginsberg, who had sent letters from Columbia Presbyterian Hospital, where he had gone for psychiatric observation after Huncke was put in jail. Jack wrote Allen to tell him that Robert Giroux had arrived in Denver and was interested in Ginsberg's poetry. Jack also asked if Allen had received any letters from Burroughs and Cassady, whom Kerouac wanted to visit after leaving Denver.

TO ALLEN GINSBERG

               July [26] 49
               [Denver, Colo.]

Dear Allen:—

This must be brief. This is all the paper I have in the empty house a-moving—I think now I know what you mean. If only you could be straight like Yeats and come right out with it—and if I too did so. I sit here at the table. Your letter at my side. [. . . .]

Now listen:—I have told Robert Giroux all about you and he is of course interested. This is the man who went to see Ezra Pound at the nuthouse with Robert Lowell. (Tell you all about details.) When he was leaving, Pound shouted from the window: "Where are you going? Aren't you eligible?" Since then Lowell went mad. Giroux is a little scared. He went to see Thomas Merton[1] at the monastery. He knows [T. S.] Eliot. He is a big intellectual Catholic N.Y. Ignu— You'll see. Bring him your volume of works to Harcourt Brace at 383 Madison—tell him your name. He knows you. He agreed that dead eyes see. But remember that he is also a big businessman like Harrington would like to be—a stockholder in the company, editor in chief, and member of the Opera Club (with Rockefellers.) Be smart, now, and don't shit in your pants. The world is only waiting for you to pitch sad silent love in the place of excrement. Okay? By sad silent love I guess I mean some kind of compromise. But a *bleak one*, see? In daylight be bleak. All set. You may be published now.

Your stories of the madhouse are so actual that I feel again as I did in the Navy nuthouse—scared and seeing through heads. I used to sit with the worst ones to learn. Be kind and allow that I sought to see. Oh for krissakes, I know everything . . . don't you know that? We all do. We even all know that we're all crazy. All of us are sick of our sad majesties. Don't be so pedantic. *Mush!*

[. . . .] I wandered around Denver the other night looking for Pommy [Neal Cassady] somehow. A black gal said "Hello Eddy." I knew I was really Eddy—was getting closer to Pommy. It was a mystic night in the Mexican-Nigger Denver.[2] There was a softball game. I thought it was Pommy pitching. I thought any moment LuAnne would sneak up behind me and grab my cock. The stars, the night, the lilac-hedge, the cars, the streets, the rickety porches. *Down in Denver, down in Denver, all I did was die.*

Then I saw your Denver Doldrums [poems] in my desk—Ah. Do you know what Giroux did? He revised the child saying from a dark corner, "I see you . . . peekaboo!" to just "I see you . . ." I asked

---

1. Thomas Merton (1915–1968), American Jesuit author of the best-selling *The Seven Storey Mountain* (1948). Kerouac dedicated two poems to Merton, published in *Monks Pond*, summer 1968.

2. See *On the Road*, Part Three, Chapter 1: "At lilac evening I walked with every muscle aching among the lights of 27th and Welton in the Denver colored section, wishing I were a Negro. . . . I wished I were a Denver Mexican, or even a poor overworked Jap, anything but what I was so drearily, a 'white man' disillusioned. All my life I'd had white ambitions. . . ."

him if he knew what he had done and he said "of course." He likes me, by the way; we're going to go to shows & operas together in N.Y. A new great friend of my life. He hitch-hiked with me so as to understand "On the Road." He is Eliot's editor, remember, and Van Doren's pal. He knows everybody—Spender[3] et al, Jay Laughlin[4] (New Directions), etc. He hitch-hiked with me in my wilderness.

I am hitch-hiking to Detroit tomorrow. No more letters to 6100 W. Center. See you in N.Y. in 2 weeks. I don't know anything about those crazy Jewish cats in your nuthouse.[5] Maybe I will in time. [. . . .]

Please do what you say—go get Dennison[6] & Pommy. I've written twice to Pommy, no answer. What's the matter? I'll write to Dennison and tell him to move to N.Y. Why are we all camping in California, Texas and Colorado? I would love Dennison to go to Europe with me. Also his trust fund would be a fortune out there, where one lives well on $30 a month. Ask Adams if this is not so. [. . . .] I want us all together before it is too late, before the Season dies from neglect (as they always do in time.) Why? Do you mind my questions? C'est tranquil ça—Excuse my soul.

As ever, Jack

---

3. Stephen Spender (b. 1909), English poet.

4. James Laughlin, poet and founder of New Directions, the publishing house that published excerpts from Kerouac's *Visions of Cody* in 1959.

5. "Jewish cats" is a reference to Carl Solomon, whom Ginsberg met at the Psychiatric Institute of Columbia Presbyterian Hospital. Ginsberg originally titled his most famous poem "Howl for Carl Solomon." On July 13, 1949, Allen wrote a letter to Jack from the hospital telling him that Solomon had revealed to him that "there are no intellectuals in madhouses." Ginsberg went on to say that Solomon "is the real Levinsky—but big and fat, and interested in surrealistic literature. He went to CCNY and NYU, but never graduated, knew the village hipsters . . . and he is familiar with a great range of avant garde styles —also a true Rimbaud type, from his teens. . . . Because of Solomon, I am reading in all the little magazines about the latest Frenchmen. One is named Jean Genet, he is about the greatest—greater than Céline, perhaps, but similar. Huge apocalyptic novels by homosexual hipster who grew up like Pomeray in jail. . . ."

6. "Dennison" was the name Kerouac gave Burroughs in *The Town and the City*. "Pommy" was a reference to Neal Cassady.

Lonely after Giroux's visit, Kerouac expanded on his feelings for Cassady in a letter to Neal, whom Jack wanted to persuade to join him on a grand European holiday after he received the second part of his advance for The Town and the City. *Ginsberg's and Burroughs's brushes with the law were still on Kerouac's mind, and he had decided that it was "much more sensible to go someplace like Italy as a 'student' than be 'beat' in American cities. . . ."*

TO NEAL CASSADY

Thurs. July 28 '49
Denver

Dear Neal—

Let me put it in a real great elaborate way, my dear buddy. Just now as I was looking for some writing paper in my suitcase (all I've got with me), I came across an old letter written to my father by a fellow printer in the winter of 1942. My father was in Lowell and the man, Oscar, was in New Haven. What kind of letter? You remember how you and I dug the old railroad men we saw all over the country last winter?—we saw them with their lunchpails in the night in Baltimore and Carolina and Texas & Bakersfield. We dug them as old workmen, we understood something about them—Well, Oscar says to my father: "Work is good down in Baltimore I hear, but it's not so good here. The weather's been freezing lately but my room is warm enough. A young waitress is now living in your old room 26 but I don't get to talk to her too much. You know me, just plodding along and satisfied enough so long as I get a warm room and good food.—God bless that man [Franklin Delano] Roosevelt." etc. This is a letter my father got long ago from another oldtimer like him. It made me wonder—and think—

Because just an hour ago I was standing in my yard looking at the great heat lightning over the plains, and to the west over the mountains. I thought the lightning seemed more intense in the mystic east (New York, Allen, etc.) and strangely wild over the mountains of the west (Frisco, you, etc.) I had a desire to go in both directions at the same time.

The oldtimer's letter is not full of desires, but stoically resigned to human limits.

Who am I to be otherwise?

II

(Let's divide the chapters.)

My editor of Harcourt, Brace—Robert Giroux, a big literary cat, the Golden Boy of Publishing right now (only 35)—came to Denver to work on the manuscript with me. B.[1] kindly took us all over (other expenses on the publisher), but the main thing is that we became close friends. I must admit that he has influenced me, to wit, he pointed out that I had no need to write about wizards like Doctor Sax, but only about people. He knew how Allen had influenced me with mad image-makings and crazy "oops!" writing. (He is however interested in Allen, I talked it up plenty, and Allen may now take his volume of works to him.) I agreed with him; I saw the *mush* in over-symbolizations . . . I even now see the reality of people as phantasy in itself (as you always did.) Reality is phantasy—*of course*!

Who are Allen and I to invent private poetic myths in a real, serious world? (A world like yours and your poor infected thumb.)

III

Do you follow my poor attempts?

Let's approach everything I want to say in this manner now:—

You and I will always be friends. I even want to help you the rest of my life—that is, with money. When I have it you will receive some. October 1950 is my date with gold, the first royalty backlog payments. Then there's the possibility of selling the book to the movies, already underway in the Harcourt office. Thousands.

But money alone is not enough, and besides it would give me no joy to just send you money when I could.

What I want is us to stop fooling around now and get involved in each other, as we should, and in work. You can't pitch tires all your life. You don't have to so long as you can benefit in the future from my efforts & "position." Don't you see the routine? How can you

---

1. Bob Burford.

be so stupid as to suppose that I've never known the fear of jail? Were the cops any kinder to you than to me when we were stopped across the country last winter?

Do you realize that you *look* like a jailbird?—(and that I try to look like one with you?)

Of all the teachers you have had don't you think I'd really be the hippest? Have you known how much knowledge I conceal in order to learn more? Why should I have to tell you this?

I'm convinced you should attempt to make yourself a writer—and an existence in it—a living. Also, there's nothing you have to learn. You know enough. All you need is the habit of work. Now that I can push your work with authority, there's no reason for you to be childish about having to write and work.

One of the big routines in society is to "look right." Old men with white hair and black-ribbon glasses "look right"—no cop, no prick dares question their freedom. It's all an evil game. I change faces a hundred times a day in knowledge and aversion of this. For too long you've let your aversion and defiance to the cheap rules of society rule your actions . . . You must begin to protect yourself by playing the game. [. . . .]

IV

I can show you the way to what you somewhat sarcastically called the "world of the big boys." It's nothing but a big bore and balloon.

See the routine?

But once in this world you need not fear the American Gestapo that hounds the American Dispossessed . . . the poor, the beat, the "characters." It's all a big hypocrisy. You will be free to live *your own way*, then, more than you think you are now. While the world is still stupid we must be wise.

Later on it will all really be a garden—I'm convinced.

V

But you must also stop feeling like the student, the novice—he who is taught by the Justins & Allens. This is your own form of Oedipus complex, to take on the role of he who's being helped, to "flirt." Remember that I've always been a lone wolf—and that even B. used to think I was "no good" because I never indicated anything else to him. It's all *inside:* why should he know? indeed, how *could* he know, unless I told him, and why should he believe it, and why should I care?

Not bullshit but real work.

Think of the enormous fund of information you have, and the mental health to write (zeal of soul), and the command of realities. What a Chekhov you can be! Why not?

How? What can I do?

I can plug your work; I can help you out with details; I can explain doubts. I can do a lot of things—and I want to [do] them because we're buddies and I can do it.

VI

Notice this, for instance:—

I have a suggestion to make:—

This Xmas I will receive another grand from the company. In order to stretch it out I plan & desire to go to Italy, where one can live very well on *$30 a month* and I can also collect $105 per month on G.I. school. Besides I want to speak Italian like Joyce, and visit his Trieste. Moreover my great editor will be in Rome in the Spring. I want to stretch out my grand till the big payoff in Oct. 1950, and dig European culture with real seriousness (language & museums & myths.) I want to bring Edie with me.

How about you? Could you come? If you wanted to bring Carolyn could you save a few hundred dollars for fare? If alone—I can swing it.

What would I do there? Just catch up on my sleep, eat, love, & write. Prices & hecticness are high in U.S.

For the other day I did what you always do. I worked in the Denargo Markets[2] from 4 A.M. to 6 P.M. unloading a boxcar-and-a-half of cantaloupe crates, 14 hours of impossible labor (for I had walked 4 miles to work at 2 in the morning without sleep since the previous night, and walked home again)—all for $13.81. Moreover I was not asked to come back because I was not as fast as the Japs.

---

2. See *On the Road,* Part Three, describing how he "worked awhile in the wholesale fruit market . . . the hardest job of my life. . . ."

(You know I spent my first grand on this ludicrous attempt to settle my family in Denver—my mother dug Paul and went back to her job in N.Y. a few weeks ago.)—(Ah me, I recall the letters I used to write to you about the blessed family idea. They can settle their own affairs now. Only my mother is still great but whether she likes it or not Edie and I are re-uniting again, my own mad chick.)

Therefore, being broke again, I tried to work at Denargo. I realized of course that the cops don't bother you as long as you're working. This is what is wanted of man today—to "stay out of trouble," "keeping busy." Old Bull [Burroughs] is always right on the subject.

But that's not for me.

I want my freedom. And right now it's much more sensible to go someplace like Italy as a "student" than be "beat" in American cities, as we both are right now.

It's safer . . . until the day when everything for me will be safe (and for you too.) Just become one of the big boys, that's all. Huncke's always said this, of course.

So Italy . . . What about it?

VII

Besides, I know literature and I would bet all on you instead of Harrington, Holmes, Allen & even Bill & Lucien, for all their finesse. Yours is the gaunt soul of a Dosty [Dostoyevsky]. Believe me.

Let's you and I revolutionize American letters and drink champagne with the Hollywood starlets. How much you want to bet I can lead us to this?

We must make specific plans. Sooner or later we should make our homes in the same block—sooner or later you must write & write —sooner yet we must get together and angle the thing out.

VIII

With your throwing arm, by the way, we could make a great southpaw pitcher perhaps. Have you ever pitched? You could inquire about the Seals' tryouts when your thumb is better . . . right in Frisco.

Still and all, Ed McKeever, Cornell coach during the war, once said at Boston College that I was the "best halfback he ever saw"— he told this to Frank Leahy of Notre Dame.

Yet I had big visions of making incarnate the mortal idea of existence in furious novels. [. . . .]

Enough of Chapters.

- -

How silly this all sounds, but it's serious.

I can't make up my mind, if I ought to go to Frisco from here before going to Detroit to pick up Edie then New York for publicity work on the book. If you know of a job I could visit you for a few weeks, and earn fare back.

Will write to Hinkle & Holmes.

I am unable to understand your love life, old man—when I left it was all LuAnne, no Carolyn; now it's all Carolyn, no LuAnne (and a broken thumb & Ray Murphy with Stiletto.) Set me straight. And another child? How you going to support your family? Ah I guess you're getting further and further from me, and that's that. I still immaturely think of life as pleasure & kicks & wherever roam. It may all be swallowed up in the world of divergences. Goodbye, Neal.

If you insist that I have a star on my forehead, go ahead.

How sad.

Details on Allen:—Jack Melody[3] (remember Xmas and the Long Island pad? television set? family?)—and Vicki and Huncke, while living at Allen's on York Avenue, loot home of detective in L.I. of $15,000 in goods and stash at Allen's, with Allen's permission. Next noon Jack Melody loses head when cops hail him for going up one-way street, and speeds off, cops in pursuit. All culprits in car. Reason for trip:—Allen carrying his letters & papers & poems to Eugene's. No other reason. Car overturns. Allen's glasses broken. Letters of Neal, Lucien, Bill, Jack, all poems, seasons, doldrums, scattered in wreckage. Allen staggers off blind. Feels the wrath of God has arrived. Jack caught, Vicki and Huncke escape in crowds. Allen wanders streets of L.I. City blind. Finally Vicki, in Melody's brother's car, with Huncke, picks up Allen and they go back to York pad, to dig the heat. No heat. They discuss. Pad full of $150 suits & a television set. Poor Jack Melody.

----

3. Jack Melody was one of Huncke's accomplices in petty crime in New York.

Knock on door. Cops come in. Big detective clue . . . phone number in Vicki's missing shoe in wreckage led to location of pad, through cat called Zaza.

The end. Big headlines & pictures in *News* & *Mirror*. Our own poor faces . . .

Everybody indicted except Allen, for whom Van Doren & Trilling intercede.[4] Allen committed to nuthouse. Cops want to know who is Lucien, Neal, Bill, Jack? (in letters.) Allen now in nuthouse—722 W. 168th Street Medical Center, N.Y.C. (6 North). Writes: "I am now become a BLEAK PROPHET—bleak thoughts, bleak eyes, bleak smile."

Is allowed to go out each weekend & will be completely free in Sept.—Lucien not troubled by parole, who know relationship. Everything really okay.

Except for Huncke who almost dies from infection in jail hospital; and says we are all just "yipping" in a pre-ordained world. No star on his forehead—not same kind.

Meanwhile, two days later, Old Bull busted for junk in Nola [New Orleans]. Car confiscated. Goes to rot in [jail], Route One, Texas, with Joan & kids.

[. . . .] Everybody separated in California, Texas, Colorado, New York, and jail.

Everybody really camping.

Jack

In Part Three of On the Road, *Kerouac described coming from Denver to Cassady's house in San Francisco, arriving in the early hours of the morning. "I was burning to know what was on his mind and what would happen now, for there was nothing behind me any more, all my bridges were gone. . . ." When Kerouac wrote* On the Road, *he used passages of Neal's letters to him in the spring and summer*

---

4. On June 15, 1949, Ginsberg wrote Kerouac that he had learned "what Van Doren means by society . . . [is] people getting together to keep each other out of trouble (or away from Tragedy) till they got an inkling of what they're getting into."

of 1949 to describe how Cassady's life had gone "from worse to worse" in his fights with LuAnne and his efforts to support Carolyn, pregnant with their second child. Soon after Kerouac arrived in San Francisco, Neal agreed to drive cross-country with Jack, who wrote, "It was probably the pivotal point of our friendship when he realized I had actually spent some hours thinking about him and his troubles. . . ."

As what Kerouac described as "*two broken-down heroes of the Western night,*" he and Cassady drove from San Francisco to Chicago in "*travel-bureau*" cars. They stayed briefly with Kerouac's first wife, Edie, in her family home in Grosse Pointe, Michigan. (Jack and Edie's marriage had been annuled in September 1946.) Finally, in late August 1949, Jack and Neal arrived at his mother's newly painted apartment in Richmond Hill, Long Island. "We were so used to traveling we had to walk all over Long Island, but there was no more land, just the Atlantic Ocean, and we could only go so far."

Back in Gabrielle's apartment, Kerouac picked up his correspondence with his New School professor, Elbert Lenrow. Lenrow had written him on September 18, 1949, enclosing an article from the New Yorker magazine on "the men in high steel" because, as Lenrow said, "certain elements in it" had reminded him of "Kerouac attitudes."

TO ELBERT LENROW

Wed. Sept. 28, '49
94-21 134th St.
Richmond Hill, N.Y.

Dear Mr. Lenrow,

Thanks for your letters, one of which reached me in San Francisco last month. I'm back in town now and absorbed in revision at the Harcourt office, but will soon be rid of work, and will call you. I enjoyed the article on the Caughnawaga Indians, knew something about them previously thru my mother, who knew some of them in the early 1900's at Lachine. Your letter from Virginia Beach was particularly enchanting . . . sea-lulls abounding therein.

Perhaps sometime this winter I can bring Mr. Robt. Giroux, my editor, to your house of an evening for music and talk. We can arrange such a matter when we meet. I told him about you.

Allen Ginsberg is at present "stationed" in the Medical Center uptown, in lieu of the shades of the prison-house. He's "under observation" and has been released but prefers to remain awhile, so they let him stay on. He has weekends off completely from Friday evening till Monday morning. You can call there (WAdsworth 3-5200) and leave messages but cannot speak to him. He usually calls back. If you call, do so during the week, mornings or afternoons. The address is A.G., 5 North, 722 W. 168th St. NYC.

A New School bulletin mailed to me reveals the fact that you are teaching a fullblown course in the classics. What? no Boethius?!!

> Your fellow Tristanophile
> (or is it Tristanomane?)
> Jack K.

Kerouac wrote his last extant letter from 1949 to Charles Sampas, the brother of his friend Sebastian Sampas in Lowell. Charles Sampas was writing a column for the Lowell Sun, *and Jack sent him a letter at the newspaper to tell him about the imminent publication of his first novel,* The Town and the City, *proudly pointing out its close connections to his hometown.*

TO CHARLES SAMPAS

> Dec. 27, 1949
> 91–21 134th St.
> Richmond Hill, N.Y.

Dear Charley:

I'm sure you remember me, Jack Kerouac, and even more your old cry for a novel about Lowell by a native LOWELLIAN (or Lowellite). In three years of work, from 1946 to 1949, during which time my father Leo died of cancer, I wrote a long novel about Lowell—and about New York City—entitled "The Town and the City."

It was accepted by Harcourt, Brace & Co., by editor-in-chief Robert Giroux, and will appear on the bookstands all over the country on Feb. 23, 1950. One of the heroes is Sammy, whose name is Alex Panos in the novel. It covers the period from the 30's on through the war and after.

It's not strictly autobiographical, since I used various friends and girl-friends, and my own parents, to form a large family, the Martin family, [who live] in an old Victorian house on Galloway Road (which is actually Varnum Avenue). So that at one point, when the hero Peter Martin meets Alexander Panos, he realizes that all his life he has seen an old ramshackle house across the river, the Panos house (which I recall could be visible from Varnum Avenue), without knowing that a great friend of his life lived there.

The first lines of the novel read: "The town is Galloway. The Merrimack River, broad and placid, flows down to it from the New Hampshire hills, broken at the falls to make frothy havoc on the rocks, foaming on over ancient stone towards a place where the river suddenly swings about in a wide and peaceful basin, moving on now around the flank of the town, on to places known as Lawrence and Haverhill, through a wooded valley, and on to the sea at Plum Island, where the river enters an infinity of waters and is gone. Somewhere far north of Galloway, in headwaters close to Canada, the river is continually fed and made to brim out of endless sources and unfathomable springs. The little children of Galloway sit on the banks of the Merrimac and consider these facts and mysteries. In the wild echoing misty March night, little Mickey Martin kneels at his bedroom window and listens to the river's rush, the distant barking of dogs, the soughing thunder of the falls, and he ponders the wellsprings and sources of his own mysterious life.

"The grownups on Galloway are less concerned with riverside broodings. They work—in factories, in shops and stores and offices, and on the farms all around.

". . . If at night a man goes out to the woods surrounding Galloway and stands on a hill . . ." . . . And it begins this way, going on for 512 pages, and dealing with everything I could think of about Lowell life and the war, and the City, and death. The last chapter is the funeral of the father, George Martin, printer, in "Lacoshua, N.H."

when the entire large Galloway family is reunited after the war and sad scatterings, at the site of their true life & origin . . . New England.

I'm having a review copy sent to you at the Sun, and only hope you will enjoy it. The book is slated for some success, if indications of advance sale (20,000 copies), advertising outlay ($7500), and the fact that an English publisher, Eyre & Spottiswoode, accepted it in proof, means anything. Several advances and a Guggenheim fellowship also came my way. I'm the last to deny amazement at this strange success.

So this brings us by a "commodius vicus of recirculation past river Eve and Adam"[1] back to the nights when we'd all bump on the Square—Sammy, Ian MacDonald, Mike Largay, Conny Murphy, Eddy Tully, yourself and others like Jim O'Dea and John Koumantzelis and so many others, and chat about what we all felt . . . an enriching background for all of us. Strange, dark Lowell. And the night I talked to you at your table in the Moody street club, only four years ago, and you advised me to stay out of Lowell. I understand that too. But it's all the same, and Lowell, like Winesburg Ohio or Asheville North Carolina or Fresno California or Hawthorne's Salem, is always the place where the darkness of the trees by the river, on a starry night, gives hint of that inscrutable *future* Americans are always longing and longing for. And when they find that future, not till then they begin looking *back* with sorrows, and an understanding of how man haunts the earth, pacing, prowling, circling in the shades, and the intelligence of the compass pointing to nothing in sight save starry passion . . . strange, is strange, how we be-dot infinity with our thoughts and poor rooftops, and hometown, then go away forever.

Where is Michael Largay these days? I hear no more from Ian. The invisible strings got tangled in the night. Sammy—I have all his letters and many poems, and scoured them for his speeches in *The Town and the City*. I wonder about his kid brothers and sisters who, in those days, sat on the porch singing like Saroyan children. And

---

1. A reference to James Joyce's *Finnegans Wake* (1939).

how, when the munitions plant was built near the foot of Stevens, Sammy said, "How green was my valley."

Hoping to hear from you soon, Charley, and that you will enjoy my contribution to the general lore and that all is well with you & yours.

Sincerely,
Jack K.

P.S. Whatever happened to Bill Sullivan, formerly of the Leader, later Notre Dame publicity? If you know, please insert info whenever you have time to write.

1950

Back in New York City in fall of 1949, Kerouac had what he later called "a season of parties" while he made extensive cuts, at his editor Robert Giroux's request, of the manuscript of The Town and the City. *When the novel was published in March 1950, it had sympathetic reviews but disappointing sales.*

In May 1950 Harcourt Brace paid Kerouac's expenses to go to Denver to publicize his book. The following month Cassady unexpectedly arrived in Denver from New York. Burroughs had moved his family to Mexico City the previous winter, and he invited Kerouac to visit him. Thinking that Jack had an income from his book royalties, Burroughs wrote him a letter in January 1950 saying that "if you want to save some of the money you are making, Mexico is undoubtedly the place for you. A single man lives high here including all the liquor he can drink for $100 a month."

In June Cassady drove Kerouac to Mexico City from Denver, a ride that began as "the most pleasant and graceful billowy trip in the world," described in Part Four of On the Road. *In Mexico Neal hoped to get a divorce from Carolyn so he could marry Diana Hansen, a woman he had lived with in Manhattan who was pregnant with his child. Kerouac became ill from dysentery in Mexico, but later, while staying with Joan and Bill Burroughs, he tried to revise his early versions of* On the Road *and* Doctor Sax *into a single book. Despite his dissatisfaction with the result, Kerouac submitted this early version of* On the Road *to Robert Giroux, who rejected it.*

In July 1950, after Kerouac returned from Mexico City to his mother's apartment in Richmond Hill, he found that his closest friends had left Manhattan. His letters from 1950 begin at this point. Lucien Carr, visiting Burroughs in Mexico City, let Jack stay briefly in his loft at 149 West Twenty-first Street. Ginsberg had been released from the mental hospital and was living at home in New Jersey. Cassady went back to San Francisco after the Southern Pacific Railroad called him back to work as a brakeman. He joined Carolyn, who had given birth to their second daughter, at 29 Russell Street and resumed their marriage.

After The Town and the City *was published by Eyre & Spottiswoode in London, Jack corresponded with his English editor, Frank Morley, and mentioned that he was rewriting* On the Road.

July 27 [1950]

[New York City]

Dear Mr. Morley,

I was hugely pleased to see that wonderful cover Eyre & Spottis-woode used [for the English edition of *The Town and the City*]. You were right, it's much better than the American one. I haven't heard a word about British reviews—unless there weren't any. If at any time you'd like to send me some I'd appreciate it.

I handed in *On the Road* to Bob [Giroux], he rejected it; I got an agent, broke off from Harcourt; tried the ms. at Farrar Straus Young . . . they didn't altogether reject it but suggested revising. Then when I started revising it, I realized I'd rather write the whole thing all over again, which I'm about to do; figure to be finished in two months. At least now I'm my own editor. The book will be much better now. My agent is Rae Everitt at MCA. Stanley Young remembers the night at the Chatham bar and at Artie Shaw's later.

Has my advance come through yet? I ask because it hasn't ap-peared in the latest royalty report. When it does my entire debt to Harcourt will be wiped out and then clear royalties will be forthcom-ing in October—not much, but a good feeling.

How are you and when are you coming to America next? It's too hot right now, I wouldn't advise it right now. It must be beautiful in England in the summer. I always wondered what an English sum-mernight must be like.

Did you meet my wonderful friend Seymour Wyse? [. . . .] My third book will be about jazz and bop[1]—with Seymour as the wan-

---

1. In Kerouac's letters from John Clellon Holmes during the previous spring, Holmes had encouraged him to clarify his ideas about "beat" and "hip." In a long letter to Kerouac on April 28, 1950, Holmes told him that "it's time we thought about our material. Call them hipsters, the 'beat generation,' 'postwar kids,' or our own displaced persons whatever you will." In Kerouac's plot synopsis of his *On the Road* book for Frank Morley, he wrote that the novel was "on the surface a story of many restless travelings and at the same time an imaginative survey of a new American generation known as the 'Hip' (The Knowing), with emphasis on their problems in the mid-century 50s and their historical relationship with pre-ceding generations. . . . This new generation has a conviction that it alone has known everything, or been 'hip,' in the history of the world. . . ."

dering stranger from England following it around the country like some 19th Century be-slouched-hatted wanderer among the Impressionists throughout France. That's not expressing it too well but you will see.

I haven't expressed my gladness and gratitude that my book was finally published in England. Though remote, the honor is like horns over the sea or something. I hope everyone in your family is fine and that you are enjoying life as ever. Skold!

Yours sincerely,
Jack

p.s. Presently I'm living in a loft very much like your hideout in the fifties. A rolltop desk, bourbon, friends . . . everything's fine.

After The Town and the City *received mixed reviews in Kerouac's hometown newspaper, the* Lowell Sun, *he wrote to Yvonne Le Maître, who had written a favorable review in a Worcester paper,* Le Travailleur, *revealing his painful identification with his French-Canadian roots: "I cannot write my native language and have no native home any more, and am amazed by that horrible homelessness all French-Canadians abroad in America have." Kerouac also suggested the difficult process of what he called "Englishizing" himself before he could attempt to write "a universal American story."*

TO YVONNE LE MAITRE

Sept. 8 '50
9421 134th St.
Richmond Hill, N.Y.

Dear Miss (Mrs?) Le Maitre . . .

Excuse me for writing in English, when it would be so much better to address you in French; but I have no proficiency at all in my native language, and that is the lame truth.

No review [of *The Town and the City*] touched me more than yours. I think it was the best review of them all. There were some in *Newsweek* and *The Times* and *The Frisco Chronicle* that appreciated, and understood the book, but yours understood me too (except for one point I'll bring up) and more than that, I liked the tone and the scope.

I am *not* Francis Martin.[1] I never was anything like Francis Martin. Francis Martin is a caricature of some of the friends I have had who were typical intellectual outcast-types, "decadent" types, from whom I admit I learned a lot but not everything—and not the most important things. Just to prove it: look closer, when you have time, and you will find that "Will Dennison" [Burroughs] the dope addict in the "City" part of the book is the exact prototype of Francis. In the original ms., this would have been more manifest, but we cut it. Francis is, in fact, the prototype of the man Will Dennison was drawn from—a wealthy Middlewestern Harvard esthete who became a drug addict. Francis is the weakest character in the book, because I never dared draining him out full. Next time I will; in another medium, another level. In Lowell I never acted like Francis. I was always with the gang. My solitudes were romantic—like the solitudes of Panos —and not misanthropic. I defend myself strongly on this point because I want you to like me. Francis was my villain.

What amazed me most about your review—which I read and re-read in Mexico City all summer—is the beautiful and elegant French tone that made it seem as though a very aunt of mine had reviewed my book. I felt humble. Your mention of my mother and father warmed my heart. Because I cannot write my native language and have no native home any more, and am amazed by that horrible homelessness all French-Canadians abroad in America have—well, well, I was moved. Someday, Madame, I shall write a French-Canadian novel, with the setting in New England, in French. It will be the simplest and the most rudimentary French. If anybody wants to publish it, I mean Harcourt, Brace or anybody, they'll have to translate it. All my knowledge rests in my "French-Canadianness" and nowhere else. The English language is a tool lately found . . . so late (I never spoke English before I was six or seven). At 21 I was still

---

1. Francis Martin was a character in *The Town and the City*, as was Alexander Panos.

somewhat awkward and illiterate-sounding in my speech and writings. What a mixup. The reason I handle English words so easily is because it is not my own language. I refashion it to fit French images. Do you see that?

Incidentally, I called the family Martin because that can also be a French name . . . Norman. It was one of the few personal clues I wanted to establish. Because I wanted a universal American story, I could not make the whole family Catholic. It was an American story. As I say, the French-Canadian story I've yet to attempt. But you were absolutely right in your few complaints on this score. Isn't it true that French-Canadians everywhere tend to hide their real sources. They can do it because they look Anglo-Saxon, when the Jews, the Italians, the others cannot . . . the other "minority" races. Believe me, I'll never hide it again; as once I did, say in high school, when I first began "Englishizing myself" to coin a term (Me—*faire un Anglais*). My mother laughed and enjoyed and loved your review too. I think you were wonderful.

My book has not sold at all. It is not even discovered. What can I say, except that the world is no good anyway and we all know it. People are all right, though. I blame the stupid channels of advertising and hooroosh that mix bad things with good—for I'll tell you, my book did not sell only because it was drowned in a flood of other books, most of which were dish water (*rinsure du pot*) and junk. It is a decade starting off inauspiciously in mediocrity and war.[2] No need to moan about it. I, personally, feel all the reward I really need when someone like you answers a good word. Hoping you'll write, and give my best to Father Morrisette.[3]

Yours,
Jack Kerouac

---

2. On Sept. 15, 1950, the United Nations forces led by General MacArthur in South Korea attacked the North Korea Communist troops, who had captured the South Korean capital in Seoul. A month earlier, the Atomic Energy Commission released a 438-page guide on civilian defense against atomic bomb attack.

3. Father "Spike" Morrisette was a priest in Lowell who had befriended Kerouac.

Still physically drained from his illness in Mexico City, Kerouac brooded in his mother's apartment over the slow sales of his novel and the collapse of his dream of an easy literary success. In the fall of 1950 he also wrestled with the problem of breaking free of the hold of his previous model, Thomas Wolfe. He wrote in his journal, "For what was the voice in The Town and the City—*a literary American voice. What is my own voice? because I am an artist, no one ever hears it nor my ideas either." In October, high on marijuana, he expanded on these thoughts to Cassady.*

TO NEAL CASSADY

Oct. 6, '50
[Richmond Hill, N.Y.]

Hello There My Dear Neal,

To you I could write a 5000-word letter every blessed day but of course a man must earn his living and plan for the future and save his energy for his work, otherwise I'd do it and keep you well-informed and well-read. Well, I have a thousand things to talk about, but where to begin? Why, begin where I feel like beginning. And when you work on your Cassady-novel, remember this tip from an old, old redoubtable hack. Harrumph! Egad! Kaff-kaff! First let me say that I have been digging the World Series and the tones of the various announcers.[1] This morning I did the World Series the honor of getting up early and blasting ahead of time. There's an announcer from Philly called Gene Kelly who is an exact replica of John Holmes (that is, dig John as a radio announcer), with the same way of *being proud of his verbs,* and so on, like when a groundball is hit, he'll say . . . "a slow, *twisting,* weak roller" as if baseball was the significance of life in itself, the things that happen in it representing in symbols of action, the symbols of (twisting) despair in the "modern world."

---

1. At this time Kerouac wrote in his journal that he wanted to create an "American Times Series to be narrated in the voices of the Americans themselves, beginning with volume I, 'Adventures on the Road' told by a 10-year old Negro boy. Later, stories and sagas told in English, or that is, in particular Americana by Mexicans, Indians, French-Canadians, Italians, Westerners, dilettantes, jailbirds, hobos, hipsters and many more. . . ."

I must say, it's mighty cool. Then quickly I turn to old reliable south-ern-accent Mel Allen, who has that simple back-country mind, like Dean [Moriarty], just pointing out things like . . . "Well, there's Johnny Mize mopping his face with a handkerchief" or "there's Del Ennis picking up a bat at the batrack." You can tell, Neal, how I dig all this; my mind, wrapped in wild observation of everything, is drawn, by the back-country announcer, back to the regular, *brake-man* things of life, and it is such a relief, and such a joy, and even such a Grace from heaven, that I always say: "Yes! Yes! that's right!" à la a fellow whose initials are N.C. (A word about yr. request for t² . . . no, I have no more now, except some left from the San Remo, some Brooklyn-grown, very poor, mentholated you might say, and not worth anything, except I knew the location of the field, which is in a busy thoroughfare, and went there one night with a gang in Tom's car and there's two cruisers criss-crossing slowly in front of the field, and all that t right under pedestrians' noses.) (You know, I'm sure you know, I would, and could, have sent you a bushel of that, spite of poor quality, but quantity.) I tell you, nothing beats the Mexican t, and I am frankly spoiled now. I did a foolish thing . . . gave lots away when I had it. Next Spring you and I'll stock up, man. Meanwhile in Calif. you can secure plenty. Well, did you get the picture I drew, and wasn't it a gone picture? Let me continue with the first train of thought: I've been thinking about *cool* for the past week almost to the point of a theory. Right under my nose I see now John Holmes and Landesman[3] et al are all becoming, or always have been, cool, as opposed to fellows like you and me . . . no word for it, but it sounds like RAW. A raw mind and a cool mind are two

---

2. T: marijuana. Burroughs wrote Kerouac on September 18, 1950, telling him that one of his friends hadn't been able to bring back any marijuana from Mex-ico City to New York. Bill cautioned Jack not to depend on drugs or waste his time with too much "solitary brooding," saying, "You don't have a habit and I would expect you to take full advantage of the freedom for action you have. You know the logical conclusion to the I've-got-it-all-inside proposition is the conclusion reached by certain Tibetan Buddhists who wall themselves in a little cell with a slot where food is pushed in at them, and stay there till they die— This is not my idea of a good deal."

3. Jay Landesman was a friend of John Clellon Holmes and editor of *Neurotica*, an early counterculture magazine.

different minds. The raw mind is usually associated with the physical life, whether athletic, work or just beat (like Huncke); the cool mind is the intellectual emphasis and the physical counterpart of it is a kind of gracefulness . . . a gracefulness that is almost effeminate. That is why Holmes, in his novel, is always referring to me as "awkward" and you as "burly" or whatever. Our feeling for music is raw, too. Don't have to explain that. The reaction is more physical, more jumping-minded, and tends from the art-of-art Tristano groove to favor the art-of-life Wynonie or Lucky Thompson[4] or Trio Shearing (not sextet) or Hucklebuck[5] groove . . . rock, rock. Same with the relationship with women: the cool man is a ladiesman, that is, a man usually to be found among the ladies, where he shines; the raw man, is, in Hal Chase's immortal words, *a lonely fucker* but a more satisfying (physically) fucker in that he knows how to go and go, but can't shine particularly in the drawing-room or perhaps even the boudoir when the lights are still on, who knows? Well, these generalizations satisfy me. I've also been thinking of *cool* with regard to my writing and YOUR WRITING, which is very important to me. The modern young writer is now faced with the problem of many voices in America. A book always has a voice, i.e., in Dostoevsky it's the anonymous monk of Karamazov[6] who has, on the surface, a prissy (almost) gossip-voice but inside of which the reader hears the enormous rushing noise of a great voice muted in the silence of books. Céline seems to have this crazy Frenchman's voice, yelling all the time and saying "Hoik! Hoik! Hoik!" Mark Twain, you can hear him just as plain, saying, "Well, *he* was satisfied," and it's nothing but a Missouri voice on the river pier. Wolfe—a great voice from the howling wilderness; and think, think, think, Neal, if Wolfe had lived and got hung up on this voice of his, and come right out and wrote a book in deliberate voice-from-the-howling-wilderness tones and substance-tale, what *that* would have been, such as, for instance, the voice of Wolfe himself walking on foot from Coast to Coast,

---

4. Eli "Lucky" Thompson, jazz tenor saxophonist.
5. Hucklebuck was a popular song-and-dance step.
6. Dostoyevsky's *The Brothers Karamazov* (1880).

which was undoubtedly his secretest, deepest thought, or among the deepest. For Wolfe was hung up on his ancestors, all of whom had "howling, remote voices like the voices of his kinsman in the hills long ago." Well, since Mexico, I've been trying to find my voice. For a long time it sounded false, of course, For a long time I labored on several other variations . . . one an outright voice for "the boys" (that is, the boys at the office, or the brakemen you see, which will be my ultimate voice); and a voice for the critics, etc., etc. Henry James is a cool voice; Hawthorne is cool. Melville in *Confidence Man* is the strangest voice ever heard in America (best of all reading for hi) (except Gogol, *Dead Souls,* for HI, especially pages 134–135) but the voice of *Confidence Man* is partly Shakespearean with a beautiful interspersion of backwoods voices and nigger voices and all kinds [of] voices. Now, I almost had the urge to TYPE OUT your last letter, the best part, or all of it, for it was the best letter I ever received and the best letter you ever wrote in your life, to show you YOURSELF how you should write, i.e., the way YOU write when you're not hung up on making a LITERARY voice and working two days on one crazy sentence. My important recent discovery and revelation is that the voice is all. Can you tell me Shakespeare's voice per se?—who speaks when Hamlet speaks? HAMLET, not Will Shakespeare, whose voice we've never really heard, except in the sonnets, and that is veiled in poesie. You, man, must write exactly as everything rushes into your head, and AT ONCE. The pain of writing is just that . . . physical cramps in the hand, nothing else, of course. (Incidentally this voice I now speak in, is the voice I use when writing to YOU.) How can I reconcile myself to printing this? I never would . . . What I'm going to do is let the voices speak for themselves. I'm going to write one book in nigger dialect, another in bum dialect, another in hip-musician dialect, another in French-Canadian-English dialect, another in American-Mexican dialect, another in Indian dialect, another in cool dialect, and I might one day write a slim little volume narrated by an effeminate queer. "My name is Roger Dun. Some years ago I had the pleasure of making the acquaintance of a simply marvelous old woman who . . . well I must say, she was simply exciting in every single respect." Or in nigger dialect: "Ain't nobody never loved me like I love myself, except my mother and she's dead.

My daddy, he done gone away so long ago ain't nobody remember what his face look like. Well, I feel lowly and blue and was like to dig a hole in the ground, and cry in it, I feels such tur'ble shame and wantsa die." Or a bum: "In 1932 I left the city of Des Moines, Iowa, and took me a hiball clear to Denver, Colorady, where I was to meet my friend Charley Nebraska One-Eye back of Sim's pool parlor on Larimer street, 'cause we was fixin' to work the harvest together as far up north as Canady. Well, Charley wasn't there, but here come old Neal Cassady down the street and I was fit to bust t'see that old reprobate was still alive n' kicking, and jess as drunk as he ever was." Or a jailbird like Huncke: "Every night I looked out the window and could see Manhattan across the river, and it was one night I was doing this when I realized I must soon go mad. A cat who was in for peddling played a Billy Holiday record in the cell next to mine; I guess I remember it all right, for I can never forget it, and it was 'Easy Living.' " Or a hipster: "Everything was solid that year. I had a pad on tenth street living with a gone little chick from Newark. In Brooklyn I knew the location of a field full of tea. That's what everybody used to say about me, man, that year: 'The trouble with Ervie is he found a field.' Well yes, well yes, I found a field and don't you know, I got high every day of the week for six months, and everything was all right." [*incomplete*]

In October 1950, after Kerouac received a letter from Stella Sampas, the sister of his old friend Sebastian in Lowell, he wrote her a short note thanking her for enclosing a "momento" of Sebastian's for him and gently chiding her for saying she was being morbid when she brought up the memory of her brother.

TO STELLA SAMPAS

Oct. 17 [1950]
[Richmond Hill, N.Y.]

Dear Stella,

Thanks ever so much for sending me Sam's old Goethean card. It brings back added valuable memories, and how can you possibly be

"morbid" sending that when you know I wanted it: we'll all be dead sometime.

How's everybody at home this Fall? I suppose Jim's[1] back in school. I sure wish I could have spent more time in Lowell that time—and more time with you and Jim and the others. Next time I visit Lowell—(and next time I visit Lowell it will be with beard & slouch hat).

Give my best to everybody. And thanks a thousand times for writing to me and sending Sam's momento. Be happy, and if you can't do that, be healthy, and if you can't do that, be good, and I know you are good, and everybody knows it too.

As ever, Yours, Jack K.

A month later, after an exchange of letters with Cassady in which Neal said he was planning a trip to New York City in January, Jack wrote his friend the surprising news that he had just gotten married a second time. Kerouac's second wife was a young woman named Joan Haverty from Poughkeepsie, New York, who had been living in Manhattan with Bill Cannastra, one of Kerouac's friends. As Kerouac told Cassady, Cannastra was killed in a subway accident, and on a sudden impulse ten days after they had met each other, Jack proposed to Joan. The marriage made Kerouac feel "healthy & living again" after the months at home struggling to rewrite On the Road.

TO NEAL CASSADY

Nov. 21 *1950*
[Richmond Hill, N.Y.]

Dear Buddy Neal,

Not much time to say much in the heat of wild manifold activities this very minute, except that your letter was to me one of the finest expressions of a man's soul I've ever read and sits among the greatest things ever written in America—yes—aside from all our personal

---

1. Jim Sampas, one of Stella's brothers.

knowing of it—and tho I cannot answer you till next week you will understand how greatly I cherish all of you. Now listen to hear: I just got married, more details later, great 20 yr. old girl, living with me Richmond, we hitch to her mother's upstate tomorrow, etc. etc. *Joan Haverty Kerouac*, married nov. 17 (impregnated on 18th)? in Judge Lupiano's residence, best man Allen,[1] & Lucien, & Holmes, & Liz (Lucien's); big party afterwards in her pad (Cannastra's former); hundred guests;[2] everything fine; wants to go to Frisco if I can land good job there; wants to go Mexcity; does *all* with me; is dressmaker, designer, model, fulfills me; am healthy & living again—here we go, we're off—can't get over your letter nor can *she*, man—all right? More next week. Hate to leave you now.

Love you so
Jack

Kisses to babies & ladies & all of sunny Cal & San Fran nite. Cannastra—he tried to jump out of moving subway, it pick't up speed, he saw pillar, screamed to be pulled back, young Puerto Rican grabbed him, shirt tore, fell against death.

1. Have bongo drums ready (Cuba-made)
2. Book jacket ready in England
3. 2 stories on market

---

1. In a letter to Cassady written the day after Kerouac's wedding to Joan Haverty, Ginsberg described the bride as "a tall dumb darkhaired girl just made for Jack. Not dumb really, since she's 'sensitive,' and troubled (trying to be on own from family in the big city at age 20), has had men (Cannastra once for a short season), but full of a kind of self-effacing naivete, makes dresses as vocation. . . ."

2. Joan Haverty remembered that she and Jack had invited only a few people to their wedding party after being married by a judge in his Greenwich Village apartment, but "when we got there [to the party] we found at least 200, almost all of them total strangers. . . . You might have expected some bride-kissing or best wishes and all that. Nothing of the kind. A shuffling parade of munchers, guzzlers and sippers just looked me over with the detached curiosity of tired tourists 'covering' one more museum. . . . By the time the night was over, the floor was carpeted with cigaret butts, the beer keg had overflowed, the toilet had been clogged up and a platter of Vienna sausage had fallen behind the refrigerator."

4. Not hi now

5. More, more, in the sense that as the nights proceed all grows clearer and simpler & *easier* and I have recovered my man-guts & can lick my weight in wildcats. What's ahead is okay—except $?

(Excuse 3c stamp—time no object, last stamp. BIG LETTER NEXT WEEK.)

The newly married couple moved into Gabrielle's apartment in Richmond Hill to save money so they could travel to Mexico after Christmas, where Kerouac was sure they would be able to live so cheaply that he could continue writing. Sitting at the rolltop desk in his "den" piled high with Joan's dressmaking material, Jack smoked a joint and wrote to Cassady while his wife showered and his mother watched a news program on television about the escalating war in Korea.

TO NEAL CASSADY

Dec. 3 [1950]
[Richmond Hill, N.Y.]

Dear Neal—

Sitting in my den that you remember which is now made over into Joan's sewing room. Past few weeks I've done more running around and more work than since 1945, I estimate. Blood tests, marriage licenses, ceremony at Judge, big party, hitch-hiking honeymoon, jobs, work, moving clothes & furniture, and all to the tune of our plans to go live in Mexico next year and the great welter of personal possessions and money hassles and madness that will involve, which I welcome most heartily. Re our annual trip to Mexico, it may be you will visit *me* down there someday, but a guy told me t'other day all the retired railroad men from USA spend their lives in Mex. Says you see them all sitting in the park on Juarez (the Prado) in the Spring. As I write this huge piles of material loom behind the typewriter like a dressmaker's dream . . . or like Céline's crazy publisher with the piles of pamphlets that go up in dust when they bash the submarine through the wall. Another welter piling up is not only the need for

me to write and sell stories, and a new job I have doing synopsis for 20th Century at home for pay, but to write that fucking Road. Down the road night; American road night; Look out for Your Boy; Boy on the road; Hit the road; Lost on the road—I don't even know what to call it.[1] My artistic problems now resemble your own. Bliazasted a moment ago unbeknownst to Hopalong Cassidy[2] who is now on tv., in shower, and find life is a dream which I am prepared to accept as a dream, or as a reality, it doesn't make any difference. Well, so I want to go to town now, and am pretty much. Have set of Cuban bongos that I do Conga beat on. [. . . .] Have not even begun answering your last 2 letters as I know you don't mind my reading your mail to others (newlywed husband talk.) Have no personal problems any more, just what will I write and flinching & scratching like W. C. Fields at sight of war news and Chinese hordes[3] in snow, whoo! Wish you would give me exact date of your arrival in NY— Incidentally plan 2 involves going to Frisco and my getting *Chronicle* sports job and Joan and I renting little house like your Russell [Street] one and her making dresses, ain't that gone too? She is originally Hollywood girl, living just off Sunset at Fountain Ave., grew up there and came to Albany at 14. Striking pix is enclosed and you must of course send back without fail as I love it . . . just guess which one. (2nd from left.) Looks like Gloria Jean in "Never Give a Sucker an Even Break" and I am W.C.F.[4] Well man, it's one of those nights when I'd much rather talk to you than write it. Please don't abandon tape-recorder: Allen and I have worked out the pygmy singing &

---

1. Kerouac's journal from this time is filled with possible names for his "Road" novel. Other titles he considered were "Souls on the Road," "Love on the Road," "In the Night on the Road," "Home and the Road," and "Along the Wild Road."

2. Hopalong Cassidy was the hero of a series of B-movie westerns from the thirties, which had a second run when shown on television for a few years beginning in 1948.

3. Five days earlier, two million Chinese communist troops had launched an attack on allied troops in Korea, and on December 3, 1950, the U.N. forces were forced to withdraw. General Douglas MacArthur, commander in chief of the U.N. forces, described the attack as "one of the most offensive acts of international lawlessness" in history.

4. The comedian W. C. Fields.

drumbeat that will stone you. Sure miss you. Joan has girlfriend in L.A. who she says is the greatest and wants you to dig sometime purely for scholastic reasons. [. . . .] if I had to hitch to Frisco to see you now, on $20, I would do it without hesitation or qualms, which was a feeling left me when I "published my book" and I thought I'd be rich and would have to spend the rest of my life avoiding hassles & beatness. Back in them for fair & love it. Love her. Physical strength too: moving the furniture I climbed those Cannastra stairs a dozen times back & forth with all kinds of loads and sometimes ran. When I had the fight in the bar I was unable to do anything like this . . . shortly after I began re-developing my muscles; and now with the mind in order I am again capable of playing football except for phlebitis of course. Well I'm only trying to explain to you that Elitch[5] is bad for muscles unless you keep going like you do all day. My book[6] is not being mentioned by the Xmas lists and not only that the critics who raved about my book have completely forgotten it . . . some who said it was one of the best novels of the year do not mention it . . . I have had the worse shitluck possible with that book and it is the same thing all the time with whatever I do . . . the curse of Melville . . . gods don't even want their favorites to have one peaceful shit in their lifetime . . . books which have a certain amount of talent, and tell a story, are rated above mine which has no talent and no easy story but was described, and as you know is, really a saga and not unworthy of a young Tolstoy: a kind of job hardly anybody can do nowadays, including Faulkner, and yet they all seemed to think it was very huge or very little, and looked around wondering what the others would say, and nobody said anything, and it became the thing, and down the drain goes my *Town and the City* like all the other shit does. To the point where today I certainly don't have the urge to do any more sagas just for my health or "posterity." Well I will do more sagas but they won't be as pretty anymore. I don't see how these cocksuckers could have done a better

---

5. "Elitch" was a code word for marijuana that Neal and Jack coined in Denver on their trip the previous summer.

6. *The Town and the City.*

job trying to fuck me up as a first & second novelist if they had laid out a blueprint in an attic. [. . . .] Now you see why my thoughts turn to Mexico; if I can land a little job with some American company I can stay there the rest of my life . . . some American money turned into pesos . . . and have five kids moreover . . . and my wife is the gal for such a life. Same dream I had in 1947 when I wrote you those wild impractible [sic] letters and Allen said my T & C manuscripts might very well be "the production of a cracked brain." Why am I telling you all this, my dear friend. Well so you'll know. And anything I write from now on is my own business and my own personal possession and have no fear that it will be useless . . .

[. . . .] What would you have done last Saturday night?—here we were in that bar on the corner near Cannastra's house, Cannastra yelling "Up your ass with Mobilgas" and the joint is full of tough hoodlums just drinkin and rarin for a fight; and Lucien with a red shirt and hair all over his face, with his girl, and the flirtations begin. The soldier whose father owns the bar says the place is closed, we can't sit in the booths; evidently doesn't want us there anyway. Well, I see trouble on all sides, and I'm just about to drag everybody out when Lucien quips something at the soldier, the soldier throws beer in Lucien's face, and Lucien takes the glass and breaks it in the guy's face. Here come six, seven hoodlums silently surrounding us; the soldier says, "That's all right, that's all right," and calmly brings the broken glass to the bar. I say to him, "Okay, okay, we're leaving." He says, "That's all right." He pulls Lucien's table out and socks him flush in the face. The girl screams, jumps up. I put my arms around Lucien and I say, "Okay, we're all leaving." Everything's going all right until one of the hoodlums pushes me, and I say, "Don't push ME!" and he says, "Who're you?" and WHAM! he socks me right in the eye. WHAM! I sock him just one in the teeth, and could have thrown ten more when I realize this is going to be murder, because Cannastra and Lucien are so masochistic, and Harrington so pathetic here, and me, how do you expect I could be anything but pathetic too? Punk hoodlum grabs my arms from behind and throws himself back on the wall with all his might to hold me pinned, kneeing me in the balls meanwhile, and the other I hit comes up and starts systematically slugging me. I dodge most of the

punches and pulla quarterback sneak through the lot and fly out that bar so fast, they'd never catch me if they chased. But the girl is crying and everybody stops. And there I am with a busted face. My first fight in six years, and only one I lost. [. . . .] I might just as well have stayed home. I don't have a New York gang to go back to that bar with me; if I did, I'd take on the two who held me, right on the sidewalk, but how can I? Where's my gang? None. Nothing. Cool New York. [. . .] Well, if I sell my talent wisely, I'll surprise you in 'Frisco this winter. Look out!—until then, write & be good—*decide to be good.* (I mean inside.) Yr. boy—

On December 23, 1950, Cassady sent Kerouac a long, handwritten letter telling the story of "Christmas of 1946 Denver" with his girl-friends Joan Anderson and Cherry Mary. Cassady called it an "in-sufferably egotistically [sic] letter," but it was apparently intended to be part of what he called the "novel" based on his life that his friends Ginsberg and Kerouac had been urging him to write since they first met. Most of the original of Cassady's letter to Kerouac was lost, but a section of it was included in Cassady's posthumous book The First Third, *published by City Lights in San Francisco.*

Neal also sent Jack a short note along with the "Christmas of 1946 Denver" narrative in which he apologized for his handwriting. Cassady added, "Seldom has there been a story of a man so balled up. . . . I know it's the style to create a fiction of a bunch of characters thrown together in a composite—like Wolfe or Proust did. But, how for one as just straight case-history? I know, no one of the characters would stand up—no living one person has all the necessary attributes to hold water in a Novel."

Joan Haverty Kerouac added a few lines to Jack's next letter to Cassady after reading Neal's letter, saying that when it arrived in the mail that morning, "Jack picked it up from the front steps and had the opportunity to read it on the subway on his way into town but that wasn't enough. He spent two more hours perusing it in a cafe-teria and didn't get home till 6:00, at which time I got my hands on it and dinner preparations were delayed another hour."

Kerouac's reply to Cassady on December 27, 1950, suggests how

overwhelmed Jack was by the letter. It seems to have helped him to trust his own voice as a writer and break free from the influence of Thomas Wolfe's fiction, so that he could write what he later called "true-story novels" like On the Road *based on his direct experience.*

TO NEAL CASSADY[1]

[December 27, 1950
Richmond Hill, N.Y.]

[Dear Neal,]

Just a word, now, about your wonderful 13,000 word letter about Joan Anderson and Cherry Mary. I thought it ranked among the best things ever written in America and ran to Holmes & Harrington & told them so; I said it was almost as good as the unbelievably good "Notes From Underground" of Dostoevsky. It was with some surprise I saw they weren't as impressed. I think it's because Holmes is really not hip to anything until it begins to sink in much later. I'm going to show it to Giroux if he will. Giroux is a man influenced in his work by personal feelings, therefore he may be prejudiced and blinded. Have no fear, there are others who will dig this for what it is besides me; Morley of England for one & even especially I think. You gather together all the best styles . . . of Joyce, Céline, Dosty & Proust . . . and utilize them in the muscular rush of your own narrative style & excitement. I say truly, no Dreiser, no Wolfe has come too close to it; Melville was never truer. I know that I don't dream. It can't possibly be sparse & halting, like Hemingway, because it hides nothing; the material is painfully necessary . . . the material of Scott Fitz was so sweetly unnecessary. It is the exact stuff upon which American Lit is still to be founded. You must and will go on at all costs including comfort & health & kicks; but keep it kickwriting at all costs too, that is, write only what kicks you and keeps you overtime awake from sheer mad joy. I used to think that Harrington & Fitzgerald were the only good practicing writers I knew; you have so

1. The text of Kerouac's letter is taken from its publication in the little magazine *Notes from Underground,* Number 1 (Berkeley, 1964).

far overshadowed them it's positively humiliating. I told Ed White in a letter that a great man had risen from his home-town. I think all this sincerely. I know I don't dream. A lot of people say I don't know what I'm doing, but of course, I do. Burroughs & Allen said I didn't know what I was doing in the years of Town & City; now they know I did. They revert & start in, re-saying, "He doesn't know," but then it will be proven allover again with disastrous boring regularity, of course I know what I'm doing. Holmes, Giroux, Harrington—all think I don't know what I'm doing. Boring regularity, etc. Because of this my judgment concerning your value is completely sound. I say this to reassure you in case you think I'm cracked, or don't think I'm cracked. You and I will be the two most important writers in America in 20 years at the least. Think that. That's why I see no harm in addressing my next ten novels & possible lifework to you and you alone. Who else? Robt. Penn Warren?[2] This established, that you are a great writer now and have only begun, let me get into details about the letter itself.

Of course you wrote it with painful rapidity & can patch it up later for the benefit of . . . and don't have to if you don't want. It will be published. It was a moment in lit. history when I received that thing & only sweetwife & I read it & knew. Ah man it's great. Don't undervalue your poolhall musings, your excruciating details about streets, appointment times, hotel rooms, bar locations, window measurements, smells, heights of trees. I wait for you to send me the entire thing in disorderly chronological order anytime you say and anytime it comes, because I've just got to read every word you've got to say and take it all in. If that ain't life nothing ain't. Do so, do so. I'm having Joan write hers in utter detail from beginning to end, including wonderful moments with old evil sexman in L.A. who lures little kids (I mean, wonderful reading moments for lascivious lads like me & you); she has just today written a glowingly pure account of her favorite mornings and fantasized them into something further & lovely. She really knows how to write from instinct & innocence. Few women can do this. Joan Kerouac . . . a new writer on this old

---

2. American novelist, poet, and literary critic (1905–1989).

horizon. I see me & her cutting around the world in tweeds, yass . . . Mierschom [sic] pipes with youknowwhat in them, he he. Then consider, listen to what I say, you're the greatest;[3] I have reason to believe that if I am to go on priding myself in my work I will have to hustle to catch you; let anybody scoff at this, I ought to know better than anybody else . . . except you.

Neal, a word or two about my plans. Joan and I have decided to get fulltime jobs till March to save several hundred bucks. In March, if I get a Guggenheim[4] (decided around last week) we will at once buy an old panel truck, load gear, and take off for 3 wonderful lazy years perhaps in provincial Mexico (cheaper than Mexcity). Texcoco, 30 miles away, 24c bus into town that I rode, pissing from the back, with Jeff, under shadow of the snowtopt volcanoes; 1c buys waterglass of raw tequila. Can live there off $400 or $500 a year. Guggenheim is $2500 or even 3 grand;—however, not to depend on such a dream of possibilities, if we don't get this dough, we intend to buy old car or truck, pack gear, and drive to Frisco; where we work till I get $1000 from Harcourt if ever they publish me again. If not we will work & live in Frisco, saving best we can, for eventual date in Mexico. This being case, when you get here, I hope you have car so I can get driver's license with you (also few lessons for sharpup). If only you weren't so hung up and could yourself save a few Texcoco's worth of years and come with us, or with the wife & kids . . . if we ever run out of $ together we could ride bus to Texas border and in

---

3. Kerouac also showed Cassady's letter to Ginsberg, and Neal was amused by their enthusiastic response. He wrote Ginsberg on May 17, 1951, that "All the crazy falldarall you two boys make over my Big Letter just thrills the gurgles out of me, but we still know I'm a whiff and a dream."

4. Kerouac's application for a Guggenheim fellowship, describing his "Plans for Artistic Creation," stated that *On the Road* was currently in its third draft. He asked for funds to help him write a sequel to it he titled "The Vanity of St. Louis." This novel "will be about 'Canucks' living in the dense complicated French Canadian neighborhoods of New England milltowns, the special and complete experience of their lives in America." Kerouac intended *On the Road* to be "the first, as the French Canadian novel will be the second in a series of connected novels revolving around a central plan that eventually will be my life work, a structure of types of people and destinies belonging to this generation and referable to one another in one immense circle of acquaintances."

a few months rake up at construction or oilfield work and come back to year of life with kicks & wives. I wish in fact you could do this with all my heart, as with Joan I will be completely happy, but with you, I would also be completely befriended and need nothing; we'd live on same street and meet in dusty alley and go down to teafields to see Jose and hang around sun. Nights, write. I'd have me wife, and me near friend nearby, and you too. $500 a year I say. No foolishness like La Vie Parisienne, but purchase of eggs from country Indians, strict haggling purchases of bread and tortilla mix and pinto beans & cheese; buy bottles water; etc. go to big city for connection as smalltown too obvious, and take great care as Bill did with odor as I say big city is hour away in car, 1 and a half in old bus. Texcoco, which you never saw, is south of Mexcity; it is hot and fine, same altitude but somehow drowsier and finer; crazy Gregors all over; Mambo in little doorway joints. It is a town with one square in middle surrounded by crumbling Spanish masonry; 3 old beautiful churches with lovely bells; fiestas almost every day and attendant fireworks; no fancy Americans like at Oaxaca and Taxco and such. We'd hang on to every cent, give the Mexes no quarter, let them get sullen at the cheap Americans and stand side by side in defense, and make friends in the end when they saw we was poor too. Comes another Mex revolution, we stands them off with our Burroughsian arsenal bought cheap on Madero St. and dash to big city in car for safety shooting and pissing as we go; whole Mex army follows hi on weed; now no worries any more. Just sit on roof hi enjoying hot dry sun and sound of kids yelling and have us wives & American talk of our own as well as exotic kicks and regular old honest Indian kicks. Become Indians . . . I personally play mambo in local catband, because of this we get close to them and go to town. Wow. How's about it? Hurry to N.Y. so we can plan and all take off in big flying boat '32 Chandler across crazy land. Bring juke, bop records, mambo records and dixieland records; typewriters, clothes, toasters, percolators, etc.

Until I see you . . . let me know when . . . I got to work now on script so I can pay Uncle Sam his bloody tax & landlord's bloody old rent & all the bloody shits together.

Jack

The day after receiving Cassady's "Joan Anderson and Cherry Mary" letter, Kerouac sat down "to write a full confession" of his life to Neal. It was the first of a series of long letters written in the next two weeks in which Jack gave full expression to his obsession with his earliest memories. This attempt to "proceed into the actual truth" of his life for Cassady was the foundation for all of Kerouac's subsequent books, beginning with the successful completion of On the Road *three months later. This was after Jack had learned from his letters to Neal that "I have nothing to offer but the words that spring from my heart and mind in this enormous story."*

TO NEAL CASSADY

Dec. 28, [19]50
[Richmond Hill, N.Y.]

Dear Neal,

The time has come for me to write a full confession of my life to you. So many things have to be discussed by me before I can even begin with what I know of the moment of my birth and its relation to the chief points of my confession, that of course I don't know where to start. In the first place there is the matter of motives: why a man should write the confession of his life to a buddy and yet have the temerity to try to claim that he does not harbor the tiniest wish to publish for money and profitable fame; a writing-man at that, a previously published writer. Then shall I say, Neal, I hereby renounce all fiction; and say further, dear Neal, this confession is for YOU, and through you to God, and through God back to my life, and wife, whatever and what-all. I urge you to consider my motives carefully; I hope I will become more interesting and less literary as I go along and proceed into the actual truth of my life. This: burn these things if you feel that the time has come for me to renounce the world; or keep them, to hand, personally, to Giroux the editor of Harcourt-Brace. I already assume that you'll not burn, but turn in, my work; but this is temerity. So many things!—I feel it will never get underway. A final statement in this poor preambling paragraph: that I wish to write the confession of my entire life to you, Neal Cassady, and send, by mail, in installments three thousand two hundred miles

· 246 ·

across the continent we know so well, through wind, rain, hail, sleet and snow, at risk of loss, in hopes of some loss, in fear of total loss, in trembling of loss, for gain of your friendship and the respect of the Lord. It has been written in the Bible, "God is light and truth." Nor will I make further talk about truth; simply to say, in this confession I will travel again the experiences already written by me for the fiction-work (T&C) and tear them down systematically; have come to believe, like you, bullshit is bullshit. Everything's got to go this time. No one can take it but you. From the very start we were brothers. Now that I have read your great work—the letter dated Dec. 23 dealing with Joan Anderson and Christmas of 1946 Denver—I feel that no one in the world, and in history, could have the strength and holy will to read in its total mass everything I have to say about my sins in the "bleakness of this mortal realm;" that, briefly, no one is as great as you, nor humbler.

Neal, hearken to my plea as I grow more natural and make real confessions that are designed & aimed to your knowing that which I know, and understand the difficulty of the undertaking. In the first place there's the feeling that you and I both know the falseness of the first and above paragraph; the stiff, necessary, opening preamble, written with the mysterious outside reader, who is certainly not God, bending over my shoulder; even the neatness of the page, not a correction, not an X, not a blot; and the fact that I write this, as you know, almost and certainly more than almost in direct challenge to your colossal achievements of the past two months (the letters, your own confession in non-chronological fragments, something I do not hope to best, but equal); the fact that we are now contending technicians in what may well be a little American Renaissance of our own and perhaps a pioneer beginning for the Golden Age of American Writings. God, God, how I'm haunted by the feeling that I am false; I can never forget that eminent gent Lucien telling me I was a sly old French storekeeper with a bag of tricks, bottom ones rotten; meaning, I've my eye too much on the last dribble-dreg of subtlest advantage. Enough, though, preambles may last forever. Only this: and if only the THIS were simpler: the opening confession shall end the preamble: I am writing the confession of my entire life, limited only by the selectivity that eliminates the obvious we both know,

simpler to say, those things we both know are of course unnecessary and if the "mysterious reader" (providing you do not burn the manuscripts) fails to understand the level of our common comprehension, then it's not our fault but a fault in American education; I am writing this confession entire to YOU because I want it to be a true and not a false or subtle confession; therefore, if this be to my advantage in the end, that is, a purer work result from it, you have every right to believe that I am doing this because it is not to my advantage to write a bad work whether published or not; and of course I already, again, assume that you will see to its publication.

I have renounced fiction and fear. There is nothing to do but write the truth. There is no other reason to write. I have to write because of the compulsion in me. No more can I say. I kneel before you in spirit and pray for honesty . . . Twinges cross my brain. These will be ironed out or nothing ever. Do you abide by this, Neal, and abide by me? And if so, dear great friend, will you continue your own work as before? From you I expect no such protestations of coy dishonesty; because you never sinned, you never were published and became the great American harlot-writer they all are; pure, you remain in your proper solemn underground, or holy hole, and I join you as of this date, Dec. 28, 1950, holy night, snowy night.

My sin—the fact that I am a subtly dishonest man generally recognized and probably by all means rightly referred [to] as a "swell guy," you see which has nothing to do with it—began, brother Neal, on the day of my birth. Before I'm finished you'll know everything about me. Value given is value received. What hath God wrought. All that. When a man is born dust takes a flyer. Dust of dust, you may as well know of my dust. My report to you in the pit of night, and to God in the pit of night, will carry me through.

If you burn these things I believe with growing conviction now that it will not make the slightest difference: my second book will still be the first book of truth I shall have written.

Enough, enough of scriveners. Still another thing; I hate to begin: I fear. I aim to employ all the styles and nevertheless I yearn to be non-literary. Nonliterary. Dribbledrags. This is the odd beginning.

March 12, 1922, at five o'clock in the afternoon, in Lowell, Mass. was the day of the first thaw. I was born on the second floor of a

wooden house on Lupine Road, which to this day sits on top of a hill overlooking Lakeview Avenue and the broad Merrimack River. From this house my mother, God bless her dear heart, lay listening to the distant roar of the Pawtucket Falls a mile away; she has told me all this. Besides of which it was a strange afternoon, red as fire; "noisy with a lyrical thaw," as I said in my fictions of the past, and that is to say the snow was melting so fast you could hear it in a million small streams under vast snowy banksides crumbling just a little in their middles from the weight of moisture. Pines dripped like the seasonal maple, made gum and gummy firsmells in the air. Great shoulders of snow dropped precipitous from their bleak wood. These descriptions are necessary at this point, for the following reason.

All my life I was fascinated by the first thaws of New England March; not until I was told I was actually born in the midst of one did I vaguely remember the day of my birth, or is this too far-fetched? Not in the least (my darkface protests across the continent to thee.) I remember it, I remember the day of my birth. I remember the red air and the sadness—"the strange red afternoon light" [Thomas] Wolfe also was hung on—with peculiar eternity-dream vividness, or if not vividness, vastness; some dream of late afternoon. Six years later, on a similar red afternoon, but in dead of frozen winter, I discovered my soul; that is to say, I looked about for the first time and realized I was in a world and not just myself. Time enough to get to that. The coincidences that have occurred in connection with late-red-afternoons—no need to say, everybody in America has a feeling for such afternoons—but so often to me, make me think I must have seen that original afternoon with eyes a few hours old. Still, this may be bullshit; and there's no way to find out till the end. And when my own son reaches out to touch me for the first time is there any knowing where I'll be then?—except that I'll be there? Will it be late afternoon? Does it matter so much? It does, and I'll return when the signs point.

The date was March 12. At this time my father was printing and publishing the SPOTLITE, a theatrical newspaper, about eight pages each weekly issue, covering local show business in Lowell, which at that time was enjoying a peak as it was all over the country. The great days of Vaudeville, and the great early days of Hollywood. To

this day I have these SPOTLITES in my closet all bound together in a big cardboard book. It has nothing to do with me except . . . when the time comes: and that time was to be 24 years later when I lay on a sickbed remembering my father's life with tears and visions. Enough to say, my father was a bustling jolly young businessman; I've already written about him considerably and pretty well in my past fictions, and I was only, and again dammit trying to "stuff" my material as of yore. No more of that!

I don't know what my father was like on March 12, 1922, nor my mother. My sister Caroline was three, my sickly brother Gerard five, I don't know what they were like. I have a picture. They stand on the wooden porch of the Lupine Road house; you almost see late-afternoon in their eyes as they look over the railing at the great Lowell world of time (the great Denver world of time, any greatworld of time). The time is yet to come for me to weep for them in these pages, dear Neal. I was born, my damned sin began. I wonder when it began.

There is a picture of me in a wickerbasket baby carriage[1] parked near the wall of a greystone garage in Centralville . . . this is the name of the section of town Lupine Road belonged . . . a picture of a plump crazy baby, rather cute actually, sort of smiling at the world, with a little hat on its head. Not a hat, but a baby-thing. No, the sin was not begun; or if so, it was not in bloom. There may have been faint notions in my mind even then in the wickerbasket that a great World Snake was worming its way up from the middle of the world, devouring dirt, excrescing dirt, inch-by-inch arriving, to find me in poor Lowell on the River; no telling. I'll explain the Snake in due time. It wasn't a star sought this lad out . . . and will you believe me Neal, this minute, I believe that Christ is the son of God, I do so believe tonight and probably now for the rest of my life, and I hope

---

1. In the 100th Chorus of *Mexico City Blues,* Kerouac wrote:

> I remember one day being parked in the wickerbasket
> Baby carriage, under huge old tree,
> In family photos we've preserved it,
> A great elm rising from dust
> Of the little uphill road. . . .

so. So I'm not "jealous of Jesus to the point of madness" like Mr. Nietzsche, Mr. [D.H.] Lawrence too; I'd say "ha-ha!" when I said it wasn't a STAR sought ME out, but a WORLD SNAKE; or a garter snake; "Ha-ha!" for nervousness of everybody knowing that I believed from early infancy, or sensed, in late-afternoon dreamy ways, that a SNAKE was coming after me. Or is this merely bullshit? How proudly we American pipsqueaks play around with the pretentious ideas of Europe. Antichrist Kerouac, the SNAKE came for him alone, no one else. I now know, the SNAKE came for all of us and caught us all, but Christ is the son of God & died for our sakes truly. Do I remind you of the similar pipsqueaks who made speeches to you in jails? (O mysterious reader, bend no closer.)

I love to digress. Actually there is nothing to remember. My family moved from Lupine Road to another part of Centralville, a house on Maiden Lane I think it was called. Several unimportant memories that may have belonged to either of the domiciles occur to me: of what point? I'm in my mother's arms; she's wearing an old brown bathrobe;[2] she's rocking me and singing; I gaze longingly at the bleak gray rooftops of the world without. How I loved my mother! How the baby loves his mother! How good it is to be a mammal! And to grow and be a man, however unfortunate and covered with sin and self-disgrace, and be foolish. For God intended it. But no more digression, huh?

No, we'll get to the agonized cock of the matter.

For my brother was sickly. His name, I say, was Gerard, which is a beautiful name, especially when it's pronounced in French. All his pictures reveal the sad little face, the soft brown fall of hair over his brow, the inner suffering, the dream: his feet are always inturned as though he was too meek, or too shy, to stand normally, and nothing was wrong with his feet at all. His little hands curl in mortification before the camera and the picture-taker. He was not long for this world from the day of his lonesome birth. There is a great similarity between my own earliest photographs and Gerard; I know now I

---

2. Kerouac described his early memory of his mother's bathrobe in Section 11 of *Doctor Sax:* "I'm sitting in my mother's arms in a brown aura of gloom sent up by her bathrobe. . . ."

imitated him through life. You will be amazed when I tell you only a few of the things he did.

We moved from "Maiden Lane," where I have no memories beyond the dream of the child, to Beaulieu Avenue, which is a French-Canadian neighborhood of wooden cottages not far from wooden tenements and the parochial schools and church known as St. Louis. Here Gerard one day found a mouse caught in a butcherstore trap and took it home to heal.[3] He made a little basket bed for it, fed it milk and cheese and just as this forgotten little mouse of ages ago began to get well the cat devoured it in my brother's absence. He cried tears. Then he took the cat and placed it roughly on the rocking chair—(I know he must have done something like this)—and said, "Mechant! mechant!" which means, "Bad one! bad one!"—"Why have you done this to a harmless little mouse that couldn't hurt you even if it tried, why did you kill a poor tiny gray mouse, she was sleeping in her little basket and you came and caught her in your teeth. Mechant! mechant! Shame on you, have shame, old vicious!" My mother heard every word of it; the text has been translated to me a million times, now it's garbled. If I could only have heard his exact words. Don't you see, Neal, I never told you, I believe my brother was a saint, and that explains all. Now you will begin to know about me. I could not live without this confession.

You doubt his saintliness? I never would allow it unless you knew all the facts, and I know you never could doubt and have it not in your soul to doubt. When he was very ill he lay in bed with his sad blue (or brown) eyes turned to the window; it was open to eternal thaws of March; and little birds came to his windowsill. He had my mother set out breadcrumbs to attract them. After weeks of this, regular whole droves and choral societies of little birds came to his holy windowsill; he spoke to them, the infant saint, and do you believe that he spoke to them of the Lamb? This is precisely what he

---

3. See the opening pages of *Visions of Gerard:* "One day he found a mouse caught in Scoop's mousetrap outside the fish market on West Sixth Street. . . ." This book, the earliest in Kerouac's "Legend of Duluoz" autobiographical chronicle, dramatizes the memories of Gerard's sickness and death described in this letter to Cassady.

talked about to the little birds: he reminded them that there were little sheep in the pasture, under blue skies and beautiful white angelic clouds, my mother heard every word. You know my mother, you know she was capable of hiding in the hall and peeking around the doorjamb to hear every dear word uttered by my little saint-brother. She reported it to me years later. There came a day when my brother thought the birds were ready for his hand. He called them to his pillow, he held out his little hand; the birds of course flew away. He tried unsuccessfully several times. When he saw the tragedy of man's alienation from the birds of heaven he cried tears. "Mama, Mama, why don't the little birds want to come into my hand; they know I won't hurt them!" "No, Gerard, they don't know, they're only little birds." "But they do know, they do!" And of course they knew, just as the cat had known, and the mouse had known, and all had known of Gerard, who was come to the world to weep.

Neal, the death of this child was a loss that must be impossible for you and I to calculate in the souls of my mother and father.

Meanwhile I was too young to know of anything of this. Let me say, the nuns in the nearby Parish of St. Louis were not blind to what was going on. When he was well enough to go to school they often let him out early when he complained about a pain in his chest, or whatever, as if they not only knew he was mortally sick but needed extra special privileges above and beyond the other normal children. Let me just add, when he died the nuns came in a solemn file to my house—but we will get to that.

Only my mother fully knew what was going on. The sight of this holy child slowly dying might have affected her mind at the time, and her stories about him may today be exaggerated, but I have verification, plus a pain in my heart, sufficient unto these pages. My father claims the same; my aunts Louise and Emma speak of him to this day in tears; and there was a priest in the neighborhood whose name I forget . . . and neighbors, and some business associates of the old man . . . who, I am told, spoke in the same way about Gerard: to the effect that he was the strangest, most angelic gentle child they had ever known.

One day he lay in the backyard grass with a hand cupped over his eyes. My mother asked him what he was doing. He said he was

watching heaven. He would say things like that very seriously, as you know.

He spoke frequently of angels and drew pictures of them. As he neared his death a tremendous drawing-technique began to come to him. He was so good, one day he drew a picture of a ship after a drawing in the *Saturday Evening Post* magazine, and when my father came home he laughed to hear Gerard had done it. There was another man with my father; he laughed too. Gerard drew still another picture to convince them and wore himself out all pale sweat to do so. Then my father did not laugh any more; it was too late to laugh. Everybody in the family must have sensed his impending death.

For the purposes of all this, I have to tell you what I was doing before I came to the last moments of Gerard's life. I was three and then four years old on Beaulieu Avenue. Let me describe it briefly, as it enters again later. First, they said our house was built over an ancient sunken cemetery; this was probably just a crazy rumor started by old French Canadian mammies that sit around by the dozen sewing and chatting in the strange red afternoons of Lowell. Nevertheless it was supposed to be true, and Gerard, my sister Caroline and I were properly scared. All along one side of the short street the houses were close together, with backyards. The other side of the street was taken up partially by the vast backyard of the St. Louis parochial school and it was precisely the recess-yard and rang with cries forever. Next to this was a tenement of about twelve families, a wonderful mad French tenement with wash hanging in mid-air and the great drowse of afternoon falling over it as I gaped from my front porch. One day, in fact, I crossed the street and sat on the wooden steps of the school's backyard to imitate my Uncle Joe and family. Uncle Joe and his family visited us frequently and when they all got settled in the parlor to talk it was a medley of voices that no one could possibly forget; mainly because Uncle Joe was a vociferous, mournful, tearstricken Kerouac-man and when he talked it sounded like "AH-BWA AH-BWA AH-BWA"; as you see not quite the usual bla-bla. I imitated this not for fun but in utter seriousness about the world. It was my Uncle Joe visiting us; I saw in the drowse of afternoon and made them all. Think, Neal, your pal Jack, three years old, sitting on the wooden steps (there were fifteen or so and each a good

twelve feet long), saying "Ah-bwa ah-bwa ah-bwa," with a serious almost gloomy little face. From the tenement, which is what I was talking about, a woman yelled at me to shut up; I hear her voice ringing in the afternoon drowse; I see the rippling wash on the line; I see the sun. And now, and soon, you will know why I saw "the house I was born in" in Mexico, won't you?—and it will all be clear as day. And Mexico because of the sun, the drowse, and ah-bwa ah-bwa of their own tongue; now do you begin to see? You never spoke my tongue nor lived in foreign neighborhoods; spent noons musing in washlined alleys among hundreds of little jabberfrogs; railed flap-tongued and wild in rubbish heaps . . . it was I, sad grownup Jack of today, mooning ragtail among the tincans and clinkers, in the hot strange sun and jabbering hum of French-Canadian time. So that the ragtail puts on his envelope of flesh, goes west where you were born, and marvels at the spacious lank land where men speak English slow and children drawl on country fences—and say, "I say Jimmy what for you brung that old browntail dawg." So it was ah-bwa, ah-bwa with me; and this was what I did while my brother died in his own dream. I knew him slightly. At least I remember practically nothing. Even today I think of Beaulieu Avenue as the street that has the same name as Scotty Beaulieu my old pal of Lowell. I mentioned the cemetery for one reason: one clear memory of companionship with the strange Gerard.

It was night. Caroline my sister and I were in bed; Gerard had his separate bedroom. Lights began flashing mysteriously on the ceiling; we wondered if this had any relation to another recent mystery, which was, the plaster in the parlor had suddenly fallen one night, and someone had said, "The souls below the house shook in their graves." We wondered: "Are they mad at us for building a house over them?" It was all too spooky to dare presume. We called Gerard and told him the lights were frightening us. He said he saw them too. He was bedridden at this time and couldn't move. We asked him what it meant. He said it was the souls beneath the house come forth to haunt us. "You too?" we cried. He was—I must say, as if —silent. (I think of Hal Chase at this moment and adjure you to remember for later, my fiction Francis Martin was Gerard as well as he was Hal, who summoned him up.) He refused to console us, as I

remember it. Actually it was a grownup boy from next door who was flashing his flashlight with the deliberate intention of scaring us; but apparently not to scare Gerard, and I even think it had all been arranged between he and Gerard to scare the little ones that night. Neal, this is all I know, or that is, all I suspect.

What night was it—before that or after—that I woke up sometime after the witching hour and saw a tall, lank figure standing above my crib in stiff watchfulness of me? My mother and sister slept just to the left of me. I barely dared to even think of calling them. The figure had wild unruly hair and seemed intent on me with hate. I drove it out of my mind at once that it was Gerard risen like a ghost from his bed of miseries—yet, it was Gerard and no one else. In utter dark of that time-night I stared back with rue at my haunter. Stiff, stiff, he never moved, never said a word, never barely breathed, and so persistent in his sullen, lidded look into my babycrib soul that I, in innocence, fell asleep impatiently, and woke up the next day to forget. These are the beginnings of my mysteries. Was it my brother?

Of course it was my brother. Who was my brother? On the kitchen floor I looked at the picture of a woman on the front page of the Boston American; with the scissors lying nearby I jabbed her in the eye. My brother—or was it my brother?—someone said: "Never do that." I never have. They say we played piggyback by the hour on the kitchen floor; why then is it so vague a memory, and why does my mother insist so.

It was a snowy afternoon, the snow was two feet deep. Everybody suddenly ran into the house and I followed wading in the drifts and yelling "Wait for me!" Nobody waited. The door was LOCKED. I cried. My mother then gave me a butter-and-sugar sandwich to munch on the porch. What was happening? Whatever was happening? Why will I never know? Let me get on to the essentials (it's now 3 A.M. Dec. 29, second day, of a task I'm not fitted for but the only one who can do it.)

I was lonely. I stood in my crib in a downstairs sickroom of some sort—possibly my brother and I were both sick simultaneously—and I cried for assistance and comfort. My mother was on the other side of the room taking care of my brother. I resented it and yelled. It was a yell has faded from the world and I wonder that I ever uttered

it. I wanted her to come to me too. My father was somewhere in the house, a vast brooding man the likes of which you sometimes see in a New York subway suddenly, coming in from Bowery nights to rest feet made completely tired from having to accommodate the weight of two hundred and thirty pounds of flesh and bone; a big man of misery, hidden in the house. In a dream I have connected with this moment when I cried for my mother in the sickroom crib, the house is bedimmed in the kind of red lights you see either Christmas or a funeral-time, to make a general brown light of gloom withal, and there are relatives; but relatives in silence, Uncle Joe and the Family suddenly grown stark and quiet in the meditation of some awful death in my house; in the dream I wonder what it all is. Somewhere in the depths of the sad brown house my father broods. Thus he brooded when I yelled. What was this conspiracy between my mother and brother against my father and me, with an innocent little sister left out? So it seemed as I howled at the rails of my sickcrib. Everything that happened then was shrouded in mystery; I swear I remember clearly the moreso I remember mystery. Suddenly, on another day, I was merely standing at the kitchen window looking at the snow fall down in little dark specks; white snow making dark specks, hmm!, and for no particular reason asked my Aunt Louise— I remember it was Aunt Louise and I was three—what it was the snow with the dark look. Such questions are answered with reduced simplicity. "Why it's snow falling, that's all." Or let me say it in French meaning: "It is the snow." I accepted it. There are several other memories, one concerning a Mardi Gras night (we celebrated Mardi Gras on a great scale), when my parents dressed me up as a little Chinaman and in the company of Gerard, dressed as himself, and my sister, old Leo my pop took us walking on the main drag of French-Canadian Centralville[4]—to show me off. The main drag was but a broad thoroughfare running between tenements and butcher-

---

4. In *Visions of Gerard*, Kerouac changed the holiday to "the Halloween of 1925, when Ma dressed me up as a little Chinaman with a queue and a white robe and Gerard as a Pirate and Nin as a Vamp and old Papa took us by the hand and paraded us down to the corner at Lilley and Aiken, ice cream sodas, swarms of eyes on the sidewalks—."

shops and a Fire Station, with a Square of drugstores and forgotten department stores of another era, and when I say another era I mean they still sold strings of twine as well as lampshades, that kind of oldtime main drag: we walked this among mysterious old crowds of my childhood and I was the hit. The improvised queue on my head I remember embarrassed me: the Chink's headtail that was so arranged to appear to grow from my skull till I feared such a thing could happen. Of what consequence a forgotten child's fear a quarter of a century ago in this Twentieth Century of recorded man?

Then my brother died. He took sick first; my mother spent the nights with him, and worked by day, and as a consequence she had a nervous breakdown and lost all her teeth at twenty-nine. She worked by day at his bedside, I mean, so that the continual stress of his death was upon her to the breaking point. He had always been sick. Always he breathed with a difficult little sigh; born with rheumatic fever in his breast, a weak heart, a poor liver, a tortured underdeveloped sinew-system and cordage that prevented him from ever pulling himself together to withstand illness and life. He had no strength; he was pale. His was a long sad face; sunken-cheeked, haunted, grim. They could have killed him with a slap on the chest. He was meek and he was doomed. Never for once did all his angels and lambs come to his aid when he needed them most; nor did heaven reach down from the blue and enfold him safely. He was from the very start (I gnash my teeth to think) ribshattered for suffering by the juices and conditional mixtures of his birth. He came from the womb an agony; the doctor shook his head at the sight of him the first week. He had knowledge of mortal suffering in his first infant glimmerings; and grew to build philosophies on that stuff as easily as the chipmunk goes for nuts. When I was sick myself 20 years later I marveled to remember the suffering of my brother for an entire nine years, insignificant and diminutive, on earth. What didn't my mother see in his eyes? How I wish I could remember his eyes and some of the things he must have said. He made my sister a regular toy house with toy furniture and toy people in one morning while she attended school, to go with her lunch-joy; then he must have had a heart of gold. They gave him a gift one Christmas, an

erector set, that became the mere worldly instrument of his almost miraculous powers of imagination: he built ferris wheels, fire engines, complicated Twenties Mack trucks, anything, anything but a Lamb and only because steel is not fleece. He even made ads for my father's theatrical papers, that the old man actually used; and he was nine. He died.

Just before he died he slapped me in the face. It is the last thing I remember before he died. It was a gray morning, my sister was going to school, breakfast was being removed from the table. Gerard sat at his erector set before the most magnificent structure of his brief career: it was huge, towering, a crane of some sort, arranged and hung in strange new ways and calculated to do a thousand strange feats. The contraption was on the edge of the breakfast table. Had he been older I'm sure he would have his second cup of coffee right then, he was so eager for his morning's work. But I had to come along and grab at his little arrangements: knock a subsidiary structure down, push the little wrench on the floor, whatever it was, disturbing him so suddenly that with understandable rage he impulsively tightened inside and his hand shot out and slapped me in the face. "Get away from here!" he cried. I mooned over that in the parlor. Gray vultures of gloomy day were feeding at the rooftops of time, I could see it outside the curtains. Gloom, grayness, faucet-ticking . . . I could see the quality of the day behind the sofa and behind the darkest corner chair. I don't know what happened from there. Bill Burroughs claims according to his amateur psychoanalysis of me in 1945 that I resented the slap in the face and wished Gerard would die, and he died a few days later.

The day he died I saw my big father come up the street from work. He had no news whatever of the death of Gerard. Knowing this I ran to him eagerly with the news. "Gerard is dead! Gerard is dead!" I sang this in the street. It was something new. Now things would change. Rumours of exciting preparations were in the air. We would all go away to Canada with Gerard and be in the bosom of things as I knew them to be; for I'd always heard, "Things aren't like they were in good old Canada, I wish we were in Canada, let's all go back to Canada." Canada brooded in the air and haunted me. Canada

was my bosom of God. If Gerard died it only meant he went to Canada; and God knows what else I knew about death and what I'm trying to hide this minute.

Well, I'm not going to hide it. I didn't know what it meant that Gerard was dead; he was transformed into an interesting better being and I was soon to look upon his face again, they assured me of that. He had temporarily left the house—to go be embalmed, as if I would know what that meant. I waited happily for his return. It was only when I saw his body (I knew it to be inside the box) lowered in the earth and dirt thrown over that my face fell.

My mother was beside herself, in the midst of her awful crackup that cost her all her teeth including several that were filled with gold, by a dentist who had joyously told her "Gold teeth never fall out!" And here her gold teeth had fallen out. Wherewith shall a man regain his salt if he has lost his savor. The holy knowing nuns came filing to my house in double line; they filled the front room with darkness and piety all dry-bones; their fingers gently touched the rosary beads with the same gentle motion that Christ uses in all the etchings and all the cheap calendar pictures, fingers languid outstretched in a holy droop, the eunuch's detachment; their lips whistled the faintest prayers; their garments were black. As phosphorescent light haloes from a hole, so their darkness haloed from the parlor, to give the lit kitchen walls a shadow without shape or border. It was a wave of dark light. It filled the house and even found its way upstairs, and may possibly have been seen coming from the chimney if I had been outside to watch. Beyond the nuns came all the others, the funeral-comers, the grimmers; and the little children brought in sad fear by stern mothers. Food cooked on the stove. My mother was prostrate in the upstairs tragedy. A cousin banged in the cellar. My sister and I stood in the middle embracing. All our firecrackers had been set off by the cousins, it was a mean Fourth of July to come.

There was rain, and a funeral: the massive arcades of the Catholic Church shone in candlelight and people coughed, and I stood at the back. Monotonous Latinities te-deumed and te-deumed to the fore of the scene. A draped coffin represented the location of Gerard my big brother. There were tears, and long files of schoolchildren terri-

fied; women blowing their noses; songs from aloft; the smell of rain-coats, and rain outside. Splendorous priests in black-and-white lace raised gleaming objects to the brown light and smoked incense at the multitude; it arrived at the back of the church in time to be smelled by me, before it was lost in the open door. Black automobiles waited outside. It was 1926. So ended my brother's life and began the gloom of my life.

The cemetery was 14 miles away in Nashua, N.H. Because of the heavy rain we sat in the car; when the coffin was lowered away my sister and my mother broke into tears. I wondered what they were crying about. It seemed so little after all; Gerard knew what he was doing in that ground, was not put there, to be specific had not al-lowed anyone to put him there, without reasons of his own. He'd come back. I felt no necessity to feel a single worry in the world.

We made preparations to move from Beaulieu Avenue at once. I went about my business. But I then began to change from a fat pink child they called Ti-Pousse, or Little Thumb for roundness and pink-ness, into a sallow weary child; washed-out thin, that day onwards; and wouldn't be able to tell you this now, if everyone hadn't told me a thousand times, and each time I don't believe it, because I don't remember a thing—I remember what I've told you. Did I not change from pink to pale? If these are the facts, then I bow. And I bow, too, to the mystery of my loneliness for Gerard that I have never been able to remember, and which must have occurred in the span of time when I first became the subtle dishonest soul I am today.

Now we come to the ways I used from that time onwards to con-ceal the dull and sullen woe in my heart from a world which might have helped me if I had given it a chance. It's not too late even now for me to repent. I have nothing to offer but the words that spring from my heart and mind in this enormous story.

I saw Allen the other day, he spent a long time sitting in an easy chair talking to me, by the light of my Christmas tree, as Joan lis-tened: we talked about Lucien's recent injuries, 1) cops hustling him out of a church drunk and dislocating his shoulder, 2) a crackup in which he was completely innocent while driving, but broke 2 ribs and foot. The doom that locates us must be met—but more of this

later, I send this off to you now, humble in the knowledge that it is not good writing at all and doesn't have to be any more. All I hope is if you enjoy. Send yr. installment. I wait. (for now) Jack

A last word, Neal: forgive me for overdramatizing in the preamble, because of course if you burned what I write to you now with such joy I could never tell it again so truly; so of course, don't burn anything but save for me, for my honest books of later. I only hope you weren't yourself shamed when you saw those awful lies on Page One. It's all part of what I want to tell you, real subtle dishonesty, bullshitting in my own face & me watching wide-awake; thus only the beginning of a long and real confession that comes from my heart to you; and incidentally to my wife too,[5] who reads every word I send you; forgive me for anything but listen, just listen, as long as you listen I'll be alright. Poor kid wanted to know why I didn't write my confession to her: so many things would have to be explained, wouldn't they?—things having to do with this country's past 20 years, jazz, the road, sports, jails, the war, places, a thousand things . . . it's better that I'm free not to have to explain too much so can rush in to piths. Incidentally I love her and still have to tell you all about her and how happy I am. Is everything all right, man? Man? (with capital M.) That's you. Now I feel better that I admitted the bullshit on Page One. On to the next installment.

Your pale pal
Jack

Fitful Ferdie, flaptit Ferdie, fossil ferdie, fucking ferdie, flip ferdie, folderol ferdie, fleckedfoam ferdie, fishtail ferdie, farty ferdie; tender tom, tamurlane tom, timorous tom, tishtish tom, tom-tom; ham herman, heart herman, hit herman, hell herman, harsh herman, hoorair herman, hoik herman, hooray herman; I say, dig doestoevsky, die-for-doestoevsky, dip-in-doestoevsky, deal-for-dusty, love-dusty, holy-dusty, dusty-what's-his-name, dusty-doody, dusty-rusty, dust of my dust and dust of your dust and dust of all dust. Henry-miller-killer,

---

5. Years later Kerouac told his bibliographer that he wrote *On the Road* in April 1951 to describe his adventures with Cassady to his wife, Joan.

henry-killer-diller-miller, henry-filler, henry-swiller, henry-luller, henry-buller, henryfucker, henrysokay. ARGH! arghand! arrant nonsense. Got letter from Billburroughswhosaysheisabouttoleavemexicotogotocentralamericabecausehehasspentathousanddollarstryingtogetcitizenship don't try to decipher I'm just killing time while Joan gets ready. Enuf is enuf andsogoodnightsweetprince.

1951

During the first ten days of January 1951, Kerouac continued writing Cassady his intense, detailed accounts of his earliest memories of childhood, experimenting with flashbacks and interjections within the chronology of his narrative, developing the voice he would use three months later to write his new version of On the Road. *He felt as if he were talking to Neal on the front seat of a car "driving across the old U.S.A. in the night with no mysterious readers, no literary demands, nothing but us telling . . ."*

TO NEAL CASSADY

Jan. 3, 1951
[Richmond Hill, N.Y.]

Dear Neal,

Now to resume. After Gerard died (and I have still more to say about his death, in fact the moment he was lowered in the earth) there was a period when I did a great deal of ruminating in the Beaulieu St. house even as everything was being readied to move to Hildreth St. In the midst of bustling and packing, I sat in the brown gloomy parlor of 1926 and had what was probably my first soul-memories. In the first paper I told you I remembered the day of my birth even now: this I did, aged four, for the first time. But I remembered still another occasion and with the same weight of heartfelt nostalgia that an adult will remember palmier years as he grows older. I remembered a long afternoon on Lupine Road when I was probably only one year old, when things were better, as my little mind well knew. This was an afternoon spent doing absolutely nothing, flat on my back in the bedroom crib, noticing with faint blurs of knowledge a few of the outside tassels of the world such as the old brown portraits of women and aunts hanging on the wall, beads in the doorway (hanging beads), profusions of pillows on old couches and particularly the heavy curtains in the windows that hid partially a great view of the outside world. At four, plunged in the terror of my brother's death and the almost worst terror of having to move to a strange other house, I remembered this afternoon with longing. I had nothing to do but bask in the world of time then; there were no fears whatever, only the glee of a growing sense that I had nothing

· 267 ·

but time, time, time to set in; absolutely no demands made on any part of my will and conscience. When I claim that I remember the day of my birth it is only a claim based on the knowledge of this second memory of a memory . . . to say it redundanredundantly.

Let me explain. I believe that memories are inseparable from dreams. When a man dreams, he can't pluck his dream-image from the air that surrounds his bed; no, on the contrary, the image and the whole material in which it sits, is already in his mind; where did it come from; it comes from that part of his brain which has stored up a subconscious vision of an actual experience. Many's the time I've dreamed of ancient scenes in my babyhood distorted only by the forgotten vision that in babyhood I conjured up. I see that room where I spent the long afternoon of bliss, the vision of it, no the IMAGE of it is stored in my mind; but I have seen that room otherwise in dreams and this was the VISION of it stored in my mind from the very moment that it happened. I entreat you to stick by me till I make everything clearer. This is not a mere "belief" of mine as I said upstairs, it is a conviction based on my own unalterable knowledge of my own mind; I'm sure that some day science will prove what I intuitively claim now. There is no distinction between memory and dream other than levels of consciousness. There is no such thing as a pipedream; all dreams come from visions of experience; they are released because they are already there in the mind.

I remember, for instance, riding licketysplit down a street near Lupine Road on a small bicycle—a bikette, by God—and the memory, the mere realistic MEMOIR of it, is Saroyanish, crazy, funny and full of fun. But since then countless dreams of going too fast on a terrible bicycle have come to me, and no doubt this was on the other level I perceived the ride on the bicycle even as I enjoyed myself. Incidentally this memory and vision belongs to the period before my brother died. It's of no importance by itself, but I must lead you on to another matter here, with which it's connected.

About the time of the licketysplit ride on the bikette my mother was visiting a French Canadian home with me; great circles of sewing-women were sitting around a round table covered with dress materials; there was a sewing machine, and red light coming from outside—no, on the other hand and to be utterly truthful, it was

night-time and the kitchen light was on. I'm almost positive it was the Gregoire home; the husband a business man associated with Pop in some way or other, no matter. Without any embarrassment whatever I allowed my mother to put me naked over her knee as she picked "worms" from my ass-hole, and this in front of a great circle of wonderful laughing women. I mention this not only for laughs, and to show you how much I've changed, but to introduce at this point a theme in my French-Canadian knowledge of the world, to wit, that there are great circles of women in this world who sit around tables and sewing machines, afternoon and night, talking and gossiping and plucking at their little ones with a grave and satisfied pleasure that only such women have. It is always the scene of great solid knowledge; they discuss superstitions with the same certainty that they discuss pork pies and how to make bread; they have gossips to exchange, and memories to unfurl, and things to point out; they speak utterly without embarrassment about the worms in their children's ass-holes and laugh uproariously about husband anecdotes; they blush and sigh and grow hungry; one woman gets up to stir the pot; there's food, and the men coming home soon. They disperse gladly and go to their own tables. Later on I'll show you how precisely this knowledge of them has affected my thinking and my decisions about life.

[. . . .] Now to return for a moment to Lupine Road, on another occasion when I sensed my brother's impending death, for dream and vision are intertwinable with reality and prophecy. It was winter, we were sledding on the snowy hill the top of which bore the imposing bulk of a "haunted castle" of some sort. I think the "castle" still stands, on Lakeview Avenue, around the block from the house I was born in. I'll return to it later in more detail, since of course it is the One Mighty Snake Hill Castle of my imagination, repeated only years later by lesser imposing "castles" and haunted houses.[1] This castle was all graystone, probably granite, and was deserted; the windows were blocked up; there were the usual rumors shouted in snowy air by little cherrymouthed kids that an evil old man lived in it. We did

---

1. Described in *Doctor Sax*, the second book in the Duluoz chronology.

our sliding up and down the hill between serried ranks of pine without fear; but few dared to come there at night. I think, parenthetically, you must at this moment be realizing that my early, my whole life, is filled with superstitions foreign to you; if so, tell me? The Catholic Church is a weird church; much mysticism is sown broadspread from its ritual mysteries till it extends into the very lives of its constituents and parishioners. Just wait, for instance, till I tell you of my fear of the statue of Ste. Therese, whose head is often seen turning by madtranced watchers; whose head I myself saw turning, head-of-stone. A haunted house is no novelty among Catholic kids and as you see all the houses I've mentioned are haunted one way or the other. To return to gists: while we were sledding on the white hill of the haunted castle one red afternoon I had a thought that my brother would die. I watched him sledding among the others with a paler, slower joy, almost grave and done-for in his methodical lipservice to fun. I knew he was terribly sick; no way to avoid knowing; but I saw with my own eyes the way he played. After he had died and been buried in that rainy earth, I sat in the Beaulieu street house remembering this prophecy in the snow.

I reviewed my whole little life. I sought to keep my soul together as well as body. I ate to live and grow; and I mused to live and grow, and even today I ask you, how else can I keep body and soul together. We were moving to another house and I didn't want to do that at all. Being a child I knew the beauty of remaining in the house which still bore the haunting presence of my departed brother; to go anywhere else would mean the deliberate beginning of forgetfulness. My brother b—yegads, I keep saying brother for mother—my mother broke into tears (it was an ordinary slip, the "br" of broke intruding on the "m" of mother)—my mother broke into tears at the sight of his usual sitting places while for me it was the best and simplest way to remember him and dote on him with gladness. In fact, I expected him back any time. But we were moving.

I spent some time on those big sunny steps in the school backyard across the street. There must have been some notoriety attached to me because of the death in my family. I probably said "ah-bwa ahbwa" among great groups of children now.

[. . . .] When Gerard hit his mortal week my mother became so sick & harried they decided to send Nin and me to Aunt Buckley's house in Nashua, N.H. The night of this decision the house was filled with relatives; it was precisely the night those cousins stole our fireworks and prematurely set them off in the backyard. I had the darkest notion the cemetery folk would get after them for that; they probably did. I don't remember the dark cartrip to Nashua and yet of course I must; and it bemuses me to think on it, that some kid at exactly the same time was taken on such a trip, from, say, Lubbock Texas to Salt Lake City, and to this day he remembers watching the telephone wires by moonlight, the ghostly hills that with his imaginary scythe (the one we talked about in Utah) (no it was Nevada) he systematically and mysteriously cut down. In fact, too, how many Americans remember their first car-rides and the phantom horse that ran alongside the car; or even the phantom of themselves that kept abreast running frantically in the earth of night, through rain, over raw clay cuts, around trees, over rooftops, never for once lagging till the car itself slowed down: I do wish I could ask Americans if this didn't happen to them too?—and if so, then these poor hasty words of mine may mean something to them, something they always knew and never thought to tell. For the New England boy like me, the phantom horse, or self, that rides along the car has to do a lot of stonewall jumping; if it's a scythe, it has to do some fancy stonewall cutting; and as you told me in Nevada (or as I told you) for the western lad it's a larger scythe that has to accommodate itself to longer spaces: so if some boy was taken on a tragic ride in 1926 across the raw land of America, as I was in New England, and swung his vast imaginary knife across the spaces of night, as I did, to cut down everything in sight merely because it was there, only a longer scythe and stranger arrangements for the cutting of ever-so-distant hills, ah well, ah well, I wish I could talk with him. Enough. This is my theme. We arrived at Aunt Buckley's house in the middle of the night and I was taken upstairs to sleep with cousins Richard and Henry. Thus began a strange week in their house and in the crazy backyards and alleys amid hundreds of screaming interesting children: great sagas went on: I sneaked down the side alley and came

around the front and there were cries. Also a dog bit me. All this time my poor brother was dying, my poor brother of whom I've said so little for lack of knowledge and perhaps memory.

Did I, during this week in Nashua, wonder at the unforgettable and enigmatic night he had come to my cribside and stood over me like a gaunt and ragged phantom? After all I knew of his great goodness, what then was this vigil in the dark, and why had it frightened me, and why did I secretly believe he probably hated me after all? Because I cannot remember this first enigma's facts maybe I'll never know an enigma again and all's been lost. He who had been my great kind brother had also been my hater in the night. In cahoots with the cemetery dead beneath the house, he had made light to flash on my ceiling, perhaps the light; this failing to destroy me, and I already informed of the prophecy of his death from the rattling crackerfires of 4th July 1925, he had no other recourse but to haunt me in the night. I feel that to him, I was the knower of his death. It has been ever since then that I feel like the knower of every man's death, every man I knew that has died. Always they die on me.

And now he had died. Nin and I were taken back for the funeral. When he was lowered into his grave I knew a great many things, and as I already pointed out, saw no reason to cry. Gerard had died because of the old sunken cemetery beneath the house; it had always been so fated; when he stretched flat in the backyard to study heaven, already the fates and shrouds were pulling him from below; when night fell and his lamby clouds were blackened, the spirits rattled for his spirit and made the plaster fall. Now that he was being put into the ground, and he was dead, I knew, as I have never known since, that death does no harm, that it is the only thing does no harm, and so I never cried. He knew what he was doing, to go join the shades that would lead him to the fleece. Rain, rain seeped into his grave and seeps into his grave today; rain seeps into my father's grave a bucket of dirt away;[2] rain, rain seeps and washes their olden bones tonight. What evil transformations have come upon my brother and

---

2. Leo Kerouac was buried beside his son Gerard in the family plot in the Catholic cemetery in Nashua, New Hampshire.

my father? On my father's skull there is a holy scowl; on my brother's bone there is a suffering stain. When I die, Neal, my face in the grave will be a bony mask with holes . . . SO WHAT AM I SUPPOSED TO DO?

I feel the guilt of my brother's death and my father's as well; and only when I die myself will this guilt go away. When dust takes a flyer it appoints itself strange pain and everlasting sorrow. This earth is where souls shroud up for a flash in the sun, and then collapse in dust. Dust to dust is exactly what we are. What agonies, what countless untold arguments in hotel rooms, meaningless purchases, foolish voyages and crazy disjoined intentions of love and lie go down the dust.

While I'm still alive I'm going on to Hildreth Street. There is a Dove in a Blackened Tree cooing its Timorous Tweet . . . come along, come along. I want to tell you next about my parapets of afternoon.

Be this artless, then I say, art is sly; truth that hath no style do not belie.

Jack

TO NEAL CASSADY

Jan. 8, 1951
[Richmond Hill, N.Y.]

Dear Neal,

Good God, man, what's this world come to, that I can't freely undertake to tell you (my friend & willing listener) every single thing I can recall about my life and deal with my memory as if it were my single moral responsibility, without feeling a twinge of guilt that I would bore "the reader." Yes, the "mysterious reader" re-entered lately; I wrote several pages that were not primarily addressed to you, only secondarily; I tore them up; they were of no value to anybody. It's to YOU I have to tell everything. How could I address God when for the better part of my life He did not make Himself manifest and gave way to the Devil so often, and forgot me. As long as you live you will have that cell of your brain in which all these things will be stored, and as you palpitate, so will these "Confessions of a So-Called

Writer" or whatever I'll call it. Many titles came to my mind (assuming publication already): "Sad and Gone," anything like that. Meanwhile the mighty framework of Joyce's *Ulysses* or the polished marvels of Pascal's *Pensées,* or even the wild and beautiful nighttime form of [Céline's] "Death On the Installment Plan"? For I still have a secret ambition to be a tremendous life-changing prophetic artist. So long as such vanity stays on, how can anything I do be worth my own weight in water? Hunble [sic] was great.

No, the thing, the villainy of the thing, is that while I don't know what my left hand is doing, I have to go on thinking that I don't know what my left hand is doing, and my right hand (well why not?) is covered in fear.

Let me just bask in the conviction that I can't bore YOU so I may continue; just as though you and I were driving across the old U.S.A. in the night with no mysterious readers, no literary demands, nothing but us telling . . . "telling eagerly the million things we know," as I said in 1947 in my crazy notebooks . . . and the miles peel off the road as we get closer to some goal that will not bring us anything but an end.

I was planning to go on with the "Hildreth Street" story as a matter of course, chronologically and just plain logically, and yet I was bored with the subject matter, and that's another reason why I tore up the past week's two attempts and not only because I forgot my grand auditor.

Then I began to think: who's laid down the laws of "literary" form? Who says that a work must be chronological; that the reader wants to know what happened anyhow, and by anyhow may be not mean any time, any where, any old thing, as the whore said to the man in the alley? Just so long as "it happened," as Allen said in the madhouse ("Anyhow it happened"), and of itself in the really bleak enigmas of time. Let's tear time up. Let's rip the guts out of reality. The man on his deathbed has wild cursorial visions that begin here and end anywhere. I am, pops, that man (stuck in "pops" to avoid the literary sound of "I am that ma-n-n-n.") Lordy and by golly, this is hard. But since there is no "reader," only you, then, why, goddamn and hellsbells, let me just take off on what occurs to me . . . from the impulse of the last installment, of course, because I wouldn't even

subject YOU to meaningless rambling. No, this makes sense, and connects darkly.[1]

I've just told you about the first four years of my life. Therefore you know it almost as well as I do. Then what would you, if you had the Strange Dickensian Vision on Market Street that I had in San Francisco in the month of February 1949?[2]

On with the story. Twenty-three years after the death of my brother let us look and see what happened to me in a vision, before going back to Hildreth street when the signs are right. Right? You know all the circumstances of my presence in Frisco at this time. But that particular night you were with Carolyn (his second wife, dear reader) and I was with LuAnne (go to hell, dear reader), and here's what happened.

It was in that low-priced hotel on O'Farrell Street . . . it began there. LuAnne and I were having a pretty good rapport. The light was out, we lay in the bed clothes on, the neon flashed in and out, and I told her all about the Great Snake of the World and how I was going to write a book about it. She listened as always, and as you know probably had a thousand other secret thoughts pertaining to her immediate plight. We were stone broke; staying in the hotel because of a friendly deskman willing to wait a week for rent; and had spent the entire night before going around completely beat for hand-outs. This is not the point. We decided to go out and eat. We were going to manage this in the following way: her friend Jean (wasn't

---

1. In *Allen Verbatim,* Ginsberg stated that Kerouac was developing a prose style in his letters to Cassady that "was the long confessional of two buddies telling each other everything that happened, every detail, every cunt-hair in the grass included, every tiny eyeball flick of orange neon flashed past in Chicago by the bus station; all the back of the brain imagery. This required sentences that did not necessarily follow exact classic-type syntactical order, but which allowed for interruption with dashes, allowed for the sentences to break in half, take another direction (with parentheses that might go on for paragraphs). It allowed for individual sentences that might not come to their period except after several pages of self reminiscence, of interruption and the piling on of detail, so that what you arrived at was a sort of stream of consciousness visioned around a specific subject (the tale of the road) and a specific view point (two buddies late at night meeting and recognizing each other like Dostoyevsky characters and telling each other the tale of their childhood)."

2. See *On the Road,* Part Two, Section 10.

it?) was living with a nightclub owner in a swanky apartment house. The owner had an old geezer on the line who wanted to meet LuAnne. She was going to go there, put on some of Jean's clothes, borrow five bucks from the nightclub owner, and come out to join me. I waited in the street. And as I told you before, I waited a hell of a long time and got so bored I went into a little bar and immediately I wanted to eat oysters because there was a sign saying "Oysters 60c dozen." I had about 60c all told. I do this often. I ordered up and ate them at the bar. Then I walked out broke. Now, waiting in a doorway for cruel LuAnne was not without its self-pitying advantages, and this I did. A sort of gangster came out of the apartment house, walked to a garage six doors down, had his car brought out, and drove right back to the awning. Filled with crazy fancies about what his life must be like, it was not without amazement that I watched a pretty young girl, an old geezer, and LuAnne come stepping out on the sidewalk and move towards the car. She was dolled up like a whore—overdressed, overanxious, furtive, undecided. She never even did me the honor of a secret sign. No doubt she saw me out of the corner of her eye; I was across the street in the door of an insurance building. I flipped my cigarette in the gutter to make a sign of my own. She teetered delicately on whore-feet in the wake of an extremely old, bald, doddering Greek of some kind. It was a grim party. No laughter rang out. The gangster threw open the back door, the girls got in, LuAnne in the back with the old Greek, Jean in front; and just as grimly the car eased off without a worldly sound and vanished in the San Fran nightlife.

Beautiful waves of pity flowed over me as I trudged home. It was impossible for me to go back to the hotel because I didn't want to have anything to do with her; extricate tangled lies, create new ones, and all the hassles of foolish life. I preferred my own pure angel soul.

In this way my soul was prepared for a strange vision. I was merely walking on Market Street, headed for Liberty Street up the curve of Mission at the foot of the hill (you know where) and just minding my own business. It was an ordinary night. Nothing extraordinary happened. The nights in California are like indoors; there's no weather, no elements. Everybody is in the big livingroom of life. Cars pass by, trolleys clang; groups scuffle by; newsboys shout, and you

look up—and there is no sky, just the ceiling of strange California time. Crowds surge around you; it's like being home in the parlor. I was going along like this: wearing my black leather jacket, unbuttoned, musing generally, thinking if you would be home or not at Liberty Street and would I have further hassles with Carolyn (or had I had them yet then)? How strange it is to be a continent away from "home" and you don't know where "home" is anyhow and all the "home" you've got is in your head. Nothing, nothing happened.

And yet as I strolled by a little fish-n'-chips joint and casually looked in, suddenly I saw a woman, the proprietress, staring at me with a kind of fear; why, I don't know. She was middleaged, a little gaunt but not starved; her hair no particular color, except I had the immediate sensation she was "English," don't ask why. She just looked exactly like all the "English" women you see in movies about London. In fact, I retract, she looked like a "Londoner" above all things, and as you know I've been to L. She looked like the frightened women in Charles Dickens movies, and mother of David Copperfield, anything you wish. And I think because I wore a black leather jacket, and was unshaven, she may possibly have taken me for a hood of some kind, with a gun—(that thought of the gun came to me, at least, because I had gone around Frisco with a gun wearing that exact jacket two years earlier)[3]—and probably was frightened either for the idea I'd bust right in and pull a holdup on the spot, or was merely casing for later. This is all in my own imagination, understand. She probably only wore a look which I took to be "frightened," and which may just have been her habitual absentminded gook-stare in those selfsame "bleak enigmas of time." She saw me, she saw "through" me—it doesn't matter, it seemed to me she was terrified of me. I didn't even stop for an instant, only looked in with really extraordinary intensity, and for no reason. I might have been hungry; by all means I was crazy. I stared right at her. I allowed myself a moment to dig the rest of the establishment. It was filled to capacity: about 20 people ranged along stools at the counter having a hearty cheap meal of fish and chips, and all of them poor people. Men with

---

3. See Kerouac's letter to Cassady, September 13, 1947 (page 127).

their wives; Negroes, little children, and a handful of real wino bums—all in the dull light of genuine beaneries. In a nonce I saw the other worker, the proprietor, her "husband," as I imagined, who was a burly Greek with hairy arms and who struck me at once as being an extremely honest and patient man of some sort. No reason whatever for this; it just struck me so. This is what I saw, this is all that happened.

I passed the joint and walked on no more than six steps, and it happened. I stopped dead in my tracks and shivered and tingled all over from top to toe; it was one of the most tremendous sensations of my life. For one full second I had no consciousness whatever of where I was, or even that I was anywhere on any sidewalk of the world; I was completely alone. An amazing notion had occurred to me; a vision, to be exact; but before I could realize it was a vision, I stood completely stoned on the sidewalk in unbelievable and heavenly rapture. For a moment like that I'd be willing to suffer a whole ten years of grimness again. For that moment I'd be willing to go back and go through all of it again . . . even the events of that night, the sad disappointment of LuAnne, the hunger, the tiredness of the long walk, the whole hard trip that took us there, anything, up to ten years before. Because if I were ready for that vision, as I was not then, I think I would be able to understand everything and never forget it; particularly I think I would know the nature of God and all the life He made, and I would be so saved nobody could find me any more. Meanwhile I stood there—for about ten seconds, the first in heavenly rapture, the last nine in contemplation of rapture (which is beatitude)—as people walked around me as they would around a post, a solid post. My feet tingled so much I thought the sidewalk had personally sent up its shivers. Never have I felt so close, so sensually close, to the actual ground I walk on. I thought I would be able to get down on the ground and talk to it—because it had come alive, and man it wasn't anything but a dirty old pavement, not mother earth at all.

Not to get hung up on the effects of this vision, let me tell you what it was, and again, it really wasn't anything: it just simply occurred to me, beyond belief, within belief, in all belief, that this woman was my mother, or properly, had been my mother, in Lon-

don, years ago, way off across the night of the world; and that when she was my mother, I was a completely rotten sort, yelled at her, stole her savings, stayed out all night and finally became a footpad and robbed people till I was caught and sent to the GAOL (my dear Neal, GAOL). As to historical time, I have a faint idea it was in Dickens' time, or the Nineteenth Century; therefore, if we count Frisco as having any reality, it was Frisco 19th Century I was standing in. Therefore (I reasoned swiftly), I had come six thousand miles across ocean and raw land to come and bother her again; and as I passed her beanery, and she saw me before I saw her, the old fright came back to her. For in the meantime her life had seen better days. Bereft of a bad son, she had left England to try a new life in America; and as America will, it popped up a Greek lunchcart-man for her ("delicately they dive for Greeks beneath the railway station. Sweet Thames, flow gently till I end my song."—Wolfe.) Gradually she readjusted herself to life, the tears stopped flowing, she forgot her evil son, who was only the product of an evil old father anyway, already the ghost of other gallows ghosts (Blimey, 'e was a 'eartless one!). The Greek was a big bulk of ugliness and hairy arms; but he was good, and he was patient, and he was kind. He had a little business and offered her partnership and security; they got married, and she became a humble New World Lady, leaving all the dark horrors of London behind her forever.

And here was her awful Jack-son returned from the shadow of the gallows, her wandering blackguard of a son, her pimp-child, her thief, returned to cheat her once more but never so crude as to try to do so right off the bat. Oh no, first he would stalk and prowl around the lunchcart, boil in his own schemes, add fillips to his everlasting persuasion-speeches, count his profits to come. "No," she seemed to say as she shot that terrified glance at me (which I recalled six steps along the sidewalk), "no, don't come back and plague your honest hardworking mother again. Isn't once enough?—can twice succeed? You are no longer like a son to me—and like your dark father, my first husband 'ere this kindly Greek took pity on a poor lost Englishwoman, you are no good, all bad, inclined to drunkenness and routs and final disgraceful robbery of the fruits of my 'umble labours in the 'ashery. Oh son! dark son! haunt me no more, hunt

· 279 ·

me not! Once, once is all! Oh my son, did you not ever go on your knees and pray for deliverance for all your sins and scoundrel acts! Lost boy!—child of the widespread dark!—depart! do not haunt my soul, I have done well forgetting you. Re-open no auld wounds. Be as if you had never returned and looked into this humbled window —flashing-eyed, keen for the blade, lusting to see my labouring humilities, my few scrubb'd pennies—hungry to grab, quick to deprive, sullen, unloving, mean-minded son of my flesh. Do go, please go! Go thou lose for gain. And see my silent Greek, he is just, he is humble, he is kind . . . Son! Son!"—as I passed and vanished—"Son!"

Suddenly innumerable real memories, a whole night-world of them, all of them distinct and miraculously English, whole images of old London and panged memories of certain streetcorners where I stood, as if I had actually and not only in the imagination lived all this, flooded through my being, and these were the precise messengers of that tingling sensation I mentioned. For they came so by themselves, I was struck dumb, and they were complete. There I stood in ecstasy on Market Street, rushing to reconstruct the events that must have transpired between my former sonhood to this poor woman in London up until this one haunted moment in San Francisco, California, February, 1949. How did I get there?

That's right where I lost it—trying to remember how I got there, for then the onrushing memory of those events tangled with my own American or "real-life" memories and everything became jumbled just like a shortwave radio at midnight that brings sounds from all over the world in a discordant but definite MEDLEY. I'd been there; I knew I'd been there; and now I'd never know how, or when, or why, or what, and life was still a foolish hassle when the vision died down and I stood dreaming on the pavement.

I never even went back for a single look into the beanery, just walked on; and I remember, I was going to tell you about it immediately, but that was the night you had gotten the pots-and-pans job and when I came in you began the joyous talk.

Considering my childhood which I have told you, what would you make of this? This is not only a fleeting glimpse of possible reincarnation but a definite sensation of the presence of God, and like the

shortwave radio, it's all in the air and is still there for me to grasp another day, and I hope to, I want to, I know I will.

Jan. 9, 1951
[Richmond Hill, N.Y.]

Dear Neal,

To continue. A new experience has touched the foundation of my soul since I wrote you the last words last night. Slowly and in due time we'll get to it, because it forms the peak-top of these foothill things. Ah man, today I understood for the first time the meaning and the truth of the Virgin Mary. When I tell it to you, you will realize, without surface pessimism, why I awkwardly brought up the dualism—the paradox—of trying to reconcile Jesus and the "black cunt" we spoke of in the Denver hotel room.

Very well, I've told you of the strange vision on Market Street. Of course I always felt like an orphan because my brother, who came before me, died to "save me," as it were, for my mother's arms (here I'm acquiescing to the pre-established musings of any Freudian mysterious-reader). But my triumph was my loss. The poor Englishwoman, who is my real secret mother, and who was the wife of my sinning foul father, rejects me in the night, and I am alone like Job on the foul-heap. It's as though Jesus was my brother and I was his flesh-and-blood Judas. Did you ever see the great Titian portrait or picture of Jesus and Judas?—the scene takes place right after the Last Supper. "There is one among you who will betray me," Jesus has said, and the disciples sadly shake their heads. From among them steps forth Judas, a tanned and muscular man, feverish for gold, trembling in his boots, to deny in Christ's face that he could ever betray him. You see his powerful trembling hand reaching out; you see the Son's pale, feeble hands hanging away disconsolate and sad from his reach, almost shrinking, but with the same "detachment of the Eunuch" as though even if Judas could betray him, betrayal could never touch his Fleece. Judas: perspiring, sun-flushed, maybe a little drunk on the Last Wine, glittery-eyed, eager (a little bit like Allen

· 281 ·

[Ginsberg] at moments) is reaching out that big hand. Have you ever seen my hand and wrist when it hangs out of a half-rolled sleeve? It's the same Judas-wrist . . . of physical strength (don't wristpull with me now I'm well again!) (or at least not with your left hand), the same sweaty muscular greedy wrist; and Jesus is looking at it with a cool sorrow in which at the same time there is the sadness of the Lamb, for he knows. Judas loves him; he wishes he could be forgiven even while he betrays;—the well known cake-and-eat-it rule. Jesus seems to be wondering how a man could be so dense, or so greedy, or so paradoxical, and so mad, sad, gone, and wild. He seems to say, "Do not touch me with this soiled and anxious hand." Judas is sorrowful too, for he loved Him well when he loved Him so. No, it's all over between them. I gaze at the hand of Christ in its delicate dovelike gesture; I think of Hal Chase. Most of all I think of Gerard. Judas is me, Jesus is Gerard. What have I gone and done; and what hath God wrought?

I never asked to be Judas and I'm sure that Judas never did; and in fact, our friend Harrington once put forth the crazy idea that Judas was a political pawn in the plot to make Jesus a martyr (a superficial modern pragmatic idea). But if I hadn't been born then how could I have betrayed Gerard; for I betrayed him merely by living when he died. He was an angel, I was a mortal; what he could have brought to the world, I destroyed by my mere presence; because if I had not lived, Gerard would have lived.

Isn't it mad, that I sense this now, and sensed it as a child, and all of it completely devoid of rational meaning; all of it merely a "sense" and a hidden conviction, and a fear, and perhaps a hope, and a thousand-and-one-mysteries.

Why, then, too, must that Englishwoman my mother drive me off into the night when it is solely her responsibility that I am at all alive! So the footpad disappeared and did never come back to plague her.

Today I was in church—today Jan. 9—thinking about what happened the first day we moved to Hildreth Street; I say this, but as you know I also had many meditations of the kind you have when you just rest in a church. It was St. Patrick's Cathedral, at eventide, or just before, so that blue light still pressed at the stained glass windows high up. I found myself in the middle of a novena. More

anon about the present . . . I was thinking over the incident of Hildreth Street, how exactly I would tell it to you, particularly how I would tie it in with everything that has come so far in these awkward disclosures of all I know on earth.

Here is what happened on Hildreth Street. It was August 1926; a pale, sickly, hot August dogday, with that terrible phosphorescent glare above the rooftops that makes you blink, even if your eyes are capable of staring into the golden sun a moment (as I was able to do until I was twenty). The trees hung like old sullen toadstools over black grass; sweat oozed from my forehead like it does from the foreheads of feverish Indian children in the jungle foothills of Mexico. Something heavy hung in the air, so that it seemed the world had become a hothouse under glass; not only that, it seemed the world had stopped turning and everything was at a standstill. Not a breeze, not a light—but a general over-all grayness, in fact a sickly paleness, above dead vegetations and silent rooftops. Hildreth Street was a fairly busy outlying street of Galloway[1] with trolley tracks in the middle, cobblestones between the rails, and modern paving laid over the rest of the road for the traffic of old architectural solemn grandfather cars of 20th Century America. I mention all this atmosphere for reasons. Then I saw the house.

It was a huge, pale, shrouded house; somewhat like the day itself; with walls of gray kello-stone, pebbles and cement combined. The yard was vast and cemeterial. In fact there was a cemetery a house away, a large one, with stones sewn among motionless grass under the bleak black trees. I really hated this after the raggedy atmospheres of Beaulieu Street. My father was in the chips in 1926; he had gone all-out to take my mother away from the scene of her boy's death, possibly trying to please her with a fancy house too. An elderly couple lived upstairs; the entire house comprised about 14 rooms in all. This is all I noticed at first.

We walked in, as the movers toiled with the furniture across the long streetfront yard, and explored the varnished hardwood halls. Little Nin was delighted; I was not. I followed my mother as she

---

1. Galloway was Kerouac's name for Lowell in *The Town and the City*.

experimentally tried all the closet doors. It was a gloomy chamber beneath the weight of a gloomy sky. My mother opened a closet door, something white flew at her, she screamed, and the thing whapped on her head with terrible vehemence. I was stricken in my tracks. "Les morts sont dans la maison!" she screamed—"The Dead are in the house!" I was too young to know what this white thing was that hit her on the head. I knew it must be Gerard. Now he was mad at all of us and not just me. He was rattling after us with a vengeance.

Little Nin was laughing; it was only an old ironingboard; when you opened the door it always flew out. But my mother was almost inconsolable; she too was convinced, I think, that it was some kind of wrath from the dead; and not only from Gerard (if at all) but from the whole mass of dead humankind among whose ranks he was now but an insignificant, diminutive member. "They made him do it!" I thought darkly. I dreaded the thought of the cemetery a door away; for if we lived over a cemetery and were haunted, what would happen when we lived next to one in the open? Ah me, my insignificant fears were only just beginning.

We told Pop about it and he laughed. One night, while sitting on the porch, he fell right through the rocker and completely demolished it. We saw the remnants of it in the morning: sticks and stones and bones on all sides of us. Let the dead bury the dead.

It was about that time I began discovering the fact that I was alive and could do things on my own. In the golden afternoon I stood on the sunporch among piles of unarranged furniture and made a complete speech, gestures and all, to a mattress leaning on the wall; I can never forget it. I can get so high thinking sometimes I can almost remember what this speech was all about and I'm positive I'll remember it yet.

In fact, soon . . . The main thing now is that I remember my mother on the afternoon of that "charade" on the sunporch: it could only have been the very day after the ironingboard gave her the ghostly slap. The sun had come out, the dogday was gone, my fears were somewhat eased, so I went into the kitchen where she stood among piles of unpacked boxes, and I said in French, "Ma, I want a butter-and-sugar sandwich."

"Why yes, my little Jean," and she simply made me a butter-and-

sugar sandwich—that is, not a sandwich, but a "beurre"—which is butter and sugar spread on a slice of bread. This I took back to my mattress on the porch and showed it how I could eat as well as make speeches. That kitchen and that sunporch, incidentally, were at the back of the house and faced the best part of the Hildreth Street environs, namely, a little brush forest, through which a wonderful path wound its way until you came to the tufts of a sandbank that overlooked literally all the rooftops of Lowell. Hildreth Street is on a ridge, Lowell is actually a valley. These were my "parapets of afternoon" that I promised to tell you about; also, later, I'll tell you of the fine dreams, amazing dreams, I had since of these sunny places which were sometimes changed into rattling night of Gerard's death haunting me. O Ghost!—to be the "brother of Jesus" and live to tell it! (I don't know seriously whether it was before 1926 or after that I came to identify my brother with Jesus.) But ain't I gay?!!—this is because, I began this page after wonderful moments with my wife, and the evening's earlier work was done in gloom and sweat. Ahwell. But to resume.

My life is like a sea, my memory the boat. Today in the cathedral, as I sat musing over the incident of the ghostly ironingboard and pondered other things to tell you about Hildreth Street, a greater, more urgent train of events occurred to me: and these events were transpiring before my very eyes.

I came into the Cathedral not only to get out of the bitter cold, but because, moments before, I had stood in Grand Central Station looking around with a futile sorrow for a place to sit and think. All there was—marble floor, rushing crowds, dime lockers, bleak seatless spaces and bright vast corners. What a thing men have let themselves in for, in this New York!—so big that it is utterly impossible to make arrangements for people to sit, or the whole world will sit. I hurried out in the cold and cut up 5th Avenue, past the (yes) Yale Club and past Harcourt Brace (yes) and swore and cursed; and cut right by the Doubleday Book store without deigning to go in and see if they had my book on display. And why should I care, when I've renounced fiction. The church is the last sanctuary in this world, the first and the last. It is the worldly edifice of the Lord; I'm done sneering at any part of it.

As you know, St. Patrick's is a Gothic cathedral, copied after Rheims or Chartres or whichever, with a rectory in the back, and a big department store across the street on 50th street. I hurried through a slamming gang of truckmen who were pushing boxes out of the department store (Bonwit Teller or something[2]) and ducked right across the street and into the side entrance of the church. (Of course I didn't duck through the "slamming gang" of workmen; actually I was across the street looking at them vaguely; I only brought them in because I'm going to use them later; and so I do, do, do renounce fiction.) It was pretty cold in the church too; I shivered for the entire hour and a half I was there; but that's a small matter.

Such lovely silence; such heights of mysterious upreaching darkness "fading among the naves"; such splendors of stained glass window, altar, chandelier, pillar, etc. etc., and as if I was thinking of that. No, I was thinking of God; even more than that I was thinking of myself and my desire to sit and think, without smoking, without fidgeting, for hours in the silence of the church. At first I sneered as all the commonplace "renegade Catholic" thoughts came to me in regimental order; but soon I was lost in real sweet contemplation of what was going on.

I must say, first, I dipped my finger in the font of holy water and made the sign of the cross, and in fact, with the nonchalance of a practiced Catholic . . . the arrogance of a Boston Irishman . . . in hopes the New Yorker "converts" might see this. I cut right along up the side aisle till I came to a suitably solitary spot. But it was too cold there, being near the door which kept opening, so I cut up further till I was in the middle of the church against the 50th Street wall. There I kneeled—with a sneer as I noticed how the New Yorkers have put a band of soft material to cushion the knees, while in Lowell as I'll tell you later I spent many hours straight kneeling on hard wood till my knees were seared with proper pain. Oh, I'd been through this crazy mill. Then I sat back and relaxed. At first I wanted to drape my arm over the edge of the pew but I thought it would appear too arrogant. This reminded me of my newspaper days in

---

2. In fact, the department store is Saks Fifth Avenue.

Lowell when I walked home from the paper in the hoary dusks of winter and made a great point of not tipping my cap as I passed St. Jean de Baptiste church, like literally everyone else was doing, especially old bow-legged Frenchmen with clay pipes who stick up a finger for the weather and say "Hallo l'pere!" which means "Hello the father!" when they see another oldtimer cutting along.

Gradually I grew to be very sad. I put away all my worries of where to get a job, how to get to California next month, what to do about my poor wife whom I had been torturing in my subtle way lately, and just merely sat thinking in church. How nice it would be to sit thinking in a church for several hours every day of one's life! From sadness I went to speculation and general philosophy. I could hear—all of us in the church could hear—the faint roar of New York traffic without. I looked up to see the blue light of evening on the mighty windows, and I thought, "If it was only 500 years ago, and in Stuttgart, and I could go up to my sacristy and write my devotional hymns and ring the bells!" and instead, outside, it was the tremendous, awful walls of Manhattan skyscrapers. Oh, what an evil world was outside, and what a really evil world it is. But then I realized that the church was such a mighty and beautiful thing, it could stand in Manhattan in 1950 with the same dignity it stood in Stuttgart in 1450; that to its lovely meaningful towers, what did "environment" matter, or history, or what men had come to and could ever come to. It was a rock of the ages. The whole weight of medieval scholarship was behind it; the unbelievable labours of thousands of impoverished artisans and mere amateur laborers; the grand inspirations of men like Buxtehude and Bach . . . etc. etc. . . . so that you see, my first thoughts were superficial, or let's just say "aesthetic."

Gradually I began gazing fixedly at the statues of Jesus and the Virgin Mary and all the angels ranged about, and my "scholarly" mind settled itself to studies of the "Catholic myth," as I so foolishly called it in my past fictions. Frankly, Neal, I don't know when it happened; when it was I began almost crying.

First there were two old priests. They came in from the back and settled themselves in a pew to my left, so that I could see them occasionally. Can you picture two old winos on Larimer Street buddying along to their daily chores, maybe just taking out the garbage

in an alley, but determined to get it done so they can drink all night? Well, with the same old W.C. Fields absentminded stumble they came to their pew and, one of them merely going in without kneeling as he fumbled with his breviary, the other took great occasion to kneel (perhaps for the both of them) and followed in. And there they began arranging their hats and bibles and whispering in loud hoarse voices, oblivious to anyone else, just like any other two-oldtimers in this world; it was this touch of real-oldtimerness that made me wince. The thing they were apparently doing was this: they were either making a novena, which is a 30-day or 40-day daily stint with a devotional purpose, to gain a certain favor from the Almighty, or they were doing something priests have to do every day or once a week. Whatever it was, they had to do it, like a job, and they proceeded at once to do it without any further hoarse whispering and figeting. Both opened their breviaries and began reading swiftly. I gathered there was so much to read and so little time to make it, so they hurried. I wondered with all my heart and soul where they would be going after, they looked so eager to get it done and cut out. Priests have a good time and do a lot of things. But gad, to see them, like any other two old guys, like seeing your father and my father in priest vestments, burly, red-faced, harassed, hurrying at their tasks, and such gentle lovely tasks, the reading of words they had read a thousand times before, all about angels and the Lord and the Lamb and the Virgin Mother, over and over again till it really becomes interesting and mysterious, enough to make my heart bleed for guys like you and me that have to haul boxes and toss tires and yell in slamming gangs to make a living. They looked like they were making a living. God knows I'm not being facetious here—or funny, or sarcastic. This was their duty; the duty of two burly men, to read of angels in a tiny book. And the biggest burliest priest had one arm nonchalantly draped over the edge of the pew just as I had wanted to do earlier. Engrossed in watching them and musing, I was surprised to see further developments had transpired in the cathedral.

A tall athletic young priest was cutting up to make a sermon; simultaneously I noted how much the crowd had thickened; and before I knew it I was in the middle of a fullblown church service. Since I

was in the church utterly given over to pure meditation I obediently kneeled, or stood, or sat at the young priest's behest and followed everyone else in so doing. He made several cryptic remarks evidently having to do with the novena everyone was on, and then began a sermon.

He began talking about how "every ambitious woman wants to see her child become successful in industry, in a profession, in some constructive field." I slapped the side of my head in despair; for by this time my meditations had carried me far from this modern competitive world into thought of a simple and medieval character. I almost sneered. Then I noticed he was starting out this way for greater punch; because then he said, "What were the thoughts of the Virgin Mother on that first Christmas night with regard to her little son? For she knew, only poverty, humiliation and suffering could save him and she knew he was come for strange reasons into the world." And from there on this fine young priest made a beautiful sermon about the advantages of humility and piety in the invisible world that will surmount the pride and decadence of the visible. I agreed with him. I almost applauded, and realized how for years I've been mechanically applauding in worldly audiences. No need to applaud in the church of the Lord. I mulled over all the "corruption" of the church, which is the worldly edifice of the Lord, and yet, assuming and saying that it is worldly, how can corruption so-called be avoided, and why not corruption in a world which has the Lord as well as the Devil in it? Shall I tell you?—red Christmas streamers hung from the pulpit, decorations, which, in the dimness, took on the exact shape of Satan as I stared; yes, Satan leered there beneath the pious young wonderful priest as he spoke to us. "I say, Father, isn't that Satan showing there?" I would have said to the old priest, and I guess he would have replied, "I see him not; Satan's seen by those he claims." I really do wonder, how many other people saw Satan in those red streamers today? But this is my "modern-art" training.

And now I must tell you of the Virgin Mary. Even before the young priest spoke of her I had seen the Light concerning her; so his words impressed me doubly. I was just staring at what I think was a brand new statue of the Virgin Mary holding her Son in her arms after the

crucifixion; at once I thought of my mother and Gerard; and other thoughts pressed in. For instance, I knew that last year, the Holy Year, the Pope had decreed, for the first time in Christianity, the dogma that the Virgin Mary had risen to heaven incarnate. For this reason a lot of churches all over the world were building special Mary statues and altars, and this was one of the newest and largest in the world. It was way over beyond the regular altar. I was amazed to see so many young girls, shopgirls, kneeling around it at the white rail. I couldn't believe my eyes when I saw first one, then another, then all of them reach out, touch the statue, touch the red flowers, and bow their heads. Such mysteries go on in a New York novena among towers. I wondered what it was all about, what the girls saw in this Virgin Mary business.

Suddenly I remembered what was wrong between my wife and myself in the past days; she'd said she felt like a "frog" sometimes in the midst of sexual intercourse; I remember it had irritated me, just like other times when she expressed regret for "the poor little thing" when she dressed a chicken for the oven. "Too sensitive for words!" I'd think—and immediately put myself on a sensual plane to further annoy her (though it's not so simple as that). Also she never considered herself worth touching when she had a period. Most of all I thought of her—on the impetus of seeing a girl exactly like her in the pew in front of me—with head bowed, kneeling, a shawl over her pretty humble head, and I almost cried to think of it. I saw how all of earthly life, with its gutty sufferings, really passes like a river through the body of a woman while the man, unknowing of these things and "clean," just cuts along arrogant. I saw how it is the woman who gives birth, and suffers, and has afterbirths dragged out of her, and navel cords snipped and knotted, and bleeds—while the man boasts of his bloody prowesses. I saw how it is the woman who suffers for the sins of man. Suffers especially more so, because the earth is so much in her, temptation drives her mad. I had even been annoyed at the poor girl lately because she conducted long secret meditations of her own in the bedroom while I "wrote." "What are you thinking about?" I'd ask slyly. What's going on in her great soul now? I'd ask myself sarcastically. Bah, bah, bah, and all that;

as if, and certainly BECAUSE I was a "writer" she, a mere girl, could not possibly have a soul like mine worthy of hours of deep contemplation.

But I saw that girls want to be pure souls too, and I mean to the extent of really putting the world behind them, like nuns. Only reason this shouldn't have occurred to me earlier, even though as a kid I feared and admired Ste. Therese, is because in America so much emphasis is placed on the sexy side as well as the housekeeping side of women. What's the difference between the original whore of Babylon with all her perfumes and the regular shopgirl who pastes lipstick on and shakes her ass before mirrors? Now it has become fashionable to smear-up for conquest, and once it was only whores who did it. If I had been a little boy of Galilee, and seen the humble women in shawls kneeling at the temple, what would I have thought of Miss Rheingold on the billboard or the Toni twins?[3] No, I saw that the girl has a soul and that her only hope is in the Virgin Mary. For if the burden on earth and dirty [sic] and blood could be lifted from one woman, then it may be lifted from another, or to be more precise, the burden is already lifted because the Virgin Mary was; just as our sins are expiated by the sacrifice of the great Lord Jesus, without any of us having to be crucified on a cross.

I no longer wondered what the gals saw in the Virgin Mary. Even then, I saw one particular girl hurrying towards the Mary altar, not as if she was eager to reach and touch it so the burden could be lifted, but primarily to shake her ass before any men who might be watching; her coat was designed exactly to show the roundness of her body and she knew it, and shook it. No, the tall, humble Joan-girl in front of me, kneeling with bowed head, was a woman who dearly and sincerely prayed for the deliverance of her soul from the perfidy of dirt.

I further noticed that there were no young men in the church, only old ones; and I knew they were all out making money or being hoodlums with all their might. If I had been a little boy of Galilee, and

---

3. Models featured in advertising campaigns for beer and for home permanents.

seen the humble young men standing motionless before the sheep, what would I have thought of the go-getter in his Brooks Brothers suit hurling himself through a revolving door with that arrogant scowl? I would have thought he was a scribe, or a pharisee, or a thief. If I had been a little boy of Galilee, and seen the old men praying at the Star, what would I have thought of the be-spatted executive hurrying from a conference? I would have thought he was Caesar. This is our world.

I wished that the church was not only a sanctuary but a refuge for the poor, the humiliated, and the suffering; and I would gladly join in prayer. The priest sprayed incense from his ciborium: everybody kneeled: I gladly joined in: no other power on this earth could make me gladly kneel, or even stand up. Did I ever tell you about the time I was in the Navy madhouse and the Admiral of the Fleet came in? —I was the only one who didn't stand up, all the other nuts did. No, I wished all mankind could gather in one immense church of the world, among the arcades of the angels, & when it came time to take of bread, I wished Jesus would reach out his hand to a single loaf and make of it two billion loaves for every single soul in the world. What else would we need besides God and the bread for our poor unfortunate bodies? And then someday we could all become pure souls—not animals and not even mortal men, but angels of heaven —and spend all our time, like the old priests, scanning the words of God over and over again till they become our only concern, our only language, our only imagery, our only wish and our only life, eternal life.

[. . . .] Am I allowed to return now to my childhood? If these pages ramble, then I am a rambler and nothing else. I want to get on and tell you about all the real fleshly wonderful people and things of my childhood in Lowell and how it lives in my brain and how it will be the only knowledge of the world I can ever have, with which to make my confession on Judgment Day.

Still more mysteries yet to come. My afternoon in the Cathedral is not the sum and crown. And when I walked out of the Cathedral, and it was dark, that slamming gang of workmen was still there across the street, and I thought: "These men must make a living in the gloom of earth; that they yell and slam, doesn't mean they are

not humble and believe not in the Lord and the Laws of the Lamb. No, it's elsewhere you must look for the villains of Gomorrhah. These are the shepherds—put to work for Bonwit Teller, poor devils, poor sodden workers of the world, cheaply paid for dearest labours. Goodbye World, I put you behind me, and Face the Lord."

In the subway everybody was going home to rest, instead of gathering in the Final Church of Eternal Joy, and I felt bad to see it. I began dreaming of a monastery. But when I came home I loved my wife, and kissed her tenderly, as she kissed me. The Lord is patient. Goodnight, sweet prince.

Jack

TO NEAL CASSADY

Jan. 10, 1951
[Richmond Hill, N.Y.]

Dear Buddy,

It could only have happened all in the same day, the same afternoon, because it belongs in my mind's afternoon. The Hildreth street house was a gloomy and shrouded place the dogday we moved in, and the signs were terrible; but in nature, which is the grassy field of men's lives while terror is only the occasional tincan near the fence, life ripples like the grass and new days mass over like lamby clouds. I quickly forgot the terror of the Flying Ironingboard and began to discover my mimic soul in wonderful day-hours. Salad days in lettuce nature, m'boy. We had an old Victrola made of wood, with a crank; and antique forgotten records about a half-inch thick.[1] These were my afternoon mambos of the time: "Dardanella," "Toy Soldiers" (I think it was called), and Sousa's marches; all old tinny things of the Twenties. I got up on a chair, put the records on, wound the crank, dropped the enormous needle, and got myself ready for the afternoon's doings. As the music began I picked up pillows from the plush sofa and threw them around the room, then dived on them, crying out the day's cry, and jumped away to shadowbox the light; return-

---

1. See *Doctor Sax,* "A Gloomy Bookmovie," Book Two.

ing finally to sit on the sofa, in an attitude of great Barrymore sadness, until the Great Vulture began to come for me, and I wrestled among the Fallen Giants (pillows).

Ah Neal, I must tell you of my Lifelong Vulture, precursor to the Adult Snake (Ouch, these Blakean capitals). My vulture I made myself, by placing third finger over forefinger and thumb below, wiggling thus to make a jaw. First it circled around my head, then dived to my arm, where it took a hearty horrible nip and I yelled the Saxon roar. Then the Little Man began to run up my arm; he was formed, of course, by walking fingers. Just about this time I'm telling you about I began creating this endless chase of the vulture and the man. Years, years after I was still doing it, and only recently I remembered it and did it again (willy-nilly hi), only now, being an adult and symbolic fool, I let my little man collapse and the vulture get him. No child in his right mind would let the vulture catch the man! Even now, over this antique L.C. Smith typewriter I'm taking to Frisco in our rattly truck next month, I'm making the vulture chase the man.

This was one of the very first self-discoveries I made, incidentally; the drama of the pillows came slightly afterwards. On this afternoon I speak of, I then went outside with a coil of rope and reclined in the wonderful lawn with my face to the trees and the sun above. Across the street, not Hildreth Street but the old road that intersected it, was a real old farmhouse with barn and fences and buckets; in which there lived a retired Fire Chief, testimony thereof:- an old red firewagon under the elm behind the barn. He wore suspenders; I did not know him. Further, Hildreth Street as I said was on a ridge, and I had the sensation of being on a ridge and overlooking the world. When, why, where, what, how, who, whichever—I don't know— but I tied myself up in the coils of the rope (ah snake!) & really expertly had myself trussed so that when the kids came out of school at four they thought someone had tied me up and left me wriggling on the lawn. "Who did that to you, little boy?" I made no answer, but martyred in silence. A group even formed to debate what to do. I writhed and moaned. In my world of vultures, giants, et al, it was not inconceivable that a monster should tie me up. It was late summer afternoon, September bugs beezed [sic] in the immense trees overhead, a coolness was coming, a leaf fell. The nuns came by and

shook their heads to see me. I was the meek foolish creator of a mad writhing role. I mused upon the entire world.

Untying myself I walked through the little bush path behind the house and came to the parapets of the sandbank overlooking the rooftops afar. I could see Aiken Street, the Aiken Street bridge, the river, the mills, and the hills beyond; my first glimpses of sad Galloway [Lowell] in the round (O what a day in Galloway without a lay). Those huge dusk-sounds came to me for the first time; "ululating," as Wolfe knew, like giant machinery of souls; with the hush of the way-yonder hidden falls, and rapids, over all. Wherefrom came this river that wound like a Snake through Mytown? Upon these Parapets of afternoon I bled to see the airs of man deepening upon his Holy Roof. I knew all the little children were coming home from school, I could hear them yell; I knew the women were pulling in the washlines from the rickety window, and gazing for a moment at the derelict day, and pulling in their heads to do supper in the darkening kitchen. I knew the old boys were crumping home on sore feet with the bacon in their hands. In the saloons the men were taking off the old straw hat and wiping the band of suffering around their brow; they lolled big tongues in heaps of brew, and yelled "Hallo l'père!" Over by the haunted castle red light was creeping on the pines; upon the roof of my birth-house on Old Lupine, blood was spreading slow; soon, soon, you could hear the put-put-put of a far-distant motorboat in the basins of the river, and hear tell stories of swimming at the Lake, picnics, pines, lappy-water and happy photographs. O motorgraphs! O telltale riverlake! O tome! O palapoot of boy! Menames are many, more than mary, prayall sacrosnake! Roofelyroof, rueboy, cementary, awes of allsand—Hallo-o-o-o-o vieux père! Ululu, ululu, bloody light beneath the shroud takes us westward to the shore by tail and coign and vasty air. Snakrecoeur! Mon peur! We jam on frere gyre are. Yes I love my brother Gerard. Oui j'aime mon frère Gerard.

I prayed the Lord my soul to keep and sowed my tenderness upon the heaptown sprawl; and wound back, along the snaky path, to the kitchen of the beautynight; and slept the sleep of fleece.

One such early Fall afternoon, the same, with initial tore-out leaf pining down to ground in dance of winterfear, I was in a little town

in Connecticut called Manchester; working in an Atlantic Whiteflash filling station; nineteen years old; one of the boys. No longer tying myself up with rope on lawns, or tossing pillows to the tune of Sousa's toot in the bleary parlor, or standing on sandybanks to see the Land of All, I was instead bending over oily motors with a grease-gun and a small wrench, one eye on my grimy work, the other on the falling leaf and the reddy coming dusk. Nothing particular was happening. The boys were jawing in the office by the stove and the cash register; smoking; every now and then, br-r-ing, a customer's car rolled over the hose and a guy run out to tend his needs. Drowse hung over. Our relationship: I was the youngest, was known to be a former college boy, and so was kidded. But one boy in particular was my loyalpal, Bob [. . .], who in laughing with the others still had eyes of real friendship for me, and always drove me home after work, to Hartford. In those days I was writing a Joyce-like novel in which I was the Dedalus; and called myself Duluoz. Let's do that now. Duluoz the Ladysman! They didn't believe some of the stories I told them about my conquests. In another station in East Hartford I once did something ghastly to prove my statements—Oh, a whole story in itself, but quick summary: A pretty young girl, about 17, wandered by the station every day and everybody had eyes for her. One drowsy noon I lolled in the grass between curb and sidewalk, in lunch hour, wearing Atlantic coveralls; she passed by; I looked at the lovely dimples in the flesh behind her knees, where soft white thigh of highschool girl meets calf thereof, that particularly tender spot, so beautifully dimpled and faint-blue-veined, you know it too; and resolved ON THE SPOT, for no other reason than those delectable dimples, to make her, come this or that. I started chatting with her in a lunch counter downstreet where she repaired; highschool girls don't as a rule hangout in workingmen's diners. I said something inane to open, like, "Don't you like Luckies better than Pall Malls?" as she reached for her pack; thus led things on to casual stroll in afternoon shades of suburbanland. Made a date with her; the following afternoon took her to an ever-so-tiny clump of bushes right outside Pratt & Whitney Aircraft; so ridiculously tiny and open, I didn't dare try anything, and instead told her all about Saroyan and poetry; and when we came out of bushes at five one thousand homecoming

aircraftworkers tooted their horns at us and yelled. And guess what!—an old Lowell buddy of mine who was on Lowell High Football team with me was one of these people, and he jumped out of the car to chat, and when the girl went on home and said she'd see me later, believe it or not, we joined some boys in the field and spent a whole hour till dark tossing football—all in that crazy wartime boomtown. These things are so mad, and so all-tied-up, I must save them and come back later, because now we're on Kitty, for that was her little name. Now, at the station I told the boys I would lay her right soon and they laughed. Following night I had regular date at her house; her mother out, we sat on parlor couch playing records; she talked about how she'd like to be married and have cottage with white fence. She was still talking about this little dream of hers and I was going to town gently; finally was in there hard and fast; and it was all over in a minute. One of those inexpressible American evenings in a girl's home-parlor, with darkness pressing at the windows, and little lace panties, and little sighs, and noises that make you jump and look over your sweaty shoulder, and the final disposal of the saggy rubber in your handkerchief. Walking home in the Autumnal night—that is, walking two miles to make a bus connection back to Hartford proper, where I had a deadwall-window room on Main Street—I passed the station where I worked with the boys and arrogantly, snickeringly, foolishly, boorishly, proudly threw the rubber on the cement of the pump-island for everybody to see when the station re-opened in the morning. And what happened in the morning is sadder yet: I arrived a little after the others, they were busy working, the rubber was still there on the ground, and no one had seen it at all, or if they had, it made no difference to them, and my little game could only succeed if I drew their attention to it.

How can a man possibly call his fellow-men to see the deflated oily rubber of his lastnight's sorrow? What worse way to boast?— and boast of what? In any case, at the Manchester, Conn. station the same kind of bullshit was going on between us boys about the girl we had last night, last week, and so on, and it was a drowsy afternoon, about four o'clock, just bout the time I lay on the grass in 1927 coiled in my guilty rope, same kind of early Fall day, and I looked up and saw across the street a pretty blonde girl and a fat

brunette girl cutting home from work in a local factory. As usual I fondled my old genitaliae [sic], I always did in those days, but Bob came running out and said the blonde was a well-known lay. "What!" I cried. "What are we waiting for, come on," and I jumped into Bob's car as quick as a flash and he hesitated none himself and jumped right back of that wheel and started the motor. The boss was right there laughing with the other boys; boss was about 35, good-natured enough fellow. "Wait a minute," he yelled, "don't you cunt-lappers know that's Agnes, she's got the biggest dose in Hartford, everybody knows that." Well we'll use rubbers, we assured the boss, and off we went; circled U-turn in the road; cut right up to the girls at the curb and I leaned out and said (because Bob was blushing): "How bout a ride home?" Quick as a flash, after consultatory gig-gles, they jumped right in the car, the blonde in the back and the fat brunette in front; and one of the other boys from the station, a great big joker whose name I forget, came rushing over and joined the party. I instructed him to get in the front seat. I was really intent and meant business, just like you in the Denver hotel with Marylou, sol-dier and Joan. Now, this is the positive truth: in exactly two and one half minutes as I sat saying nothing and the others chatted, I turned to Agnes, she turned to me, I grabbed her by the shoulders, kissed her, and right quick from some instinctive sense shoved my hand right up her dress and came up with her box shining golden in the golden sun. I'm even inclined to believe this all happened before the car was in high gear; I'm positive I was conservative saying 2½ minutes, tremendously so. I remember I had the feeling the car was only just starting to roll when I came up with her lovely vaginal heart in my hand. I got immediately a hardon, told Bob, ordered him in fact to drive to the woods. Right then the fat brunette began com-plaining: "Say, what's the meaning of this, who do you guys think we are anyway? You think you're pretty wise, don't you; well, I'm getting out."

"Ah, come on, honey," said Bob with his smile, "we're only taking a detour to your house, it's a nice Autumn afternoon, you'll be all right, don't you like our company?" and he made an inane joke and she giggled a little and was appeased for a moment. And the big lug

had his arm over the back of the seat and nodded to everything. But my lovely Agnes and I said never a single word, just lay sprawled on that backseat with me, with her legs spread and her thing to the light and I was all over her with crazy wonderful joy. "Hurry up," I kept saying, "find a nice hill someplace." And the brunette starting whining and complaining again, and as usual, it's always the ugly girl who takes it upon herself to chaperone the passionate pretty one: well, this time it didn't work.

We got to a little ravine in the woods and parked the car. I ordered everybody out and told them to go for a walk, especially also so as to assuage the frightened one, so off they went, the three of them, and I was left alone with my lovely Agnes. We didn't talk. In a jiff I was in; but for some strange reason I couldn't come; all 19-year-old cockmasters can't come, you know this as well as I do. They concentrate all their available energy on getting girls and then they can't come; they even use some of the most amazing tactics in the world to make a girl and they can't come; they waste years of their lives thinking, plotting, charming, hustling, sweating to make a girl and they can't come; they are completely fanatic like a veritable Ahab about "tail" and like Ahab they are impotent before the whale when the time comes. Fellows and the girl up on the hill (I glanced once out the backwindow as I pumped) looked exactly like three people in an illustration for a romantic *Saturday Evening Post* love-triangle story; and they said later they were having one hell of a laugh watching the car bump up and down for the entire twenty minutes it took me to come. Fat brunette wasn't laughing, but the boys were. It was almost worth the trip. They tried to tip her in the lorny leaves but she complained and pushed and whined and they gave it up; meanwhile she claimed the right to worry about my lovely Agnes. So everybody sat down in the grass and settled to watching that car jiggling up and down—as if no one was in it, because Agnes was stretched waydown with her head on car seat, one leg on floor, other on back of rest, and me hunched over like a bull. An abandoned car jumping up and down as if the motor was on and the rods were jumping. Agnes and I didn't say a word; she just took it all—100 horsepower of energy—and came three, four times to my final one,

and when we finished she said, "I thought I'd die you fucked me so much." That's about all she said. I threw the rubber out the window and came out and hailed the others. Then I paused.

Standing on the hill, that lorn threesome cast a long shadow over the brown-green grass and the leaves that was the saddest dayshadow I'd just about seen in all my born days. I felt like yelling for joy and madness. I was completely bushed and pumped out, so happy; already hungry for my nightly 80c steak in Main Street saloons; I urged Agnes to give me her address. She walked around the back of the car and washed some, and come back, never saying a word, and faced the other three as they approached. The brunette was just about to say something when old Bob grabbed Agnes and pulled her in the car for laughs; Agnes tripped right in there, and we had to take another walk up the hill. The fat rouged brunette was so sore she began whining again about . . . cops finally. Nobody paid attention. I wandered off alone to enjoy the red afternoon, leaving Big Lug and brunette alone to sore devices, and sat in a copse with a leaf in my mouth. Bob had his bang; he came out and called Big Lug; Big Lug went down and got his bang; and then we all drove home happy except brunette. We dropped them off in town, said goodbye, waved, and off we went back to the station to finish up work for the day.

The boss wanted to know how it was. We told him; all had big laugh; and then drove home to Hartford with radio blasting away and all the smoke of the town puffing up in front of us. And yet that night, I sat in my lonely dusty room brushing cockroaches off my typewriter as I wrote some terribly sad story—I cannot remember which one. But I will know later.

CHAPTER WHATZIT

Discovering oneself in little childly charades, in general finding the world, so that someday you can grow up and pile into a woman's soul for no other reason than personal commanding need—as the old sun slants over your endeavor's joy—leads to the first childish sexual experience within conscious memory. Just before I started going to school I was introduced to two little twin boys who lived up that intersecting country road the farm was on. I might have met them myself; but because their older sisters were friends of my moth-

er's I was taken there one evening with the express purpose of providing chums for me. They were five years old, like me; one was blonde; the other dark, with a little moonscar on his cheek. Because of this scar I called him "Banana" (in other words a banana-moon scar), but he immediately disliked my calling him Banana. So whenever his blonde brother conspired with me against him, we whispered the name Banana over and over again; in French, "banane." The sisters were devoted ladies who were actually taking care of little orphan nephews; and are still doing so today. (There's a punchline to this incident will knock you out.) The mother was dead, the father gone; and the sisters, who worked, in shoeshops, by the way, lived in this house with the twins and their decrepit blind father. I won't —I will mention the name, Marchand. Most interesting of all was the house. It was a huge rambling weatherbeaten wooden shack of a thing, really a splendid old heap, on top of a hill that formed the ridge-top of the general Hildreth Ridge overlooking Lowell; it had an enormous raggedy yard full of old wrecked cars. Now, Neal, picture if you will old wrecked cars in 1-9-2-7! Such dilapidation, sad sorrow, grime and ruin and broken wreckage is utterly inconceivable. Among these ghosts of pre-World War I wrecks the twins and I played day-in and out. There was also an old sagging barn. Behind their house, with its broken turrets and towers and stainedglass windows, stretched a vast country field, bordered by forests in which Gypsies were known to have stayed only a few years before. Beyond the Marchand house, beyond the junkyard in the back, was, among other things I will tell you, a haunted abandoned house on a hill under pines—everpresent, everpresent. Coming in towards my own house on Hildreth there was a bakery, a strange bakery set far back on a lawn and looking more like a modern funeral home; and finally a real long-faced New England Victorian house, with mysterious draped windows, occupied by another two elderly sisters and a little boy who was reported gravely ill. This will give you a picture of the twins' house. The school we were all about to attend was cattycorner across the dirt country road from the rambly Marchand house—a regular redbrick school with gravelyard and coatshack. To get to all these wonderful things which were next on my agendy after the Hildreth lawn, you only had to walk a block uphill.

Banana's real name was Ovila; his brother was Robert. We discovered a wonderful thrilling game; we went under the rickety porch of the house, which was high enough for us to stand, and there, in the sand and ruckus of lost years, we took long interminable pisses that were only imaginary after the first ten seconds of actual urination. We also faced each other at times, but this was not necessarily necessary. I recall the peculiar thrill of these operations: I don't know if you felt the same at five: but only because I was hidden from the world, with fellow-hiders, in the darkness under the porch, it was indescribably amazing to be absolutely free to air my little tool for as long as I wanted. We were little Catholics; undoubtedly we'd been told what to do with our tools, i.e., keep them out of sight and no bones about it . . . Well, you understand this, I mean the tremendous little kick & excitement of exposing the greatest dimmest secret; even the pleasure of the cool air entering the pants through the fly, etc. and most especially the gleeful seclusion altogether. Later on, at ten, I felt and remembered these moments when I hid in the closet with my little cousin whose name I have now sadly forgotten for the moment; my little cousin asked me to tie her up and leave her there, we whispered in the dark about it. The Lord could see us, underporch and closeted, but for the moment his wrath was postponed because it had to be done first, or, of course, there can be no atonement without sin, and you have to sin before you can learn the Lord's presence. Thus the Eden apple and all that. Yes, the Lord could see us but for the moment he was Himself the Snake of Temptation, if that's possible, because if not, why didn't we run? We learned the Lord ALLOWED it. The come-uppance came after, and it was intended. And it was fun. O world.

Arising from these pissadventures beneath the porch, I became curious about little girls, and one Saturday night—but wait, this comes later in its own time and I was telling you about the twin boys. I brought them up for a special reason; and tried, artistically, to make you see them (but failed because I've abandoned art). But no harm was done or has been done. Ovila—Banana—is the one I want you to think about. Would you suppose that this dark little boy of twenty-four years ago underneath the dark porch in haunted old Lowell, across all those unbelievable night-years in the world round

the globe and in the broad complicated forlornities of poor mortal time, should have come and wandered the drear pathways of life in his own sufferings and strayings—risen like a ghost from this haunted boyhood of your buddy's—and come, in plain ordinary day, to tick-tocking ordinary afternoons in hallways, on foot and human, across the sweep of your own eyeball? That he did, because you have met Banana, but I didn't have time to tell you.

Yes, 23 years after these dusty incidents of olden day, you and I arrived in Richmond Hill in a '50 Chrysler in the company of a meek man from Detroit, on a bright cool Autumn day, to 94-21 134th Street, my mother's new apartment; unpacked our filthy gear we'd lugged all the way from a crooked little door in Russian Hill, San Francisco; climbed the stairs—and as we did so, talking and yelling up to my mother, we dodged a fellow in the hall who was coming down with a paintbrush and some cans, a plain-looking, stained youth you'd never give a second looksee to; and this was Banana himself I now tell you; and to me, as to you, it's a matter of wonder and rare speculation.

How comes it? And do you recall, the first thing my mother did was complain that "Vila" was gypping her in a modest way—she confided to us in the kitchen while he was downstairs with his brother, not the twin Robert, however, but a REFORMED GANG-STER, whom you also brushed shoulders with on the sunporch—that he had done a good paint job but was certainly getting his from the deal. Remember all this?

Unobtrusive time! If we hadn't taken that exact cable car on Hyde Street, Frisco, and rode downtown; and hit the exact old man's saloon on 3rd and Market; and slept at Henry Funderburk's just the night we did; and got the ride with the Queen in the Plymouth, and imitated Bill Burroughs' driving in Nevada, or talked of Imaginary Scythes in that same state (between Reno and Battle Mountain); and stolen that softball on Broadway, Denver, or played catch on 27th and Federal with the kids (when I brought you shoes); and dug the bop on North Clark after the long ride in the Cadillac and the stop of Ed Uhl's; and got stopped by cops on Hastings Street in Detroit, and got that exact ride from the Chrysler corporation employee and arrived just at the time we did on Times Square when they were tearing up the street, and got just so "by a cunt hair" lost on the way to my house by taking wrong-way one-way streets, you would never have met Banana at all because he was just leaving as we arrived, and we had come 3,200 miles and he had come (so far as your eye-ball is concerned and the truth of all my lifework) I say he had come twenty-three years and countless, countless miles, via his own modest travels and a hitch in the Pacific with the armed forces, and all the weight of his own suffering and strange existence on this broken earth; he had come that far—and there she was. Time is a woman . . . because time is the earth.

No you would never have met Banana and I would never have known this.

Do you know that I don't care if this ever gets published or not and that this is the only "writing" I'll ever do?

This masturbatory world!—a retired Navy admiral in his memoirs refers contemptuously to the "fly-fly boys" of the air force, to "trigger-happy aviators" and Washington "politicos" and "unification boys" and I, this is the only "writing" I'll ever do, note that contempt. Men everywhere sit on their own insignificant pot, they dandle the gland all gloom.

Be that as it may. See how all things swirl together in unison, how they connect darkly. Forasmuch, we're on the subject of dealing with those things in this part of my childhood that are connected with you; you don't dream there's still another thing; a most amazing connection however exists. Now, please to remember, in my one and only novel "The Town and the City," on page 395, top, there is reference to a haunted house and a field in one of Peter Martin's dreams. Let me proudly quote: "And then, with the whole world rumbling with doom and dark, the scene shifted to a field, the weather turned gray and pallid, and Peter—little Peter, about five years old—was standing in the middle of the field filled with terror. On one side of the field was an old abandoned house—the 'haunted house' of Galloway. Nearby was the house in which a 'little boy' had died, a boy 'like Julian, his brother.' And there was an old shack in which 'gypsies' lived, the 'pockmarked gypsies who always kidnap little boys.' And Francis was on that side of the field too, possibly living in the haunted house, or in the house where little Julian had died: that seemed most probable. In the field itself Peter stood terrified by a further danger—the 'drunken men' who got drunk and fell on children and killed them, because 'when men are drunk they weigh a thousand pounds.' (This was a popular superstition among Peter's little chums of yore.) One of the drunks was lying senseless there in the weedy swamp. But on the other side of the field, in a vista of space, with the sun shining, there stood a bunch of tall rawboned youngsters, including his brothers Joe and Charley, around a kind of tractor plow, talking and smoking. Nearby was his father's car, the old Plymouth, and his father himself sitting in it and smoking a cigar and looking at a roadmap (just as he used to do on Sundays long ago in New England)—*and all of it in the great light of a plain, with mountains beyond."*

The underlining is mine just now, and for a reason.

Now, you will note how this dream is as a vision of the things I'm telling you about tonight, the house of the twins, the field, the haunted house, the "gypsy forest," et cetera and plainly so. You will also note "five years old," which was my exact age. You will further note, that it is a kind of dream-fear of homosexuality and clearly connected to the incidents of showing ourselves under the porch. I made the gypsies "pockmarked" on purpose for the plot "Town & City," in which Waldo, the queer, is pockmarked; & gypsies are generally pockmarked. You will, and have already in fact, come to note that "little Julian" had died; and bear in mind that I mentioned earlier the little boy who lived on the corner (near the bakery) who was reported gravely ill, who lived with two elderly sisters. Now I might as well report, he later died in that house . . . two houses from the haunted house itself. Please be a witness to this . . . parenthetically: that in the fiction of "The Town & City" I gathered those informations which had truly & sincerely to do with my life, but I muddled them for the sake of "art" and not only that but foreshortened them, as in this convenient dream in the midst of the "plot." Actually, the whole story of Peter Martin, as such, is contained in this one dream, which is not an integral part of anything in the book, at all . . . just a passing impression. His dualism, his hatred of Francis the dark one, and his love of Joe the bright one—Francis representing mystery & gloom & haunted houses, Joe the plains and the broad clouds and the everlasting joyousness of America—is all there in one package. At least with relation to men, or Man. On the one side there is death, sin, hauntedness, darkness and drunk; on the other, bright spaces and a "tractor plow." (Remember your dream of HOME, how we walked over my plowed fields?—after the crackup of the Pontiac with the hipsters?) Please notice also the connection between all the queer business . . . pockmarked Waldo, Francis— and the amazing (private) fact that a PLYMOUTH appears in this dream, the selfsame Plymouth of that queer who drove us East just in time to meet Banana as he was just leaving, which ties every-thing up.

But the connection that YOU figure in is this: in 1947 when we planned to go West together I formed a vision of you . . . in fact, if you can remember, we took a bus from my house on Crossbay Blvd., Ozone Park, for a short ride to that little old library half-mile away, and talked on the way about "wranglers" in the West. I was saying that there were two kinds of western youths, the wranglers and the city boys, properly the city college boys; to be more specific, there were Ed Uhls and there were Hal Chases in the West. I mentally placed you as a wrangler. That is the only reason why—the ONLY reason—I threw in (and just now underlined) the part about plains and mountains, in other words, Colorado and Denver itself, because you came from there. I'm saying to you, when I wrote that last line of the paragraph in my "Town & City" labors, I was specifically referring (tho not mentioning) with respect to you, so that you too stood around the tractor plow with Joe and Charley. This is how you are therefore strangely connected with the scene of these events in my life twenty four years ago, in haunted old sad Lowell of time.

So now I'm free to tell you about "Saturday night" and my interest in little girls, as I started to do. Next installment. In the near future, too, when the old signs start pointing again, I'll have to rush you back pellmell by the scruff of the neck, poor man, to Beaulieu St. because at supper the other night my mother told me some amazing things I had forgotten, or could not possibly have remembered, hav-ing to do with all, all.

Yrs, Zagg

On January 10, 1951, Jack got a letter from Neal saying he was coming to New York in February. In high spirits Jack put aside his epistolary narrative and described the plans he and Joan were making for their "big trip to the last coast."

TO NEAL CASSADY

Jan. 10 *1951*
[Richmond Hill, N.Y.]

Dear Neal,

Just got your letter of allsquare agreement; I guarantee, barring accidents, 50 bucks for our trip and am getting part-time job to add 60 or so to this. I make about $35 per week on scripts; add $15 part-time, that's 50, and Joan makes 30 starting Monday as house-keeper;[1] by Feb. 8 or properly 9th (last workday), we'll have the dough. Meanwhile I still pay rent at home. We will lay out boxes and bookcases on floor of panel truck and put mattress on top for one sleeper during non-stop flight to Frisco; beside it, a pile of fur-niture, not much, and blankets to cushion. I see everything working out fine; a thousand hassles that will only be wonderful because we are taking that big trip to the last coast. I feel wonderful about it. Now in answer—(I feel wonderful about it, I mean fun, fun, tops, tops, great, great, wonderful, grand, fine, magnificent, this is it.) Our crazy plans of 1948 Spring actually taking shape somewhat. In an-swer: I did receive your dream-letter about Burroughs and Hubbard. Would you believe, the mazing coincidence is that Bill's name is Wil-liam Seward Burroughs and I used to know a tall young bum called Big Slim William Holmes Hubbard my buddy of the nuthouse[2] who planned a break with me with breadknives to get to freights that ran behind nuthatch but we got caught and sent to Washington Big Hatch with five guards and straitjackets (knives discovered under our pillows.) All absolutely true. So when Bill's ghost turned out to be

---

1. When Joan's Christmas job in a department store ended, she found another full-time job and Kerouac began writing film script synopses for Columbia Pictures.

2. The Navy psychiatric ward in Newport, in the spring of 1943.

called Hubbard I shivered I tell you. [. . . .] Matter of fact, if we do really Go, we will go to Poke [Poughkeepsie], stay night, take Joan to Albany, rush east over fatal road Mike and I had crackup on (N.Y. Vermont line) to Lowell, dig everything, even Boston, rush back Albany, down Poke for another night, back to N.Y. and off. And Joan says if we cut down thru Washington on way to Denver her Colonel father may throw a few bucks in our knapsack if he feels like it and at same time we dig big Wash cocktail parties, etc. All this is malleable material and we'll do it all; including your Pop, which I will love and wait for. In any case the raw skeleton plan is complete. You've thought it out to a perfect T. I wouldn't dare alone because of no knowledge of truckmotors and all; I would dare but wouldn't like so much. Besides we have portable radio and will have music all the way; also old truck floorboards will send up our heater heat. I bring mambo drums and you bring flute and we play on side of road when Joan spreads peanutbutter on bread or whatall. Cold all the way, shivering mad adventures, then suddenly down the Sierra we come to wonderful green Sacramento fields. Ah. Home.

[. . . .] Please, please try to get that Russell St. apartment because it will be near and on fine wonderful Russian hill I love & Joan loves to heartell. Where's Divisadero? Never mind, I'll look it up at once. Carolyn's attic saves my soul; ah wonderful. Tell her a million million thanks. Will give us start.

Another letter on filmy paper due in 2 days with next installment. OK? Saving Elitch for you. Put the cat to sleep and wind the clock.

Zagg

L*A*T*E*S*T B*U*L*L*E*T*I*N

– – – — – – – – – – – – – – – – — – –

Just got your most recent letter about no Ekotape and re-arriving N.Y. only to re-return SF Feb. 3.

Joan and I immediately getting jobs to save at least $150 for great day when 3 of us head west, yessir, that's who's joining you.

Various plans feasible: RR passes . . . or old $95 panel truck . . . or hitch-hiking for us. Time not yet to discuss that (few articles).

Only to tell you, okay man, we're going back with you to SF to begin our new life.

Mexico if & when I get writing-loot only.

Frisco: we get unfurn. apt., move in, get jobs & build from that . . . nothing but bare floor, mattress (if possible), and mambo records on jukeboxpicolo . . . the rest no matter . . . candles, bread & jam.

T question: all gone except equivalent of 3 . . . no sense . . . hold it for Feb. 3 or Jan. 23, whatever date thou arrivest . . .

Who now living at 230 Divisadero? Any other likely apts. around? Can Hinkle keep eyes open? Who lives Helen Hinkle's former apt? All such. Joan and I already in SF as you see. Who lives at Liberty apt. where Carolyn was. Help. Here we go.

I will take any work at first; later see Chronicle people and United Press people.

Big SF man already. Can't wait. Finally doing it. Ain't you glad, ain't I glad? Good old frisco I love it.

We have great trip across continent again, with my lovely now.

Very glad to hear of you & C. [Carolyn] together again; my favorite.

RR passes fine; explain further; will I have to be Mr. C. and she Mrs. D.C.?—and if so, how can you get free RR ride if you too are Mr. C.

My idea is: if we could get cheap old panel truck, load gear, mattress-bed in back, drive to Frisco, move in, then sell truck for same or slightly lesser price. (Added advantage of cooking our steaks on side of road.) You have license; you buy truck; I help you drive to Coast. Otherwise I have to get license & I already failed once.

If no truck, I put gear in packing crates, and we go with your RR passes. If you have to pay part of the RR fare it come to a lot of money. Old car better, huh? Think with me.

Let me hear at once.

One more thing, did you get first installment? If so where do I mail next ones, or shall I hold for you? Have 2 more already. By May I'll have me $1000 advance on new novel, hey what?—only a REAL BOOK this time.

Godspeed to N.Y. and my door; sleep at my house.

Your pal,
Jack

P.S. Installment, no I mean, letter I wrote last night pasted on to this for kicks and future ref. Read on—but it's dated 24 hours since news of your new decisions.

Writing to Ginsberg at home in New Jersey the next day, Kerouac mentioned his copy of Pierre; or, the Ambiguities *by Herman Melville, which had been published in a new edition in 1949 with an introduction by the psychologist Henry A. Murray. Murray had said that in Melville's "quasi-autobiographical novel," he "was not writing autobiography in the usual sense, but, from first to last, the biography of his self-image." To Murray, "*Pierre *is at no point a transcription of fact; everything has been completely recast by Melville's shaping will." Finally, "Melville's impelling intention in writing* Pierre *is better defined by saying that he purposed to write his spiritual autobiography in the form of a novel, than it is to say that he was experimenting with the novel and incidentally making use of some personal experiences." Kerouac might have been influenced by these comments a short time later, when he and Joan moved into an apartment at 454 West Twentieth Street in Manhattan that Joan had found for them. Once settled, Jack decided to make a fresh start on* On the Road, *recasting the book as a confessional picaresque memoir about his adventures with Cassady.*

TO ALLEN GINSBERG

11 Jan. 1951
[Richmond Hill, N.Y.]

Dear Al,

N. is due in town Feb. 8 at which time Joan and us migrates to Frisco in old truck. Will you please be kind and return my Melville to me before then? anytime in N.Y. bring it to Lou's or Holmes. Gotta see you before then and during time N. gets here for last talks. Please don't stop your novel & become disinterested in perfidious misadventures of your friends & their eventual dooms that need explaining. I gave L. wrong impression of state of my weddedness (if in case he said anything and you wrongly pondered.) Any jobs? Drop me card & let me hear. N. and us going thru Denver to pick up old N. Sr.[1] from pokey; at last I will meet W.C. Fields. Whither goest thou, O America, in thy frantic truck at night? Whee!

Yrs,
Unstable of the Lamby Clouds

In February 1951 Cassady made a brief trip to New York City to see the infant son he had conceived with Diana Hansen the previous year. He could not supply transportation for Jack and Joan to come back with him to San Francisco, and Kerouac described their last sad meeting in the final pages of On the Road, *watching as Cassady's counterpart Dean Moriarty "ragged in a motheaten overcoat he brought specially for the freezing temperatures of the East, walked off alone." In the middle of February the Guggenheim Foundation contacted Kerouac about his grant application, and he wrote two letters to the literary critic Alfred Kazin, whom he had heard lecture at the New School on nineteenth-century American writers, asking to use Kazin's endorsement of* The Town and the City *as a reference.*

In his first letter to Kazin, trying to establish a common ground with the distinguished man of letters, Kerouac was at his funniest cataloging sludge piles of obscure books and authors in Fourth Avenue used bookstores to illustrate the vanity of anyone's ambition to be a writer. Carried away by his own rhetoric, Jack described his life with Joan Haverty as an entrapment in "an American Tragedy roominghouse newlywed marriage all soaked in dolors." Perhaps he resented Joan's insistence—she had not gotten along well with her mother-in-law, who spoke French with Jack and catered to his late-night culinary whims—that they move out of Gabrielle's apartment and spend money to rent their own place in Manhattan. Kerouac's description of his marriage was in marked contrast to his romantic characterization of Joan six weeks later when he wrote in the last

---

1. Neal's father, whom the Cassadys visited in Denver in 1952. Carolyn Cassady described the visit in Chapter 31 of *Off the Road.*

pages of On the Road *that she was "the girl with the pure and innocent dear eyes that I had always searched for and for so long."*

TO ALFRED KAZIN

Feb. 20, 1951
454 W. 20 Street
New York, N.Y.

Dear Mr. Kazin,

Last Fall when I made out my application for a Guggenheim Fellowship, Bob [Giroux] was shocked I hadn't used your name as a reference. I wanted to round out the list with names of female pundits along with Mark Van Doren and Carl Sandburg. Last week the Guggenheim Foundation sent me a form letter asking for supplementary material in the matter of my application which will "tend to establish" my case for the award. Could you now drop them a note for me? It would be doing me a great favor, my poor miserable half-assed practical life depends on this fellowship. I want to stretch to three years in Mexico to write a bunch of books. At present I'm trapped—an American Tragedy roominghouse newlywed marriage all soaked in dolors. I enclose some remarks you made that Bob sent me to make it easier if you want to use them.

Thinking out the idea of writing you last week I thought in another way, about your "Walker in the Streets."[1] I read that you were bringing out an anthology next. I can understand the pain of your poor long hesitations and long thoughts. We're not all different. The critic isn't supposed to make a "mistake" when he jumps to the art. But I say he can, I say I can. I say you can. You don't revere Carlyle like I do but he was a man of rich mistakes of which, I think, only the richness is left. Besides I consider you "creative" more than critic, as did everyone else in 1948–49 when you "blew" on Whitman, Melville, Twain, Thoreau and Emerson so marvelously. I myself don't read anything contemporary (you know young punks, and I don't have time or money), but I would read avidly every word of "Walker

_____

1. The title of Kazin's book was *A Walker in the City* (1951).

in the Streets" [sic] because it's just what I want to hear and I know
the man who's doing it (not personally but well-enough). Lots of
people are waiting for something like "Walking in the Streets" [sic]
—fiction is become FETID. [. . . .]

In the spring of 1949, after I'd had my advance from Harcourt, I
began haunting old bookstores on Fourth Avenue to get myself a
classical collection. Instead I wound up being depressed at the sight
of vast piles of useless and meaningless dusty literature, particularly
from the 19th Century. . . . "Ridpath's Life" . . . "The Military
Writings of Abner Doubleday" . . . "Puck of Pook's Hill" . . .
"The Works of Samuel Parr" . . . (collected) . . . Saintsbury's histories
. . . manuals by Craik . . . the clergyman's translation of the Bellum
Catilinarium of Sallust . . . Nathaniel Parker Willis, his prose and
verse . . . Whittier, Holmes and Lowell . . . Samuel Parr's celebrated
preface to the edition of Bellenden . . . the philosophy of Christoffer
Jaboc Bostrom . . . Frith's two-volume life of Leech . . . the works
of Susan Edmonstone Ferrier and Ivan Alexandrovitch Goncharov
. . . Morley's life of Cobden . . . the scientific works of Luigi Ferdi-
nando Count Marsigli . . . John MacLeod Campbell . . . the Early
Recollections of Joseph Cottle . . . Taine, Renan, Thureau-Dangin,
Michelet, Fronde, Bulwer Lytton, Edmond de Goncourt, Horace
Walpole, G.P.R. James, Jeremy Bentham . . . I had visions of the
treatise on Cervicabra arundinaceum [sic] used in the alley by old
Nebraska One Eye just blown in from Omaha . . . of rain and wine
falling on all of them. And I said to myself, after Shakespeare and
Dostoevsky, what? How about the works of J. Russell Mowris—this
is the name of an actual 90 year old white haired man I met in the
subway who wrote a considerable number of books and showed me
some from his briefcase.

What does it matter what WE do?

Outside of that, everything is fine. So last summer I wrote . . .
"The suitcase containing all my worldly clothes was gripped in my
blistered hand. I sweated onOward [sic] all anew, to whatever was
my life, to a smaller promised life than the life they talk of everywhere. Strange neons overtopped the scene of my own tragic birth.
I quivered forward to my own mysterious conclusion. I was convinced something would come of it for me. Faith was a skeleton, and

that my rack. Mad under the skies, and had to be, I ground ahead as the moon raced across my eyes with her clouds making a radar screen before her, but not much to my surprise." [. . . .]

I even gave this up in despair. At present I'm moving right along on another tack. By the way, call me sometime, CHElsea 2-9615, for a coffee chat, if you have time.

Yours,
Jack Kerouac

TO ALFRED KAZIN

Mar. 1, 1951
454 W. 20 Street
[New York City]

Dear Alfred,

I did fill out my regular Guggenheim from last Fall but now they want "supplementary material which will tend to establish my case."

Enclosed is a statement you wrote when my book came out that Bob Giroux never used because of your advisory position at H[arcourt]-B[race].

Could you sign this and send it to them, or send it back to me?

What—isn't Pineapple street[1] where you were born?—did you go back to your birthplace?

Wonderful to hear your book will be ready this Spring. Then I'm sure you can relax like mad in Europe. Just in time for the chestnuts . . . I mean the ones that bloom. Good luck!

As ever,
Jack

In March 1951 John Clellon Holmes brought Kerouac the manuscript of his completed novel Go, *a fictionalized account of the lives*

---

1. Kerouac had originally typed Kazin's address as 339 East 58 Street, New York City, but the envelope was forwarded to 91 Pineapple Street in Brooklyn.

of Ginsberg, Cassady, and others in their circle. Soon afterwards, on April 2, 1951, Kerouac began a three-week stint of marathon typing of a new version of On the Road, *scotchtaping together twelve-foot sheets of paper that Bill Cannastra had left in his apartment. The novel nearly completed, Kerouac learned that Ginsberg had told Cassady about it in a letter. "Worried you might get wrong impression of what I was writing," Jack wrote to Neal, going on to tell him that he'd just about finished a story that "deals with you and me and the road." There was relief as well as apology in Kerouac's tone when he confessed to his friend that he'd "telled all the road now. Went fast because road is fast . . ."*

TO NEAL CASSADY

May 22 1951
[Richmond Hill, N.Y.]

Dear Neal,

Want you to know I didn't ask Allen to write you a letter about "your doom" and that in fact my book about you is not about your doom but about your life and I know your life in many respects better than Allen does . . . not sluffing Allen but I was worried you might get wrong impression of what I was writing. From Apr. 2 to Apr. 22 I wrote 125,000 [word] full-length novel averaging 6 thous. a day, 12 thous. first day, 15,000 thous. last day.—10,000 thous. devoted to Victoria, Gregor, girls, weed, etc. Story deals with you and me and the road . . . how we first met 1947, early days; Denver 47 etc.; 1949 trip in Hudson; that summer in queer Plymouth and 110-mi-an-hour Caddy and Chi and Detroit; and final trip to Mexcity with Jeffries—last part dealing with your last trip to N.Y. and how I saw you cuttin around corner of 7th Ave. last time. (Night of Henri Cru and concert). Plot, if any, is devoted to your development from young jailkid of early days to later (present) W.C. Fields saintliness . . . step by step in all I saw. Book marks complete departure from *Town & City* and in fact from previous American Lit. I don't know how it will be received. If it goes over (Giroux waiting to see it) then you'll know yourself what to do with your own work . . . blow and tell all. I've telled all the road now. Went fast because road is fast . . .

wrote whole thing on strip of paper 120 foot long (tracing paper that belonged to Cannastra.)—just rolled it through typewriter and in fact no paragraphs . . . rolled it out on floor and it looks like a road. Now Neal I want to tell you—your doom is of no concern to me simply because I don't think you're doomed at all and in fact I expect your soul to get wilder and wilder as you grow older till at ninety you will be a great white-haired saint even if a "blank" brakeman (Allen's wds.)[1] Fuck it, in fact you know you will wind up in Mexico with your family if you have any sense . . . but even if you don't . . . It's not your doom; I been worrying all day that Allen made you sad; made you say about blind-spots cock cancers and what not. Another thing: pay no attention, partially [sic], to material of last January dealing with Virgin Mary girls . . . cunt is all and I know it. I don't harken back to Black Christ Cunt at all . . . I know cunt is all, I live cunt and always will and always have . . . saying this to assure you I don't renounce the one thing you hold dear but hold it as dear. To forestall, therefore, this psychological development in your brain possibly . . . "Jack wrote about Virgin girls . . . now he has turned on me and spells my doom." All Allen's own mind. I believe in your energy, your loves, your greatness, your final and magnificent grandness like Whitman's and I believe in your LIVING and not your DYING (I'm not a Cannastra, a Ginsberg, a Carr). I believe in everything about you except you dying and if you die I won't know what to do with myself in this world, in the special compartment which is reserved for you, the other reserved for Joan. I love you as ever and not only that I don't want you to die. Clear?

---

1. Ginsberg had written Cassady that Kerouac had nearly finished a book about him but needed help with the ending of the story: "Jack needs, however, an ending. Write him a serious self-prophetic letter foretelling your fortune in fate, so he can have courage to finish his paean in a proper apotheosis or grinding of brakes."

Cassady got into the spirit of things by supplying a few alternative endings for *On the Road*: "Tell Jack I become ulcerated old color-blind RR conductor who never writes anything good and dies a painful lingering death from prostate gland trouble (cancer from excessive masturbation) at 45. Unless I get sent to San Quentin for rape of teenager and drown after slipping into slimy cesspool that workgang is unclogging. Of course I might fall under freight train, but that's too good. . . ."

And I love Carolyn and I love your children and I love women and I love life and celebrate and believe and let's hear no more and this is the way I'll be till ninety.

If book sells, I get advance immediately, June, and take off at once for Mexico, bus, things slow freight, arriving Mexcity, look for cheap pad, settling down temporarily till other developments and other books (will now write all my books in twenty days.) Of course since Apr. 22 I've been typing and revising. Thirty days on that. Will be my routine . . . starting with my own life, pure aspects, no fiction, till I can invent like a Dostoevsky and of course I know how and can and will. As for you, don't wanta hear another word about your inability to decide whether to say "although" or "till" or "rather" or such shit in front of a sentence . . . How many times do I have to tell you the letter about Joan Anderson is an American masterpiece and so are you leaving it to ME to sweat to publish it. Now you also know why I haven't written lately—novelwork—and soon as I finish I write you huge letter telling EVERYTHING about N.Y. Jerry Newman[2] gossip, etc. All. Don't have to write back—let me write all our letters.

Jack

P.S. I was waiting to finish my book to write to you & surprise you.

Soon afterwards, Kerouac's world collapsed around him. His wife learned she was pregnant and later said that she refused to have an abortion when Jack told her he didn't want her to have the child. Joan insisted he move out of the apartment, and later she went back to her mother's home in upstate New York, ending the marriage. Jack handed the manuscript of On the Road *over to his editor, Robert Giroux, and brought his things to Lucien Carr's loft on West Twenty-first Street. On his last drunken night in his own apartment, Kerouac began a letter to bring Cassady up to date on recent developments. Jack had discovered writing* On the Road *that coffee was*

---

2. Jerry Newman was a New York friend and jazz enthusiast who had founded Esoteric Records.

best for "real mental power kicks." Back on alcohol while he wrote the letter, he told Neal that "with a few brews my fingers flail and less than fly as usual."

June 10 *1951*

[New York City]

Pops,

Now I sit here, with a sore phlebitis foot, my book finished, handed in, waiting for the word from Giroux, a book about you and me, I sit here, my wife's not here, she's at her mother's, presumably to-morrow I move out and we part, I don't know what to do, where to go, on June 20 I may have a thousand dollars or more, meanwhile I stay with Lucien and Allen in loft which Liz-girl left, where do I go, what do I do now and I write to you old pal with a few brews on my left, my black cat sleeping, the last night in this pad [. . . .]

And what I really wanted to do was write you a big letter about the night in back of Jerry Newman's record store blasting with Mezz Mezzrow[1] and the owner of a Harlem niteclub and a colored gal and the music we played and recorded etc. and the kicks I got digging people but personal tragedy since obtruded my plan and all I want to talk about is myself, damn it son of a bitch. I get as much hung up, man, as you ever did in your most hungup days and at a time after I really wrote a great book, my very best, one of the best to be published this year anywhere (or next Jan.) and wrote it too in 20 days as I say and I feel the pull and strain of having to type with a rusty typewriter like this and a dull ribbon that won't enact my tones and so, also; with a few brews my fingers flail and less than fly as usual. I tell you another, I wrote that book on COFFEE . . . remember said rule. Benny, tea, anything I KNOW none as good as coffee for real mental power kicks. If you were here and since you can't talk any more I would regale you with the story as it stands . . . of me

---

1. Jazz clarinetist and co-author with novelist Bernard Wolfe of Mezzrow's au-tobiography, *Really the Blues* (1946).

. . . but have to bat out. You know I dig your pain in any kind of writing. Remember! COFFEE! (try it, please.) You are a great writer Neal and if don't believe me maybe you will believe me when everyone hails me as great writer within next few years. Immediately starting still another novel, this summer, soon as I sit somewhere whether banks of Seine pad or anywhere . . . 3c glass pernods in Casablanca country; or anywhere; Peru, Mexico City, great Marseilles, or Seymour-London, anywhere. [. . . .] Too drunk to write and Ah Neal and I had so much MUCH sonof did to tell you . . . tomorrow continue.

Now I'm in Lucien's loft—alone—cold rainy afternoon—tossed & pitched all night long—Ah shit man I think I'll just go to Mexcity and build me a topflight pad & relax in coolness, kicks, food, mistresses, main once-a-week etc. heh? Get me an LP record player & great LP Charlie Christian album[2]—Burroughs leaving Mexcity he says[3]—I will dig Mex on lush this time and explore great Mexico. How awful it would be if I hadn't writ this On the Road!—Got my next book ready to write HOLD YOUR HORN HIGH, jazz novel —won't go Europe till I can really spare $300 roundtrip tickets. Anyway my soul is hungup right now & I gotta make a move soon . . .

Please write me a letter.

Jack

---

2. Charlie Christian was a jazz electric guitarist who died of tuberculosis in 1942.

3. Burroughs had left Mexico City for his first exploratory trip to South America, hoping to be initiated into the use of the hallucinogenic drug yage by the local Indians. He wrote Kerouac in May 1951 that Jack's letters reflected "some staggering misconceptions on the subject of Mexico . . . Mexico is not simple or gay or idyllic. It is nothing like a French Canadian naborhood. It is an Oriental country that reflects 2000 years of disease and poverty and degradation and stupidity and slavery and brutality and psychic and physical terrorism. Mexico is sinister & gloomy & chaotic with the special chaos of a dream. I like it myself, but it isn't everybody's taste, & don't expect to find anything like Lowell down here."

Cassady's response to Kerouac's letter was to invite Jack to live with him in San Francisco, despite the impending birth of his and Carolyn's third child. "Sad buddy Jack" replied with more bad news—Giroux had rejected the manuscript of On the Road.

June 24, *1951*
[Richmond Hill, N.Y.]

Dear Neal,

Your offer exciting and generous and warm and true—I love you for it. But must tell you that I am completely fucked. Giroux didn't take my book. Harcourt won't publish it, tomorrow I have to get agent like beat young first novelists do only worse. Giroux says HE likes book[1] but is sure the President of the company and the Sales Manager won't—even tho it's "like Dostoevsky" (he says) they don't even read Dosty and don't care about all that shit and bums etc. Giroux says Harcourt expected me to write AGAIN like Town & City and this thing so new and unusual and controversial and censorable (with hipsters, weed, fags, etc.) they won't accept.

Because of this, Allen re-reads my book and decides it is really beat after all. Lucien thinks it's shit. John Holmes still stands by it. I know you would like it. Anyway here I go. Don't know what to do. Have no money to even GO to your attic; and once there, would have to work; and have necessity of writing further book in peace & silence. Nothing to do. First step, I go south to rest my mind and soul in South and eat sausages & eggs cooked by my Mom and Lucien's psychiatrist be damned (and Allen's too.) There I wait for word from my agent (Wm. Morris). If nothing, I come back to NY and SHIP OUT—(If I can)—because man, once and for all, I must I don't care how get to Mex City for peace and writing. [. . . .] If I can't ship

---

1. Giroux later had a different memory of what happened. In 1989 he told the editor Keith Jennison that when Kerouac unrolled the "scroll" manuscript of *On the Road* in his office at Harcourt Brace, he asked Jack, "How the hell can the printer work from this?" Then, according to Giroux, Kerouac "stormed out in a rage. I never read a word of it."

· *320* ·

out and don't sell book—where else can I go but your attic? As I say, Neal, listen, really, it's not right for big grownup man to interfere with home of married brakie with tux-back and THREE children and busy normal wife. It promises fuckups. But I'm so glad and warm about offer—look, write to me please, at this address, we'll discuss, I'm going to be reading and taking walks in Kingston No. Carolina, so write. [. . . .] Yr. sad buddy Jack

Burroughs had sent the manuscript of his first novel, then titled "Junk," to Ginsberg and Kerouac in January 1951 before leaving Mexico City on his trip to South America. Jack had read the book before making the fresh start on On the Road *in April 1951 and credited the opening paragraphs of "Junk" and Burroughs's straightforward prose style as literary influences, telling Neal years later that he "was imitating a kind of anxious Dashiell Hammett of Wm. Lee" in that version of* On the Road. *At the end of July 1951 Kerouac acted as Burroughs's agent in trying to place "Junk" with New York publishers, as in Jack's letter to James Laughlin of New Directions.*

TO JAMES LAUGHLIN

July 30, 1951
[Kingston, NC]

Dear Mr. Laughlin,

I would have sent along the ms. of "Junk" sometime ago but the author suggested from Mexico that he wanted to make changes first. And now all of a sudden he's disappeared to Ecuador or Peru and his wife[1] can't find the deletions and new chapters we know he's written.

With this in mind, that he wants to delete some parts (including

---

1. Burroughs's common-law wife, Joan, wrote Kerouac on July 9, 1951, that "Bill is going to case the situation further south and send for us when he settles somewhere." Joan admired *The Town and the City*; she wrote Jack on February 28, 1950, that it was the first book she'd read "in about four years (since Benzedrine)."

parts about Wilhelm Reich[2] I understand) and add a new chapter or two, I'm sending this to you as is.

Thanks very much for the letter and for considering the request. I really hope you like this.

Yours sincerely,
Jack Kerouac
c/o Carr
149 W. 21 Street
New York, N.Y.

In August 1951 Kerouac went into the Veterans Hospital in the Bronx for another treatment for the phlebitis in his legs. After nearly three weeks in the hospital he wrote a homesick letter to Stella Sampas describing his brief marriage, and then he wrote to Neal Cassady with the unhappy news that his estranged wife was suing him to pay for her prenatal care.

TO STELLA SAMPAS

[postmarked August 30, 1951]
Kingsbridge VA Hospital
Bronx, NY, NY

Dear Stella,

I've been 3 weeks in this hospital getting treatment for an old injury. Much solitude led to thoughts about Lowell until now I just have to re-visit home—soon as possible. Have you ever remembered, in the darkness of a midnight in some strange room, whole spates of crystal-clear time from your childhood? I want to re-visit the tenements of Centralville where I jabbered on the porch with little kids long before I even knew how to say "door" in English—I want to re-visit the mysteries of my past, which is my job; the mysteries of

---

2. Wilhelm Reich (1897–1957) was the controversial psychiatrist whose design for an "orgone box" to rejuvenate his patients was used by Burroughs. On March 11, 1947, Ginsberg wrote to Reich asking him to suggest the name of an analyst to help him discuss his "psychic difficulty" as a homosexual.

my source, my soul, the things that now teach me the meaning of universal love . . . I just wanted to explain it a little and didn't elaborate, nor succeed too well. In any case, Stella, I should like also seeing you—your new bar—the folks—and (being poor) I was wondering if your brother still made those weekend trips between Lowell and New York; if so I'd like to ride with him, find out where he is & contact him for the ride. Is he still stationed in N.Y.? Please write soon, at 94–21 134th St., Richmond Hill N.Y., my mother's house, so I'll know. I expect to leave the hospital this week, (Friday) cured (can't smoke any more, though).

As for my "marriage," that fizzled; it'll teach me not to ask a girl to marry me the first night I meet her—and be wary of any quick acceptance of such a crazy proposition. Luckily I have no money (I earn $25 a week doing home synopses for 20th Century Fox), and am sick, and she can't make her escapade a profitable one. Forgive and forget.

Give my best to your folks; and I hope to see you soon.

Fraternally,
Jack

P.S. On each visit to Lowell in the past eight years, it was midwinter—now I yearn to see late Summer on the Merrimac at dusk, and Pine Brook, etc.
PP.SS. My best to Jimmy.

TO NEAL CASSADY

Friday August 31, 1951
Kingsbridge VA Hosp.
130 W. Kingsbridge Rd.
Bronx, N.Y., N.Y.

Dear Neal—

If you were wondering, at exactly 4:30 P.M., California time yesterday, Aug. 30, what I was doing, what your old blood brother was up to, then gaze at what he was doing at just that moment.—he emerged, propelling the wheelchair in which he sat, from the darkness of the hospital movie basement with its pitiful representation of the Strip in Hollywood starring Mickie Rooney etc., into the side alley beyond the side exit, over a rollboard doorsill, and found himself immersed in terrible horror; for here, an apple core's throw from the silver screen and the hundreds of G.I. patients in the audience (a circle of darkness, attention, and lively communal joyment) was the sound of a church organ playing funeral fugues, the smell of the morgue (a door from the movie room), the presence of the meat-wagon, or death car, long, black, sleek Cadillac coffin Eight; not an ear's tit from the gay jazz music of the screen. So he, your blood brother, horrified lest he stumble with his nose on the decomposed death-stench of this hospital earth, wheeled back into the dark theater, disturbed patients in his haste to go around the back (with consummate speed pushing the wheel, hard-wristed), and came out a further distance from the funeral which was taking place, as he could now see in the architecture, on top of the movie(!), as if a category lay in the fete above its opposite, unbeknownst each to each. Not just only that: but rolling to the bottom of an incline in the general mortuary yard, reaching grass where invalids dreamed in the Bronx night, the organ music pursuing, your blood brother came upon a fence over which tortured trees lifted and then bent their primary bough as if almost anticipating the fence to grow higher, beyond which, green, bright, sad, was the transparent swimming pool called Four Chaplains Memorial, filled with children and pretty girls (the organ music playing on, its hymn of all-woe beneath their cries and splashings), the pool of life, which would never have existed if the S.S. Dorchester, that yr. blood brother sailed in 1942 just before it sank with the chaplains, had died. Woe and saddest death on all sides, he, yr, faithful brother, sat a long time there in the dark steeped in the joyous melancholy of the organ, the funeral remembrances of the ship, how dirty the old tub was, the children, the girls (nurses) with upward optimistic tits like a young man's thoughts, smelling [. . . .] the inexpressible cheesy old horror shitstink of morgues that even in the wide Bronx night imparted onto the very grass and shrubbery a powerful subterranean discouragement, like steamheat from the hole of Calcutta—but enough now, I haven't got a typewriter, I write in bed . . . (and a cute little French Canadian nurse, giving me a sleeping pill, says I can't sleep because of a guilty conscience con-

· 324 ·

cerning the Catholic church: of course I can sleep, I want free goof-balls; of course I'm guilty, I'm after knowledge, not salvation, or salvation thru knowledge anyhow.) Better to sew up: if you wrote to me recently, understand that I didn't receive yr. letter because I've been in this hospital since Aug. 11, the day I was supposed to leave for Mexico with Lucien, a thing I had planned for months as Allen watched with silent beady eyes every move Lucien made, then suddenly I was ordered to the hospital, Lucien was amused; indifferent, and Allen suddenly decided to go with Lucien, and they went without visiting me in the hospital; since which time, the loft locked, any mail has had to wait in the downstairs rusty box, subject to the thieveries of Puerto Ricans or drunken queer friends of poor dead Cannastra. And I've been anxious to hear from you [. . . .] Incidentally, apropos of everything, get high on good shit and open the pages of Malcolm Lowry's "Under the Volcano" for the end of the line or at least the best (for you) since Proust & Joyce—try same thing with Wm. Faulkner's "Pylon"—but certain parts of "Volcano" are our personal meat. Oh, how I yearn to get to Frisco—on Oct. 25th I get royalties. My wife, having sent the law after me for support, has never given me the affection I still need from somebody, anybody [. . . .] Write, 94–21 134th St. again (back with my mother).

Jack

Out of the hospital, Kerouac was jailed briefly for nonsupport by Joan Haverty. At the beginning of October he congratulated the Cassadys on the birth of their first son, whom Neal and Carolyn named John Allen after their friends John Kerouac and Allen Ginsberg.

TO NEAL CASSADY

[postmarked October 1, 1951
Richmond Hill, N.Y.]

HURRAH FOR JOHN ALLEN CASSADY

Dear Neal (& Carolyn)—Reason I'm so late answering your heart-warming letters is because my fool former had me put in jail for nonsupport when I'd already promised a doctor-bill $5 per week in private and so she got judge to order it thru court. Cops screeched up to house in 2 prowlcars. I was in cooler with poor Spick husbands for 30 mins. Got myself new set of seaman's papers. Have decided to do something drastic. Oct. 25 I get Frisco-travel money; is brakie job still open by then? are they open now? later than Oct. 25? Important to answer. I'm not lamming from pitiful pittance but my last week's script pay was 18 bucks and I gotta get a bigger job—also to send my Ma 10 a week. Yes I can work on rr.—leg healed, dont worry. Very confused, my mind reeling, hardly time to think of writing, too many goils, excitements, conflicting plans, wishes, all balls nevertheless. Letter follows.

Jack

A week later, Kerouac told Cassady that he had begun the "re-writing" of On the Road *(he had already retyped it onto standard sheets of paper from the twelve-foot sheets he'd taped together as a long roll in the original manuscript). This was more than a minor revision of the novel; it was a completely new recasting of the story in what Kerouac described as "my finally-at-last-found style & hope," a method of literary composition he developed more fully later that month into the writing method he called "spontaneous prose."*

TO NEAL CASSADY

Oct. 9 '51
[Richmond Hill, N.Y.]

Hey Neal—

Just for kicks I'm sending you these 3 now-typed-up-revised pages of my re-writing ROAD . . . to show you that "Dean Pomeray"[1] is a vision—and also my finally-at-last-found style & hope; since writ-

---

1. "Dean Pomeray" was Kerouac's pseudonym for Cassady in this version of the narrative, which became the book titled "Visions of Neal," later published as *Visions of Cody*. In the published version of *On the Road*, Cassady was called Dean Moriarty.

ing that I've come up with even greater complicated sentences & VISIONS[2]—So from now on just call me Lee Konitz.[3] *Tomorrow I go to find me a ship.* I assume brakie jobs unavailable in Frisco; besides, sea-going is more movement, more ports, more money saved, better for me.

Incidentally this ROAD now is really a book & will make something—Try reading it on your tape, slowly. I already made a tape of jazz writing at Newman's back room.[4] Want to earn money at sea so I can devote my genuinely hung-up artistic interest to *this* shit—and more to come. Man I'll tell you all about this and everything else as soon as I get to Frisco which will be either a (one 1) voyage or even en route to one—S.I.U. ships New Yorkers to Frisco berths, pay fare from N.Y. Going to sea I'll see more of you than any other damn way—I say this from love and it's true—O what times we get when I hit Frisco loaded with loot & maybe Persian hasheesh & we carry wire recorder to little Harlem & also use it to record fucking-sounds in beds, etc.—all the while everything cool 'cause I'm big drunken seaman on leave. Give my love and dearest fondest all to Carolyn, & congratulations on her third flawless childbirth. Solid? Right. WRITE AT ONCE, I BE HERE TILL OCT. 25.

Jack

Finally Kerouac accepted Neal's offer to let him live in the attic room in the Cassadys' small house in San Francisco. Planning to stay awhile on the West Coast, Jack took a job with the Southern Pacific and continued his spontaneous prose experiments rewriting On the Road *and recording on Neal's tape recorder. Cassady was working*

---

2. Kerouac used his new prose method to change his novel from what he called "just a horizontal study of travels on the road" to "a vertical, metaphysical study" of Cassady.

3. Lee Konitz was an alto saxophone player. With spontaneous prose, Kerouac felt he had found a way to write that gave him the spontaneity of a jazz musician.

4. Kerouac used a tape recorder in the back room of Jerry Newman's record shop.

on his autobiography, beginning with his earliest memories in Denver, and Kerouac read his manuscript as it progressed. Before leaving New York, he had discussed publishing a version of On the Road *with Ginsberg's friend Carl Solomon, who was working for his uncle, the Ace Books paperback publisher A. A. Wyn. Once in San Francisco, Jack tried to interest Carl in taking Neal's book too.*

TO CARL SOLOMON

Dec. 27 1951

[San Francisco]

Dear Carl

How are you, you old foof [sic]. This is a Spanish typewriter but I have a lot of important things to talk to you about so don't worry about ?, etc. Received your letter and read it carefully both Neal and I. We read it while at work for the Southern Pacific tossing heavy bags of mail [. . . .] I was up all last night a rainy night doing a two hour tape recording one hour of it the entire tale of Dr. Sax by myself while Neal and Carolyn and kiddies slept and rain fell on the roof. In other words I guess I have a novel. All I have to do is type it etc. and I'm writing in this quick crazy way because theres NO Time in Frisco have to run to Union Hall do a thousand things. Im going to write you a long letter from the ship I get understand? The purpose of this one letter (right now the recording of Neal on flute and me on drums interrupts my purpose) is to tell you TWO THINGS:

1/ Im not gone off from A.A. Wyn. I'm only gone off to earn money on my own hook so that when I do sell my book it wont make any difference and anyway it isnt finished yet. [. . . .]

2/ NEAL IS WRITING A GREAT NOVEL AND ALREADY HAS over 20,000 great careful words written. This is Dean Pomeray itself . . . I told him to send it to you at once but of course Neal cant believe it when I tell him that its anything [. . . .] write back and tell Neal to send on because he's bashful and dont believe.

Listen Carl, I've decided not to do the Dean Pomeray but at once start on my own downtown red brick neon in Lowell because the latest things I wrote and have been writing "about Neal" suddenly and curiously are really about myself [. . . .] Meanwhile the news that Scribners took John's book was good news for all of us.[1] It gives added incentive to Dean Pomeray's own self-written book. I understand, don't worry [. . . .] why Scribners would take John's book and not mine. Please PLEASE dont worry about my not joining your stable [. . . .]

Neal's book is magnificent. If you think I had the thing down . . . he himself is completely conscious not only of the old barbershop and the old B movie and bouncing his tennis ball downtown streets of Denver and the bum flops and poolhalls [. . . .] And if you start with myself and Neal for writers you're going to be starting a publishing house that will someday count (and Ansen and Ginsberg, don't lose any of these.)

Carl I have to catch that ship and run

So I'm off

I'll try to write again soon before I leave [. . . .]

Jack

---

1. Holmes's novel *Go* was published in 1952 by Scribner's, which turned down an early version of *On the Road*.

1952

During the winter and early spring of 1952 Kerouac lived with the Cassadys in San Francisco; he was on the West Coast when his daughter, Janet Michelle Kerouac, was born on February 16, 1952, in Albany, New York. Neal helped arrange a job for him as a baggage handler and yard clerk on the Southern Pacific Railroad, and while Jack continued to send money home to his mother, he tried to evade paying child support. Besides his "high times" as Cassady's buddy in San Francisco, Kerouac also "swam in the sea" of his own words at the typewriter as he continued what he called "sketching" his new version of On the Road, *which he was then calling "Visions of Neal." It was his attempt, he later told Ginsberg, to create "a big multi-dimensional conscious and subconscious character invocation of Neal in his whirlwinds."*

Kerouac was still trying to help Burroughs place his manuscript of "Junk," and in San Francisco he dropped a note to James Laughlin at New Directions to see if Laughlin was interested in reading a revised version of the book.

TO JAMES LAUGHLIN

Feb. 24, 1952
[San Francisco]

Dear Mr. Laughlin,

I'm still wondering if anyone has read W. Denison's[1] "Junk" yet; if so, I'd like to recommend it again, and say that it has prose and considerable archive value. I'm out of town now and Allen Ginsberg is Denison's connection in New York for the moment. Ginsberg recently received a revised version from the author down in Mexico City; it's smoother now and not so weird and Reichian. It's at present the best book and rawest story on the subject. It would be a shame if it was eventually swallowed up by cheap paper covered 25 cent Gold Medal or Signet books like "I, Mobster."

Sincerely,
John Kerouac
c/o Harcourt Brace or c/o A. Ginsberg
383 Madison Ave.   416 E. 34 St.
New York, N.Y.   Paterson, N.J.

---

1. Burroughs's pseudonym.

· 333 ·

On the day of Kerouac's thirtieth birthday, he wrote an exuberant letter to John Clellon Holmes that gives a sense of his excitement writing spontaneous prose five months after his discovery of this literary technique. It also reveals Kerouac's instinctive feeling that he wouldn't be able to sustain the pace of this new writing method: "Please tell this to Allen, [I] feel that I have completely reached my peak maturity now and am blowing such mad poetry and literature that I'll look back years later with amazement and chagrin that I can't do it any more . . ."

In this letter Kerouac enclosed a fragment of another letter written to Holmes on February 8, 1952, on Neal's birthday, describing a wild night he and Neal had together in San Francisco. Carolyn had found from past experience that making them leave solved nothing. Not knowing what else to do, she postponed any action. Jack and Neal were so relieved she hadn't barred them from the house that all three shared a giddy sense of relief that they were still together. Soon after this incident, while Neal was away from home for several days at a stretch working as a brakeman, Jack and Carolyn became lovers, with Neal's tacit consent.

TO JOHN CLELLON HOLMES

March 12, 1952 my, and your, birthday
[San Francisco]

Dear John,

Old friend, think, I wrote you such mad letters in the past three months that I couldn't bear to mail any of them . . . and filed them for my own use; someday you may see them, I assure you, didn't miss anything; but I only want you and in fact don't ever you dare think I would "put off" writing to you when what I actually do is practice . . . my letters to you. Tell me now, but you're not here; and also listen, I dont want you ever to think I'm not talking to you when I'm talking like this. I know you're there; you know I'm here, we understand each other right well. Enclosed in this present epistle you will find some of the unmailed letters which explain themselves . . . but do you realize and believe also that I cant remember whether I did or not, write you a letter, or mail you scraps; I certainly did write

Allen, twice, and Carl; believe me [. . . .] Now listen, I have a
thousand and so many things to tell you, naturally I dont know
where to start, in a way its a good thing youre not in Frisco, I'd write
myself out talking everything to you as Ive been doing these past few
years of our friendship—wait till you see On the Road! I finally made
it! Our long coffee clutches were not in vain, not botches, we both
made it, but as always boasting or that is blowing a louder horn than
you I hastily jump in and reassure you, this Road that I have here,
25 cent, better than any hair pomade youve EVER known my dear
Mrs. Hick, but wait, a thousand gray days have passed everything is
in the air, wild things haunt the meaning of the night, we're all set
now the two of us to blow our tops apart in a terrible cojoonery of
wild demeanors and dasimodos. . . . I meant to say Quasimodo, the
hunchback, Oh yes, Oh ho, this will give you, ladies and gentlemen,
up steps Jack Kerouac now earnestly beginning his letter to John
Holmes not only for posterity fuck you all but for John Holmes too,
later, later, I'll quote later, dont push me now, I'm tellin old John,
here, old hardcock hardman John Holmes whose wife flew the frit-
ter,[1] for which we all raise beer tankards because the Indians bit the
dust anyhow; what can we do, in New Orleans we piss in the river
and play poker, we get married six times if not seven; we get hauled
in by the law; we've been shat and puked on and fuckedup and laid
low and made our wild potlatch screeches in the raging Dostoyev-
skyan fires of heroism throwing our mothers' dearest possessions
within and withal, why there are more Ippolits than Idiots you Imagine, and think of the great news of Allen Ginsberg that undoubtedly
means that we're all coming into our own at last, I for one, please
tell this to Allen, feel that I have completely reached my peak maturity now and am blowing such mad poetry and literature that I'll
look back years later with amazement and chagrin that I can't do it
any more, but nobodys going to know this fact for 15, 20 years, only
I know it, and maybe Allen, I certainly of course know Allen is

---

1. John and Marian Holmes had separated. In the earlier letter to Holmes, Kerouac had written, "I'm terribly sorry to hear about you and Marian. What are
you going to do without her? I think you're in love with her and should get her
back at once and make her mind."

blowing, always has, did long before me, really did, and will continue to grow; we all start early or late but start, and then blow like mad, but where was I, I started, you see just like when we're talking down 7th avenue and have so many subjects and minds swinging in the tits of passerby girls that with their thighs and our cunts intermixed and all them neons and beoms and fleons and grewons, and Scott Fitzgerald Columbia jews cuttin down the street with a hold your and a whoo whoo and all the wild kicks of absolutely lastplace greatest in the world and King of America, Manhattoes. You cant beat New York City.

Ho New Orleans hear that? Hear that you goddamn motherfucker Frisco; you pissy ass Seattle, you dullpoke old Minneapolis St Paul, you lakey crakey flakey Mineeapolakey, you wild up Duluths of the blue moose and doggerel of the snow, you hoar river, you beginning wildlands, you never did piss on me enough did you damn river? hey John, I'm talkin to the river, dig me talkin to the river and lettin you listen, like opening the stops very fast in a terrific good saxophone and now, at last, I announce to you, I've become a tenor man, an alto man, excuse, alto man, on Neal c-melody alto I been learning ever since the wild visions of musical pure truth I got on peotl (talk about your technicolor visions!) I blew like mad all my first day and but now, and now, I blow, a few weeks later, with perfect Stan Getz pearly tones and never miss the key but always, that is almost always, really occasionally miss the note itself, usually miss the note, but the key is there, the wild heartbreaking soft harmonic hint of all our hong song hearts, the central pit and prunejuice of poor old Jazz, mind you, pit and prunejuice,

It just came to my lips then and my fingers now, wow, I'm telling you John, everything, everything, everything is so mad (as I write to you Oscar Peterson is blowing like a sonofabitch on one of his new records, that great emphatic left hand, and people saying "Ho!" in the background as he bignecks to his work, dig that gone verb, fig that bone verde, merde, shit, I dont know where stap or stort, dig? But now let's get on the beam, I want to continue, I got this sax and can blow it real well now; but also, and I could prove by sending you a record I made, on tape, of me, on a number, but instead, passing thru New York soon as a seaman, where I'm incidentally and hurray gonna make my home again with my mother, or either that or hide singly in Manhattoes and get my kicks, get ready for the eventual day of the writing of the novel THE MYSTERIES OF AMERICA (only in New York I can write that one, that's the vantage point of the center). On the road!! but on! Mexico calls me, I may go to Mexico for two weeks very soon, just for t— [. . . .]

There's a rusty freighter chugging out the Golden Gate under great San Pablo mts. and I wish I was on and off to Hongkong [. . .] but next night, hear this, working my poor ass off in the cold night with mailbags, my pitiful $35 pay pops out of my dungaree watchpocket and I never find it again, goddam my soul and yet look how good I feel and what a fine wild truthful and complete and real good letter this is; o boy, I can hardly wait to see you, and Allen and everybody, but let me pause awhile in my orisons

> Do you think I'm crazy?
> No no no I'm not
> Jack

PS You want news but I cant organize this news I have in one letter—see you soon, within 6 months.

> Note date, February 8, 1952
> Neal's birthday

Dear John *(Holmes)*

> All, all by that inhuman
> Bitter glory wrecked.

O champion scribbler of the night! how do you go by your fourwalls this mid-matin, how do you fare in your doldrums and consequences, and your—

If all the words of man could be placed on this one page I'd place 'em. But enough have I boasted to you these many years. [. . . .] Frisco is mad, absolutely mad and almost perfect city at the end of the American continent and culture; from here on, it's not west, it's South, the word is South, and the word in LA is only East. Between

Frisco and LA lies the jumpingoff plank of California, stationed somewhere and guarded in the darkness by angels. Neal has just said, less than a half hour ago, that in California everything (in Frisco especially, not LA where he has been) there is the feeling that everything is golden, light, nothing's going to happen, miracles are not rare, and most of all everything seems unreal and undangerous and actually nothing ever happens to anybody, which is true [. . . .]

Most beautiful girls in the world in Frisco. It's a bloody shame. O what a tragic Saturday Neal and I had 3 weeks ago. Coming home from work in dark of night, musing on my freepass incoming to Frisco train, I'm thinkin about Neal, red neons, night, and instead, enroute home, get few beers in the wildest bar in America, corner 3rd and Howard, paddy wagon's there every hour, we just got to drink there you and me sometime but anyway I get high drunk, drop money on floor, am panhandled, play Ruth Brown wildjump records among drunken alky whores [. . . .] cut around corner to little Harlem scene of the great jam sessions of 48 and 49 (about Dean and Chad), only girl I laid in town so far is in there, colored b girl, gone woman, Marie, I hook up in there with her niece tall lissome black Lulu, call Neal feverish with excitement (he's in bed fucking) he rushed out, came down, in middle night, station wagon, all pile in, rush to find four foot connection Charley, he's on street, wham, tea, first thing you know, in his room, strip poker starts, and Lulu has to lose! In a dead giggling silence she began undressing before us— great tits, shoulders, legs, thighs, belly, belly button, perfect Betty Grable all over—wham, and Charley who's a 4 foot sexfiend born raised in Panama where his father is numbers racket and 4 foot too, has eyes on her, Neal is saying "Sh-h-h-it," whatever, and I'm watchin, and whoo, her girlfriend's watchin, fresh out of reform school she is (name I fergit), told us about conditions there, how when girls go fruit they put em in cottages alone, all girls go fruit, black girls go fruit for mexican girls, Neal spends entire rainy days hiding from his wife listening to these stories from the five colored sisters and cousins hangin around Marie's housing project shack pad, with lazy men around, Neal sits on bed blasting and giggling with the girls all day—Lulu gets embarrassed and dresses, re dressed; from then on, disaster, Neal runs off to get t from wife, she waiting in night, now sobs, I, drunk, bring two girls into dark house, we stand breathless by baby sleep crib as Car[olyn] sobs and everything and throws us out, and off we go, 2 girls and me and Neal, bleary, driving into woods of California for orgy, but one girl cops out, Lulu stay with me, but Lulu pass out, and we spend whole day driving aimlessly and with that vague jawed but tremendous rocky fatalistic and tragic obstinacy of Neal and his fathers and the great raw hoboes and hardy winos of death and experience in the world, Neal just drives and drives having switched to old 32 pontiac tragic jalopy of the mist, we go up and down unbelievable Shakespeare cute hills of California countryside, warm day, hawaiian shirts, forests, we take girls back to project, a brother comes to carry Lulu out, pays no attention, off they go, Saturday late afternoon, the red sun falls on everything, night's coming, wild whooping Saturday night[1] and Lulu's already drunk and ruined her coat; well, Neal and I return to house crestfallen, to wife rocking baby hysterically in dark house. [. . . .] [incomplete]

In the spring of 1952 Kerouac wrote to Burroughs in Mexico City asking to stay with him after leaving the Cassadys. The previous September, when Burroughs had returned to Mexico City from Panama and Ecuador, he accidentally shot and killed his wife in a drunken accident. At a friend's apartment Bill had taken out a pistol and suggested to Joan that she balance a glass on her head so he could play William Tell. He fired and the bullet entered Joan's forehead an inch below the glass, killing her instantly.

Released from prison on bail, Burroughs remained in Mexico City waiting for the case to be settled. He began work on a second novel, later published as Queer, *and invited Kerouac to join him immediately: "Why don't you come right on down here now?"*

---

1. This night is described on pages 331–332 of *Visions of Cody*, "Tragic Saturday in Frisco . . ." where Kerouac incorporates the text of this letter. Carolyn Cassady gave her account of "what really happened" in Chapter 28 of *Off the Road*.

April 3, 1952

Orizaba 210—apt 5

Mexico, D.F.

Dear Jack,

I can't make any definite arrangement with you because I don't know when or how or by what route I will leave Mexico. When I do know will inform you. Also it is not for me to decide how long I will remain in Mexico. Once the case is settled, the Immigration dept. allows me 5 days to pack up and get out of the country with the alternative of forcible deportation to the U.S. [. . . .]

I am relieved to hear of the liquidation of Old Bull Balloon, and the advent of Bill Hubbard.[1] My novel is coming along. Expect to finish it in 2 or 3 months more as I don't write from scratch in fact I can't. When I write it is simply a question of putting down in some sequence what is already there. The excerpts from your novel sound mighty fine. Of course, the *Finnegans Wake* kind of thing can only be fully appreciated in context of the whole work, which in the case of this kind of writing more than any other, is an actual amoeboid-like organism.

With Marker[2] away I got another habit. Start cutting down to-morrow. With plenty codeine there's nothing to kicking a habit. Done it 5 times in the past 2 years. This habit I got partly for my health. I was convalescent from jaundice and wanted to cut out drinking completely for a month or so.

Been seeing a lot of bull-fights. Good kicks. Going to a cock fight this evening. I like my spectacles brutal, bloody and degrading.

Why this arbitrary date the 18th for your arrival here? Why don't you come right on down here now? Right at the moment legal pro-ceedings are immobilized by Holy Week. I asked the secretary how

---

1. These were pseudonyms for Burroughs that Kerouac used in his early drafts of *Doctor Sax* and *On the Road*.

2. Lewis Marker, Burroughs's lover, and the "Eugene Allerton" of Burroughs's *Queer*.

come no court this week and she say: "Because we are Christians" (unlike some other people who shall be nameless).

I am due in court Monday, and if the ballistic experts are there, and the judge ain't in Acapulco, and Jurado shows, maybe I will be acquitted or convicted or something definite. No word from Allen. My best to Neal.

As Ever,
Bill

Before leaving New York, Kerouac had been so desperate to be published that he accepted a $250 advance from Ace Books and signed a contract giving them an option on his next three books. Thinking that the Ace mass-market paperback format, primarily sold in drugstores, meant a shorter book, Jack began to type up a 160-page book about Cassady from sections of the manuscript he was calling "Visions of Neal," planning to submit it to Solomon under the earlier title of "On the Road." Kerouac also proposed that Ace publish the detective novel that he and Burroughs had written based on what Kerouac referred to as the "Lucien murder." Uneasy that Ace was not a quality publisher, Kerouac urged Solomon to persuade A. A. Wyn to publish the longer version of On the Road *in a hardcover edition.*

TO CARL SOLOMON

April 7 [1952]
San Francisco

Dear Carl,

There's no leeriness on my part concerning papercover books . . . fact of the matter is, Burroughs and I wrote a sensational 200-page novel about Lucien murder in 1945 that "shocked" all publishers in town and also agents . . . Allen remembers it . . . if you want it, go to my mother's house with Allen and find it in my maze of boxes and suitcases, it's in a manila envelope, entitled (I think) I WISH I

WERE YOU,[1] and is "by Seward Lewis" (they being our respective middle names). Bill himself would approve of this move, we spent a year on it, Lucien was mad, wanted us to bury it under a floorboard (so don't tell Lucien now). If you publish it (some hope!) I'd like it re-titled and re-authored, by John Kerouac and whatever Bill's calling himself now (Sebert Lee I think).

But here's my main idea in this note (and apart from fact that I feel you're okay and wish you'd like me more), I have an idea we could publish ON THE ROAD regular hardcover *and* papercover, extracting 160-page stretch for 25c edition (the sexy narrative stretch, I'll designate it when I mail in full manuscript some time soon). This is no dope idea, this is real money idea, the stretch of my ms. that begins, "I first met Neal Pomeray in 1947 but I didn't travel on the road with him till 1948, just the tail end of that year, at Xmas time, North Carolina to New York City 450 miles, and back to NC, and back to New York City again, in 36 hours, with washing dishes in Philadelphia, a teahead ball in Ozone Park, and a southern drawl evening drive in Rocky Mount in between. And in all that time Neal just talked and talked and talked. We had met in 1947 when he first came to NY from Denver with his first wife, the 16 year old LuAnne Sanderson of Denver and LA where her sadistic handsome father divorced from her mother, was a cop; Neal, all bare ass standing in the door of a cold water pad when we first knocked on the door, me, Ed Gray, Hal King. They were students at Columbia University, close friends of mine, Hal was a dear close friend at the time; they told me Neal was a mad genius of jails and raw power, that he was a god among the girls with a big huge crown wellknown wherever he went because he liked to talk about it and made frequent and assertive use of it. Also the women talked about it and wrote letters mentioning it, and sometimes frantic; a reader of Shopenhaur [sic] in reform schools, a Nietazshean [sic] hero of the pure snowy wild West; a champion. In the door he stood with a perfect build . . ." and so on for 160 pages, going through our 4 trips in 40

---

1. This novel had several titles, including "The Philip Tourian Story" and "The Ryko Tourian Novel." The final working title was "And the Hippos Were Boiled in Their Tanks."

states. If that isn't pocketbook perfection, what is? But my only fear is you wouldn't publish full ROAD in hardcover . . . believe me, Carl, the full ROAD will make Wyn a first-rate reputation.

J

—and t'would be foolish to sacrifice reputation for quick profit; and besides I wouldn't stand for it, *so let's do 2 editions.*

In the spring of 1952, when his lengthy visit began to wear out his welcome at the Cassadys, Kerouac wrote more frequently to Ginsberg, whom he regarded once again as a buddy after enduring what he later told Allen were Neal's "stony silences." Ginsberg had sent Jack some of his poems and a description of meeting the poet William Carlos Williams in Rutherford, New Jersey. Kerouac missed his friends in New York, but he couldn't return to the East Coast because his wife was insisting that he contribute to the support of their daughter.

TO ALLEN GINSBERG

> March or April [1952]
> [postmarked April 8, 1952
> San Francisco]

Dear Allen,

OKay keed, glad you liked my whatnots about your poems. [. . . .]

Appreciated yr. thing about you and Williams—I saw him, it's a classic night, he's 68, what's he got left . . . good thing he was at least a doctor, I feel shame all the time from all this poetry, I don't know how the hell I manage to live with myself being so open and cuntlike and silly like ROAD will be and you will your tragic "sandwich of pure meat"[1] made me shudder and wish I could help you on

---

1. Later Ginsberg developed the imagery:

> A naked lunch is natural to us,
> we eat reality sandwiches.
> But allegories are so much lettuce.
> Don't hide the madness.

> ["On Burroughs's Work"]

Judgment Day . . . not in the face of God but your own when you realize . . . That pix of you and Lucien, he says yr. poetry is amusing in it . . . he looks like a successful snob, you look like a hipster from San Remo but I love you don't doubt that part of it.

I'm just being Lucien like now. News of Bill's book astounding— I *knew* it, who else writes a full confession, hamstring your cunty old Merton's in a hogfarm, blah, Bill is still great; I wrote 2 weeks ago and asked him to take me to Ecuador with him, am waiting for his reply [. . . .]

If he sends for me, my third novel will be underway immediately . . . it will be about Bill sinking into South America, no title as yet, as vast as "On the Road," tell Carl. Also tell Carl I'm sending in "Road" completed and neatly typed and all considered and pruned no later than [mid-]April so I can start on novel No. 3. I want to hit onwards, one of these years I will knock off 3 masterpieces in one year like Shakespeare in his Hamlet-Lear-Julius Caesar year—I didn't ask you to go to Paris with me because I need you, I was only being kind to a fellow writer and being traditional, fuck you too.

Ti-Jean X X X

I am typing up the entire Joan Anderson chapter of Neal's to stone Carl with.

Next: Hey, how lucky you are to have a home address like that Paterson home of yr. Paw's even tho as I know there, you, a ghost, etc. feel like an outsider and crazy but worse than that unliked or strange and from-mars, but me, I have a terrible guilt and no-home and will never feel the same again on account of that cruel cruel little bitch [. . . .] I'm getting awfully tired of roaming and now (keep it to yourself for christ sake) my mother writes that cops are haunting the house and priests are calling on her wanting to know my address, tell Eugene it's that Goddamn Brooklyn Uniform Support of Dependents and Abandonment Bureau of the DA there, the bastards want to change the country to "meet a problem," there're one million men in this country trying never to see their wives again and these socialistic think-they're-well-meaning-pricks are trying to "solve" that, you and yr bureaucracy, Tit, dont tell nobody but I have to leave even Frisco in due time of course shit man I wish I was innocent again [. . . .]

PS Tell John Holmes "Go, Go, Go" was the title of a story I wrote about me n Neal in a jazzjoint, it was Giroux made up the title; he call his novel "Go" is a good idea for him, I got nothing to do with it, he wrote and asked me if it was one of my old rejected titles, jesus christ what am I supposed to be jesus christ [. . . .]

I'm a wino in frisco temporarily.

John Holmes is a latecomer, or that is, a pryer-intoer of our genuine literary movement made up of you, me, Neal, Huncke (as yet unpublishable) and mebbe Lucien someday . . . just like other literary movements, and therefore John Holmes is really riding our wagon without knowing where actually it's headed (but you know and I know). (Boy) [. . . .] Neal is great, his book is great, I'm disappointed in Carl's intelligence telling him to study Mickey Spillane,[2] what does he think our boy is, an idiot? Would I write a book about a dope?

In May 1952, after arriving at Burroughs's apartment "with seabag, the dust of great Mexico" on his shoes, Kerouac wrote Ginsberg a series of letters describing his trip down to the border with the Cassadys and his life with Burroughs in Mexico City. Jack also asked Allen to act as his literary agent and wrote to his friend in great detail about his new writing method of spontaneous prose.

TO ALLEN GINSBERG

May 10 [1952]
c/o Williams (Burroughs)
Orizaba 210, Apt. 5
Mexico City, Mexico

Dear Allen,

It took Bill and I 10 days to find this splendid typewriter and ribbon and only recently we resumed work on our respective books.

---

2. Mickey Spillane was a best-selling "hardboiled"-detective-fiction author whose novels featured graphic descriptions of sex and violence.

I have no idea how it could have been possible for Hilda, Joan's siren friend from Albany (you know, the brunette) to write, a month ago, a letter to Kells'[1] wife telling her I was coming to Mexico unless somebody in New York who knows my movements is hipping her and possibly Joan, not that it matters but why? Try to figure this leak for me, it ain't right.

Neal left me at Sonora, Arizona on the Mexican border. He had his car with the seats all out (station wagon) and had pillows and babies and Carolyn all gypsied and happy in the back; I left the happy domestic couple and started on my new adventure, at dawn. Crossed the wirefence into Sonora (it was NOGALES Arizona excuse me into Nogales Sonora I went). To save money I bought 2nd class bus tickets south . . . it became a tremendous Odyssey[2] of bouncing over dirt roads through jungles and changing buses to cross rivers on makeshift rafts with sometimes the bus itself fording the river up to the wheeltops, great. I hooked up soon enough (around Guymas) with a Mexican hipcat named Enrique by asking him, as we stood in front of some nepal cactus, if he ever tried peotl; yes he had; he showed me you could also eat the fruit of the nepal for the palate; mescal is the peotl cactus. He started teaching me Spanish. With him he had a handmade radio repair ohms and amperes gadget for appearances; also it was one of his crafts (he's 25) but actually we ended up using it for, pour cacher la merde, if you dig, which we picked up in an Oriental village or town called Culiacan, the opium center of the New World . . . I ate tortillas and carne in African stick huts in the jungle with pigs rubbing against my legs; I drank pure pulque from a pail, fresh from the field, from the plant, unfermented, pure milk of pulque makes you get the giggles, is the greatest drink in world. I ate strange new fruit, mangos, all kinds. In the back of the bus, drinking mescal, I sang bop for the Mexican singers who were curious to hear what it sounded like; I sang "Scrapple from the Apple" and Miles Davis' "Israel" (excuse, it was written by Johnny Carisi

---

1. Kells Elvins, Burroughs's friend.

2. Kerouac described this trip in "Mexico Fellaheen," included in *Lonesome Traveler:* "When you go across the border at Nogales Arizona . . ."

whom I once met in Remo) (wearing checked topcoat with fur collar). They sang me all the songs, did "Ah ya ya ya yay yoy yoy" that Mexican laugh-cry; in Culiacan we got off bus, me, Enrique, and his 17 year old footman tall 6 foot Indian Girardo; like a safari we started off down hot dobe streets of midnight, straight for the stick hut Indian outskirts of town; near the sea, in the Tropic of Cancer, hot night, but pleasant, and soft, no more Friscos, no more fogs. We came to a gigantic space between the dobe town and some huts and crossed in the moonlight; one dim light ahead, in a stick hut; E. knocked; door was opened by white garbed Indian in big sombrero but with downturned Huncke-like Indian face and scornful eyes. Some talk, we went in. On the bed sat a big gal, Indian's wife; and then his buddy, an Indian goateed (not by style but didn't shave) hipster-junkey, in fact opium eater, barefoot and tattered and dreaming on the bed-edge, and thin, Huncke like; and on the floor a drunken snoring soldier who'd just eaten some O after lush. I sat on bed, Enrique, he squatted on floor, Big Girardo stood in corner like a statue; the host, scornful, made several angry remarks; E. translated one of them, "Is this Americano following me from America?" He had once gone to America, to L.A. for maybe 12 hours, and someone rushed . . . well he is hero of the gone heroes tribe of Mexican Fellaheen[3] Afternoons and Mexico (I saw the Lord Star from a bus) gave me a medallion to look at which was either torn from his neck or from another torn, see, but I think it was torn from him but he recovered it and he gestured showing how this American (maybe cop) tore it from his neck in L.A., that's what he did, was crucified in Los Angeles and returned to his Night Huts. thus anger . . . Understand, Allen, that everything is going on in Indian dialect Spanish and that I am digging everything, all of it, almost perfectly, with my French Canadian mind in the middle of the Dakar village.

---

3. Kerouac used "Fellaheen" to describe the indigenous peoples of the Americas. Carolyn Cassady adds, "I could never tell exactly if he used the term to mean the 'essence' of a culture, unspoiled by exterior influences, or as Spengler used it (where Jack got the term), who says it means the 'residue' of a culture after it has collapsed."

I thought I was beyond Darwin's chain,
A phosphorescent Jesus Christ in space, not a champion
   of the Fellaheen night
With my French Canadian mind.

Then Scornful, who was very husky and goodlooking and dark, handed me a pellet and instructed my boy Enrique (who was squatting on the floor pleading for friendship and coolness but had to go through certain tests, just like two tribes meeting) so I looked at the pellet, and said Opium, and Scornful laughed and was glad; pul'd out the weed, rolled several cigars, sprinkled O in them, and passed around. I got high on the second drag; I was sitting right next to the Indian Opium Saint who, whenever he succeeded in breaking into the conversation, made apparently vacuous or maybe mystic remarks that they in their practicality and hepness avoided—everybody, young Girardo, blasting. I got high and began to understand everything they said, and told them so, and chatted in Spanish with them. Scornful brought out a statue he'd made in Gesso . . . you turn it over and it's an enormous cock; they all put it on their flies seriously to show me; laffing only a little, and on the other side a, I think, woman of some kind, or human figure. They told me (it took a half hour, with writing in my notebook) that in Spanish the other word for Gesso was Yis, or Gis. I showed them things like Zotzilsha, the Bat God; Yohualticitl, Lady of the Night; Nanahustl, Lord of Lepers; Citalpol, the Great Star; and they nodded (from my notebook). Then they apparently talked about politics, and at one point, by candlelight, he the host said, "The earth was ours," "La terra esta la notre" or however . . . I heard it clear as a bell and looked at him and we understood (about Indians I mean) (and after all my greatgreatgrandmother in Gaspe, 1700, you know, was an Indian, married my ancestry French baron) (but so they say in the family)—then it was time to retire, the three travelers went into Huncke's hut and there they gave me the choice of the bed or the ground, the bed was a straw pallet on crisscross sticks with a piece of cardboard for insulation under which the Saint Junkey kept his fixings and shit. He was offering his bed to all three of us, it was too small, so we stretched out on the ground with my seabag as a common pillow, I tossed with

Girardo for the outside position, I lay down, Huncke went out to get some shit, and we blew out the candle. But first Enrique promised to tell me all the mysteries of that night in the morning, which he later forgot. I wanted to know if there was a secret underground Indian hipster organization of revolutionary thinkers (all of them scornful of American hipsters who come down among them not for shit or kicks but with big pretenses of scholarship and superiority, this is what Scornful indicated) and not with pure Allen Ginsberg-like friendship on the corner on Times Square is what these Indians of course want, see, no bullshit, and they need Hunckes. In Frisco, the last week, I visited Lamantia[4] with Neal, he is living in the former stone small castle overlooking Berkeley Calif. he was reading "The Book of the Dead,"[5] was reclined in a sumptuous couch with furnishings and turned us on, three friends from Calif. U. dropped in, a psychology major who is apparently his Burroughs, a tall handsome owner of the house (who is somewhat the Jack K.) lounging on floor and sleeping eventually [. . . .] and a young eager intelligent kid who was like you; this was his circle, and of course he was being Lucien, they talked about psychology in terms of "I saw that damned black background to the pink again in yesterday's peotl," "Oh well (Burroughs), it won't hurt you for awhile" (both snickering). [. . . .] Lamantia showed me his poems about the Indian tribes on the San Luis Potosi plateau, I forget tribe name, they deal with his visions on Peotl, and they, the lines are,

arranged

like

this, for effect, but more

complicated.
But I was disappointed in Neal that night for not at least digging [. . . .] as I told him later, we were like two Italian mountain peasants allowed by local nobles of the castle to chat with them for a night and had failed on account of Guidro talking about his cart and horse

---

4. Philip Lamantia, San Francisco surrealist poet (b. 1927).

5. W. Y. Evans-Wentz's translation of *The Tibetan Book of the Dead*, regarded by Ginsberg as a "parable of waking existence as well as after death journey."

all the time. This made Neal mad, and the next night, for the first time in our lives, we had a fight—he refused to drive me to Lamantia, outright. He made up for it the next day (at Carolyn's urging because she loved us both) by buying a Chinese dinner, my favorite. But when I left Neal at Nogales I felt an undercurrent of sad hostility and also that he had hustled me there awful fast instead of the picnic we were going to have by the side of the road in Arizona or Imperial Valley even. So it goes, I dunno. But Neal was great and generous and good and my only complaint is cheap, i.e., he never talked with me any more, just "Yeah, yeah," almost sullen, but he was busy, but he is dead, but he is our brother, so okay, forget it. He needs another explosion, I can tell you that much; for now he is all hungup on complete all-the-way-down-the-line materialistic money and stealing-groceries anxieties and Nothing Else, positively. Carolyn has to stay in the house for months at a time while he works every day, 7 days on railroad and other jobs, to pay for things they never use, like cars; not a drop to drink in house usually, no shiazit any more, nothing, and Neal always gone. This was my observation; Carolyn is a great woman. I think it will work out when they move to San Jose, in the country, and then C. can at least grow a garden and get her kicks in sun, there being no sun where they live now, or nothing, although I never was so happy in my life than in that splendid attic with 11th edition Encyclopedia Britannica . . . but my complaints are the least of it, and I want to tell you in person later, and you understand, I dont want to appear to be the ungrateful brother-in-law guest yak-king in behind their backs which I aint, I was happy and secure for the first time in years and the first thing Neal said was, "Do anything you like, man." But to Culiacan: the candle out, I lay awake for an hour listening to the night sounds in the African village; footsteps crunched close to our door, all three of us stiffened; then they moved on; and sounds, rhythms, beasts, insects. Huncke came back and slept, or dreamed. In the morning we all leapt up simultaneously and rubbed our eyes. I took a crap in a 1000-year old Indian stone crap-per in the outdoors. Enrique went off and got me about 2 ounces of shit for only $3, which is expensive down there but I had dough they knew. Then I got high again and sat listening, squatted, to noon sounds of village, which is a cooing, crooning, African, world Fellaheen sound, of women, children, men (in the yard was Scornful with a spear splitting twigs on the ground with great strokes of perfect aim, chatting and laughing with another spear wielder, mad); Huncke just sat on bed with eyes open, moveless, a dead mad mystic Francis I tell you, down. Enrique rolled enormous Indian joints, laughed at my American sticks I rolled. In fact they roll em just the size of Lucky Strikes so they can smoke on street unnoticed, round, firm. Then I got shakes (from no eat and bouncing for days) and they wondered at me; I sweated. Scornful went out and brought me hot food; I ate happy; they gave me hot peppers to revive my system; I drank a pop with it; they kept rushing out for soup, etc. I heard them high on tea discussing whose food it was . . . "Maria" . . . they gossiped about her; I saw enormous complexities of Indian noontime gossip and love affairs, etc. Huncke's wife came in for a brief giggling look at me; I bowed. Then I was surrounded by cops and soldiers. Guess what, all they wanted (tho my heart sank) was some tea; I gave a lot of it away. "I'm going to be arrested in Mexico finally," was my thought but nothing happened, and we left, safari, waving, and cut; in the heat of the day Enrique made us stop in the old church for a minute to rest and pray; then we moved on, left Girardo in Culiacan with tea and 20 pesos, got bus for Mazatlan, were entertained by young intellectual busline employee (two Mission Oranges) (at sidewalk crazy cafe) who said he read Flammarien [sic] . . . I told him I read existentialists, he nodded, smiled. Enroute to Mazatlan, Enrique got a woman who offered us her house and food for 10 pesos in M. that night, Enrique accepted cause he wanted to lay her, but I didn't feel like being a watcher of Spanish lovers, but I agreed; in Mazatlan we took our gear to her two aunts' house in the Dakar slums (you know Mazatlan is just like an African city, hot and flat right on the surf, no tourists whatever, the wonder spot of the Mexicos really but nobody hardly knows, a dusty crazy wild city on beautiful Acapulco surfs) and then Enrique and I went swimming, blasted bombers on sand [. . . .] The beach at Mazatlan when we look'd at the girls five miles away and the red, brown, and black horses in the distance, and the bulls and cows, the enormous verdures, flat, the great sun setting in the Pacific over the Three Islands, was one of the great mystic rippling moments of my life—I saw right then that Enrique was great and that the Indian, the Mexican, is great, straight, simple and perfect. Towards late afternoon, bussing now from Guadalajara I slept; there is no more beautiful a land and state than that of Jalisco, Sinaloa is also lovely. We arrived in Mexico City near dawn. Not wake up Bill so instead walked in slums and slept in a criminal's hovel for 5 pesos, all made of stone and piss, and blasted, and slept on miserable pad . . . he said to look out for the gunman. I avoided his learning Bill's address, for obvious reasons, told him I'd meet him that night in front of post office, went to Bill's with seabag, the dust of great Mexico on my shoes. It was Saturday in Mexico City, the women were making tortillas, the radio was playing Perez Prado, I ate a 5 centavor [sic] powder candy that I first dug 2 years ago with Bill's little Willy;[6] odors of hot tortilla, the voices of the children, the Indian youths watching, the well-dressed city children of Spanish schools, great clouds of the plateau over piney thin trees of morning and future.

Bill was like a mad genius in littered rooms when I walked in. He was writing. He looked wild, but his eyes innocent and blue and beautiful. We are the greatest of friends at last. At first I felt like a beat fool brought to a far flop in a land of centipedes, worms and rats, mad with Burroughs in a pad, but not so. And he persuaded me to stick to him instead of Enrique, somehow got me not to meet the kid that night, and I aint seen my saint Enrique since . . . that is, a guy who could teach me where, what to buy, where to live, on nothing-a-month; but instead I turned my mind again to the great St. Louis of American Aristocracy and has been so ever since. Wasn't that right decision? The kid, I mean, I feel sorry for standing him up—but Bill cant afford any contacts save Dave you know, his position is delicate. His "Queer" is greater than "Junk"—I think now it was a good idea to put them together, with "Queer" we can expect big Wescotts Giroux and Vidals[7] to read it avidly, not only Junkie-interested types, see. Title? "Junk or Queer" or something . . . hey?

---

6. After Joan Burroughs's death, their son Willy had left Mexico City to live with Burroughs's parents in Florida; Joan's daughter Julie went to live with Joan's parents in upstate New York.

7. Critic Glenway Wescott, editor Robert Giroux, and novelist Gore Vidal.

JUNK OR QUEER   OR JUNK, OR QUEER   JUNK AND QUEER
But title must have indications of both. Bill is great. Greater than he
ever was. Misses Joan terribly. Joan made him great, lives on in him
like mad, vibrating. We went to the Ballet Mexicano together, Bill
danced out to catch bus; we went on a weekend to Tenencingo in
the mountains, did some shooting (it was an accident, you know, no
doubt about it anywhere) . . . In the mountain canyon there was
depth. Bill was up on the hill striding along tragically; we had separated at the river in order to go separate ways—always take the
right road Bill had said night before about cobblestone road and
asphalt regular road to Tenencingo—so but now, he was taking left
road, climb along ridge to mouth of cut, and back along, to road,
avoiding river—I wanted to in the inexpressible softness of Biblical
Day and Fellaheen Afternoon wash my feet at the place where the
maidens left their cloth parts, and sat on a rock shook spiders from
it first but they were only the little spiders that watch the river of
honies, creek of God, God and honey, in the flow of the gold, the
rocks are soft, the grass just reaches to the lip, I washed and laved
my poor feet, waded across my Genesee, and headed for the road
(holes in my shoes now, I'm at my last ten bucks in this foreign land),
interrupted just once by canyon where depth and tragedy made me
circle further, met Bill in a Tenencingo soda fountain waiting. We
came back that night, after turkish baths, etc. Bill's Marker has left
him; I have had two women so far, one American with huge tits, and
a splendid Mex whore in house. Met several great Americans . . .
but they all got arrested yesterday for weed, tell you their names later
[. . . .] Bill and I want huge letter from you about Wyn situation,
for both of us (my ms. coming soon, 530 pages); more news about
Genet, first-degree murder? news about everything, and again I want
to know where are the first 23 pages of On the Road goddamit! (Will
insert into ms. for me?

                                                    Write   J

On the Road is a very great book, but I may have to end up daring
publishers to publish it . . . but he who publishes it will make money
. . . you'll see why, when.
Why dont you roundup a few dollars (including 10 pc of B's advance)

and come join us . . . we're heading South in 3 weeks . . . we're going to find that yage in Ecuador,[8] you know [. . . .]

What do you think of subtitling it [*On the Road*] A Modern Novel ???? (like Modern Jazz)

[. . . .] I schmeck twice a week with the old master . . . He talks to me all the time, I listen . . . what a relief after Neal's stony silences. I'm through with living in America, you know.

We also intend to go to Rome.

TO ALLEN GINSBERG

May 17 1952
[Mexico City]

Dear Allen,

Just sent *On the Road* to Carl c/o office; it should arrive Wednesday 21st or Thursday or Friday (or Tuesday). Didn't know you wanted to see it first.

You read it before Carl; show him this letter. Also ask him for my letter of minor instructions.

I also insist you take 10% from now on and be my agent.

First 23 pages have sent back to you and just fit em in.

Love,
Jack

TO ALLEN GINSBERG

May 18, 1952
[Mexico City]

Dear Allen,

Bill says he will write you a letter contesting your "fear in the dark" reasons for not coming down—while at the same time he doesn't want you to leave until "Junk or Queer" is settled, natch. We want you to become big hip New York agent and later editor

---

8. See Burroughs's letters to Ginsberg about his trip to South America from January to May 1953, published as *The Yage Letters* (1963, 1975).

now, if we make money you can open yourself an office, handle the mss. of everybody . . . Holmes, Harrington, Ansen, Neal, yourself, Carl, Hunk. By the way, where *is* Huncke?

I myself am leery of going into dark jungles with Bill . . . he scares me with stories of snakes . . . "they have a boa there that's really tree-bound until the age of so and so then it takes to the water" (in a bored yawning voice). And the malarial mosquito takes a dip with its ass when biting you, it's different from regulars; and the danger of sleeping on the ground is a certain kind of viper with so much venom that there's no cure, you just die. And the Auca, man-killing tribe; and lawless provinces and lawless towns like Manta on the coast; and the staple diet in jungle is monkeys, etc. But I will go if I have the dough, of course. At some point, keep this to yourself, possibly en route from Ecuador to Paris, I will zoom thru New York for a week of reunions and kicks on the sly, mebbe a month hey?

I know you will love *On the Road*—please read it all, no one has read it all yet . . . Neal had no time, nor Bill. *On the Road* is inspired in its entirety . . . I can tell now as I look back on the flood of language. It is like *Ulysses* and should be treated with the same gravity. If Wyn or Carl insist on cutting it up to make the "story" more intelligible I'll refuse; and offer them another book which I'll commence writing at once, because now I know where I'm headed. I have "Doctor Sax" ready to go now . . . or "The Shadow of Doctor Sax," I'll simply blow on the vision of the Shadow in my 13th and 14th years on Sarah Ave. Lowell, culminated by the myth itself as I dreamt it in Fall 1948 . . . angles of my hoop-rolling boyhood as seen from the shroud. Also, of course, now that *On the Road* is in, I'm going to start sketching here in Mexico . . . for the general basis of my Fellaheen south of the border book about Indians, Fellaheen problems, and Bill the last of the American Giants among them . . . actually a book about Bill. That's two things. And at any leisured moment near libraries (say, if I lived on the Columbia campus, or in Paterson, or a cheap room near 42nd and 5th Avenue), I'm going to execute my Civil War novel which I want to parallel Tolstoy's 1812 hangups in 1850's, in other words a historical novel, a big personal Gone With the Wind about Lucien-like cavalry heroes and Melville-like Bartlebies [sic] of draft riots and Whitman-like nurses and especially dumb soldiers from the clay hills staring into the gray mist and void of Chickamauga at dawn. Learning facts of Civil War as I go along. But I'm not sure which (of the first two) ideas will be completed first . . . should be "Doctor Sax."

Now here is what sketching is. In the first place, you remember last September when Carl first ordered the Neal book and wanted it . . . Sketching came to me in full force on October 25th, the day of the evening Dusty and I went to Poughkeepsie with Fitzgerald—so strongly it didn't matter about Carl's offer and I began sketching everything in sight, so that *On the Road* took its turn from conventional narrative survey of road trips etc. into a big multi-dimensional conscious and subconscious character invocation of Neal in his whirlwinds. Sketching (Ed White casually mentioned it in 124th Chinese restaurant near Columbia, "Why don't you just sketch in the streets like a painter but with words") which I did . . . everything activates in front of you in myriad profusion, you just have to purify your mind and let it pour the words (which effortless angels of the vision fly when you stand in front of reality) and write with 100% personal honesty both psychic and social etc. and slap it all down shameless, willynilly, rapidly until sometimes I got so inspired I lost consciousness I was writing. Traditional source: Yeats' trance writing, of course. It's the *only way to write*. I haven't sketched in a long time now and have to start again because you get better with practice. Sometimes it is embarrassing to write in the street or anywhere outside but it's absolute . . . it never fails, it's the thing itself natch.

Do you understand Sketching?—same as poetry you write—also never overdo it, you should normally get pooped in fifteen minutes' straight scribbling—by that time I have a chapter and I feel a little crazy for having written it . . . I read it and it seems like the confessions of an insane person . . . then next day it reads like great prose, oh well. And just like you say the best things we write are always the most suspected . . . I think the greatest line in *On the Road* (tho you'll disagree) is

"The charging restless mute unvoiced road keening in a seizure of tarpaulin power . . ." This is obviously something I *had* to say in spite of myself . . . tarpaulin, too, don't be frightened, is obviously the key . . . man, that's a road. It will take 50 years for people to realize that that's a road. In fact I distinctly remember hovering over the word "tarpaulin" (even thought of writing tarpolon or anything) but something told me that "tarpaulin" was what I'd thought, "tarpaulin" was what it is . . . Do you understand Blake? Dickinson? and Shakespeare when he wants to mouth the general sound of doom, "peaked, like John a Dreams" . . . simply does what he hears . . . "greasy Joan doth keel the pot (and birds sit brooding in the snow) . . ." However, I got very tired of blowing all that poetry and am now resting and getting hi and going to movies etc. and trying to read Gore Vidal's "Judgment of Paris" which is so uglily transparent in its method, the protagonist-hero who is unqueer but all camp (with his bloody tattoo on a thigh) and craptalk, the only thing good, as Bill says, are the satirical queer scenes, especially Lord Ayres or whatever his name . . . and they expect us to be like Vidal, great god. (Regressing to sophomore imitations of Henry James.) If Carl publishes Genet in drugstores all over America he will have done a service to his century.

[. . . .] You want me to send (my dear agent you are now boy) some sketches, etc. well it's all in *Road* . . . be sure and extract what you like for individuals and publications. I am equal on the whole thing, it's all good, all publishable . . . You can make short pieces out of any part. Send jazz parts to *Metronome* [. . . .] We can show *Road* to Scribners or Simpson or Farrar Straus (Stanley Young). If necessary, change title to Visions of Neal or somethin, and I write new *Road* for Wyn.

But methinks none of such crap necessary. Isn't "Queer" great?

Jack

After driving Kerouac to the Mexican border, Neal and Carolyn Cassady continued, with their three young children, on their car trip to visit Neal's father in Denver, and Carolyn's parents in Tennessee. Kerouac wrote the Cassadys after they returned home to California, alerting them that he might be shipping out of San Francisco if he landed a job as a merchant seaman.

May 27th 1952
c/o Williams
Orizaba 210, Apt. 5
Mexico City, Mexico

Dear Neal & Carolyn,

By now you must be back from Tennessee. Word from my mother and sister indicates I must have some mail up there . . . forward it on to me care of this address, we'll be here for another month, or at least I will, there's the possibility Bill will be here all summer before he can travel. I finished typing the book[1] on this splendid typewriter and sent it in; and on Bill's advice made Allen my agent; I suppose Allen may take it seriously and really go to work, I don't know, don't care, if they don't like my book it's too bad for them. I'm going to go back "to sea," that is, make another concerted effort to get going on the ships and get me a union book. . . . I wrote to Al Sublette[2] asking him where to meet him, where shipping is best, etc. Norfolk and New Orleans are supposed to be good, better than Frisco; on the other hand I might have to go all the way back to Frisco but that'll have its compensations in that I'll be seeing you again and can get some more wonton.

Neal, are you back on fulltime railroad?—and did the baggage room break up yet? how's Hoppy's position now? By the way, boy, I am of course indulging in a perfect orgy of Miss Green & can hardly see straight right at this minute, whoo! 3 bombs a day. On the way down me boy I blasted with Indians in stick huts in an adventure unparalleled in my long years of searching the sprale [sic].

---

1. A new version of *On the Road*. Ginsberg remembered that Kerouac got his three-book contract from A. A. Wyn at Ace Books on the basis of the chapter in a manuscript (later published as *Visions of Cody*) describing Cassady playing football in Denver. See Part Two of *Visions of Cody:* "Suddenly out on East Colfax Boulevard bound for Fort Collins Cody saw a football game going on among kids in a field. . . ." In a letter Kerouac wrote to Carolyn Cassady on August 10, 1953, he described the roll manuscript of *On the Road* as "the one I wrote 1951 where we make those transcontinental wildtrips written in simple old prose."

2. Al Sublette was a friend Kerouac introduced to the Cassadys in San Jose.

. . . You know, after I left you that morning, Nogales (Sonora) suddenly woke up and began playing parades in the street and fiestas
and kicks and I drank all day in a wild poolhall-bar-restaurant-
saloon two-part joint, also got burned for a fin (Mexican, 5 peso, 60
cents) by a connection . . . no reflection on Mexico, he was a American Negro, the bastard . . . memories of Frisco burns . . . . but here
way down in the Big Indian Town an American hipster friend from
L.A. laid 5 ozees[3] on me free . . . and I get more from Indian tribes
in the montanas when Bill and I and Dave go hiking and shooting
among the wild deer.

A thousand things to tell you . . . in fact, not the least in importance I already started *Doctor Sax* and have 20,000 written . . . or
more . . . writing, high, in the afternoons, while Bill sleeps . . . or is
out . . . at night I take 5 mile hikes around town, sometimes in the
remote out-part slums where Fellaheen dogs are the only living thing
awake . . . or rats. . . . I walk the long muddy dobe alleys . . . . or
go down to Organo the new whore street (1 peso, no bull) that is a
gas to just walk . . . . but, also, alas, to my sorrow in having to
confess, there was a 17 year old girl named Luz who induced me
to go upstairs with her into a little room with ceiling so low I had
to stoop, either that or let my head stand normal between senseless
beams . . . three cots, each surrounded by flimsy blanket curtains,
with bouncings . . . we had to stand and wait and watch a wild gay
whore playing kittenishly with the pecker of the man she just engaged
on the street, a well dressed giggling Ling of a Chinese; then little
Luz and I got one of the curtained cots, and she just plopped back
there with her legs openbalance relaxed to go (openbalance) and I
must confess tho I licked my chops in thought of all this I felt a little
like a bastard . . . one peso . . . 12 cents . . . but she apparently
welcomed all comers (ahem) and in fact seemed to enjoy herself and
to think that she was born just to lie there 20, 30 times a night and
get her dough with an honest f . . . sc . . . an honest . . . ah,
ahem, hey, now, whap, lookout, here's a quotation from *Doctor Sax*:

---

3. Five ounces of marijuana.

(Doctor) Sax and Smiley got into (of course Sax had a Butte name)—into a tremendous game of pool watched by 100 Butteans in the dark beyond the table lamps and its bright, central green.

SAX (won the break, breaks) (Crash) (the balls spin all over)

SMILEY (out of the mouth like a cigar and a yellow tooth) Say Raymond-O, don't you think this romance has gone far enuf?

SAX Why do you say that, Pops? (neatly rubbing chalk to cue as 8-ball plunks into corner pocket in the mill.) Anything you say, Pops.

SMILEY Why (bending over the table to take a shot as Sax protests and everybody roars) m'boy, it sometimes occurs to me, not that I haven't been to see the doctor late-ly (grunting to take a shot) (with cue)—the perfect disposition for your well-known little ten dollar ass is over by the table benchers there with the Pepsi Cola box and farnitures [sic], whilst I becalm myself in a dull weed (puffing cee-gar) and aim this rutabaga stick at the proper ball—white—for old yellow number one—

SAX But I sank the 8-ball!—you can't shoot now!

SMILEY Son (patting the flask of Old Granddad in his back pocket with no deprecatory gesture) the law of averages, or the law of supply and demand, says the 8-ball was a goddam Albino 8-ba-w-l (removing it from pocket and spotting it and lining up white cueball with a flick of his forefinger to a speck on the green beside it, simultaneously letting out a loud fart heard by everybody in the poolhall & some at the bar precipitating various reactions of disgust and wild cheer, as the Proprietor, Joe Boss, throws a wadded paper at Smiley Balloon's ass, and Smiley, position established, whips out a bottle to the light) (said flask) (and addresses it a short speech before taking a shot—to the effect that alcohol has too much gasoline in it but by God the old Hampshire car can go; promptly thereafter re-pocketing it and bending, neatly and briskly, with amazing sudden agility, neat and dextrous, fingertip control of his cue-stick, good balance, stance, the fingers all arranged on the table to hold the cue just so high, just right, pow, the old man pots the yellow one-ball into the slot, plock, and everybody settles down from the humor to see a good game of rotation between 2 good players and though the laffs and yaks continue into the night, Old Bull Balloom and W C Fields never rest, you can't die without heroes to look after.)

Please write, somebody . . . let me know what it was like in Tennessee and your plans for San Jose,[4] and the children, etc.—with luck I'll be seeing you soon off an MCS ship, I'll ring the doorbell with dry martini mix and Shakespeare . . . "Ah, isn't it g-r-r-and" like Henri Bleu (Henri Bleup).

Uncle Jack

Early in June 1952 Kerouac wrote Carolyn Cassady after Ginsberg had sent on a letter she had written to him about Jack's visit. Kerouac's interpretation of Neal's attitude toward his relationship with Carolyn was one of Kerouac's most explicit comments on the affair. He was careful to make clear to Carolyn that he could offer her no future with him, but urged her to move the entire Cassady household to Mexico to enjoy what he described as "the endless kicks of Mexico," not far distant from where Burroughs planned to start a "Hipster Colony" in Ecuador as "an island in the coming Soviet and Totalitarian invasions of the world . . ."

TO CAROLYN CASSADY

June 3, 1952
Mexico City

Dear Carolyn,

I was very glad to see that letter you wrote Allen, he sent it for me to see, I had no idea my mail hadn't reached you (one letter to

---

4. The Cassadys planned to move from their house at 29 Russell Street in San Francisco.

Tennessee, one to Frisco later), and no idea too you and Neal had stopped agreeing on an agree-basis . . . and what? once more wrangling in the pursy house . . . Take it easy, don't fight, latest word from headquarters of the Orinoco over here is, you can't work in Mexico but you sure can live in Mexico cheap. So I say, Neal, if you want to live in Mexico all you gotta do is work about 4 months on railroad per year, everything here incredibly cheap, more than I thought, Bill lives expensively in American neighborhood, you can live for nothing in Mexican neighborhoods in the city (swanky hotels on mud streets at 8 bucks a month etc.)—but also entire beautiful stone houses with gardens, fireplaces, vistas, at $27 American a month . . . and in the country, outside town, same thing for less . . . and stick huts for nothing I guess . . . Food is low . . . I buy 2 and a quarter pounds of filet mignon (2 1/4 is a kilo) for 11 pesos or 11x12 cents or $1.34 American dough, this is therefore FILET MIGNON 60 cents a pound. . . . hamburger here is only 18 cents a pound CIGARETTES 6 cents a pack RENT $20 a month ICE POP FOR THE CHILDREN 1 cent ICE CREAM CONE FOR POPPA CASSADY 3 cents or 6 cents large SECOND CLASS BUS FARE FROM NOGALES TO MEXICO CITY $6.00 . . . 1500 miles, like from New York to Denver, Frisco to Denver. . . . But enough of that, you can see. And listen Carolyn, you could have come through with the car that morning, no charge, and we could have driven fifty miles around or anything at no charge (and bought stuff) . . . and seen a fiesta in the afternoon in the gay little city of Nogales, you have no idea what it is ten feet beyond that wire fence.

In your letter to Allen . . . how can I have enough of the Cassady clan? including the children? hey? I am glad to hear that Neal has a sustained interest in me, the bastard postures the other way, so naturally, but, ah, um, ahem, ah,—of course he'll rise again . . . and is risen now but as Allen said in a recent letter to me, "Who knows what personal disgust and rocky glare lies beneath Neal's seeming 'silence'—after all that's happened he now has the right to sink into a fit of disgust."—which I wish I could do, it would take the silliness out of me. . . . (I get it on peotl, by the way, disgust, I just ate it twice more times here with the hipsters of Mexico City and Bill too, I'm not going to take it any more, definitely toxic on the eyes and stomach). Neal is a successful provider because he knows how to work . . . Allen and I never learned tire recapping or braking or any of those difficult or special trades or even tirechanging . . . I know that Neal will miss (while in Mexico) working . . . and while working in U S will miss Mexico . . . if that's what you're going to do. It can be done. I think it would solve problems . . . especially if you take care and find yourself an ideal little *house* here in Mexico with garden and yard for Cathy, Jamie and especially Johnny, guaranteed low rents available, no higher than $30 or more likely $20 and if you want to make it in Ajijic or Oaxaca, or Taxco (artist colonies) definitely even less, $15, sometimes $10 a month rent for a house . . . this will solve the problem of freedom to move around and leap in and out of doors and get high and dig not only Mexico but the life of families in the sun and yards and kicks all over and with a car how could you miss the kicks the endless kicks of Mexico, the picnics in Chapultepec park among the Indians, the drives to the floating gardens of Yoxichimilxico, (dont believe I spelled that right WCFields) . . .

Now listen Carolyn—I have to go to sea to buy a trailer for my mother to put in my sister's backyard (this is confidential on account of Joan) . . . (my stuff will be there, my home headquarters in the world)—but if you and Neal (and I'll probably see you soon) really plan to make it Mexico then I'll be in on it with you . . . (and'll have some sea money and more peace back home). We can all live down here in a house . . . sometimes I'll be either at sea, or staying at home in Carolina, or visiting Bill in Ecuador,—Neal sometimes working in California (4 months) and the other 8 writing The First Third in his house in Mexico, with imminent advance . . . sounds logical and awright to me . . . don't want to force anybody . . . In 4 months Neal you can save close to $2000 can't you? . . . that's 40 a week in Mexico, a huge sum of $330.00 pesos in Mexico, per week, plenty for you and family the year round Doctor bills included PENICILLIN buy in drugstore, shoot in drugstore, price: one dollar not ten dollars, half a million units. All medicine, docs cheap, very modern. Bill Burroughs says he's going to found his farm on an Ecuadorian high jungle river not far from coast and invite Hipster Colony of anybody hip come down and found an island in the coming Soviet and Totalitarian invasions of the world . . . so we'll also have a backway out. As for discussing the emotional complexities of the matter, ahem, harrumph, egad, I really feel like Neal incapable of dealing with such big abstract problems of love and mystery or at least I feel incapable but will say, or throw in my hat into discussion, with: There is an anxiety in you for Neal to love you in a certain way. What is that certain way? (ask yourself, or answer all) that certain way is lost in a tangle of shrouds if you ask me, I tell you I've always been convinced life is a spook. Many's the time I wanted to hold your hand or kiss you, merely as acknowledgement that we were all in the car heading for the world unknown, but felt the jealousy-kick just as much as Neal, and so played up to it, and didn't do what I wanted—this is the fault with accepting balloons of abstract possibility become real fact with bannerline headlines we put across the mind . . . confusing the level of reality with the level of imagination, myth, or possibility, or "value" (jealousy is a hassle over value, which is an abstract idea)—I dont think Neal was jealous, he just didnt know what we expected him to do, and we didn't either, I personally felt quite calm about the whole thing and still do except for qualms about how you feel, both of you [. . .], in other words, I accept loss and death, and if you offer me some of your life I'm very grateful but I know that nothing will come of it, of life, but death, so it really makes no difference to any of us what happens now and soon. . . . Eternity is the only thing on my mind permanently, and you are a part of it. One good thing about Mexico, you just get high and dig eternity every day.

> Write soon. . . . Neal write/also or
> Jack

p.s. You remember Wig the bassplayer in Frisco? with the Mephistophelean goatee and great driving bass-style. . . . Neal, sold us thru that Johnny with umbrella Fillmore night we waited with Roberts poolhall connected Wig took a cut of our shit, I saw him blow bass Club 299 and elsewhere . . . ah well, he came to Mexico City, played bass with local Mexican bop men and one American baritone sax called Hood and piazickedup and went back to Frisco and got wife and her car from bonds (not real wife) and came back down permanent and wants to open hip bop joint and who does he connect with for his heavy habit but Bill . . . and's been around every day . . . house is mad, full of young fisherman New Orleans blond hipsters with crazy little wives and one blond kid from Frisco who just got into a horrible life & death fight with Mexicans in wild bar of roads (Americans started it) almost got killed . . . but laughs and blasts and lot of rocking fools down here okay but I like my Mexico with just a simple plain single American friend Bill and I hope someday you and cut along in my highs and mystic writing and visit $3 (3 peso) whores of Organo street, man it outdoes em all, ah, me. . . . But I've got to break the monotony of the continual high ecstasy of Mexico (I mean t) & coolness of surroundings which makes kicks guilt-less and work a pleasure, work like say shopping, you know how you and I went shopping for groceries in Frisco, then picture you and me cuttin in stationwagon high to a Mexican market for our groceries, the hassles and mad scenes and in Mexico nobody hurries, there's absolutely no count left, no reason to rush, no more memory of—just a lot of Indians in a big huge 3 million encampment being adventurous weird and Bohemian in the eternal soft weather outdoors with stone and wood and flour and fruits and juices—long darkhair sleek Indian of Mexico, lookout . . . . . . when the moon shines, and I eat peotl, and blast, and drink pure pulque from an urn, I can see the United States glimmering on the plain and South America the other way, I got owl eyes in the hoot, hoo doo you too.

And Oh incidentally, to conclude this massive epistle, I have already written a third of *Doctor Sax* (45,000 words) in this past month in Mexico . . . in case I catch on like wildfire in New York with *On the Road* I got another masterpiece ready for the press.

I am leaving here late in June, bound for sea-job anywhere, mebbe New Orleans . . . I'll send new or forwarding sea-address and also leave it with Bill who himself poor fellow will soon have to have a forwarding address to the South . . . he's losing his bail money to crooked lawyers, but is free, and will be going to Panama soon to establish a home for himself and Willy . . . maybe Ecuador if he sees fit; his folks have moved to Florida permanently, with antiques and flowers, and Willy . . . Bill will send for Willy. Julie is lost in Albany with Joan's folks and Joan in general dark Albany ah, phew. I love you both and hope I dont bore you with my long talks. Forward my mail. Kiss the grail. (So Burroughs says "That Wig ain't got no energy & besides he aint no morsel neither." etc.)

Kerouac's next two letters to John Clellon Holmes, the first one written the same day he wrote Carolyn Cassady, continued to describe the euphoria he felt with the unlimited supplies of drugs in Mexico City while he lived in Burroughs's apartment. Midway in the writing of Doctor Sax, Kerouac felt himself at the height of his creative powers, on the verge of discovering "something beyond the novel and beyond the arbitrary confines of the story . . . into the realms of revealed Picture . . . wild form . . . my mind is exploding to say something about every image and every memory . . ."

TO JOHN CLELLON HOLMES

June 3 [1952]

[Mexico City]

Dear John,

Whoaps, hoa, hold on there boy, remember I's the geezer's that's a gonna write "Hold Your Horn High" all about that thar cityslickin Lester Young and his broad Billy [Holiday] and other friends and interconnections in the development of jazz since 1935 on—on to Zoot [Sims] and Wig [Gerald Wiggins] now—so hold off, recall I told you this, re-remember, don't tromp on my Lester and my Miles—find yr own Lester, cream yr own Miles—I personally will confine myself to making Seymour [Wyse] the central image of Appreciation, Lester the central image of Lonely Blow—Billy's his woman (I've known several women like Billy since I saw you, including one Indian woman, one Negro, and Billy herself I saw sing in Frisco and talked to her with her dog in my arms)—but not to prove anything, so okay John what I want to stress: "Afternoon of a Tenorman" and "Hold Your Horn High" were two different ideas with set goals—the only thing that's changed in my idea is the title (because modern tenormen lean their horns on their haunches and that's allright ayen't it?) Are we set? [. . . .]

On a peotl high I wrote you a very sullen letter about this which you can have if you want. [. . . .] Now high as I write this. Everything clear above. Hope to hear from you. How's the folks? Who's the hex? What's the hoax? Where's the axe? How's the hix? I got hicks. Crash, bla—(savy wavy line)—rather than make mistakes and erase them I just decide to type on anyway . . . that's why I don't compose my books in typewriter . . . I goof the machine. Hasn't Allen received my "On the Road" yet? I think it's lost on the road.

I paid only 30 cents postage on it, I'll never see it again, I was trying to save money, I am a desperate Indian. Please check to Allen . . . [. . . .]

Jack

P.S. Yr literary comparisons (Bird as Melville, Tristano as Hawthorne) are a great idea . . . one typical of you, i.e. more cerebral and bookish than any I might have—yet what I wanted to point out in this letter, gathering all the top jazzmen together IN ANY COMPARISON group in a blow-blow-blow whaling jazz-bop Whirling Vision Story or even tight-knit "movie" epic is still basically the book I was going to write, and how can I write it and publish it if you're going to do literally the same thing. That's what I want to discuss (remember Spring of '51 the 20-day "On the Road" I wrote at Joan's on 20th street when I left out New Years 1949 material from story because it covered your GO territory?) In fact Allen recently wrote me a letter asking if he could use "hoods of rain" because he'd seen general hoods of rain in "Doctor Sax" ms.—needless to say that is an example of great tact, great gentility, which I figure we will have to use in this friendly tangle of materials. Do I sound like a lout? In fact by God tell me if I do—

P.S. "Jazz musicians most perfectly epitomize the often sorry, and fabulous, condition of the artist in America"—that's the meat of your Tenorman book, isn't it.[1] Mine will epitomize the sad sick night of subterranean America blowing ecstasy by the Moon of Eternity . . .

---

1. Holmes had begun his novel about a jazz musician, *The Horn* (1958). He dedicated it "For Shirley, who listened and for Jack Kerouac, who talked."

the shadow of a golden horn on a nightclub wall, with smoke and sick faces and Zoot steps out to chew the sad wrangle of our dreams-&-goofs on the mouthpiece of his horn . . . Zoot (whose friends I met down here shooting in the vein by a broken window in lower East Side Norman Mailer subterranean hipchick coldwater beat pad).

Mostly it will be the joy of the jazz era and the subsequent coolness of the bop era, and words to describe the music—but why do I go on [. . . .] So there are three stages in the Jazz story

(1) Lester-Seymour in the Swinging days (cold Baltimore nights
in 1938–1943)

(2) Neal-Slim Jackson in the back alley-go-days (Frisco
in 1944–1949)

(3) Al-Stan Getz or Zoot in the Cool Fifties (Subterraneans
in a cooling goof 1950–1952)

And the chapter about Billy [Holiday] I am going to call *The Heroine of the Hip Generation* [. . . .]

TO JOHN CLELLON HOLMES

June 5 [1952]
[Mexico City]

Dear John,

Dig this, PEOTL EATERS OF THE HIP GENERATION: It was only a customary (I'm writing this as I go along) week in the life of Bill and I when all of a sudden, to break the calm or paralysis of our long after-dinner conversations dominated by his massively informed and never-endingly sour and severe pedantry full of richnesses and prizes and unspeakable sophistications of speech, comes along a gang of young American hipsters: first young tall blond B. in Levis and bohemian saddlestrap shoes and strange little yachting cap on head, once owned a motorcycle, once fished his own boat in Key West— a kid of the crazy generation of the Fifties, anxious to find his way through the maze with a string of hip signs, with little hip wife . . . seven year old kid, two others . . . 28 . . . and real nice, good smile, nice kid, sweet boy in fact, that's your thought, he's a sweet boy, he's hip, he's all right, he's real cool, and his wife too, and they have some peotl and give us some so Bill and I are settling down mashing

up our peotl buttons into a green little dish [. . . .] so Bill and I eat
the peotl and get the usual results: first you feel within minutes the
wild toxicity of the poison . . . "these green apples have a toxin in
their tree" . . . "old peotl cactus grooking in the desert to eat our
hearts alive" . . . a charge like a high Benny drive . . . then nausea,
and finally the desire to vomit but you can't without great difficulty
and if you do anyway you will lose yr high at great cost, and for
two hours absolute, absolute misery. So Bill gets going on some miserable line . . . of something, anything, to keep alive . . . he begins
with . . . "Ah, I feel awful, I feel worse than if I was suddenly a
prisoner in the High Andes, a penalist in a town like Quito up on
the High Andes all dark and windy and cloudy all day with incredibly
dirty old Indian women sitting by a wall huddled in their robes
against the cold wind and across the street you see an old man with
his hands in his cape, nothing to do but sit and already night is
coming if that's what you're waiting for, sort of an unpleasant cold
wind coming up, you know it'll be a cold night, and as I step off the
bus to enter the Penal House I'm strapping my leather belt of the
leather jacket because of the cold wind that's just swooped down
from the Andes and I look at my leather belt buckle with a feeling
of complete and irrevocable hopelessness. The Penalists are allowed
to sit around the stone square all day, the Landlady of the Penalists
won't have them hanging around the rooms, besides she only wants
them around for meals and Sunday afternoon's one tea . . . Penalists
can buy one candy bar a week, in the one store in town, and can
stand around looking at the candy they're going to buy on Sunday
but have to stand behind the Customer's Line. I am treated with
greater contempt by the old bitch in the Penal House because she has
some paranoid idea I'm a privileged snob on account of my brown
leather jacket and gray felt hat. So I sit all day huddled in my jacket
and hat in the cold dirty winds of the High Andes. None of the
Penalists know how they got to the Penal Town, they only know one
thing: that they can never leave. This is because of an impassible
mountainpass, can only be attempted with guides, and anyway there
is an Escape Consultant for the Penalists who wish to escape but he
is an old fumbler and doogler Major Hoople[1] idiot boasting about

---

1. Well-known character in *Our Boarding House* cartoon.

the past, filling out endless papers, works his hobby in the evening, by day has a regular weatherbeaten indoor bench placed outdoors under the Square tree and the Penalists wait for their turns in the other benches as the endless interview drags on. Finally some of the old Penalists become dotty and yell out at night, 'Well, boys—got the guide all bought for Monday morning . . . wish me luck,' and a great silence permeates the gloomy halls of the Penalists," and Bill is dismally surveying the floor and realizes he is not in Hell which is at least hot, but in Eternity which is so cold . . . He told that story to prevent himself from vomiting. Isn't it great?

So we got high on the peotl and I went out and walked around feebly in the moonlight of the park with no coat on wanting to sit in the grass and stay near the ground all night by moonlight, with the lights of the show and the houses all flashing, flashing in my eyeballs not in technicolor riot but in a great flapping of light that clapped over my eyes in intervals, as if, and I knew, light was a throb, and is. Bill got on a talking kick. The next morning Wig arrived from San Francisco, a bop bass player I'd known vaguely there, but he came to Bill's for stuff and so I met him, he played with Shorty Rogers and the new group out there. Shorty Rogers trumpet, arranger; Jimmy Giuffre on tenor and the great Art Pepper on alto, Hampton Hawes on piano and get his piano, and the one and only "Haw!" Shelly Manne on drums (with a French horn and a tuba also), and bass, a group that Wig says is the "First indication that California can do something the East can do; Shorty Rogers doesn't blow like Miles [Davis] at all, he blows entirely different, for my money better" (with which statement I find hard to agree, I heard the entire new album on 33 by Shorty Rogers and his Giants and he doesn't blow like Miles, but his own way (of course, as Wig himself says, you can't compare these things) . . . So Wig's in town, has a big car, and suddenly says to entire assemblage gathered in a hipster possessed afternoon in Bill's pad and my pad, B. the blond hipster, his wife, Don, Dave, an Indian girl his wife, [. . .] "You wanna hear some music?" "Yeah" so we drive over and pick up his speaker, 33 modern sleek machine and a whole case of longplayed bop albums mind you, and come back, hook up in bedroom, set up music, and first Wig plays Stan Getz and the Swedish group with Bengt Hallberg on piano, the marvelous Lars Gullin on baritone, great rhythm section —first music I'd heard in months... months... then that night Wig wigs and goes to sleep and leaves machine to me, by now we're in stone cottage out in woods and got fire going and outside is raining and got weed, peotl highs again, Bill high, and I play everything in albums and for the first time in months contemplate the music of bop ... also play Bartok, Walton quartet, Villa Lobos . . . till late next day, play all the Bird albums including the marvelous blues he blows and the choruses he interchanges with Miles on an album called Modern Sounds in Jazz, featuring its Creator Charley Parker, name of album, a blue album, a must, Miles plays a solo in there as pure as wood.

[. . .] Someday I'm going to write a huge Dostoevskyan novel about all of us. If I could only stick to novels long enough to tell a few good big stories, what I am beginning to discover now is something beyond the novel and beyond the arbitrary confines of the story . . . into the realms of revealed Picture . . . revealed whatever . . . revelated prose . . . *wild form*, man, *wild form*. Wild form's the only form holds what I have to say—my mind is exploding to say something about every image and every memory in—I have now an irrational lust to set down everything I know—in narrowing circles around the core of my last writing, very last writing, when I am an old man or ready to die, will be calm like the center of whirlpools and Beethoven's quartets—I love the world, and especially do I love the external eye and the shining heart of pure heart-to-heart mornings in a sane eternity, with love and security, but at this time in my life I'm making myself sick to find the wild form that can grow with my wild heart . . . because now I KNOW MY HEART DOES GROW . . . SALUD! HEALTH! JOY! WRITE TO ME SOON! LOOK FORWARD TO A HUGE JOY IN THE VERY NEAR FUTURE—I see it in yr cards, in the sky. Someday I am going to be a hermit in the woods . . . very soon now I'll visit my site.

Jack

Acting as Kerouac's agent Ginsberg read the rewritten version of On the Road *when it arrived at Ace Books. Ginsberg's letter to Kerouac on June 11, 1952, detailed his response to his friend's new writing style. Allen began with the comment that as a commercial property, "I don't see how it will ever be published . . ." Even more devastatingly, he said he thought the book was "great but crazy in a bad way" and went on to imitate what he called Kerouac's "junkyard" style of spontaneous prose. Ginsberg concluded by advising his friend to "cut out the comedy and crap and personalia jackoffs, for leanness and humanness." In his own poetry from this period, Ginsberg was still attempting to write academic verse. In San Francisco three years later, when he sat down to compose "Howl," he discovered his own way to use Kerouac's technique of spontaneous prose. Twenty years later, when both Kerouac and Cassady were dead, Kerouac's manuscript was published posthumously as part of* Visions of Cody. *Ginsberg wrote an introduction to the book in order to praise Kerouac's literary achievement, reading the text as "a giant mantra of appreciation and adoration of an American man [Neal Cassady], one striving heroic soul."*

TO JACK KEROUAC
FROM ALLEN GINSBERG

Wednesday, June 11, 1952
[New York City]

Dear Jack:

Allright, the manuscript arrived a few days ago, on the road [sic]. Carl read it, I read it once, and Holmes has it.

I don't see how it will ever be published, it's so personal, it's so full of sex language, so full of our local mythological references, I don't know if it would make sense to any publisher—by make sense I mean, if he could follow what happened to what characters where.

The language is great, the blowing is mostly great, the inventions have fullblown ecstatic style. Also the tone of speech is at times nearer to un-innocent heart speech ("why did I write this?" and "I'm a criminal"). Where you are writing steadily and well, the sketches, the exposition, it's the best that is written in America, I do believe. I'm not stopping now to write you praise-letter, tho maybe I should etcetc. but on my mind I am worried by the whole book. It's crazy (not merely inspired crazy) but unrelated crazy.

Well you know your book. Wyn I'm positive won't take it now, I don't know who will. I think could be published by New Story people in Europe, but will you be revising it at all? What you trying to put down, man? You know what you done.

This is no big letter [. . . .] I will, all by myself, read book second time, next week, and write you 20 page letter taking book section by section figuring my reactions.

For an on the spot minute guess:

1. You still didn't cover Neal's history.
2. You covered your own reactions.
3. You mixed them up chronologically, so that it's hard to tell what happened when.
4. The totally surrealistic sections (blowing on sounds and refusing to make sense) (in section following taperecords) is just a hangup, hangup.
5. Taperecords are partly hangup, should be shortened and put in place after final trip to Frisco.
6. Sounds like you were just blowing and tacking things together, personally unrelating them, just for madness sake, or despair.

I think book is great but crazy in a bad way, and *got*, aesthetically and publishing-wise, to be pulled back together, re constructed. I cant see anyone, New Directions, Europe, putting it out as it is. They wont, they wont.

HODOS CHAMELIONTOS in Yeats is series of unrelated images, chamelian [sic] of the imagination diddling about in the void or hangup, meaning nothing to each other.

Should keep *Sax* into framework of a myth, a FRAMEWORK, and not violate framework by interrupting Sax to talk about Lucien's formerly golden hair or Neal's big cock or my evil mind, or your lost bone. The book is the lost bone, itself.

On the Road just drags itself exhausted over the goal line of meaning to someone else (or to me who knows the story); it's salvageable. I mean it needs to be salvaged. Your handing up the whole goddam junkyard inclooding the i agh up erp esc baglooie

an't you read what I'm shayinoo im tryinting think try i mea mama thatsshokay but you gotta make sense you gotta muk sense, jub, jack, fik, anyone can bup it, you bubblerel, Zagg, Nealg, Loog, Boolb, Joon, Hawk, Nella Grebsnig. And if you doan wanna make sense, shit, then put the nonsense on one page boiled down to one intense nervous collapse out of intelligibility (like Williams did in a section of *Paterson,* scrambling up the type, and followed it real cool by a list of the geological formations of shale, etc. under the fuckin Falls, and then went on to say "This is a poem, a POEM.") and then go on talking like nothing ever happened cause nothin did. Nothing jess *interrupted* something. But nothing juss keeps breaking in out all over the joint, you'll be talking along, and say—"he come out of the room like a criminal"—then you'll add—"like a shrouder" (whoever heard of?)—then you'll add—"like blac kwinged rubens"—then you'll go poetic and say—"like pinkwinged Stoobens, the hopscotch Whiz of grammar school, hopscoth, the game of Archangels, It's hevvin, it's clouds, meanwhile he was alla time juss commin out of that room," but you got us not only up inna clouds, via Steubenvill and urk ep blook, but via also I am JK interrupting myself.

Well maybe it's all three dimensional and awright aesthetically or humanly, so I will re re re read your whole buke, puke annal (and jeez, Joyce did it, but you're juss crappin around thoughtlessly with that trickstyle *often,* and it's not so good.) reread your whole book I will.

and give you a blow by blow account of *how it comes off.*

And incidentally dont be too flabbergasted flip at my foregoing because I Allen Ginsberg one and only, have just finished cutting down my book from 89 poems to a mere perfect 42, just to cut out the comedy and crap and personalia jackoffs, for leanness and humanness,

It is ACTION WHICH IS DEMANDED AT THIS TIME. That's what he sez, though god know what kind of action he talkin about.

Even before receiving Ginsberg's response to his rewritten book about Cassady, Kerouac felt his life closing in on him in Mexico City. He finished Doctor Sax *just as he began to run out of money and he grew surly when Burroughs refused to feed him indefinitely. Even*

worse, Burroughs and Kerouac quarreled over Jack's plan to store marijuana and peotl in the apartment; Burroughs was out on bond and feared a long jail sentence in Mexico if the police discovered large quantities of these substances in his place. By June Kerouac wrote Holmes self-pityingly that he was surrounded by "doom. . . . I don't know why. What have I got? I'm 30 years old, broke, my wife hates me and is trying to have me jailed, I have a daughter I'll never see, my mother after all this time and work and worry and hopes is STILL working her ass off in a shoe shop; I have not a cent in my pocket for a decent whore."

"Yearning to get back to food and drink and regular people," Jack asked Neal to wire him twenty dollars so he could return to his mother, telling Neal, "I sure wish I was with you right now Buddy, sharing a last glass of tokay and with that fine blonde kerouacass gal serving up hot pizza in the pie plate, goddam I miss you."

After Ginsberg's rejection of his "spontaneous prose" book about Cassady, Kerouac's depression increased to the point where he wrote a letter to Carolyn saying that her life "would have been impossible" with him, and describing his state of utter destitution: "My shoes are torn, my seabag's torn, my raincoat's been stole, I have 60 cents American—I really am getting fucked again by the publishing business, they just won't publish me any more. . . ."

Gabrielle Kerouac had given up her apartment again and was living with her daughter Nin in Rocky Mount, North Carolina. In mid-July 1952 Kerouac joined them and took a job in a textile mill, his morale shattered. The next month he wrote a bitter letter to his editor Carl Solomon and publisher A. A. Wyn about their rejection of the new version of On the Road. Shortly afterwards Jack shot off a furious blast at Ginsberg for joining with the others in putting him down: "if instead you were men I could at least get the satisfaction of belting you all on the kisser—too many glasses to take off."

August 5, 1952
[Rocky Mount, N.C.]

Dear Carl, Mr. Wyn, Miss James:—

Hemingway says that before 1927 all his stories were returned by editors "with notes of rejection that would never call them stories, but always anecdotes, sketches, contes." Thus only a few years ago even Hemingway with all his clarity was considered unprintable. What happened in the few years since? "Ulysses" which was considered difficult reading is now hailed as a classic and everyone understands it. Even "Finnegan's Wake" is beginning to be understood. By the same token, and in its time, "Sister Carrie" sat for years in a publishing house because it was considered unprintable. By the same token, and in its time, I believe "On the Road" because its new vision roughs against the grain of established ideas is going to be considered unprintable for awhile to come.

When something is incomprehensible to me ("Finnegan's Wake," Lowry's "Under the Volcano," "Delilah" by Marcus Goodrich)[1] I try to understand it, the author's intellect, and passion, and mystery. To label it incoherent is not only a semantic mistake but an act of cowardice and intellectual death. Between *incomprehensible* and *incoherent* sits the madhouse. I am not in the madhouse. The masses catch up to the incomprehensible; incoherent finds its way to an intelligently typewritten page.

In exchange for this compliment, your calling "On the Road" a "thoroughly incoherent mess," what am I to do, mail you an I.O.U. for $250 and the contract? And if you don't return the manuscript of "On the Road" will it be my understanding that you want to buy this 523-page 2nd novel by a young writer of reputation here and in England for $250?

This is what will happen: "On the Road" will be published by someone else, with a few changes and omissions and additions, and it will gain its due recognition, in time, as the first or one of the first

---

1. Marcus Goodrich's *Delilah* (New York, 1941) was a novel about a U.S. Navy vessel.

modern prose books in America; not merely a "novel," which is after all a European form; and its publisher will be proud to have it on his list because it will live, like "The Town and the City" will live and like "Doctor Sax" will live. And all you will have succeeded in doing is putting another cookbook on your list to fill the gap I leave. You can spin a thousand neat epigrams to prove that any cookbook is better than the wild visions of Neal Pomeray and the Road. But not when the worms start digesting, brothers and sisters.

I didn't write "On the Road" to be malicious, I wrote it with joy in my heart, and a conviction that somewhere along the line somebody will see it without the present-day goggles on and realize the freedom of expression that still lies ahead [. . . .]

I wish I could make felt the thousands of hours of anxiety and hard work that have gone into the past year since our contractual association began. Multiply that by 12 years, when I started writing; and always without enough money to live like other people, never sufficient clothes, and on the road actual starvation. [. . . .] You might as well ask Michelangelo to cut David down to livingroom size for all you're going to get out of me in this "revision" when I have a thousand books to write. [. . . .] Last week I was working in a mill. (Rocky Mount textile mill.) Without the first installment of the advance it is a physical impossibility to do any revising work on this controversial manuscript. Please let me know what you intend to do as quickly as possible. I should like to get "On the Road" on the road to its eventual publisher.

Yours bitterly,

TO ALLEN GINSBERG

[October 8, 1952]

This is to notify you and the rest of the whole lot what I think of you. Can you tell me even for instance . . . with all this talk about pocket book styles and the new trend in writing about drugs and sex why my On the Road written in 1951 wasn't ever published?—why they publish Holmes's book which stinks and don't publish mine because it's not as good as some of the other things I've done? Is this the fate of an idiot who can't handle his own business or [is] it the general fartsmell of New York in general . . . And you who I thought was my friend—you sit there and look me in the eye and tell me the *On the Road* I wrote at Neal's is "imperfect" as though anything you ever did or anybody was perfect? . . . and don't lift a finger or say a word for it . . . Do you think I don't realize how jealous you are and how you and Holmes and Solomon all would give your right arm to be able to write like the writing in *On the Road* . . . And leaving me no alternative but to write stupid letters like this when if instead you were men I could at least get the satisfaction of belting you all on the kisser—too many glasses to take off. Why you goddamn cheap little shits are all the same and always were and why did I ever listen and fawn and fart with you—15 years of my life wasted among the cruds of New York, from the millionaire jews of Horace Mann who'd kissed my ass for football and now would hesitate to introduce their wives to me, to the likes of you . . . poets indeed . . . distant small-sized variants of same . . . baroque neatpackaged acceptable (small print in the middle of neat page of poetrybook) page . . . Not only have you grieved me now by your statement that there is nothing in *On the Road* you didn't know about (which is a lie because at just one glance I can see that you never knew the slightest beginning detail of even something so simple as Neal's worklife and what he does)—& Solomon pretending to be an interesting saint, claims he doesn't understand contracts, why in ten years I'll be lucky to have the right to look into his window on Xmas eve . . . he'll be so rich and fat and so endowed with the skinny horrors of other men into one great puffball of satisfied suckup . . . Parasites every one of you, just like Edie said. And now even John Holmes, who as everybody knows lives in complete illusion about everything, writes about things he doesn't know about, and with hostility at that (it comes out in hairy skinny legs of Stofsky and "awkward" grace of Pasternak,[1] the sonofabitch jealous of his own flirtatious wife, I didn't ask for Marian's attentions . . . awkwardness indeed, I imagine anybody who walks on ordinary legs would look awkward around effeminate flip-hips & swish like him)—And the

---

1. Stofsky and Pasternak were the names that Holmes gave to characters based on Ginsberg and Kerouac in *Go*.

smell of his work is the smell of death . . . Everybody knows he has no talent . . . and so what right has he, who knows nothing, to pass any kind of judgment on my book—He doesn't even have the right to surl in silence about it—His book stinks, and your book is only mediocre, and you all know it, and my book is great and will never be published. Beware of meeting me on the street in New York. Beware also of giving any leads as to my whereabouts. I'll come up to New York and trace down the lead. You're all a bunch of insignificant literary egos . . . you can't even leave New York you're so stultified . . . Even Corso[2] with his Tannhauser chariots running down everyone else has already begun to pick up . . . Tell him to go away . . . tell him to find himself in his own grave . . . My heart bleeds every time I look at *On the Road* . . . I see it now, why it is great and why you hate it and what the world is . . . specifically what you are . . . and what you, Allen Ginsberg, are . . . a disbeliever, a hater, your giggles dont fool me, I see the snarl under it . . . Go ahead and do what you like, I want peace with myself . . . I shall certainly never find peace till I wash my hands completely of the dirty brush and stain of New York and everything that you and the city stand for. . . . And everybody knows it . . . And Chase knew it long ago . . . that is because he was an old man from the start . . . And now I am an old man too . . . I realize that I am no longer attractive to you queers . . . Go blow your Corsos . . . I hope he sinks a knife in you . . . Go on and hate each other and sneer and get jealous and . . . My whole record in NY is one long almost humorous chronicle of a real dumb lil abner getting taken in by fat pigjaws . . . I realize the humour of it. . . . and laugh just as much as you . . . But here on in I'm not laughing . . . Paranoia me no paranoias either . . . Because of people like you and Giroux . . . even with G. you fucked me up from making money because he hated you . . . and came in with Neal that night and Neal right away wanted to steal a book from the office, sure, what would you say if I went in your N O R C and stole things and made fun of it . . . and Lucien with his shity

---

2. Gregory Corso, a young poet Ginsberg had met in Greenwich Village in December 1951, shortly after Corso's release from prison, where he had served three years for his part in a robbery.

little ego trying to make me cry over Sarah and then telling me at the lowest ebb of my life that I would be awful easy to forget . . . He must know by now unless be-sotted and stupid with drink that it is so about everybody . . . how easily one may disappear . . . and be forgotten completely . . . and make dark corruption spot in dirt . . . well alright. And all of you, even Sarah I don't even care to know any more or who will ever hear of this insane letter . . . all of you fucked me up . . . with the exception of Tony Manochhio [sic] and a few other angels . . . and so I say to you, never speak to me again or try to write or have anything to do with me . . . besides you will never probably see me again . . . and that is good . . . the time has come for all you frivolous fools to realize what the subject of poetry is . . . death . . . so die. . . . and die like men . . . and shut up . . . and above all . . . leave me alone . . . & dont ever darken me again.

JACK KEROUAC

By this time Kerouac was back on the West Coast, where Cassady had arranged a job for him on the Southern Pacific as a student brakeman. After staying a short time with the Cassadys in their new home in San Jose, Jack took a room in a Third Street flophouse hotel, where he lived as cheaply as possible in order to save money to return to Mexico. There he wrote the spontaneous prose sketch "October in the Railroad Earth" about his work on the Southern Pacific, drinking a "fifth of tokay no tea." After Holmes sent him fifty dollars, Kerouac wrote to thank him and describe how he felt being rejected by friends and family.

TO JOHN CLELLON HOLMES

Sunday Oct. 12 [1952]
As ever, whereabouts is *dead secret*
c/o Cassady
1047 East Santa Clara St.
San Jose, Calif.

Dear John—

Here I sit in my little room in Frisco Skid Row, the first time in weeks I've had to sit & write in response to your letter and check. I just come in from work, will be going out again in 8 hours, work sometimes 24 hours a day, have no time whatever for anything but sleep, I get in my double bed with bop on the radio, a poorboy half-bottle of Tokay wine, the shades drawn, & I try to rest and think: "Some lost song is beating in my soul, that I have not sung, and cannot sing"—the star of my sister, I remember her pale little face in holy snows of Lowell, now, like all America, she's grown cold-hearted, blank, money-anxious—ah, she used to make little holy cards—my mother angrily retorted, in a letter, "So you want to roam & leave—well, *don't you dare do anything that will dishonor your father's name*—(!)"—[. . . .] The days of *The Town and The City* are all forgotten—I start West in the rain—John, you think I'm a self-made martyr? I go 3,000 motherfucking miles, sleep on railroad porches, in Salvation flops, eat out of cans—in Hickey, N.C. I stand in the drizzle exhausted, one saves me—I stay at Ed White's in Beverly's backyard—we cook weenies, drink Tokay—I make love to big Swedish student-girl Edeltrude—Mrs. White motherly packs me lunch, I hitch to Salt Lake (after a day spent sketching Neal's entire Denver area) and sleep in motel garage, hitch straight to Neal's door via wild trips, including Australian history professor anxiously from top of oil pole, in Nevada desert, scanning horizon for swimming hole—"nothing I like better than swimming, ya know?"—we end up on little slimy rocks of Tuckee River [. . . .] I was bored with the job in Rocky Mount, with $5 in my pocket I lifted my seabag up and walked out my sister's backdoor ("Never mind presents from China, just mail me $50 room & board for the month of August.")

[. . . .] In San Jose, Neal's big house, Neal's frantic working with me out on railroad—I learn—can't stand position in his house, leave to live in my Skid Row retreat (near the Wildest Corner in America, 3rd & Howard, around the corner from the Little Harlem where they blew so much in 1949)—Neal I don't like any more; he's somewhat insultingly abrupt & even beginning to put on that familiar American pseudo-virility of workingman & basket ball players, "tough guy"—when I try to talk about literature he makes it a point to change the subject to money or work or "bills," him & his bloody bills—[. . . .] I'm not American, nor West European, somehow I feel like an Indian, a North American Exile in North America—in New

York I'm a Peasant among the Solomons, that's why I never make a cent off the huge productivity of my crazy pen—there's something else in me—maybe because I have an Indian great-great-grandmother—or have strong Quebec Plain Peasant feeling and general weird Catholic mysticism—& a streak of truly Celtic superstitiousness—[. . . .] I accept your $50 in the spirit of gratitude, and I need it too, it will be added to my winter writing stake—I'm ready to write a super *Town & City*, a book of 1,000 pages. *On the Road* it will have to be called, The Neal Road I'll change to "Visions of N.P."—Already started my super book, not only about the hip generation but another fictional arrangement of my family life—[. . . .] If it wasn't for the railroad now, people would instantly recognize me as a true hobo—the bo's on Third St. all do—A HOBO LIVES LIKE AN INDIAN.—Nevertheless, the glory of it all is, I am a gifted writer and my soul is pure—& big to live—[. . . .] Write to me care of Neal's, I get my mail there—we hardly talk to each other but Carolyn is close to me and I go there to drink wine with her—Neal apparently wrote another letter to Allen explaining why he can't talk to me—I ought to throw my 2c in & explain why I can't talk to him—but I would say this, it was him stuck his head in my door in Ozone Park and outlined the reasons why we should be friends— now that he has the soul of a baboon clearly showing, I wonder I forgot seeing it then right in the door—Gad, the mistakes I've made, the time wasted—the forgetting of lonely nights in cheap hotel rooms with my father & mother making little cold suppers cheerfully— every time we'd touch the lace curtains a shower of dust fell, & Pop would say, "Perk up, Jackie pauvre Jackie, we won't always be poor & abandoned," and my mother'd say, "Oui, and look, here's the bread, the ham, the butter, the coffee, the little cups, we've got everything we need."—and how I loved Mary Carney's[1] dark sad face, & wanted to marry her at 16 and be a brakeman on the Boston & Maine railroad—only an ounce of my hundredweight life—to have a real asshole like Cassady come along & con me like a yokel into

---

1. Mary Carney, described in *Maggie Cassidy*, was the Irish girl Kerouac fell in love with during his senior year at Lowell High School.

listening to his crap & believing in his kind of franticness & silly sexfiend ideas—it will all come back, John—Please stay my friend thru life, it'll be long & dark.

As ever, Jack

In his Skid Row hotel in San Francisco, after answering his early-morning calls to report to his job on the railroad, Kerouac also wrote a conciliatory letter to Ginsberg, greatly relieved to learn that Allen had liked the Doctor Sax *manuscript and wanted to continue as Kerouac's literary agent.*

TO ALLEN GINSBERG

Nov. 8 1952
[San Francisco]

Dear Allen,

I read your letter many times. It's very nice, you are very nice to understand my writings. I felt honored. Doctor Sax is a mystery. I'm going to leave him the way he is, but not for the same reasons as *On the Road* (enraged, etc.) but because I really like it the way it is, a few things you suggest I will do, like bleak Blook and the child. Doctor Sax is only the top of the pot about Lowell . . . the truth buried insane in me, in my head that becomes so inflamed sometimes. I'm trying to speak to you brother to brother,—like we were French Canadian brothers. Literature as you see it, using words like "verbal" and "images" etc. and things like, well all the "paraphernalia" of criticism etc. is no longer my concern, because the thing makes me say "shitty little beach in the reeds" is Pre-Literary, it happened to me to think that way before I learned the words the literateurs use to describe what they're doing,—At this moment I'm writing directly from the French in my head, *Doctor Sax* was written high on tea without pausing to think, sometimes Bill would come in the room and so the chapter ended there, one time he yelled after me with his long gray face because he could smell the smoke in the yard. You know I was mad at you, but you know it doesn't take me long to stop, and many times I wanted to write you and say "Well, you understand, sometimes I get mad," etc. I always thought you my little brother, my little petushka, even tho you're jewish, because you're like a little Russian brother. Lucien has always said to me not to get mad at you—if I get mad, to get mad at those who try to hurt me, like himself? Neal got mad at me, he wasnt talking to anybody, he hung the phone on me, I got me a fine little room in Skid Row at $4 a week and I was arranging myself so well (and writing a big new novel like *Town and City*) that I was happy for the first time in years, and was saying to myself, "Well, Neal has always been crazy, since the day he put his head in my door at Ozone Park and was making me believe he wanted to learn to write," quel bull shit eh what? But I was sleeping one night on the railroad, on an old ratty couch, hard asleep after 3 days and 3 nights of work and no sleep,—Neal was bent over me, hung over me, laughing, "*There* you are buddy! Come on, now, come on, now, no words, come on, now," so, me, I am here to try to be nice, I go along with him and move back to his house, and then CAROLYN gets mad at me, etc. Bitchy people, I hate people, I cant stand people anymore,—The phone just called me gotta go to work again, I'm sick and tired of it—This is why it took me so long to answer you, the railroad.

Let's let John Holmes handle *Doctor Sax*, another thing about your letter, and you, always afraid it isn't "right," etc. like Arthur Schlesinger Jr and Adlai Stevenson and the Harvard Law School and United Nations and Dean Acheson ready to fly at any instant with a detailed appraisal of something . . . for what? for what? for what? for what?

See?

Go is alright when you see it between book covers, it's sincere, each page . . . Truman Capote, Jean Stafford are full of bull on every page . . . so Holmes is better than they I say.

Ah I'd love to see you, maybe I will this Xmas according to my plans of travel. Good Morning to the whole gang.

Your friend
Jack

ps When you said to yourself "Oh that stupid Kerouac hasn't bothered to put in a plot, just left an undigested mass of images and references etc." you weren't remembering were you that once it was LOVE animated our poesies, not no anxious techniques. Yes the digging by you of Balzacian jewelpoint (and ah I can't) it means you REALLY did comprehend the book like I thought nobody could, our clairvoyance is together—my good boy.

In December, after Kerouac was laid off by the railroad, Cassady drove him down to Burroughs's apartment in Mexico City, where Jack planned to live for a while under his mother's maiden name ("Senor Jean Levesque") so his estranged wife couldn't locate him. Jack had invited Carolyn to go with him on a vacation in Mexico, but Neal insisted on making the trip with Jack instead, so that he could bring back a new supply of marijuana. After Neal returned to California, Jack wrote that he was "ready" for Carolyn's visit, but she gave up her plans to join him because Neal was so hostile to the idea. In Off the Road *she wrote that Neal said, "Serves him right for stealing other men's wives."*

TO NEAL AND CAROLYN CASSADY

Dec. 9 [1952]
Orizaba 210
[Mexico City]

Dear Neal & Carolyn—

I took a little dobe block up on Bill's roof, 2 rooms, lots of sun and old Indian women doing the wash. Will stay here awhile even though $12 a month is high rent. But perfect place to write, blast, think, fresh air, sun, moon, stars, the Roof of the City. All ready for your visit, Carolyn, I even bought Mexican pottery to brighten my 2 cells. Tonight I'm buying 3 dozen oysters for 35 cents equivalent (expensive) and frying them in butter, with imported Chianti for a chaser, & French bread. Every morning it's steak & eggs which I buy for 30 cents and cook up. Also I am stocked on goofballs, bennies, a little laudanum, & Nescafe. Bill just finally left Mexico, last night, how sad. They were asking for more bond money. He bequeathed me knives, holsters, daggers, medicines—I feel like Neal that I'll never see him again. Dave also blew town, for reasons of his own, the new government cracked down on pushers. And now finally today even Garver leaves—and I'm completely alone on the roof. Now or never with a great new novel long anticipated from me in N.Y.—Day & night lonesome toil—

Neal, enclosed you'll find note for picking up last half of November check. SEE HOPPY IF HASSLE—Send it on to me registered mail, at Orizaba 210, address envelope as follows in my Spanish name:

> Senor Jean Levesque
> Orizaba 210
> Mexico City, D.F., Mexico

(OR IF CAROLYN COMES, LET HER BRING IT)—(EASIER)—

This is my name now, here—the address is too hot to use "Kerouac"—Cops come looking for escapee Bill who jumped bond —see? Then I'll cash check at big bank.

Carolyn, is you coming?—Thomsons coming?—Let me know— write—Love to Cathy, Jamie, Johnny & All

Jack X X

(TURN INSIDE)

Dear Carolyn—

Just got your letter. Did Neal get home that night? Thank you for forwarding my mother's letter. I am unbearably lonely in Mexico, I guess I'll never be satisfied with anything. Now that I have regained my regular love of life, of people, specifically of Neal & you after October's Darkness, the old human loneliness has come back to wash against my rock, ah me—But what can any of us do with our time?—which runs out while we wait, yawn, & worry—Ah phooey—Please come visit me, Carolyn, my little pad is all ready— All the fresh air of the Indian Plateau blows into it—Maybe you could drive down with Al Sublette for protection, he wouldnt bother you like Conductor Lou Wolfe if he knew the purpose of your visit & if Neal said okay—Mexico, you'll see, has all the practical advantages but the soul yearns broken everywhere. That's funny about Jamie playing Jack & Jill all day long. I can hear it now—

I'm trying to rest my feet for railroading next spring—I've begun my work on the final-chance big novel—

Come on & get your vacation with me!—We'll have wine, tea, & oysters at midnight—we'll go dance the Mambo—

(As usual, Neal did nothing, just like in the dream I had, he rushed into Mexico City & rushed out with his tea)—

NO MORE PAPER

X X J.

In San Francisco Kerouac had discovered that Holmes's novel Go *had sold out in the bookshops. After the success of his book Holmes was asked by* New York Times *editor Gilbert Milstein to write an article titled "This Is the Beat Generation," which was published in the* Times *on November 16, 1952. Jack was sent a copy of the article by Stella Sampas because it included his name. Lonely in Mexico City without Burroughs or Cassady, Kerouac thanked Holmes for mentioning him and admitted that he thought he and Allen had no talent for journalism because of their "secret wildness."*

TO JOHN CLELLON HOLMES

Dec. 9, 1952

Address Envelopes Here in My

Spanish Name

Senor Jean Levesque

Orizaba 210

Mexico City, D.F., Mexico

Dear John,

Just arrived in Mexico last week, Neal drove down, procured needs & went right back. Burroughs left for Panama via Florida last night, skipping bond which was becoming exorbitant because his lawyer also shot someone and had lammed to Rio, leaving Bill's case hung.

Bill Garver is also leaving, & old Mex Dave left last night, and I am all alone in Mexico, in my rooftop block (BILL'S ROOF) among the old Indian washwomen, to write that long-awaited epic of poor & lost in the darkness . . . Will keep you posted on the legend of Du-luoz's life, with all the weight this connotes, denotes—So that further books can be dense spates from this Duluoz World, such as *Dr Sax* already is, & *Road of Neal* visions, as you'll see.

Neal finally read *On the Road* & flipped; on tape recorder, with relish.

Oh I'm lonesome! Listen John, come on down here & see me, spend a month talking—& screwing. And bring Allen!—Bring Lil Allen!

Next Spring I may take up your invitation to live awhile & write in Old Saybrook house, will still have money to pay my board too —Am swooning for a New England Spring again!—Oh the poet *bur-rows* too much nowadays—hey? I have a desk, the Indian Plateau clouds are bright & serene outside—rabbits & chickens peck at the stone roof—Tonight, high on benny, I shall lie on my back in this room plotting the chapters of the Duluoz Life—What title? No se—

Your *Beat Generation* article liked by everyone. I see you have considerable journalistic talent, like Lucien—something Allen & I don't have, from secret wildness. You have voice of authority. Thank you for mentioning me. I received a letter from Sebastian's sister in Lowell, she saw it, says: "I'm terribly glad that you're not entirely ignored. To know that you have so much to give us poor mortals and yet no one holds out his hand, 'Beats' me."

[. . . .] How's progress on "Go" and on reprint "T & C" and "Doctor Sax" and your "Decent"? Let me know real quick, let's roll up a ball of correspondence now that I am free from railroad work for some months.

"Go" is out of stock everywhere in California—apparently the title is selling like wildfire, so for God's sake tell Scribner's to send out more copies to the outlying bookstores, they're losing money & so are you.

Oh let me know about Dell Books!—If they turn it down, what for? I can abridge it and add sex to it myself, & improve it, too! Old

Giroux took out my cunts—recall? Scenes of Liz, Ruth, Mex girl,—etc.

Burroughs is gone at last—3 years in Mexico—lost everything, his wife, his children, his patrimony—I saw him pack in his moldy room where he'd shot M all this time—Sad moldy leather cases—old holsters, old daggers—a snapshot of Huncke—a Derringer pistol, which he gave to old dying Garver—medicines, drugs—the last of Joan's spices, marjoram, new mold since she died & stopped cooking—little Willie's shoe—& Julie's moldy school case—all lost, dust, & thin tragic Bill hurries off into the night solitaire—ah Soul—throwing in his bag, at last, picture of Lucien & Allen—Smiled, & left.

Kerouac's last extant letter before leaving Mexico City was to Stella Sampas, telling her that he had just written Doctor Sax, *"a strange dark book" about their hometown, as well as a novel titled* On the Road *"which is a vision of America that is so wild none of the publishers understand it," and confessing that his "dearest hope" was to make a home in Lowell once again with his mother.*

TO STELLA SAMPAS

Dec. 10, 1952

PLEASE ADDRESS MAIL TO ME
MY SPANISH NAME, THUS

Sr. Jean Levesque
Orizaba 210
Mexico City, Mexico

Dear Stella,

Your beautiful letter reached me in California as I was preparing to travel to Mexico, so the delay—I've not been ignoring your letters but they've been finding me in out-of-the-way-places like Montana & here, and late, and I didn't know what to say—during a recent long, dark depression with thoughts of suicide sometimes. But now —I'm so glad to hear about your job with Mr. Weinberger—your story about climbing the stairs in the Giant Store—O Giant Store, when will I ever see it again!—and your symphony, the symphony that you want to make of your life—do so, do so! Thank you for sympathizing with my "literary obscurity"—it's a bitch—I have to work on my feet for a living, on railroads, and my feet are & have been bad for 5 years, from swelling of the veins—I've been in several hospitals, stopped smoking—The rich homosexual literati of New York at first offered me alluring scholarships and then withheld them when it became apparent that I wouldn't be famous [. . . .] But what they don't know is that I am going to be famous, and the greatest writer of my generation, like Dostoevsky, and someday they'll see this and the emptiness of their lives spent chasing after fashions & glittering Italian islands—when the soul of man is weeping in the wilderness, and little children hold out their hands for the love of Christ—

Ah I wish Sammy had lived—what a great man he would have been—Wars don't advance mankind except materially—The loss of people like Sammy, and even Johnny Koumantzelis, and even Jimmy Scondras, makes the earth bleed, & kills something—Billy Chandler, Chuck Lozenu—so many were killed—from Lowell—for nothing. The survivors build new apartment houses and think they've gained an "era"—they've got an error [. . . .]

Stella, hold fast to your beliefs, and the symphony of your life let it ring—I envy you your opportunity to take long walks in Lowell at night—the Grotto on Pawtucket Blvd., the charging restless ghost houses of foam beneath the Moody Street bridge, the sad, great trees of Stevens St. & Pawtucketville—the tenements of Centralville, Aiken St. & Market St.—the dark railroad to Billerica, the stars above the railroad earth—the little bridge over the Concord in So. Lowell—ghosts of Thoreau paddling the Rosemont Basin by night—Stella, I've just written a strange dark book about Lowell called *Doctor Sax*—you'll hear about it, tho it isn't at the publishers yet—I'm now writing a bigger novel than *Town & City*—about Lowell—I've also written a 550 page novel called ON THE ROAD which is a vision of America that is so wild none of the publishers understand it—but it will be discovered later, for my position in this generation is a whole lot like Ezra Pound in his—It was Pound influenced Gertrude Stein and she influenced Hemingway; it was Pound influenced T.S. Eliot; but where is Pound? In the madhouse. What are his works?

The foundations of 20th Century American letters—I've been in the madhouse once and will be in the madhouse again—but it will be because of love. [. . . .]

My dearest hope is to come back to Lowell, with my mother, and make a home—eventually get married again—to some girl that loves me, not hates me—hate is madness, my wife I believe is insane—But it's too late—But nothing can prevent me from returning to Lowell, and revisiting the house where I was born, Lupine Road, Centralville; and the house where my brother died; in the night I can return to Lowell and walk all I please those hallowed streets of life—So I'll be seeing you in Lowell in May—if I can make it, and intend to—Good luck, excuse this sentimental letter, love to whole family.

Jack K.　　(Write)

LATER—3 HOURS LATER
P.S. But you must be my lucky leadingstar—because after I'd written the letter to you I strolled down to the union hall and as a culmination of several years sporadic waiting while working at land jobs such as brakeman or sometimes just simply hitchhiking bum, why, I got a job on a ship going to Korea and to shuttle from there to IndoChina, Saigon, Japan, Hong Kong and Manila—be gone 4 months—come back & make my mother a nice cash present for all the years she supported me while I wrote & now the years she goes on slaving at shoe shop skiving machine while I roam—

Stella, this means a new era in my life—it harkens back to Lowell dreams of Oriental travel—it will give me an opportunity to create some new novel undisturbed by money & food problems—God smiled on me this morning—somehow you have something to do with it—And so, some time after 8 months, 2 trips, I shall visit Lowell & bring you a nice gift from China or someplace in commemoration of this great day in my previously rapidly darkening life—Give my regards to your Ma & Pa—& to Jim when you write—As Sammy said in 1940 running after the Boston train in a snowstorm the night Bartlett [Junior High School] burn'd down, "I'll See You Again. . . ."

Jack

Abandoning his "dreams of Oriental travel," Kerouac left Mexico City and hitchhiked to New York to join his mother for Christmas when he learned that Gabrielle had left Rocky Mount and rented her own apartment again in Richmond Hill. Ginsberg wrote the Cassadys that he had seen Kerouac in Manhattan, when he "came in in time for New Year's cried drunk & high in cab at dawn on way home. . . . I keep thinking he has no adult society and marriage world to write about and keeps repeating lament for Mother." Jack stayed in Allen's place on the Lower East Side, where he scribbled a note to his friend after a hectic holiday party at Lucien Carr's.

TO ALLEN GINSBERG

[December 28, 1952
New York City]

Allen—

I've been digging your mad little pad and I took the terrible liberty of borrowing The Complete Oeuvres Genet, upon my word I won't lose it and'll return it very soon—The mystery not only of the French language but Genet's dawn—I didn't tell you about the thieves and fairies of Mexico and the one they call Negress—*Negra*—Also, yr. radio is superb, Lester Young in the afternoon on WHOM or Vivaldi on WNYC—Please tell Lucien I don't even remember falling asleep —Too much drinking & excitement for me—Your letter to Williams I never dug before for good language—You & John make me very happy. LIFE IS A LARK NOW. Show Sax to VD![1]

Ti Jean

---

1. VD: Mark Van Doren. See letter to Ginsberg, May 1954 (pp. 413–414).

1953

As Kerouac had told Ginsberg, Doctor Sax was merely "the top of the pot" about his memories of growing up in Lowell. After he settled into his mother's apartment in Richmond Hill, he began to write another book to follow Doctor Sax in the chronological series he was then calling the "Duluoz life." This was the book about his high school romance with Mary Carney, which Jack described as "a serious study" in his next letter to the Cassadys. Back with his mother, he found his mood lightening and he even jokingly apologized for not helping Neal the previous month on the long drive from San Jose to Mexico City.

TO NEAL AND CAROLYN CASSADY

Jan 10 [19]53
[Richmond Hill, N.Y.]

Dear Neal & Carolyn—

If you want to write to me address envelope to Mrs. G. Kerouac, 94–21 134th St. Richmond Hill N.Y. and put return address upper left corner and she'll know it's for me and hand it on, otherwise, using Holmes' address, I dont get letters soon enough as he spends most of his time out of town in Connecticut and I dont see him anyway, having buried myself in writing-work in a concentrated crack at it before I give railroading further thought this year, my legs being bad, etc., and have two novels plus Road, Sax, and Town & City underway. Neal, will you please send me the 2nd half November check c/o Mrs. G. Hope you havent already sent it to Mexico, it'll be stolen. Send it to me now; otherwise I'll have to cash one of my travelers checks, one of the last, for pocket money & chow money.

In Mexico, after you left, I in 5 days wrote, in French, a novel about me and you when we was kids in 1935 meeting in Chinatown with Uncle Bill Balloon, your father and my father and some sexy blondes in a bedroom with a French Canadian rake and an old Model T. You'll read it in print someday and laugh. It's the solution to the "On the Road" plots all of em and I will hand it in soon as I finish translating and typing. The other novel is a serious study of the 16 year old love affair with Mary that I many times warned you and told you about I'd write so now I'm writing it.

· 395 ·

Uncle Bill Balloon is a boomer and I have a few railroad things written that'll give you a laugh.[1] If you dont write that book about the Coast Division of the S[outhern] P[acific] I will.

New York is great, I like winter weather, storms, snow, long walks in overshoes, will go and live in French Canada eventually with Ma and really make it for the storms and health up there. I find Allen, Holmes and everybody incredibly tiresome; their trouble is, they're dull tools; they think they're fascinating people I'm sure. I find me myself and I the only interesting person to talk to around here. I have no girls, no money, just write and sleep; that's my life, I'm alright; no more talk of death, crap, no. Our last trip to Mexico was marred by my not knowing still how to take my foot off clutch while stopping and at the same time ponder problems of where to park, what to do; and you getting sore, thinking I did it on purpose, especially as I said I did it on purpose, but truth is, I didn't do it on purpose, dont know how to drive, just typewrite. [. . . .]

But this is the way the world ends, everybody alone, that's good, that's how you started, remember? Everybody dead in the cemetery; husbands live with their wives; the 4:19's on time; Texas sheriffs wear stars, etc. Sironia Victoria Texas with little Xmas lights in dark bungalows and main line at end of street, I, high, dug in walk, sick of Indians. Etc. Lucien now wears heavy mustache and hornrimmed glasses, looks like old awful editor; Allen is getting fat-faced and ugly; Ansen looks like a regular pig and is as stuffy; Helen Parker's old and motherly; Holmes (made $20,000 on GO) (will inherit $80,000 from family) eats in expensive restaurants and spends all his time chasing and hailing cabs with his coat flapping anxiously;[2] everybody's in his heaven, God made the world, I'm okay too and get hi once a night and still believe and still love you.

Jack

---

1. This was the manuscript of Kerouac's story about working as a student brakeman, "October in the Railroad Earth."

2. See Kerouac's description of his friends in *The Subterraneans*, after Holmes ["Balliol MacJones"] got a $20,000 advance from Bantam Books for the reprint rights to *Go*, "an unheard of sum and all of us beat types wandering the Beach and Market Street and Times Square when in New York." Bantam never published the paperback edition.

Early in February 1953 Kerouac mentioned in a letter to Carolyn Cassady that he had lunched with Malcolm Cowley, an editor at the Viking Press, to discuss his writing. When Cowley insisted on revisions in his manuscripts, Kerouac refused to listen to him, telling Carolyn that Cowley turned out to be a "semi-pedantic Vermont professor type with a hearing aid and said if I took out the fantasy parts of Sax *the just stories of boyhood growing up Massachusetts would make me $50,000." Kerouac was unhappy that Ginsberg had called him "a holy fool" for refusing to revise his manuscripts for publishers after Ace Books turned down his new book about Mary Carney, ending their three-book option. Later that month Ginsberg sent Kerouac a draft of a publicity release that he had written with Carl Solomon to announce the publication of Burroughs's* Junky *(published by Ace Books under the pseudonym William Lee). Allen asked Jack to send him a "plug for Bill as intense and hi-class as you can make it," but Jack angrily refused.*

Feb. 21, 1953
[Rocky Mount, N.C.]

Dear Allen and Sirs:

I do not give my permission for my name to be used in the notes prepared by you and A.A. Wyn and Carl Solomon for David Dempsey's *New York Times* literary notes column. I do not want my real name used in conjunction with habit forming drugs while a pseudonym conceals the real name of the author thus protecting him from prosecution but not myself and moreover whose work at the expense of my name is being bruited for book trade reasons.

In this "rough draft publicity" I do not want *The Town and the City* mentioned in juxtaposition to *Go,* by association hinting at some unprofessional and artistic semblance, and I deny permission to place my name next to Clellon Holmes as a co-expert on the *Beat Generation.*

Especially I do not want to be misquoted as saying that I "dig the pseudonymous William Lee as one of the key figures of the Beat Generation." My remarks on the subject of either the pseudonymous author William Lee or the generation are at your disposal through the proper channels, from my pen and through my agent.

Yours most respectfully and strictly business,

> John Kerouac
> c/o MCA
> Mrs. Phyllis Jackson
> 598 Madison Ave.
> New York, N.Y.

Kerouac returned to the West Coast when the Southern Pacific called him back to his brakeman job. He moved from his hotel in San Francisco to San Luis Obispo, arriving shortly after Cassady nearly severed his foot in a railroad accident. When Jack wrote his mother he glossed over his boredom living in San Luis Obispo, but in his letter to Cassady he complained to his injured friend about having to work full-time on the railroad.

TO GABRIELLE KEROUAC

> Sat Apr 25 '53
> [San Luis Obispo, Calif.]

Dear Ma—

Enclosed is the first letter I wrote, from Frisco

Now I'm in San Luis Obispo, and here is my address:

J.L. KEROUAC
COLONIAL HOTEL
103 SANTA BARBARA AVE.
SAN LUIS OBISPO, CALIF.

Ready to go to work—I won't make much more than $80 this end-of-the-month but things will start rolling in May, and by Christmas I'll have $2,000 saved, or bust. Yesterday on my time, to learn the job better, I worked in the mountains.

In 2 months, San Luis Obispo will have 2 television stations. In the paper, as you see, they advertise lowprice trailers—also houses, but they're all in the thousands of dollars. The best idea I think will be for us to start in a trailer, for about a year, till we get a start.

Maybe in San Jose would be better—all TV channels from Frisco and great warm weather. But I wanted to study "Obispo" as a town; it nestles in the mountains; the work is more peaceful. One thing sure—California is beautiful and ideal and will be our home . . . down here 250 miles south of Frisco, or up in San Jose 40 miles south of Frisco. In "Obispo" we could live right on the sea—

My nose was a very serious infection; when I went to see Neal at the railroad hospital they gave me a million units of penicillin, and pain pills; for 3 days my eyes watered with migraine pain from that swollen shnozzola; the doctor said the infection was in a bad spot, close to the eyes, so you see I wasn't "lamenting" about nothing . . . it was the continuation of that "poison."

Ma, I have a great little hotel room, $6 a week; I cook steaks, eggs, toast, coffee; I have a view of great mountains over the little sleepy Nashua town; in back the trains pass, I walk to work in 1 minute; the sun is warm, the birds sing in my window; at night I curl up & get a good sleep to the tune of crickets. You haven't lived till you've lived in California . . . you'll see.

Ma, instead of going down South 4th of July, come visit me, I'll get you some passes for half the way, you can ride a nice train all the way; when you get here you'll have a whole week to see California before starting back, I'll lay off work & show you around. Think it over. P.S. Neal is going to N.Y. Xmas, we might travel back with him, he wants to. He broke his leg [sic] falling off a boxcar— He won't work till Spring 1954—He'll probably get 8 or 10,000 bucks—with that he can make a fast start on some business or other—the railroad pays accident benefits—Xmas he wants to go to N.Y. in his station wagon. So we'll see then.

Meanwhile, I'll work, & send you papers, & save money.

Coming to California has brought me back to life again. I realize now I shouldnt have left last year. I only went to N.Y. to see you. Boy do I hate N.Y.! Never again—

How is my kitty? I hope he's still around Xmas so we can bring him back.

Let me know about Nin's visit & any news . . . about yr. arm.

Remember, quit when you've had enuf, all we have to do 1) make a start here in a trailer, any old trailer, the rest can come later— You'll see I'm right. Well, Ma, goodnight now, please mail enclosed note to

> Phyllis Jackson (my agent)
> M.C.A.
> 598 Madison Ave.
> New York, N.Y.

Love & Kisses, Ti Jean X X X

TO NEAL CASSADY

> [April] '53
> [San Luis Obispo, Calif.]
> Hello to Carolyn

Dear Neal—

Things are slow in SLO but I imagine no faster in San Jose. This place is like a rest sanitarium. I am now completely healed & ready to return to the feverish intensities of the big city. I am racking my brain trying to figure my next move in life. One of them will be a month in the forest in the mountains, sleeping out & fishing for subsistence. (JOHN THE BAPTIST) After that, Mexico, and this time a cunt will live with me. Until then, R.R. work. But what am I to write? I'm afraid I need Miss Green to write; can't whip up interest in anything otherwise. But that is a lesser matter, especially as I'm writing a letter to a man with 3 children who has worries, and an injury. Still, what's the sense of living if you don't get what you need. And I need food, rest, girls, dope, wine, beer, and Old Granddad. Also I am bored. I would like to live on yr. front divan when you get home from the hospital and pay you $10 a week room & partial at-home board & that would add $40 to yr. month's rent and help you. The $56 you owe me I guess we'll have to forget now. I don't covet what's been spilt. So off work & after rest I'd have some kicks at yr. house instead of sitting naked in a San Luis Obispo railroad hotel room watching the high school girls come home at 2.

So write & let me know when you'll be home & I'll hustle up to San Jose board[1] before it's too late.

Loss & tedium of life are driving me slowly inside insane—I've tried every angle of my mind to figure what to do—to get out of the dilemma of *half* wanting to live (because of sex, no direct contact also with my needs), and *full* having to work (because of economic trap). God I don't set store in anymore—ain't no good or evil, it's just the way a person likes to do—Jesus Christ was a liar, *jealous of the Pharisees,* & afraid of the black cunt & chose the Cross—

I don't even believe in Melville or Wolfe any more—& even Proust & Joyce I wonder why they bothered—I am a world weary *ennuyez* with a cameo ring, my dear. Write—c/o SLO Crew Clerk.

Jack

Kerouac had planned to stay in California working as a brakeman until Christmas 1953, but by midsummer he was so bored that he impulsively signed aboard the S.S. William Carruth, *bound for Alabama, New York, and Korea. In August 1953 he wrote Carolyn Cassady that he had jumped ship on the East Coast when he decided he didn't "want to be in steel trap prison ships with disagreeable stewards and what not . . . besides I was lushing tremendously and so much I stopt drinking for a month thereafter."*

Back with Gabrielle in Richmond Hill, Jack spent increasing amounts of time in the East Village with Ginsberg and Burroughs, who stayed with Allen for three months while they edited an epistolary book of Burroughs's letters to Ginsberg In Search of Yage *(January–May 1953) before Bill left for Europe. Kerouac had a brief, intense love affair that he described in* The Subterraneans, *a novel written in his mother's kitchen in October in three all-night marathon typing sessions fueled by Benzedrine. Both Ginsberg and Burroughs were impressed by the manuscript, which Allen described as "Too much Jack once in awhile, but not fatal." In November 1953 Kerouac heard once again from Malcolm Cowley, who offered to show*

---

1. The names of each day's railroad work crews were posted on a board.

Kerouac's manuscripts to Arabelle Porter, editor of the prestigious paperback series New World Writing.

TO MALCOLM COWLEY

Nov. 21, 1953
[Richmond Hill, N.Y.]

Dear Mr. Cowley,

When you hear from Arabelle Porter, if she wants any excerpts of mine, let me know and I'll act on that. I'm glad you're trying to help me get published someplace now. I see from the latest *New World Writing*[1] where Libra or Gore Vidal is trying to tear you down to lift himself up to position of big new dean critic which is such a laff he's just such a pretentious little fag. They told me in 1950 that the homosexuals were very powerful in American Literature—since then what's troubled me is not that, so much as the certain dull individuals who happen to be homosexual who have grabbed off the limelight and therefore the temporary influence, second rate anecdote repeaters like [Paul] Bowles, pretentious silly females with flairs for titles like Carson McMullers [sic], clever dramaturgists, grave self-revellers too naive to see the shame of their position like [Gore] Vidal, really it's too much, think I'll come out soon and make a statement—every single original musical genius in America, for instance, has been to jail or prison; I assure you the same holds true for literature; this is the time.

Let me know about Arabelle; my new agent is Stanley Colbert of Lord & Colbert, 109 E 36.

Yours,
Jack Kerouac

---

1. The series *New World Writing,* published by the New American Library, was an anthology of international avant-garde writing dedicated to publishing "the best of the new work we see, by writers of many and various aspirations, traditions and talents."

Less than two weeks later, after Ginsberg decided to move to California, Jack wrote a letter to Carolyn Cassady about a short-term job that Neal was trying to arrange for him in San Jose.

TO CAROLYN CASSADY

Dec. 3 '53
[Richmond Hill, N.Y.]

Dear Carolyn—

That parkinglot job sounds like it's made to order for this old philosopher. With a guarantee from you or Neal that it is there and not a changeable by-the-time-I-get-there deal, I am ready to take off at the first possible moment, which is, the day after Xmas, by bus, arriving around Dec. 29 & ready to work & glad to be with my 2 buddies again for another New Year's Eve.

As you know, Ginsberg won't get to San Jose till February at the earliest. He has made the astounding discovery that the New World had a "Greece & Rome" of its own & you can get there by 2nd class bus.[1]

I have $30 to my name & hope to earn some in Xmas rush baggageroom work if possible in this overcrowded frosty fag town; the least of which I can say for it. I always end up knocking off a couple more prose masterpieces ere the publishers repeat & make known to me thru masks of "luncheon" & "contracts" their dark contempt for the dedicated prophetic & pure scribbler beholden to no contract but that which the stars drew up, in the end, to no revision but Time's own sea of it, to no commercial slant but the sun's on the commerce of the brow, to no hope of earning but the harvest after sleep.

God is alone, and I'm better off because of it. It'll be more important for me to know—in the Apocalypse of the Fellaheen to come, when all culture & civilization are done—that the shallow-eyed potato is the best potato, then t'would be for me to know the sum of

---

1. After Burroughs left New York City on a Greek freighter bound for Europe, Ginsberg had visited Burroughs's parents in Palm Beach before going on to Havana and Mexico, where his destination was the Mayan ruins in Yucatán.

my Advance, what J. Roger Critic said, and the politics of reprint rights . . . reprint indeed, and of what tweedledee in a tweedledum world. In Strawberries,[2] take note of best producing runners—cut down the others. All my life and all my lifework ahead of me, during which I make it my hobby to feed myself, before God. Irrigate only in hot July & August, not before or after, except in a dry Spring, of which beware.

Purple thoughts for a parkinglot & a chance to avoid an Eastern winter, & see my little Jamie. Hire out as brakeman in the Summer rush—head for Thanksgiving Mexico, return Spring of '55 new senority.

As ever & same old,
Jack

---

2. Neal was attempting to grow a marijuana crop in the field next to the Cassady home.

1954

Arriving in San Jose in time for Neal's twenty-eighth birthday on February 8, 1954, Kerouac lived with the Cassadys while Neal tried to teach him how to handle the job on the parking lot. The strain of the ménage-à-trois was too much for Kerouac, especially after Neal forgot he had invited Jack to live with him and began to make what Carolyn described in Off the Road *as "oblique cracks about Jack's presence as a freeloader on the family." In this tense atmosphere, Kerouac's sense of self-pity escalated, as expressed in a letter to John Clellon Holmes.*

TO JOHN CLELLON HOLMES

Feb 19 [1954]
[San Jose, CA]

Dear John—

Thanks for sending the record, but I left home to come out here before it arrived but all's well and good. Had another harrowing trip featured this time by a 200-mile freight ride on an open flat car huddled in thin blanket going 80 m.p.h. along dewy midnight Coast surf and so cold and disgusted I kept giving "p-r-r-t" Bronx cheers thru the blanket nose-wrapt at the actual surf familiar to me by rail and then by coastwise sea last summer but sight of which now I disdained imperiously to allow to be graced by my eyeballs . . . singing "He made a bum out of me" ("He" the Conductor who made me ride outside the crummy) . . . and in Watsonville I ate grass finally and spoke compassionately to several bugs, and if you think I'm crazy you shall be pitied.

I thought you were in Europe, thus delay. Why should there be nothing left of your guts?—in that connection, 'tis better to dismount the lion and walk on yr. own two feet, for if you can ride a lion you can also speak to lion—and Burl Ives[1] anyway may be hungup on "career" and suffering of ego thereto attendant. Be wiser, Thou art.

Thy friend, Jean Louis

---

1. Burl Ives was a popular folk singer.

P.S. Ginsberg's in Yucatán gazing at "our equivalent Greco-Roman classical ruins of the New World" and impressing old rich ladies—

After two months at the Cassady house, Kerouac fought with Neal over the division of a pound of marijuana. Jack angrily moved into a skid row hotel room in San Francisco and then returned home to Gabrielle in Richmond Hill. There he asked Carolyn to forward a letter sent to him by Alene, the young woman he had called Mardou in The Subterraneans.

TO CAROLYN CASSADY

[April 22, 1954
Richmond Hill, N.Y.]

Hey

Please send my mail on, I finally got home in one piece, quite starved and the better for it; hunger makes you angry; anger makes you understand yourself; etc. Ha. I have a letter from Alene I'd like forwarded, at least; know you're wondering where I am before forwarding. Hope you got yr money by now, whatever it is, and all yr ideas about karma come true;[1] personally I dont believe in karma; and just found out I'd made a dreadful mistake, thinking Emptiness had preceded the Now World; a big mistake; it's not that the world is "empty," but, that you say about it, it neither IS, or, IS NOT, but merely a manifestation of mind, the reflection of the moon on a lake; so the next porkchop you eat, remember, it's merely a porkchop reflected off water, and your hunger, and you the hungerer, Narcissus you. . . . but for purposes of this world, I say let wine and porkchops flow, anything to put us asleep, or put ME asleep leastways Who

---

1. Shortly after New Year 1954, Carolyn and Neal discovered the writings of Edgar Cayce and became adherents of his theory of reincarnation. Kerouac had begun to study Buddhism, and his philosophical arguments with the Cassadys had not made it easier for them to live together in San Jose.

me? Who you? Who you ever be who ever I be send what ever is. Someone was trying to tell me something, maybe, and I want to see.

J

P S How unreal.

Thinking that Ginsberg had arrived from Mexico to stay with the Cassadys, Kerouac wrote a long letter from his mother's apartment to relay the gossip about their mutual friends on the East Coast and to tell Allen about his discovery of Buddhism. Jack offered to send Allen "a 100-page account of Buddhism" he had typed up from his reading notes in the San Jose Public Library entitled "Some of the Dharma," but he cautioned Ginsberg that "it's the only copy, we must take special care with it, right?" Kerouac also quoted from his first book of poetry, "San Francisco Blues," written in his room at the Cameo Hotel "in a rockingchair at the window" after leaving the Cassadys in March.

TO ALLEN GINSBERG

[early May 1954
Richmond Hill, N.Y.]

Dear Allen,

Starting last Friday afternoon drunk on wine, and ending this morning sober, with bat in between in town seeing Kingsland, Ansen, Holmes, Cru and Helen Parker, here's a big semi-silly letter; reason I wont throw away silly parts is because they may amuse you and you would be amused instead of not amused. They were written drunk, are gossippy, but maybe funny; first 4 pages . . .

I am enclosing a bill letter from Bill in Tangiers[1] containing material I'm not sure you've seen, and that I want you to be as sure of sending back, as I am right now of returning your Acavalna Paper. Be sure now! [. . . .]

I recently had an affair with a junkey girl call'd M. A.—that you may know of, friend of Iris Brody's, saw me and Kells in his yellow

---

1. Burroughs was sending letters to Kerouac from Tangier asking for news about Ginsberg in Mexico.

jeepster in Cuernavaca in 1952; knows everybody, but is so hot and so Camille like suicidal and crazy I cant follow her around; she just went to hospital for an overdose, for instance. And it's too late anyway for me to love, to love love, that is, or love women, I mean. I mean sex and involvement and commonlaw marriage like, or I'm talking thru my hat. [. . . .]

I've been getting sillydrunk again lately in Remo and disgusting myself a la Subterraneans. I want to live a quiet life but I am so weak for booxe [sic] booze. I am very unhappy and have nightmares; when drinking; after a week of abstinence, I am happier than ever before in life, but slowly become bored and wonderin what to do now; am writing two big books[2] only because have nothing else to do and it would be a shame to waste all that experience in "talent"—as Carolyn says—and generally speaking, I have crossed the ocean of suffering and found the path at last. And am quite surprised that you, innocent, novice-like did enter the first inner chamber of Buddha's temple in a dream; you're going to be saved—There would be rejoicing and hossanahs [sic] in heaven if anything once in heaven WERE a thing, or could rejoice, where rejoicing is a naught—heaven is nothing—

Let me see you conceive of nothing while you live, and I give you heaven. [. . . .]

> Little anger Japan
> Strides holding bombs
> To blow the West
> To Fuyukama's
> Shrouded Mountain Top
> So the Lotus Bubble
> Blossoms in Buddha's
> Temple Dharma Eye
> May unfold from
>   Pacific Center
> Inward Out and Over
> The Essence Center World.

---

2. "San Francisco Blues" and *Book of Dreams*.

This is from my new book of poems SAN FRANCISCO BLUES that I wrote when I left Neal's in March and went to live in the Cameo Hotel on Third Street Frisco Skidrow—wrote it in a rockingchair at the window, looking down on winos and bebop winos and whores and Cop cars—and I quote it to draw your attention to the fact, we have consistently been clairvoyant of each other's minds for years now, this poem has "bubble" in it which you used with Buddha in your letter (tho you deleted it for "balloon")—and it hints of the temple, the inner chamber, of the Mongolia wall, of which, incidentally, I too have a dream, in BOOK OF DREAMS (which I'm now finishing the typing of)—

The dream, is, "Dreamed of being in some kind of hardship pilgrimage with a man and woman in some Mongolian harshland and when we got to the Fellaheen town of the rippling-tree which had a gray cement factory color and dismalness I said 'However in your town here I could pose as a prisoner of yours, in fact, in reality, I am your prisoner, according to the facts,'—'Yes, that's a fact,' they said much and innocently pleased, especially the woman—they might have been Mongolian—I walked on the sidewalk ground carrying my rifle stock down as befitting a prisoner and they rode the point of our vehicular or animal travel-gimmick that had carted us across the Siberian wastes—I secretly mistrusted their joy, we had started on some Jesus pilgrimage by the wall, now they were letting their thoughts be affected by matters of war (there's a war)—but I trusted them finally."

A thousand other examples of our clairvoyance oneness later. L. I saw, as I say, went to his house one Sunday afternoon, bringing a pint of whiskey cause I owed him 3 bucks from another night, and tho C. was like displeased, I insisted we mix it all up with ice in a bottle to take to the park with us, where she wanted to sun child, so on the park L. and I are belting from this magnificent huge cocktail and here comes H.P. and BRUCE AND TOMMY and sits with us, and then I got to go for a leak in Washington Park toilet so I walk with Tommy across, and we pass STANLEY GOULD who says, "Who is that, Tommy Parker?" and here comes GREGORY CORSO with black skin tan of Scandinavian ships and cut his hair off in crew cut and looks like great beachcomber poet and he takes my Buddha book and reads one line coldly, but then says, "I know it's great, you can't lend it to me, can you?"—"No, I gotta have it by my side all the time."—"I know," he says, and we talk about you, and he says, "When Allen gets back I wont pay no attention to him, fuck him"—I say, "Why do you talk like that about Allen, whatsamatter with you and Allen?"—"Fuck him," he says, like agonized over something . . . I warn Mary A. not to hate Gregory, like she wants to do, I tell her, "He's no different than you, all is the same essence," and over comes hepcat to talk to us.

I was at Helen P.'s and had a ball and then ALAN ANSEN came with WILLIAM GADDIS[3] and I didn't like Gaddis cause it seemed to me he was making Ansen unhappy . . . I put my hand on A's head and rubbed his head and he went off with Gaddis and came back again to me 'n Helen and we got drunk in the night and danced the mambo . . . sweet Helen in the morning put on her easter bonnet and went to work down the streets of Village—good brave gal— Finally got rid of JACK ELLIOTT the singing cowboy who apparently was costing her a lot of money but poor Jack, he cant work, he's like the robin, he sings . . .

So I walk down the streets of the Village with JACK ELLIOTT [. . . .] and he's playin the Memphis Special, and other songs, and we run into BILLY FAIER, a great banjo genius from N'Awrleans, and bang BILL FOX drives by and I stop him by yelling at his car, and he comes out, and I say, "Bill, give these boys an audition for Esoteric"[4] and we have a songfest and a hundred and two school children gather around to listen and up comes an old Frisco wino with his bottle and broken pulpy nose and he likes Jack Elliott's singin so much he says, reachin in his shirt, "By god, boy, I'm gonna give you my lass sandwich."—"I'm from Oklahoma meself"—and the sun goes down—and I have a pimple on my nose—

ALENE L. calls me on the phone, it seems she's now a hardworkin waitress at Rikers restaurant on Columbia campus at 115 and Broad-

---

3. The novelist William Gaddis is portrayed as "Harold Sand" in *The Subterraneans*.

4. Esoteric Records, the small New York record company founded by Jerry Newman, specialized in avant-garde jazz.

way, so I go to her house, bringing ms. of *Subterraneans,* as promised, and I tell her I still love her and we hold hands goin down the
street, cause you know, boy, I love all women . . . but instead of
being big swain I get drunk with JORGE D'AVILA Ed W's boy and
his great buddy from Puerto Rico HERNANDO, who is the very first
person I have met in this world who has completely and instantly
understood the words of Buddha . . . a great cat, you meet later,
architect, so far . . . You see Allen, all there is to Buddha, is this—
All life is a dream—but later, I'll explain later . . . it isn't AS IF it
was a dream, it IS a dream . . . see? So I get drunk with the boys in
the West End and JOHNNY THE BARTENDER is still asking for
his copy of *The Town and the City,* and at midnight I take a peek
in Rikers, and there's Alene rushing around on little twinkling legs
with her arms sawing along her thighs, real intent on being "Sane"
and just madder than ever if you asks me. [. . . .]

JOHN HOLMES, I rush up to his place at 123 Lexington and ring
the doorbell and he's laboring up the stairs with a bagful of gin, and
we go in, there's Shirley,[5] we get drunk, I rush out and fetch Mary,
she jolts, we go back, we play old Billies, old Lesters, it goes on, we
pass out, next day when Shirley goes to work me and Mary and John
go to a 3rd Avenue bar and drink and talk all that day and I say to
John Brothers Forever, and mean it.—Shirley comes home at night,
sees three drunk lushes bums in her room, sighs, leans against door
just like Marian, and all it's the all same thing again as Marian, and
John "writes" during the day, and they havent published *Go* in pock-
etbooks, for some reason, and he's "broke"—he says, "In 1952 I
had a lot a money, but now" . . . and he is sad. For money I guess,
but we talked, and made up okay, and of course he asked about you
with concern & intelligence. But he is suspicious of the reason for
my visits—so I'll leave him alone. [. . . .]

SEYMOUR I done heard about, from SAM KAINER. I was over
to Mark Van Doren's house to pick up *Doctor Sax* where I'd left it,
with his son CHARLES. Mark wasnt there and had already written

---

5. John Clellon Holmes had divorced his first wife, Marian, and married his
second, Shirley.

me a note saying that Sax was "monotonous and probably without meaning in the end," saying at first, "quite a work but I dont know where to place it," whereby I realized he is really nowhere, face it, but Charles was friendly, he is having a novel published by Giroux soon (my dear) and he had his sweetheart with him who is all gushing and fascinated in my talk about Buddha and wants to know how to practice dhyana and Samadhi and Samapatti and in comes a gang of young kids, and Sam Kainer, I say, "Sam Kainer, where'd I hear that name?" and of course!! it's the cat who lived in Seymour's pad in St. John's Wood all this time, blasting with him, conducting bop session, he wears a goatee and is very cool and Phillip Lamantia like and hep—and says Seymour for awhile was Ted Heath's band manager, Ted Heath big band like Woody Herman in England.

JERRY NEWMAN I went [. . . .] with him to antique shops where he got lamps for his huge new CBS style by-his-father-billfooted studio which is the most beautiful, vast thing you've ever seen with soundproof walls so we could have screaming agonized orgies in there and nobody'd ever know (right around the corner from Holmes) and where he is makin big records and big money now—and says he will have big sessions with Brue Moore and Allen Eager and Al Haig.[6]

BRUE MOORE I finally met, with Gould my Buddy, and Brue says he's from Indianola, Mississippi, not far from Greenville, on River, and says, "Lets you and me drink wine, you think I drink whiskey, you ought to see me drink wine, we'll go down to the Bowery and light a fire in the alley and drink wine, and I'll play my horn"—with Gould, we'll do this, in October. Be sure to be with us. Melville I'm in Love With You Always.

NOW LISTEN ALLEN, DO NOT FAIL to look up, if possible, Al Sublette, at the Bell Hotel at 39 Columbus St. Frisco, with or without Neal, so Al can take you around the Great Frisco and show you, remember and dont fail . . . he's a great boy, and sell me to him, please, he mad at ma, at me—big mad good boy and maybe

---

6. Brue Moore was the tenor saxophonist then appearing at the Open Door in Greenwich Village with Allen Eager, also on tenor sax, and Al Haig, pianist.

the first hep Negro writer in America maybe, if he digs—Not that he's avant garde, he's, understand, a straight simple hepcat with a GIANT FLAIR FOR WORDS, a wordslingin fool, dont know it, a real POET in the sense in which it was known in Elizabeth's time, and, not surprisingly, a wino, and jolts too. I just could write epics about his vision of America, 's what I mean, Al.

PHILLIP LAMANTIA, Ed Roberts, Leonard Hall, Chris McLaine, Rexroth,[7] look them up while you're in Frisco. It's your big chance to dig the Berkeley axis—Is Saint there? . . . Jaime's house . . . big peotl heroes like Wig Walters obtain from there; dig Wig if you can, the "Cash" of Bill's JUNKIE novel. [. . . .]

And of course, for your beginning studies of Buddhism, you must listen to me carefully and implicitly as tho I was Einstein teaching you relativity or Eliot teaching the Formulas of Objective Correlation on a blackboard in Princeton.

Here, first, is the correct bibliography:

TEXTS FROM THE BUDDHIST CANON KNOWN AS DHAM-MAPADA. (Samuel Beal, London and Boston, 1878).

LIFE OF BUDDHA, or BUDDHA CHARITA by Asvaghosha the Patriarch, translated by Samuel Beal (Sacred Books of the East, vol. 19)

THE GOSPEL OF BUDDHA by Paul Carus (Open Court, Chicago 1894).

BUDDHISM IN TRANSLATIONS by Henry Clarke Warren (Harvard Oriental Series Vol. 3, Harvard U.P. 1896) Also in HARVARD CLASSICS.

THE BUDDHIST BIBLE, Dwight Goddard (Goddard, Thetford, Vt.) This is by far the best book because it contains the Surangama Sutra and the Lankavatra Scripture, not to mention the 11-page Diamond Sutra which is the last word, and Asvaghosha's Awak-

---

7. Kenneth Rexroth (1905–1982), San Francisco writer and radical political activist. Ginsberg went to see Rexroth with a letter of introduction from William Carlos Williams.

ening of Faith, and the Tao. The Buddhist Bible uses sources—
from the Pali, the Sanskrit, the Thibetan, Chinese, Burmese and
modern.

BUDDHIST LEGENDS E.W. Burlingame (Harvard Oriental Series
Vol. 28, 30). These are commentaries on the 423 Aphorisms, very
rich.

THE DIALOGS OF THE BUDDHA, DIGHA-NIKAYA (long dia-
logues) (Rhys Davids, Oxford 3 vols.).

VISUDDHI MAGGA by Buddhaghosha, trans. by P.M. Tin (The
Path of Purity, Pali Text Society, Translation Series 11, 17, 21).

THE SACRED BOOKS AND EARLY LITERATURE OF THE
EAST. Volume 18 India and Buddhism. (Parke, Austin and Lip-
scomb New York-London).

There's more and you will undoubtedly be telling me what to get
if you get into this, which I advise and in fact insist on with all my
heart heat and argument and brotherliness. I don't mean to put down
Cayce, for after all he did say, "Practice, then, brotherly love, kindness, long suffering and patience," he was no charlatan when it came
to the business at hand, he was no charlatan anyway.

Now Allen, as Neal or Carolyn can tell you, last February I typed
up a 100-page account of Buddhism for you, gleaned from my notes,
and you will see proof of that in several allusions and appeals to
"Allen" and I have that here, if you really want to see it, I will send
it importantly stamped, it's the only copy, we must take special care
with it, right? "Some of the Dharma" I called it, and it was intended
for you to read in the selva [sic]. Some of it is now, I see, useless,
because mistaken, or written on tea, or other faults, but it may really
give you a sendoff into the above tomes, which is my wish.

Listen, you must begin with the Life of Buddha by Asvaghosha;
then if you can, read the Surangama Sutra next. This is how I found
path, but the paths of the many are many to the one path.

Your adventures in Mexico I am reading and re-reading, they are
very sad, you only fragmentize, I can't wait to hear the Dakar-like
details later, for poetry reasons. [. . . .]

My Brooklyn in the dream is true, because I often have such dreams of the vast Brooklyn, I ride on endless els, and rust yards, etc. and (tell this to Neal) last week I worked 2 days on the New York Dock Railway as Yard Brakeman, right down on the Brooklyn waterfront, at Moore McCormack Pier 15—switching cars off the floats, where railroad meets sea, it was my destiny to finally make that job—$18.35 a day—but that phlebitis junk bump is holding me up, my job is braking cars and the arm cant do it—so I took a month's sick leave, must get some trypsin (parenzyme) the miracle drug—I enclose little note I wrote to Neal about the weird eastern railroad signs so different from ole SP.

Bill in Europe[8] is really so sublime, so accurate—we must make a movie, or better, more seriously? I claim you should sit down and write VISIONS OF BILL IN EUROPE, à la Vision of Neal, and we'll publish later when we get $500 to buy and maintain our handpress in Mexico City or Phnarktown [sic]. Incidentally, concerning the press, I no longer want to "run it," you run it, but I still offer my services as handset printer . . . worries of business way beyond me now, only humble la-bours with hand okay, I have garden in my yard and beanfield now you know, and potatoes, etc.

[. . . .] Close yr eyes, cross yr legs under you, practice slow in-breathing and outbreathing, think, "I am breathing in, I am breathing out," then you think "There is the breathing in, there is the breathing out," and soon essential mind will begin to shine in you and you will begin to experience your first samadhi. [. . . .]

And now, I suppose, this is enuf for now, you must be tired of all these words, so goodnight my good one and dont be mad at me (none of ye).

Jack

Living with his mother in the spring and early summer of 1954, Kerouac felt a contentment reflected in his letters to Ginsberg and the Cassadys in California. For a time he contributed to the house-

8. Burroughs had been living in Tangier since January 1954.

hold income with his railroad unemployment checks, and he led a "quiet meditative life" studying Buddhism and tending a small vegetable garden in the backyard of his mother's apartment building in Richmond Hill, preparing dinner and drinks for her when she returned from her job at the shoe factory. Trying to ride the ripple of attention over Holmes's novel Go, *Kerouac had given the title "Beat Generation" to the original manuscript of* On the Road, *and his new agent Sterling Lord was circulating it among publishers. Neal's foot injury had healed, and he had been awarded a cash settlement from the railroad, most of which the Cassadys invested in a new house. By the end of July, as Jack told Carolyn, he was longing for Neal to drive "the lonesome American roads" to the East Coast and take him back to San Jose, where he hoped to join Ginsberg at the Cassadys'.*

TO CAROLYN CASSADY

[May 17, 1954,
Richmond Hill, N.Y.]

Dear Carolyn,

I was so glad to hear from you; it isnt that I'd soured on you, but that I thought you and Neal had soured on me after my lapses into impatience and irascibility in that time. As I look back on it, I exhort myself for always, and in that particular instance, ascribing so much self-individuality to myself as to allow the Kerouac-Me all kinds of rights, such as and including, leaving San Jose for the purpose of digging the city, which I really was going to do anyhow and was only looking for a proper time or even an excuse, which Neal certainly furnished, in his own self-individual blindness, by telling me we'd agreed I'd buy the whole pound [of marijuana] for $20 when as far as I can remember it was supposed to be 50–50, and when I protested sincerely, saying, "I didnt say that! I didnt say that hey!" a gleam came into his eye and he said "But dont you remember?" and that same day, dividing the oolong on a piece of paper with a line drawn by me in pencil through it to divide when we wrapt it all up in our individual greedy packs he insisted that I had also agreed he'd get the powder (due to piles picked) which was another one I

didnt hear, whereby I said, "The next agreement will be in writing."
I remember that while I carefully picked up my oolong drop or leaf
by leaf, sometimes a dry crackly would fly and lend itself to Neal's
pile, and I'd think "What kind of losing is that, when accidentally
you give?" and then when Neal stole the powder I thought "What
kind of gain is that, when deceiving on purpose?" So it comes out
now, I was really sore at Neal on account of that deal, and his wanting to borrow ten from me was just the excuse I leapt at to make
my dissatisfaction felt. Then, from frying pan into fire, I went to Al
Sublette's, and drank, and recidified [sic] my spiritual gains to where
I was blotto and bleary again and far from wisdom. (At least I didnt
hear him.)

But now quiet meditative life in my room and in the sunny yard
where I have planted a vegetable garden, and turning down requests
from beautiful girls over the telephone wanting to "fuck and suck"
(quote), this no lie, and reading my bible book, and practising meditation, I see all the mistakes I made, all the mistakes you and Neal
made, I recognize once more as on that brilliant, radiant, sympathetic, sinless original night when I arrived remember on the freight
train and we drank beer and argued the dharma,[1] realize once more,
we're all the same, we three, and for us to fight is as silly as can be.
(Everybody is the same; I never hit a girl but I might have had in
previous lives.) But now I dont think I'll ever return to California,
so wont see you for ages, unless some crazy ride in cars is proposed
by someone around here or I get a car myself, which I will do, '47
Station Wagon, if I sell "Beat Generation" to some publisher, currently it's supposed to be Little Brown in Boston. Then, yes, carbum-
ming around land, I would return to San Jose, and see you, and
already look forward to that, tho, nothing is real, all is a dream, yet,
we should get together once and for all and have a real battle because
I still say you have been duped into belief in ego and self-nature and
immortality by Cayce, who in every respect is radiantly right, ex-
cepting the matter of ego-personality as an entity, an atman, that

---

1. Sanskrit word for truth, or the duty, the law. Kerouac's preferred translation
of "dharma" was "the meaning."

lasts from life to life. With what material, I pray you, does an entity carry itself over; what is that essential permanent and indestructible stuff and suchness of the stuff that makes what you call a soul?—if it isnt just your tremendous clinging to ego-personality. But I aint even warmed up on the subject and now I'll switch to Allen a minute. I dont think anybody need worry, he may be on purpose being silent and mysterious and trying to make people worry; bet you ten dollars that's what it is. There's no danger in Mexico so much. Besides I think Allen is already back in New York, hiding, I saw him on the corner the other night; I was very drunk, yelled out "Allen!"; he was standing in beat coat, tanned, tangle-haired, mad looking, and just stared back at me like flipped village intellectual; being drunk, the world was unreal anyway, and not only did I think "It's probably not Allen" but "if it is Allen anyway it doesnt matter" and I went on as tho it was a dream; I wouldnt be surprised if it was Allen. I wouldnt be surprised too if he'd gone mad finally, like his mother, I expect that some day, definitely. My wish is, tho, that he comes to San Jose and has his wits and excitements and goes on being like he was, tho it'll be time for him, too, to realize the futility of all such clinging to arbitrary conceptions and notions as abound in his intellectual world alone. I need not say I love Allen, he knows it himself from telepathic messages which I've been sending him, and from intuition concerning the round of intentions and now knows. Burroughs letters from Africa hysterical worryings of junkey.

So your lawyer ended up getting all the loot, and you end up with what originally the railroad offered you, and now Neal cant make the board anymore. And all because you wanted more, more, more, always more, more, more. I'm the same way, dont blame ya. But there's got to be an end to clinging, I say. And I do hope Neal gets back on the board, if only so I can, some summer in the future. For sake of your S[an] J[ose] life mainly.

Fact, I might go to El Paso in the Fall and make it down there, living in Juarez and workin Texas. If you cant make the board any more, change railroads. Railroads are going out, I hear; trucks taking the business. Worry, sorrow, there'll always be a mess when you try to deal with the discriminatory activities and work of sentient excited multitudes. Teach yr children simplicity, cook up big stews, and all stay home goofing in the overgrown yard. Send them to school and teach them culture-cravings, buy expensive meats, castrate the hedges and mow the lawn and plant rock gardens and fancy swings and all be harried and worried, go ahead. You'll see.

I was collecting railroad unemployment here, but now they dont think I'm trying hard enuf to get a job, and so cuttin my checks off. When they do, I will tell them to go to hell . . . but now I wont even bother to do that, and in my deep mind, I see no reason to even say anything and for that matter to even collect said checks and no reason to live because life is not worth living. But since you've got to do something to tarry the time along, even tho in our deep minds, yes, as you say "There's just no time or space, and you know all," yet you've got to get your food every day at least and worry about your close ones . . . compassion. But now let me tell you how I think now.

If, for instance, you and I do meet some day in the future, it wont be you, or I, but someone like you, and someone like me, drawn together for same reasons. I think that's what Buddha means, when he says, "I was that deer," or "I was that prince countless kalpas ago," he means as we'd say, for instance, in Brothers Karamazov I am Alyosha and you are Katerina Ivanova . . . assigning roles. I have the greatest Buddha book here, the Jataka, or Stories of the Buddha; a monk who quits the religion because he's tired of trying, is reminded by Buddha he was in another life a young desert traveler who almost gave up until the caravan leader told him to split a rock, out of which water spurted as high as a palm tree; "you were the boy, the caravan leader was just I." A woman monk has a baby from her marriage after she's joined the order; the phoney head of the nuns disordains [sic] her; she goes to Buddha, who saves her; tells her she was once a deer, big with kid, who didnt want to die, so went to the deer king, who pleaded to the king's hunter in her name; "you were the deer, the Deer King was just I." It strikes me like assigning roles in already existent dreamlike legends. The Buddhists are an-atman, dont believe in any essence of soul that exists either now, or carries over; it is this. Look out the window at the tree; it exists because it is, it doesn't exist because it is a dream; it neither is, nor is not; it partakes of no reality, and partakes of no non-reality; it's merely a

dream, a vision, a phantasm, the moon shining on the lake, an eva-
nescent dew, a flash of lightning, a shadow (like the past, like the
future), a bubble. Eternity is a dream, the present moment is a dream;
you know it in yr bones. Nothing is real, yet no conception such as
that nothing-is-real, is real either, or non-real; no arbitrary conceptions of what is, or is not, wears any validity, in a world which is a
dream. When you die your consciousness departs from participation
in the dream, your body drops off; Essential Mind, which is beneath
consciousness, is the thing with which you're going to realize that
you've died; it is Everything. You will be returned to All, the sensation will be "I didnt realize I had no self but was merely partaking
of the nature of all things, which is a dream"—which is error drifting
on the surface of essential mind, possessing in its dreamlike nature
the same dharmakaya as non-error—Because life is a dream, how
can you cling to it? If you believe that you have a self-nature, you
deceive yourself into thinking arbitrary conceptions about yourself
that give you the illusion that you are real and in the Cayce case,
that you can go from life to life as a self-entity carrying yr ego forward to perfection. But nothing is high in perfection, nothing low,
all things partake of the same nature, which is a big dream. Look at
the tree; it is because it is, and it is not because it is a dream. . . .

Why is it that we feel compassion in our bones, when once I saw
my father fall on the floor because his legs had gone dead in the easy
chair, a surge tore at my heart, of something which you wouldnt
expect to happen in a loathsome, unlocatable, tormented, non-self-
natured, accidental composite of molecular groups of flesh and blood
and bone, universes of this blank and bleak in a void and made to
move in tormented vegetablized directions* (*molecular groups of
atoms, world-spheres with no center and no selfhood suddenly worrying in this dream—) . . . if the message of compassion wasnt coming from the center of the universe of Essential Mind, saying,
"They've all wanted to take enfleshed form and take a crack at action
in the dream and they were all damn fools"—O dont you remember
when you were a little eye flying around the world looking at it
eagerly, wanting to join in the fun, like a little spermatozoa flying
around the fetal egg and trying to get its little head in to swell, among
a million brothers and sisters, shouldering its way into the world, in

the womb of the woman in the middle of the Womb of the Dream, leaving that heaven, that moveless emptiness void of spontaneous and radiant effortlessness, that golden dream deep in the womb of mind, to take a crack at dark sad ether, at six million discriminated anxieties and self-misleadings about "happiness," the slew of suffering on all sides in the name of some gutsy human idea, some divinity without lucidity and without self cause, liquid as water in a dream, unsatisfyable as a drink of dream water in a thirsty mournfull dream, the lugubriousness of it all, the mindless selfbelief and malicious flailing to hunger after hungering, the cry on all sides "More life! More life!" and all the time *the dead know better* . . . stop the monkey mind of the universe, I say . . . We just think that we're being born, when we're born . . . We just think that we've got a self nature, when we think of ourselves . . . We just think that we're dying, when we die . . . It is like the castle of the Gandharvas, castles in the air . . . a world reflected in a mirror—the end.

Let me know about the little ones who know that God is Pooh-Bear[2] and that the rainbow went in the water . . . May the vajra raja enlightening diamond radiate beams upon your house and remember to have a big spacy backyard for Old Jack who may yet pitch a shack back yonder and grow latelife beans and grapevines . . . I've been invited incidentally to live in a monastery 30 miles north of Paris, L'Eau Vive by name, at Soissy sur Seine,[3] and have a place to go if I get fare money, so . . . Write and let me know all the news about everything.

All my love
Jack

---

2. See the last paragraph of *On the Road:* ". . . in Iowa I know by now the children must be crying in the land where they let the children cry, and tonight the stars'll be out, and don't you know that God is Pooh Bear." Kerouac revised this ending in the various typescripts he made of the original 1951 roll manuscript of the novel.

3. See Kerouac's letter to Robert Giroux, late summer 1954 (p. 444).

[summer 1954
Richmond Hill, N.Y.]

Dear Allen—

From the 2 letters I received from Bill and you today,[1] after silences of a month, I perceive that you should get together on a permanent basis in Mexico City. You should get a couple hundred dollars together and put a down payment on a good house in a poor district of Mexico City, with enclosed garden, and have teas to which Paul Bowles[2] is of course never invited. Upstairs in a room you can start stacking up the first printing equipment—you're going to publish things yourself, and create a sensation in the higher literary world. You will live lives of delicacy, solitude, easeful poverty (that is, do your own shopping, count pesetas, cook, buy 5-peso rum & ice & mix with Mexico colas & have big American parties with sex girls & visiting heroes). The Coast is dismal, expensive, full of heat, meaningless Super Vice Squads, bicyclists with no balls, shoddy Ken Rexroths of the Castle, humble Mexican fieldhands looking for Fudgicles, railroads of steely death ready to be fucked by Asians. You and Bill—archeologist exiles in Indian Mexico going to French movies on Saturday nights, rowing in Chapultepec Park on Sundays . . . (with girls, or alone with girl). Old Jean-Louis generally mostly around & probably inveigled to invest in the house . . . in 5 years, Oriental decors. [*incomplete*]

---

1. Ginsberg was still traveling in Mexico. On May 24, 1954, Burroughs had written Kerouac saying that he had "picked up on Yoga many years ago. Tibetan Buddhism and Zen you should look into."

2. Paul Bowles (b. 1910), an American novelist living in Tangier. Burroughs later complained in a letter to Kerouac, on August 18, 1954, that when he first moved to Tangier, Bowles had cut him socially by not inviting him to parties.